The Bolero School

This book is dedicated
to the peoples of Spain
and their devotion to their
great cultural heritage

'As for me,
I can explain nothing,
but stammer with the fire
that burns inside me
and the life that has been
bestowed on me.'

Federico García Lorca

Lecture: Poet in New York,
translated by Christopher Manse

(Lorca in Columbia, October 1929)

The Bolero School

An Illustrated History
of the Bolero, the Seguidillas
and The Escuela Bolera:
Syllabus and Dances

Marina Grut

including
A Prologue by Alberto Lorca
and
The Escuela Bolera in London
in the Nineteenth Century
by Ivor Guest

DANCE
BOOKS

A CIP catalogue reference
for this book is available
from the British Library

ISBN: 1 85273 081 1

Cover illustration:
'Baile del Candil'
(dance by lamp light).
Illustration digitally enhanced by
Nicolai Grut, Feedback Video,
Toronto, Canada.

Publication of this book was made
possible by generous support from:

The Radcliffe Foundation
The Carina Ari Foundation
The Heritage Dance Foundation
and Dr Charles Zwerling
The Spanish Dance Society

Contents

Acknowledgements   vii
Prologue by Alberto Lorca   xi
Foreword   xv

PART 1: The History of the Bolero

Introduction   3

1 The Seguidillas   13
2 The Bolero   45
3 Regional Boleros   63
4 The Bolero as the National Dance of Spain   77
5 The Escuela Bolera   109
6 Main Centres of the Escuela Bolera   119
7 Dances and Dancers of the Escuela Bolera   129
8 The Pericet Family   161
9 Biographical Information   173

Appendices to Part I

I   The Escuela Bolera Dance in London in the
    Nineteenth Century *by Ivor Guest*   211
II Some Theatres in Spain   217

PART II: The Pericet Syllabus

Codified Steps of the Escuela Bolera   225

PART III: The Codified Dances

Bolero con Seguidillas (Goya)   283
Bolero del Candil (Goya)   288
Seguidillas del Candil (Goya)   290
Bolero de Caspe (Regional, Aragon)   297

The Pericet Versions of:
Boleras de la Cachucha   301
Boleras de Medio Paso   308
Cachucha   319
El Olé de la Curra   327
Jaleo de Jerez   335
La Macarena   345
Panaderos de la Flamenca   353
Peteneras Boleras (Andaluzas)   358
Seguidillas Manchegas   369
Sevillanas Boleras   377
Soleares del Maestro Arcas   386
Zapateado de Maria Cristina   390

Bibliography   397
Index   401

Colour plates between pages 144 and 145
and pages 208 and 209

Acknowledgements

I am particularly grateful to:

The Radcliffe Foundation.
The Carina Ari Foundation.
The Heritage Dance Foundation and Dr Charles Zwerling.
The Spanish Dance Society, without whose generous assistance the publication of this book would not have been possible.

Ivor Guest for his genuine interest, knowledge and help in reading the manuscript, for generously allowing me to reprint his article on the Escuela Bolera dancers in London, and permission to quote from his books.

Professor Bengt Häger for understanding the need to preserve such a heritage and for helping to do so.

Richard Glasstone for reviewing the manuscript.

Ralph Pemberton, the knowledgeable linguist and guitarist, who translated beautifully and endlessly for me and advised me on musical matters.

Conchita del Campo for the endless hours that she willingly spent proofreading through the codification of the exercises and dances, her welcome comments and caring interest.

The teachers and dancers with whom I studied through the years for this particular part of my research, because this is part of a larger work on the dances of Spain:

Eloy Pericet in Madrid, for many hours of study and for the photographs of his family, as well as answering endless queries, and Angel Pericet for giving up his holiday to teach me when Eloy was away.

Mercedes y Albano, in Madrid, who guided some of my first Spanish steps in Spain and through whom I first learned about the Escuela Bolera, and who led me to Eloy Pericet Blanco for further study.

My friend Joan Fosas of the folk company Esbart Dansaire de Rubí, Barcelona, for sharing wonderful dance treasures of the east coast of Spain, as well as unforgettable moments with his family: Rosa, whose beautifully made costume, for Bolero de L'Alcudia is pictured in this book, we treasure it in Washington DC, her husband Pedro and their children Nuria and Meritxel in Rubí, Barcelona.

Vivacious Carmen Gordo for much information and many historical regional dances.

The lovely dancer, Consuelo (Chelo) Cano Concuero, for her loving help on the Goya Seguidillas dances.

Enric Marti i Mora from the Department of Traditional Culture, 'Lo Rat Penat' of Valencia, for his instruction of Valencian dance and folklore, to me and my company in Washington DC.

Two of my American pupils: Nancy Sedgwick, Executive Administrator of the Spanish Dance Society in Washington DC, who danced the steps for hours for our mutual benefit; and Paula Durbin, who put on tape some of the dances and who checked some questions that I had on the Escuela Bolera syllabus with Luisa Pericet in Buenos Aires. She also passed on news clippings about the Pericet family in Argentina. We had many interesting discussions via e-mail on the Escuela Bolera.

Mary Ann Shelton, who prepared the 1989 Escuela Bolera exercises for word processing.

Irina Campbell (Montes) for her beautiful dancing of some of the Escuela Bolera treasures and for recognising the value of the Spanish Dance Society examination syllabus.

Professors Nancy Diers Johnson, Maida Withers, William Pucilovsky and Carl Gudenius at George Washington University, whose loving support and encouragement of my theatrical endeavours made my stay in Washington DC so satisfying and happy.

Jasmine Honoré in Cape Town, who suggested that I had a 'feel' for Spanish dancing and sent me to study with that indefatigable Elsa Brunelleschi in London, where I stayed with her and her family and was given access to her books and music. I met many fascinating people in the dance world in her home. She was unique in her excellent teaching of castanet playing and imparting Spanish dance as a whole, and not just flamenco.

Carlos José Gosalvez Lara for his knowledgeable assistance at the Biblioteca Nacional in Madrid, and others there who helped me with such patience and kindness: the librarians Isabel Ruiz de Elvira and Cristina, Maria Victoria Salinas, and the assistant Maria Sol Alonso-Cortes.

Audrey Harman of the Royal Ballet School Library in London, always cheerful and caring with her assistance, as was Elena Jack of the Royal Academy of Dance library.

José Blas Vega for his erudite research, kind assistance and gifts of valuable books and papers.

Aurora Pons, former Director of the Ballet Nacional de España, for discussions and for advising about the shoes worn in the various *Escuela Bolera* dances.

Arcadio Carbonell, of the National Ballet School in Madrid, the Royal Conservatory, for being my very genial host on recent visits to Madrid and for putting his large library of music, books and prints at my disposal. Nothing was too much trouble in his efforts to help me.

Pilar Llorens, who has sadly passed away in 1999, for her excellent research into the early dance of Barcelona, which she has shared here with us. She is a great loss to Spanish dance.

Maria José Ruiz, Marta Carrasco Benítez and Cristina Marinero for their ongoing work on Spanish dance and the heritage of the research on the Escuela Bolera in Seville.

Roger Salas for inviting me to participate in the fascinating and valuable symposium in Madrid in 1992, the Encuentro Escuela Bolera, and for his writings. (I hope that my contribution added by the reporting of things actually happening today in Spain.)

The inimitable José de Udaeta, a great educator and communicator, for his revelations at the 1992 Encuentro Escuela Bolera and on many others, punctuated with much shared laughter, and also for permission to print many of the illustrations that he has collected through the years.

Luisillo for opening my eyes to the possibilities of transposing Spanish dance successfully into the theatre and for helping, for many years, to trace the people who could teach me the unknown dances I yearned for – and for generously lending me his studio for lessons on these dances.

Alberto Lorca, a great gentleman, for helping with so many things – locating addresses, people, photographs – for his delightfully wicked sense of humour, and his beautiful choreography.

The book *The History of the Spanish Theatre* by A.D. Shergold and the research by Anna Ivanova in her book *The Dancing Spaniards*. Both had access to information beyond my resources.

Knud Arne Jürgensen of the Royal Danish Library's Department of Theatre, Dance and Music for his book on the Bournonville dancer Ferdinand Hoppe, and other material. He helped me almost a quarter of a century ago to find a picture for my book *The History of Ballet in South Africa*, and to our mutual delight we met up again at the Swedish Royal Ballet's 225th celebrations in Stockholm in 1998.

Kerstin Wiking and Eva Karlsson in Stockholm, at the 'Bildarkiven' of the National Museum of Art, who went far beyond the call of duty to find Spanish dance sketches of the *bolero* and other dances drawn by Swedish artists, as did Grethe Hallberg.

Anja Musiat of the archive and library of the Royal Theatre in Copenhagen, and Ida Poulson, curator of the Royal Museum in Copenhagen, for the time and trouble they took to trace pictures for me.

Karin Högberg of Zornsamlingarna, Diane Liddy of the Hispanic Society of America and Christopher Ketcham of the Phillips Collection.

Enrique Breytenbach, a friend indeed, who is always willing to draw sketches for the books that I have prepared for the Spanish Dance Society, as well as this one.

Two pianists, Judith Binding and Maureen Blaydon, who have helped me on many occasions.

Sherrill Wexler for her wish for such a book and for her constant encouragement for me to write it and get it published.

My colleagues Marina Lorca and Rhoda Rivkind for their support in many ways throughout thirty-five years of friendship, and all who have helped me through the years.

Sharon Sapiensa for collecting photographs of Matilde Coral, Maria Jesus García, 'Toni' Muñoz and Theo Dantes for photographs and visual material from Valencia, Robert Harrold for the photograph of the exit from the Pericet Studio.

Vicky Kurland Ramos for discussions when she taught from my notes and Gillian Hurst for clarification of Cecchetti steps.

Cecily Robinson, for teaching me not only ballet, but how to 'dance' and not just move to music, in far-away Cape Town, and for being the most inspiring teacher that I have ever encountered.

Sanjoy Roy has my gratitude for the initial editing of this extremely difficult manuscript.

Liz Morrell for so willingly guiding the final moments of this book and its illustrations with care and devotion to detail. Patrick Donnelly for his painstaking work on the illustrations.

The writer's retreat, Die Boekehuis, Calvinia, South Africa.

My children Vicky, Edmund and Nicolai for their genuine interest and support, and most of all to my knowledgeable, patient and generous husband, Mikael, who not only encourages and assists me in all I do, but who changed and enriched my life from the moment we met.

Prologue

Alberto Lorca

Marina says that I am the last living mammoth of Spanish classical dancing and because of this she wants me to write about my experiences. It all began in September 1944. I was 20 years old and had never set foot in a theatre. I had never seen a ballet. Then a friend, Roberto Carpio, took me to visit the Teatro Español [in Madrid] and when I stepped onto the stage I realised that my life had changed forever. I had to live in the theatre, on the stage.

At that time I was an extremely handsome (young) mammoth, with a very impressive body, built up by all sorts of sporting activities, athletics, swimming . . . and I had a fine ear for music. As a result, two days later, I was on stage with other boys and girls dancing a polka, choreographed by Carpio.

Soon afterwards people told me that I was wasting my time and that I should go to an academy and learn how to dance properly. So I went to the Pericet school, located in the middle of a traditional (*castizo*) quarter, at Encomiendo Street number 10. The room was 6 × 4 metres. In the middle the planks were worn down by years of stamping (*zapateado*). You needed pack-horse ankles to survive! There was a lovely old lady pianist of indeterminate age and there was also a cat; these two merged in one's senses.

The *maestro*, Don Angel Pericet, sat in front of a balcony and went through the Escuela (the classical school of Spanish dance) exercises. That meant all the different existing steps very cleverly put together in groups or 'families'. Then there was Conchita. She was the sister of Angel and Luisa. When teaching – she used to sit right in front of you, face to face – she played her castanets and we had to follow her. We worked for 20 or 30 minutes, just to play the four verses of *Sevillanas*. This was the way we learned.

And finally, Luisa, my unforgettable teacher, who then taught me how to dance the four verses. This was the very first thing we learned. Once you could dance the steps, move your arms and play the castanets of that choreographic jewel of Andalusian dance, when you were able to dance those four *Sevillanas* properly, and only then would she go ahead with the rest of the dances, an enormous repertoire of *Boleros, Seguidillas, Malagueñas, Jotas* and so on.

From all over came pupils such as Elvira Lucena, Pacita Tomás, Carmen Sevilla, José Luis de Udaeta, Juan Magriña. Harald Lander came every year from Denmark and he could leap very high. Once Luisa had taught him all the required *port de*

Alberto Lorca archive

bras, his jumps were only half as high as before. Then she asked him to add the playing of the castanets, and that was that: his leaps were down to 14 inches.

There were those pupils that approached the Escuela Bolera like refined dances executed by countesses or marchionesses. Luisa always explained to me how mistaken those people were, because none of those aristocrats had the necessary strength and stamina (*fiatto*) to go through with it, nor could they play castanets well enough. Furthermore, most of them would not have had the guts to visit the sites where those dances – *Bailes del Candil*, *Corraleras* and so on – took place. In those places, as in the film *Saturday Night Fever*, the (*Bolero*) dances were executed as a contest: how high you jumped and how many *coplas* or verses you could perform in a row. This was the way you could charm the girls, and it left very little chance for the aristocracy.

Performances started. My first engagement came from Udaeta. He wanted me and two girls to dance with him in *Aida*. As I had never used make-up before, I chose a very dark brown colour for my face and body and, just to be a little exotic, I made up my ears in turquoise blue! My mother asked me later what kind of flowers I was wearing.

The second engagement came from a German called Mr Duisberg, who was a famous director of the Scala Theatre in Berlin. I had a real ball! I was dancing some *Goyescas*, Viennese waltzes, Brazilian sambas, gallops, polkas . . . We stayed in Barcelona for three months and in Madrid as well. *La joie de vivre*!

With all the money that I had earned, I decided to learn as much as I could. I did ballet with the excellent Danish teacher in Madrid, Karen Taft, flamenco with La Quica and the great Estampio, choreographer of the *Zapateado de las Campanas* and the *Baile del Picador*. When I came to him – he was already 70 – he used to work with us in his bedroom slippers with rubber soles. Can you believe it? Many years have passed and I still can't understand how he managed it.

In 1946, when I was working on my first choreography for myself, the studio door opened and there she stood: Pilar López in person. She asked me to go through my routine, so I did. She stood up and said '*Gracias*', and disappeared. I should have felt miserable, but I didn't. I was not in the mood for that. Two weeks later, while she was on tour in Andalusia, she called me to join the company that very evening. She had to dismiss three gypsies, and needed to replace them. Alejandro Vega and Manolo Vargas were already in the company and I was to be the third replacement.

I made my debut dancing a lovely ballet by José Greco, with his wife Nila Amparo, to music by Infante. The plot was a bit like that of Jerome Robbins' *Fancy Free*: the girl flirted with José and us and, finally, the four of us left her alone. That happens. In that performance I also danced *Bolero Liso* and got ten curtain-calls. When I crossed Pilar on stage she said, 'You're fired!' She had a delightful sense of humour and sense of fun. Once, while performing *The Three-Cornered Hat*, we danced in two lines. The boys were going backwards to the end of the stage and the girls going the same way but facing the boys. She had made good use of the movement and when I looked at her she was wearing an enormous false moustache that she had kept hidden in her in her corsage while facing the audience. Another time, when we came out of a rehearsal, the streets were crowded as never before. An Arab king or prince of a little-known country was visiting Franco. As the cars passed with the populace acclaiming them, I noticed Pilar next to me, arms up, playing castanets furiously. I could not believe it. We could have been jailed for this. This was the woman who created the most beautiful choreographies and kept Spanish dance in its purest and most glamorous form.

On one of the many cruises to South America we had to take the boat from Cádiz, where we arrived the day before we were due to sail. Pilar called a few old flamenco friends to organise a party. When we – Pilar and five members of her company – arrived at an enormous place with stained glass windows and very long tables with plenty of seafood, ham, cheese, fried fish and gallons of wine and whisky, we were thunderstruck. There we were met by a crowd of 10 women (the youngest aged 65) and 15 men, all singers, musicians and dancers.

I remember that one old woman was shy of eating in our presence, but after some glasses of *fino* wine everybody began to lose their shyness and started to play and sing. The oldest woman said, 'Anyone who cannot restrain themselves can come and dance.' It was a magic night. They all danced, no matter if they were wearing canvas sandals or felt slippers. The whole evening was a lesson in wisdom, femininity and power, a lesson in traditional old flamenco singing and dancing (*cante antiguo* and *baile antiguo*). We finished at ten in the morning and went straight to the boat.

At that time Pastora Imperio was performing every night in a flamenco club (*tablao*) called *Gitanillos* which was owned by her son-in-law Gitanillo de Triana, a very famous and excellent bullfighter. We went there just to admire her marvellous arm movements (*braceo*). Amongst others Maleni Loreto, Rocio Jurado, La Nepompa were onstage too in this very *tablao*. And we can't forget Carmen Amaya and Lola Flores, two well-known artists of unmeasurable talent, temper and grace.

Nowadays when I go to a 'flamenco' performance and I see four guitarists, four singers, two *palmeros* (hand clappers), two drummers with a wooden box (all of them with microphones) producing an unbearable noise, I remember us, with only one singer and one guitarist, stamping our *zapateados*, playing our castanets, doing our *palmas*. The audience and we ourselves could hear the music and the singer perfectly. Nowadays the flamenco is no longer what it used to be or what it should be.

I had the chance to see the best flamenco shows, sometimes with Malena and Macarrona. The star of the show always sat at the end of the semi-circle near the audience, always dressed in a dress with a long train (*bata de cola*), always in white. She was the last to perform, at all times an *Alegrias* dance (*Por Alegrias*). Those dancers always had to go through all the sequences required in the *Alegrias*: *salida*, *falseta*, *castellana*, *escobilla* and *ida*; altogether only about six to eight minutes at the most. At present the girls do not even know how to handle the long train of the dress (the *cola*), and, worst of all, they don't have the sense of timing. They dance – to an *Alegrias* beat but completely ignoring the *Alegrias* sequences – for 20 or 30 minutes, mostly stamping (*zapateados*) like boys. After ten minutes one wishes one had not come.

To conclude, let me say a few words about a delightful friend with a great sense of humour, a good mother, a good grandmother, and married to an intelligent, witty and loving husband. I have never known a person so tenacious, persevering and devoted to Spanish dancing as Marina. That makes her an expert on every field of this art that we love so much.

Thank you Marina. I love you.

Alberto Lorca
Madrid, 19 May 2000

Foreword

Whatever research I present is done with humility. After fifty years of Spanish dance experience I am in awe of the vastness of the field. This book is for dancers and dance teachers and anyone fascinated by the richness of Spanish dancing. It contains what I, as a dancer and teacher of ballet and Spanish dancing and director of Spanish dance in the theatre, have gleaned from lessons with many teachers in Spain and elsewhere; from texts in the books and manuscripts that I have studied; from asking questions of whomever I thought knowledgeable about Spanish dance and music. It is not enough to dance, it is necessary to know what and why, as Otero so wisely says in his book *Tratado de Bailes* (Seville, 1912). Those interested in the connection between ballet and Spanish dancing and in flamenco will also find many matters of interest.

I have tried hard to acknowledge all my sources. Above all it is from my own direct experience of this fascinating field of dancing that I have drawn certain conclusions. I have tried to create a book which I wished had existed for me when I was starting to learn about Spanish dancing: a place where answers can be found. Each section can stand on its own, and there may therefore be a slight amount of repetition, brought in for clarity – but, I hope, not much. Some photographs are very old and therefore not clear, but their relevance is obvious.

The codified steps and dances are of use when studying the detail of the dances. After a class one may wonder which foot a step started on, or which arm or castanet rhythm was used to accompany it. It can save endless worry and pass on the correct version to posterity. This is why I decided that only one version of the exercises – that of the Pericet family and from one teacher, Eloy Pericet Blanco – should be notated. In performance these steps may have slight variations even by members of the same family. Each dance is written out in a manner suited to the particular dance. I hope that this section is as error-free as possible. It is gruelling work to codify all the aspects, the arms, timing, castanets as well as steps for someone else to read and understand. However, it may help someone when they go to study in Spain, and detail can be added to by that person.

Of the vast field of Spanish dance one can only scratch the surface in a lifetime of study. The two companies that I have recently worked with – one Basque, Argia in San Sebastian under the revered Juan Urbeltz, and the other Catalonian, with the dedicated dancer Joan Fosas of the Esbart Dansaire de Rubí in Barcelona and

José Otero Aranda
José de Udaeta archive.

with the inspired choreography of Albert Sans – both have several hundred dances in their repertoires, none duplicated. One group performs only Basque dances, the other's dances are confined to the regions along the east coast of Spain. This will give an idea of the amazing number of dances of infinite variety in this country. There is erroneous data in print, quoted and requoted by researchers who know the literature but not the dances. I have tried to correct what I came across and not add to this. This book deals with some aspects of this vast heritage. It is so difficult to obtain information that a dancer needs to know on this subject, especially in English, that I wish to share what little I have gleaned, with the hope that someone will find it of interest and of use to build on in the future.

JOSÉ OTERO

TRATADO

DE

BAILES

SEVILLA, 1912

Cover of *Tratado de Bailes*

Part I

The History of the Bolero

Illustration 1
Don Angel Pericet Carmona
José de Udaeta archive.

Introduction

The Salient Features of the Escuela Bolera

Food For Balletic Thought

During my research I serendipitously came across similarities between the Escuela Bolera and the Cecchetti and Bournonville methods. The Bournonville style in Copenhagen is now the only remnant of the old nineteenth-century French style of ballet, which shared that period in dance with the Spanish style of classical dancing. While this style is still preserved in Denmark, though recently precariously so, the Spanish equivalent remains in scattered dances, sometimes badly reconstructed in several parts of the world, including in Spain. However, there the Pericet family have, through the twentieth century, retained it intact from the teaching of their grandfather, Angel Pericet Carmona.

The Style

People tend to look only in past centuries when they do research, forgetting that Spanish dance is alive and continuously evolving. Few serious scholars write about Spanish dance as it is in the present. I once asked José de Udaeta when the style of the Escuela Bolera (the classical *Bolero* school of Spanish dancing) changed from what it originally was in the nineteenth century. This prompted him to speak of this at the Escuela Bolera symposium in Madrid in 1992. Although books and manuscripts were constantly being written about the Escuela Bolera, it was amazing that no one had ever remarked before on something so fundamental. As late as the 1940s, the whole way of performing the arm movements in the dances was changed by Angel Pericet Jiménez from the way it was danced in the nineteenth century, the era when the *Bolero* was known as Spain's 'national dance'.

Placing of Arms and Body

I first studied the Escuela Bolera steps and dances in London with Elsa Brunelleschi. There was a slight forward lean or tilt of the body, and the arms were held forward and slightly open to either side of the head, a placement considered essential in the eighteenth century by Requejo, a dancer from Murcia, when he was trying to restore the *Bolero* to its former glory. He went further, saying that the elbows should be no higher than the shoulders, harking back to the era when heavy

Illustration 2
An illustrated page from the chapter 'Le Bolero' by guitarist/composer Ferdinand Sor(s), from the *Encyclopédie Pittoresque de Musique* of A. Ledhuy and H. Bertibi, Paris 1835.

epaulettes did not allow for the arms to be raised higher. These position of arms and body can be seen in all engravings, lithographs and figurines of the eighteenth and nineteenth centuries. The movements were small rounds of the arms, as they also were in flamenco earlier in the twentieth century. The *rodazánes* (*ronds de jambe*, or rounds of the leg) were in front, and small. Later I found everyone in Spain dancing the classical dances upright, with great extensions of arms and legs and the *rodazánes* to the side and elevated. No one told me why. Perhaps they did not know. (When I studied with Enrique 'El Cojo' in Seville in the 1960s, he too demanded that I change the use of arms in flamenco to wide generous gestures.)

When I discussed the changed arm positions with José de Udaeta, he said that Angel Pericet Jiménez, the present generation's father, had changed this in his teaching. In discussion with my teacher, his son Eloy Pericet Blanco, he said that his father had indeed done so when he moved to Madrid in the 1940s. However, Udaeta stated at the Encuentro Escuela Bolera Symposium that he had studied in Seville with Rafael, the brother of Angel Pericet Carmona, who had continued to teach everything in the old style. Thus today the generally accepted position of the body is upright with the arms over the centre of the head, the *rodazanes* are to the side, with a high extension of the leg, and there is a more generous use of the arms. It has caused a lot of confusion as some teachers still teach the forward tilt and position of the arms, and the *rodazánes* in front. Dancers are often told that it is 'old-fashioned' and out of date. The original soft use of the arms is still used today in Valencia in their regional dances. In fact the usual position found in the Escuela Bolera dances, with one arm above and to the side of the head and the other low and to the back, is called the Valencian position, and shows the connection in the Escuela Bolera with an inheritance from that region. It can be seen in the lithographs of Fanny Elssler and her contemporaries. Compared to the nineteenth century, in the present day classical ballet the positions of the arms tend to be less rounded and sometimes held slightly further back (Richard Glasstone, personal communication).

No emphasis was placed on keeping the knees straight or on extension of the legs, and today some teachers feel that this is how the Escuela Bolera should be performed. However, this could be a matter of poor teaching, because I think that several centuries ago in Spain, Esquivel de Navarro was advocating the straightening of the knees and a turn-out of the legs.

Pierre Rameau, the author of *The Dancing Master* (Paris, 1725), wrote down the arms for ballet in almost an exact description of the work of the Spaniard Requejo, who had tried to restore the *Bolero* to its former status and glory. In other words, he was trying to go back in time to the original arms used when dancing a *Bolero*. In speaking of the arms, Requejo stated that they must be used as a frame to the body. These were Rameau's sentiments as well. He was the teacher of Isabel Farnese of

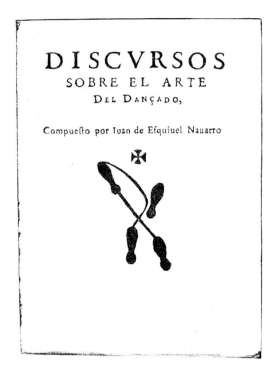

Illustration 3
Treatise on the Art of Dancing, compiled by Esquivel de Navarro. Published in 1642.

◆ See colour plate 1

Parma, who married Philip V of Spain in 1714. Some historians think that Rameau influenced the use of arms in Spanish dance, but the elements described, such as the use of the body with *épaulement*, so entrenched in Spanish dancing, and positions of arms and feet, can be found in the dances of Spain centuries before this period. They are typical of some of the regional dances in many areas across the country. The influence could thus have flowed in the opposite direction, through Spanish dance to ballet.

However, in another way, ballet performances in the eighteenth century did change the way the classical *Bolero* was presented in the theatre. The lavish spectacle of ballets caused the *Bolero*, from being a couple dance, to become presentations using several couples, while many steps were also added to the repertoire of the Escuela Bolera. It also made the Spaniards form a method of teaching that style of dancing, something unheard of before or since. Today the Spanish Dance Society offers a method for Spanish dance teaching as a whole, but this started outside Spain, by a group of teachers in South Africa seeking to improve the standard of Spanish dance teaching outside Spain. It has become an international organisation and has been adopted by the Spaniards as well. Examinations are held annually in all the major cities and towns in Spain. It has become particularly popular in Andalusia.

Spanish dancing is such a vital force, it could not but have influenced ballet. In the case of Rameau it is tempting to think that he was influenced by the way Spaniards used their arms.

Ballet's Direct Inheritance from Spanish Dancing

Arms held with hands resting on shoulders. Men dropped their tired arms thus to rest them from the heavy épaulettes. Used to teach poise by RAD; seen in the dance *Seguidillas del Candil*, from the Goya era.

Fingers placed under thumb. The Royal Academy of Dancing used this at the barre. In Seville, Matilde Coral still uses it to teach wrist movements (*Muñecas*).

Arm position across the chest. In Cecchetti this appears with *pas de bourrée, pas de chat* and during a *port de bras*. It is also seen in the dance *Peteneras*.

Blasis's 'Mercury' position. This is known in Spain as the Valencian position and depicted in sketches of Fanny Elssler in *La Cachucha*. Seen in the *Peteneras* and *Boleras de la Cachucha*.

Shared Inheritance

Stepping to the side at the start of a pas de bourrée. Ballet (Cecchetti): Cecchetti *pas de bourrée couru*. Escuela Bolera: *pifla y pas de bourrée*.

◆ See colour plate 2

Lean away from the leg (cambré) when it is lifted to the side in 2nd. Ballet (Cecchetti): *degagé à la seconde.* Escuela Bolera: *escobilla hacia delante y tres destaques.*

Arms used in circles in Spanish dance. This was misunderstood by foreign choreographers such as Bournonville and possibly Petipa. Ballet (Cecchetti): ballet step travelling. Escuela Bolera: *vuelta de valse.*

The Spanish way danced with a little beat. Ballet (Cecchetti): full *contretemps.* Escuela Bolera: *retortillé dos paso de vasque y vuelta fibraltada.*

Small run ending with a point. Ballet (Cecchetti): *pas de bourrée, dégagé* and *fouetté.* Escuela Bolera: *batararaña.*

A very similar exercise for rounds of the leg. Ballet (Cecchetti) *ronds de jambe* with a hop, turning. Escuela Bolera: *rodazánes en vuelta.*

A ballonné exercise. Ballet (Cecchetti): *ballonné à trois temps.* Escuela Bolera: *ballonné, dos pas de basques y vuelta fibraltada.*

Typical Escuela Bolera steps with no Balletic Influence

Golpe punta y talon
Lazos
Soubresu
Sisol, dos jerezanas bajas y dos altas.

Misunderstandings when Foreign Choreographers Portray Spanish Dancing

Vuelta de valse
The use of circular arm movements in Spanish dances, used by Bournonville, who moved them from side to side from a position over the head.

Sevillanas chorus step
Used by Massine, Bournonville and possibly even Petipa, who do more of a *balancé* with a lot of swayback in the body. This sway is not used in this step by Spaniards. In fact, Spanish dancing requires tremendous upright discipline of the body, and control.

Escuela Bolera is not ballet with castanets
It is usually thought that the Escuela Bolera is ballet with a Spanish accent. This is a total misconception. A ballet dancer would be hard pressed to dance these dances without extra study. First, there is the addition of playing castanets, no mean feat to sustain while jumping. Then the arms are used in circular movements, totally different from ballet, although the arm positions used in ballet are taken from Spanish dancing – including the positions mentioned above.

Ferdinand Sor(s) (see p.4), a famous Catalan guitarist and composer who spent most of his life in exile in France, England and Russia (because he backed the wrong side when the French invaded Spain), wrote of this difference between ballet and Spanish dance. He claimed that the rules for the arms and head, the head and the feet and the carriage of the shoulders are contrary to those of the French dance. If by 'French dance' he is referring to ballet, it is not the contrary, merely different, as I described above. Sor was not a dancer, and it was difficult for him to analyse dance. The movements of feet and legs are not different at all, the steps are. Sor said that M. Coulon (possibly the teacher Jean-François Coulon, 1764–1836) had great difficulty teaching the Spanish dancer Mlle Mercandotti the French dance because she already performed the *Bolero* in the characteristic way, and that she eventually mastered it to the detriment of the Spanish dancing. This is hard to believe. Any dancer worth her salt should be able to master different styles. It may not be easy, but it is possible. Certainly a dancer who is ballet-trained already has the technical basis for part of the classical Spanish dance. Each is a training in its own right.

Sor also wrote of the French dancer Mme Lefebre (Lefèbre in France) who performed in Seville with her company of French and Spanish dancers for Napoleon's brother Joseph and the invading troops. It is amusing that he says she changed the way that the Spanish dances were performed and yet was applauded by the Spaniards; so her changes must have been acceptable. Yet those who applauded were amongst the conquered, and one can imagine that they probably had little choice, or wanted to flatter the invaders.

Another misconception is Sor's statement that the *cabrioles* and the stamps, performed several times successively with a flat foot derive from the Gypsies; the stamps were already present in Spanish dances when the Gypsies arrived. The *cabrioles* are only performed today by the Gypsies to 'send up' non-Gypsy dancing, when they perform *Bulerias*, and in that particular case they use those from the *Aragonese Jota*. The stamps Sor referred to are typical of the Escuela Bolera. Interestingly enough, today they have been modified and can be danced by doing a *sostenido*, or toe dig and stamp, which is more elegant. They appear in *Boleros* and in *Sevillanas Boleras*, the classical version of the *Seguidillas* from Seville. They also appear in Zorn's notation of the *Cachucha*.

The Steps
Many steps in ballet come from Spanish dance – beaten ones from the Basques for example. Most of the Escuela Bolera steps are from regional dances: some with little beats in them, some with twists of the foot on the ground (*bordoneos*); or on the half-point (*lazos*) with legs turning in and out as in a Charleston; *punta y talon*, with the toe digging (turned in) at the side and then the heel dig (turned out). There are many others: *batararaña*, a glissade and then a point of the foot to a front corner; *cuna*, rocking over on crossed feet, as in a sailor's hornpipe; turns with the body bent, over and under, forward and backward. The Spanish *glissade* is more like a 'step-close', although in some studios they are jumped as in ballet. The balletic steps are mainly to be found in the final three sequences of the third

course, or Tercero Curso, of the Pericet Syllabus. They are very difficult – *brisé volé*, *entrechats cinque* and *six* and so on, steps from Russian dancing for the men with deep *plié* and jumping out to the side up on the heels; and also jumped turns in the air. These are not found in the most popular dances from this period, but beats and pirouettes are found in the *Boleros* such as *Bolero de Medio Paso* and *Boleras de la Cachucha* and *Bolero Liso*, with its free choreography.

Perhaps this is the moment to note two peculiarities about two Basque steps found in ballet that are also different from ballet. When the Basques beat their legs, in an *entrechat six* for example, they beat in front first. This is the way they still perform and count their beats at the Paris Opera (Richard Glasstone, personal communication). When the Basques do *rodazánes* (*ronds de jambe*), those on the ground are always outward and those in the air always inward.

I recognise that the step known as *matar-la-araña* ('killing the spider') may have come to us through the tongue-in-cheek corruption by Rodrigues Calderón in his book *Bolerologia*. He satirises many things in it. Eloy Pericet maintains that there is no such name for this step, but that it is called *batararaña*. Has this joke perhaps been handed down to posterity and been taken seriously?

Within the Escuela Bolera's remaining syllabus and in the dances there is no *pas de chat*. I have seen the dance *Olé de la Curra* mistakenly presented with many *pas de chat*. In the Pericet system there is no turn with a *développé*, referred to in Spanish as *destaque doblada* (Eloy Pericet, personal communication).

Dances

What does Blasis mean by noting down the dance *Seguidillas 'Taleada'*? Could this be a printing error? No such dance as *Taleada* can be found, nor could the knowledgeable Spaniards produce evidence of one. The *Seguidillas Jaleadas* is mentioned in print, and there is Saldoni's *Boleras Jaleadas*, but both with a 'J'. A Jaleo was a type of dance. The *Boleras de la Cachucha* has alternating sections of *Bolero* and *Cachucha*, with the *Cachucha* sections referred to as the *Jaleos*. The dictionary definition of *jaleo* is a racket or uproar, and it is used in dance to describe the hand-clapping and shouting that often cheers on the performers. Was it a misprint or a misunderstanding on the part of Blasis that has come down to us?

There is a reference to a *Jota* in Baron Davillier's book about his travels in Spain in the nineteenth century. In the illustration by Gustave Doré, who accompanied him on his journey, it was clearly a *Bolero*, one danced by mourners. His citation can lead to others quoting him and continuing the error. It led to my own contribution to the 1992 Encuentro Escuela Bolera symposium in Madrid about two Valencian *Boleros*: the above dance of mourning, named *Mortitxol* (death of a child) as performed by the Esbart Dansaire of Rubi, Barcelona; and another Valencian dance, predating ballet, also performed by that company, the *Bolero de L'Alcudia de Carlet*. The steps performed in that dance are relevant to those in the later Escuela Bolera, which should therefore not be assumed to come from ballet.

As a ballet-trained Spanish dancer, I was able to recognise the Basque *Gabota* in the 'Vestris Gavotte' which was demonstratated by Sandra Hammond at a history conference in the USA in the 1980s. Had I not learned the *Gabota*, I could not have

Illustration 4
Danza del Velatorio, Valencia.
Sketch by Gustave Doré.

made this comparison when I saw the Vestris version. Musically, and in the steps, there is a direct connection. The Basques told me that the French ballet-master Jean-Georges Noverre (1727–1810) studied in Zuberoa, which would be on the French side (Juan Urbeltz, personal communication). Did Noverre teach a gavotte to them or did he take back that gavotte to Paris, and through his productions teach it to Vestris, through whom, in turn, it has come down to us? If someone were to look closely I am sure there would be many such instances to be unearthed.

Regional Similarities

Another intriguing matter is the cross-influence between regions. I came across the *Peteneras* in Valencia danced as a jolly, bucolic regional dance in triple time. In Andalusia this dance is solemn and deep, and counted in rhythmic cycles, or *compás*, of 12 beats. Then I read that the *Peteneras* in Andalusia was originally a dance of light gaiety. Perhaps the solemn words were added later to this melody? Yet who knows whether the *Peteneras* of Valencia is not the old version, now abandoned in Andalusia after the Gypsies took it and imposed a deeper mood of interpretation upon it? As I write in the chapter on the *Bolero*, it involves a cross-culture connection that came from the oil and silk routes that led to the dances exchanging regions. Who knows today who gave what to whom?

♦ See colour plate 3

Illustration 5
The Pericet family of 'Don Angel' Pericet Carmona, in Seville around 1920. Eloy Pericet Blanco Archive.

As with the Valencian dances termed 'Escuela', the name and connection may stem from either direction, but the development is firmly Andalusian. Two lithographs of Mariano Camprubí and Dolores Serral show them depicted with one hand on the hip and the other just hanging loosely down. This position, and the one seen in Elssler's famous picture with one arm overhead and the other slightly behind, are typical Valencian poses. The latter is called the Valencian position in the Escuela Bolera and the former is used in Valencian dances, for example the *Fandango de Hortunas*, which starts in that position with the arm on the hip while the dancer marks time with a slight hip movement, waiting for the right moment to start the dance. In the same way, the *Peteneras* of the Pericet family starts in that position, hand on hip centre stage, and on the commencement of the dance moves into the Valencian position.

The Pericet Family

Having been passed on to each successive generation of Pericets in a direct line, as taught by their grandfather, the Pericet method is all that remains of the exact steps and dances of the Escuela Bolera as it was in the nineteenth century. They thus go back to the first Angel Pericet (Carmona, 1877–1944) and his teachers of that era in

Seville, Amparo Alvarez (La Campanera), so beautifully sketched by Doré, and Maestro Faustino Segura. Whether the changes of style and steps are changes for the better is a matter for debate. Should the style remain for posterity with rounded open arms, and a forward tilt of the body, or be allowed to evolve and therefore change?

The Pericet connection is by no means our only link with the Escuela Bolera, but it is the most direct link over the centuries. There are many other teachers of this classical school (mentioned in the following chapter) in Barcelona, Seville, Cádiz and Málaga. Maria Mercedes León, for example, speaks of her contact with the daughter of a teacher in Madrid called Maestro Roy and of how he taught many more steps and certainly more intricate beaten footwork than found in the Pericet heritage. This could, of course, be Roy's own choreography.

I have codified the steps that remain in the Pericet Syllabus and some of the important dances of the Escuela Bolera in the Pericet versions. Other dances, such as the folk *Seguidillas* and *Boleros*, have also been included to record them for comparison and to preserve them for posterity.

Demonstrations of the links between Cecchetti and the Escuela Bolera

The links between the 19th century Cecchetti ballet syllabus and Escuela Bolera steps and style were shown at the following three lecture-demonstrations directed and presented by Marina Keet in London:

The Royal Academy of Dancing Assembly on the 2nd January 1998, with dancers: Gillian Hurst, Fiona Willsher, Sandra Doling and Hugh Rathbone.

The Cecchetti Society Day on the 26th July 1998, with dancers: Jaime Coronado, Conchita del Campo, Sandra Doling, Lourdes Elias, Gillian Hurst, Hugh Rathbone and Yuri Uchimi.

The Royal Opera House, 'Beyond Flamenco', presenter Deborah Bull for the Artists' Development Initiative Programme on the 23rd July 2000, with special guest artists Marina Lorca, Carlos Robles, and with Jaime Coronado, Conchita del Campo, Sandra Doling, Lourdes Elias, Gillian Hurst, Hugh Rathbone, Nancy Sedgwick, Nuno Campos, Francesca Frölich and Ella Barker; pianist, Judith Binding; singer, Peter Burroughs; guitarists, Angus Cruickshank and Jingles.

Dances showed the development from the *Seguidillas* through regional *boleros* and Escuela Bolera, as well as the influence in Hispanic America.

1

The Seguidillas

Origins

The *Seguidillas* from Castilla la Nueva or the region of New Castile, is of great historic importance. From the *Seguidillas* arose the famous *Bolero*, known as the national dance of Spain in the nineteenth century. The *Seguidillas* is thought to be the oldest original Spanish dance in Spain after the *Danza Prima* of Asturias. When looking at dances from Ibiza one wonders at this claim, as the steps there seem far more primitive. However, the *Seguidillas* is intrinsically Spanish, with no foreign influence. The great Spanish playwright Quiñones de Benavente (1866–1954) maintained that all the current Spanish dances stemmed from it – a slightly exaggerated view, which nevertheless shows how highly it was regarded.

In type it is direct and bucolic, though structurally broadly the same as a *Fandango*. It does not have the same sensuality as the *Fandango de Huelva*, but is more rustic, like the various *Fandangos de Verdiales*. Tomás de Iriarte, when writing of the *Fandango* asks, 'Which is the barbaric country whose inhabitants do not like to hear the strains of their folk dances?' – a cry for preservation which should be heeded.

In origin the *Seguidillas* comes from a particular verse type which has certain characteristics in form and rhyming. It goes back many centuries, but was at its height of popularity during the seventeenth century and was cited by authors of that period. It continued to be popular long into the eighteenth and nineteenth centuries, and versions of it such as the *Sevillanas* are thriving today and still danced as a living social dance, not just preserved by folk groups.

La Mancha: The Home of the Seguidillas

The original *Seguidillas*, the *Seguidillas Manchegas*, as its title denotes, comes from La Mancha (like Cervantes' Don Quijote), the bare plain between the mountains of Toledo, Cuenca and the Sierra Morena. The name La Mancha comes from the Arabic 'Al Mansha' meaning 'the dry land' or 'wilderness'.

The *Seguidillas Manchegas* is referred to by Miguel de Cervantes Saavedra (1547–1616) in *El Ingeniojoso Hidalgo Don Quijote de la Mancha* (Part 1 published in 1605, Part II in 1615), in chapter 18 of the second part, according to the *Encyclopaedia Britannica*. However, an even earlier mention of this *Seguidillas* was made by Mateo Alemán (1547–1614?) at the end of his novel *Vida y heches del*

♦ See colour plates 4 and 5

Picaro Guzman de Alfarache (1599), in which he wrote that the *Seguidillas* has replaced the *Zarabanda* in popularity. Although it is difficult to find traces of the *Seguidillas* before then, researchers have found verses of that type as far back as the fifteenth century.

The *Zarabanda* had been condemned by the clergy in the sixteenth century, together with the *Chacona* and the *Escarramán*, yet it did appear in the Corpus Christi Festival in 1593. But the condemnation must have assisted in its demise and replacement in popularity by the *Seguidillas*. Music and dance play an important part in the emotional life of people, and are usually the first to be banned when religious or political factions feel that they could rouse unwanted political emotions.

The sixteenth and seventeenth centuries saw the *Seguidillas* play an important role in village life. It also gained popularity in the capital, Madrid, which is situated in the cultural region of New Castile. Unusually for a peasant dance, it was even included in elegant soirées. Engravings depict the various steps from it. It featured in all the popular festivities, especially at the Prado, which in those days was a meadow on the hilltop outside Madrid. There the capital's people, the *majos* and *majas* (as the ladies and gentlemen of the middle class of that period were called), gathered on Sundays and danced. The artist Francisco José de Goya y Lucientes (1746–1828) has depicted and immortalised these occasions in his paintings.

What remains of these dances – a *Seguidillas del Candil*, a short *Bolero*, a *Tirana del Zarandillo*, a *Fandango Antiguo*, a *Jota de la Pradera* and *Fandango del Candil* – are still performed by the Coros y Danzas of Madrid. This group cel-

◆ See colour plate 6

Illustration 1.2
Seguidillas from
Ciudad Real.
Sketch by
Enrique
Breytenbach.
Marina Keet
archive.

ebrated its fiftieth anniversary on 23 May 1999. Originally they were assisted in the reconstruction of these dances by the musicologist M. García Matos, and then later they were trained by Carmen Gordo. They were directed by Carmen Cantero from 1974, and from 1998 they came under the direction of Jorge García Ávila with the principal dancer Concolación (Chelo) Cano Concuero conducting the rehearsals.

The *Seguidillas* becomes a dance of infinite variation once it leaves its original Manchegan form. It is a couple dance, but the couples may form one or more lines, or they may form circles or double circles. In technique, it migrated from its rustic origin of jumped steps to be stepped or stamped, as in the *Seguidillas* from Seville, the *Sevillanas*.

Always Seguidillas in the Plural

Composing *Seguidilla*, or the verses, was a popular pastime both in the country and in cities. The verses were set to music, and to this a dance was added. The verses were printed, sometimes with pages decorated with woodcuts, and sold in the streets. *Seguidillas* is always referred to in the plural, as this includes all its forms – poetry, music and dance. The singular refers to the verse alone, or to verse with music.

The verse, which came first, can have four lines in which the first and third are heptasyllabic, and the second and fourth pentasyllabic. At times this order can be reversed, as in the example below. It can, however, also have seven lines. García Matos goes into much greater detail. What needs to be noted is that in the danced version, what is known as the *copla* or verse, actually consists of three small

NUEVAS SEGUIDILLAS

En las que un fino enamorado esplica sus amores, burjándose á Cupido y pintando al mismo tiempo la hermosura y perfecciones de su querida dama.

Cupidillo me abrasa
con sus incendios,
mas como son Cupidos
muero por ellos:
　Que es fuego dulce,
que cuando mas abrasa
menos consume.
　Cuanto mas tiraniza
mas le deseo,
porque con sus rigores
crece mi anhelo:
　Que mi destino
se alienta en lo tirano
como en lo fino.

Ofreciendo á tus aras
mis sacrificios,
nunca logro la dicha
de mis alivios:
　Porque inhumano
no se rinde á lo dulce
ni á lo tirano.
　Siempre tuve por dichas
sus sinrazones,
porque en él las locuras
son discreciones:
　Que como es ciego,
no distingue lo altivo
de lo discreto.

Illustration 1.3
Nuevas Seguidillas, by kind permission of Carmen García Matos.

'verses' divided by the *estribillo* or so-called 'chorus', where there is no singing but just strumming on the guitar. The *estribillo*, or chorus, is danced at the start of the dance as an introduction. The *Seguidillas Manchegas* from Ciudad Real is a neat example. The following translation is by Ralph Pemberton:

Copla (verse)

First small verse (*copla*):

'*Son las que canto*	(5)	What I sing on the
Seguidillas Manchegas	(7)	Seguidillas from La Mancha;
Son las que canto	(5)	What I sing on the
Seguidilas Manchegas	(7)	Seguidillas from La Mancha;
Son las que canto	(5)	These are what I sing

Here the chorus or *estribillo* is played.

Second small verse (*copla*):

Son las que canto	These are what I sing
Porque las Sevillanas	Because the Seguidillas from
No valen tanto	Seville aren't as good;
Porque las Sevillanas	Because the Seguidillas from
No valen tanto	Seville aren't as good.

Here the chorus or *estribillo* is played.

Third small verse (*copla*):

Las Mancheguillas	These beauties from La Mancha
Suenen a cascabeles	Sound like the jingling
Las Mancheguillas	and ringing of bells;
Suenen a cascabeles	They sound like the jingling
Y campanillas	and ringing of bells

All this is considered to be one verse. Pemberton writes that 'Mancheguillas' also has a second meaning: women of La Mancha. *Cascabeles* are spherical like sleigh bells, while *campanillas* are normal hand bells; so the last line refers to the effect of the music, and at another level, to the sound of the voices.

There are, of course variations to this theme. One example is an amusing verse that compares men to bees which flit from flower to flower.

Con las abejas	
yo comparo los hombres,	I always compare men to bees my child,
yo comparo los hombres,	To bees . . .
yo comparo los hombres,	
yo comparo los hombres,	
chiqillo, con las abejas.	

Illustration 1.4
Distribution of the
Seguidillas, in the shaded
areas, according to the
musicologist García Matos,
sketch by Enrique
Breytenbach

Later the words warn that the bees seek to plunder the flowers, but sometimes flowers can have thorns!

Another example with seven lines is:

Mi madre me ha mandado	My mother has ordered me
que no te quiera,	Not to love you;
y yo le digo: Madre	But I said to her, 'Mother,
si usted la viera...	If only you could see her.'
Quedó tamaña,	She was so taken aback,
y moriendose el labio	That biting her lip,
dijó: ¡Caramba!	She said, 'Lord in Heaven!'

The word in the last sentence should be *mordiéndose*, but without the 'd' it is quite southern, more Andalusian.

What can not be seen in the written text is the pause of one beat after a word:

'Son-las-que-can-to (5) – pause
Se-gui-di-llas-Man-che-gas (7) pause
'Son-las-que-can-to (5) – pause
Se-gui-di-llas-Man-che-gas – (7) NO pause
'Son-las-que-can-to (5)

These pauses give the verse its rhythm and the lack of a pause make the last two lines flow into one and gives the poem the four lines. As with verses of other

Illustration 1.5
'A collection of the finest verses of the Seguidillas, Tiranas, Polos to be sung to the guitar. Volume I, by Don Preciso. Which, in spite of being frivolous, reflect the joy and wit of Spain.'

folk songs like *Jotas*, the words are an expression of very personal feelings and thus a vehicle to convey the poet's ideas on a great variety of subjects pertaining to humour, romance, current affairs, politics and so on; the words keep the songs alive and are the reason for their survival.

Replaced by Other Dances

García Matos says that the *Seguidillas* continued to be popular in the cities until the nineteenth century. It was sung under windows of loved ones, in the plazas and in the streets. In the country it held its own with the *Bolero*, *Fandango* and the *Jota*. Then the dance was replaced by other popular dances of the day to fill a social function. Recently, however, it has re-emerged to become almost the national dance of Spain, and in its form from Seville, the *Sevillanas*, it is definitely a popular social dance, danced in the south at all public gatherings and celebrations, and in special *salas* or venues.

A Description of the Seguidillas in 1740

Writing under the pseudonym of Don Preciso, Juan Antonio de Iza Zamácola o Ozerin collected and published the best verses of the popular regional dances – the *Seguidillas*, *Polos*, and *Tiranas* to be sung to guitar accompaniment. He gives the following description of the *Seguidillas* as performed at that time, around 1740, here in a translation by Ralph Pemberton:

Once a young man and young woman have appeared in the middle of a room, facing one another at a distance of about six feet, the chorus figure or prelude is played, after which the beginning of the *Seguidilla* is sung. For the *Seguidillas* Manchegas, the first line of the verse is sung, and for the *Seguidilla Bolera*, the first two lines, although these should take up only a total of four *compáses*. The guitar continues to play its completed phrase (a type of *passacaglia*), and, once the fourth compás is reached, the singer begins the *Seguidilla*. Then the dancers break into the dance, played with their castanets, and this goes on for nine *compáses*, at which the first part ends. The guitar plays the repeated figure once again, as the dancers change places by performing a slow simple promenade. The singing begins again at the fourth compás, and then, for a further nine *compáses*, the dancers perform those variations that are characteristic of their particular school of dance, thus completing the second part. Once again they change places, returning to their original positions and the third part follows the same pattern as the second. At the ninth *compás*, they stop simultaneously, together with (as if unexpectedly) the voice, the guitar and castanets, with the room in silence and the dancers remaining motionless, adopting beautiful poses with the term *bien parado*. The latter phrase means well stopped, or held.

The musicologist García Matos comments that, in all probability, this had always been the truly characteristic form of the *Seguidillas*, and it has been preserved up to the present day. The Bolero, which originated from the *Seguidillas*, took it over with hardly any changes, because it consisted, and continues to consist, 'of three similar parts, known as *coplas*, with a break after each *copla*, known as the *bien parado*, which provides an opportunity for the dancers to rest while the guitar plays its repeated phrase.'

Compás

Pemberton explains that:

In Spanish, *compás* can refer to the flamenco *compás* or to what other musicians refer to as a bar or measure. It really comes to the same thing (especially in *Sevillanas*); it's just that some bars are 12 or 6 beats long from the viewpoint of flamencos. Needless to say, 'bars' is really intended when the word *compás* is used, although 'measures' is a little less definite somehow, and would be a good word to substitute for *compás(es)* in the translation. A further complication arises in counting the 'measure' in *Sevillanas*, because in the traditional form the guitarist is playing in 2/4 while the dancers (I believe) count in 3/4, producing a nice counter-rhythm; but each will, therefore, finish up with a different number of bars for the same number of beats. In modern *Sevillanas*, as performed in *salas rocieros* or nightclubs, discos, etc., the guitarist, band or other accompanists also play in 3/4, presumably as a concession to the dancers.

He goes on to say, perceptively:

By the way, doesn't the second quotation imply at least one difference, i.e. that the *Bolero* dancers remained at *bien parado* between *coplas*, whereas the *Seguidillas* dancers performed a *paseo*?

This is quite correct. One comes across this in the Pericet versions of the classical *Peteneras Boleras* (where castanets are played throughout the introduction to each verse, with the dancers static) and *Boleras de la Cachucha* and *de Medio Paso* for example. There is a version of *Peteneras*, where charming dance sections between the *coplas* have been added by Mercedes y Albano. These are to the sections where, in the Pericet version, the dancer stands still and plays castanets.

Illustration 1.6
A performance in a public
square in Valencia in 1862
showing the covering used as
protection from the sun.

The Most Well-Known Seguidillas

C.G. Hartley calls the *Seguidillas* 'that most graceful dance which every child is taught . . . It is the "*Seguidilla*" with its gracious memories, which gives life to the "Feria"'. The Feria is the most famous festival held in Seville after Semana Santa or Holy Week (at Easter), where the *Seguidillas Sevillanas* is danced endlessly, tirelessly day or night.

As mentioned above, this *Seguidillas* from Seville is currently the most popular social Spanish dance for old and young. It is known simply as *Sevillanas*. From *Songs and Dances of Spain* (published by Sección Feminina de F.E.T Y de las J.O.N.S.) we learn that the most famous *Seguidillas* versions come from Seville, Córdoba, Malaga, Lucena, Montilla and El Alosno (in the Province of Huelva).

García Matos states that it was also first known as *Seguidillas*, then as *Seguidillas Sevillanas* and later simply as *Sevillanas*. Nowadays *Sevillanas* is danced not only at festivals all over Spain, but also in special bars (cafés), where people gather just to dance *Sevillanas*. (There is even a restaurant in Edinburgh, Scotland, where people go to dance *Sevillanas* to guitar.) Like the *Seguidillas* from

◆ See colour plates 7 and 30

La Mancha, it is a couple dance, but it was first performed as a solo in the nineteenth century by the dancer La Campanera (the teacher of Angel Pericet Carmona).

Corraleras, The Early Theatres

At the beginning of the twentieth century *Sevillanas* steps were bounced rather than stepped as they are today; they now show a marked flamenco influence. There are various types of *Sevillanas*. The *Sevillanas Corraleras* comes from the word *corral*, meaning cattle-pen (originally for wild animals). It was the first word used to describe a theatre in Spain. In the same way that theatres in the rest of Europe grew out of market places, the Spanish theatres seem to have started in the earthy plazas, or squares, where people gathered to sell horses and do some other trading. The owners of the buildings around these plazas had ringside seats for the performances! Special boxes were built below balconies to house spectators, and the king and queen often reserved one especially for themselves. There were several theatres by this name in Madrid during the eighteenth century, the Corral de los Caños del Peral, the Cruz and Corral del Principe and in Valencia the Corral de Val Hubert and Olivera. The latter two seem to have been pulled down quite early on at the order of the Church.

In an engraving from a Valencian performance one can see how the balconies of the houses around the square became translated into the balconies in indoor theatres. Strung across the tops of the houses are coverings, attached on either side to the buildings and forming a shelter for performers and the theatregoers. This was eventually to become the roof of a permanent theatre as we would know it today. Theatres in Europe grew up in the market places where entertainers went to earn a living performing to the shoppers. Typical examples in London would be regions of Covent Garden and the Haymarket.

Sevillanas Varieties

Many of the various types of *Sevillanas* can be seen in the film *Sevillanas* by Carlos Saura (a video of the film was made in 1992), including personal improvisations. It is the subject of the verses and the words that affect the title, such as those with religious or biblical references; others have references to pilgrimages. The style could be classical, or *corraleras* of pure folk origin. Often the *Sevillanas Rocieras* is played on the three-holed flute, which is played with one hand, while accompanying it with the other by striking a *tabor* slung over the shoulder. This is struck to keep the rhythm. García Matos says the flute is called a *gaita*, the same word used for a bagpipe. It has a hauntingly beautiful sound and is also the instrument used for several of Andalusia's regional dances such as *Fandango de Huelva*. Together with the flute and drum accompaniment, split reeds are banged against the hand, giving an added unusual rustling sound. *Sevillanas Boleras* can be accompanied by piano or *bandurrias*, lutes and guitars, or simply a guitar. More detailed information about these dances will follow later (pp. 36-43).

The Music

The music of the *Seguidillas*, like the dance, is very uplifting and is in 3/4 or 3/8 time, allegretto (not so lively) in Castile and allegro (lively) in Andalusia. The usual accompaniment is guitar, but some villages have a band composed of *bandurrias* (which play the melody), guitars (which strum the rhythm), *panderetas* (which follow the rhythm) and very often a *laud* (lute), triangles and *yerillos*.

In the countryside, to accompany the music or singing, blowing or passing the hand across the mouth of a large jar also produces a sound that is often used, with or without guitar accompaniment. A bottle with an indented pattern is scraped with a metallic object to produce another percussive accompaniment. This is especially used over the Christmas period by children doing their rounds of carol singing. All these instruments provide the rhythmic percussive acompaniment.

Anacrusic

The difficulty of the *Seguidillas* is that the music is anacrusic; that is, there are one or more unaccented notes before the stress comes on the first note. Some of the steps for a *copla* may start on these unaccented beats from the former section. The song starts on some of these endings of the *estribillo* and the steps throughought the first verse of *Sevillanas* are the last three beats of the *estribillo*. This trend is echoed in the later *Bolero*, where the count starts on the last beat of a bar and goes over two bars.

Modernisation

The *Sevillanas* music in recent times has certainly taken on a markedly Latin-American influence. Instead of the usual solo voice, groups of singers take part in Hispanic-sounding treatment of the melodies. When they do, it is usual that a solo voice still sings the introductory passage or *salida*. There is certainly a vast range of recordings available of different very modern treatments of the old structure. It is because of this renewed view of the music that it has kept its grip on the public. No one has changed the basic structure of the dance even though more personal interpretations have crept in. It shows how steeped the Spaniards are in their own culture and how the dances in the various regions have evolved and become enriched by the local people. There is no other country with such strong traditions kept so alive and current. Thus the *Seguidillas* made an exciting comeback in the 1980s. However, today anything goes and sometimes a piano is mixed with guitar sections as well. Improvisation is the theme of the times and the way the guitar is played and the songs sung has a strong Latin-American influence.

Regional, Not Flamenco

Another influence is that of the flamenco performer on the music and singing. This folk music has come to be interpreted more and more in a flamenco form by singers and guitarists. This personalisation is typical of flamenco and probably inevitable, because Andalusia, the home of the *Sevillanas*, is also the home of flamenco. Thus a sung form with complex personal embellishments, like those of

SEVILLANAS

Illustration 1.7
Sevillanas.
Marina Keet archive.

Illustration
1.8
Pilar López
dancing
Seguiriyas.
Pilar López
archive.

flamenco songs, has crept in. The interpreration has become so individual that it often cuts out the dancer and becomes more *libre* or free and often very slow for the singer's use, almost like the spontaneous bursts of song, *saetas*, or 'arrows' of song, improvised during religious processions. This does signify that the rhythm of *Seguidilla* rhyming still appeals to the locals as regards improvisation.

The Flamenco Seguidillas, the Seguiriyas

Of interest is the flamenco *Seguiriyas*. This is the corruption of the word *Seguidillas*, as it is known to the Andalusian Gypsies. Early on it was a happy dance, and we will see later how it influenced the Valencian *Bolero de L'Alcudia de Carlet*, both musically and in the steps, which were jumped, in keeping with the early *Seguidillas*. Later it was to become a very *jondo* or deep flamenco song, supposedly first danced to by Vicente Escudero in the twentieth century. The original flamenco dances were limited, with distinct divisions for male and female. This distinction disappeared when dancers tried to enlarge their repertoire by adding the dances of the opposite sex to their own. They also added dances to new music, formerly only sung or played on the guitar, as was the case of the *Seguiriyas*. We do not know exactly when the *Seguidillas* changed from a bucolic romp to a tragic lament.

The Hemiola: Two Counts of Three and Three Counts of Two

The *Seguiriyas*, the flamenco descendant of the *Seguidillas*, can actually be danced to the regional *Seguidillas* music. *Seguiriyas* belongs to the flamenco family of dances counted in cycles of 12 beats. The accents fall on the counts of 3, 6, 8, 10 and 12, as in the usual flamenco, but in a different sequence. This way of dividing the *compás* is known as a hemiola.

When fitted into flamenco mode, the *Seguiriyas* rhythm changed sequences from the usual flamenco 12-count cycle starting from 1 or 12, to one that starting on the eighth beat. It is musically notated as alternating bars of 3/4 and 6/8 time. Some teachers dispute the fact that a 12-count phrase should be called a *compás*. They maintain, correctly, that a *compás* is actually a bar. However, all the dances in the *compás* of 12 counts fall into sequences: two sequences of three counts and three sequences of two counts:

1, 2, 3; 1, 2, 3; 1, 2; 1, 2; 1, 2

(Counting the sequences in this way would avoid many problems and endless arguments!)

This is known as a a hemiola. The accents fall on counts 3, 6, 8, 10 and 12:

1 2 **3**; 4 5 **6**; 7 **8**; 9 **10**; 11 **12**

What matters is where the count starts. In *Alegrias* it is usually 1, in *Soleares* and *Bulerias* the dancer usually starts accenting the steps on 12 (note that the

Bulerias sections within the *Alegrias* are also counted thus). In *Seguiriyas* it will be on the count of 8.

The *compás* of *Seguiriyas* is often counted by dancers as:

1 and; **2** and; **3** and a; **4** and a; **5** and;

1 and   is one sequence of two counts (8, 9)
2 and   is one sequence of two counts (10, 11)
3 and a is one sequence of three counts (12, 1, 2)
4 and a is one sequence of three counts (3, 4, 5)
5 and   is one sequence of two counts (6, 7)

Thus it can be seen that the three sequences of two counts have been divided and cut off from each other, two falling at the beginning of the rhythmic cycle and one at the end. This is also the way dancers learn it, but to illustrate how it falls into the rhythmic cycle of 12 beats, to which the *Seguiriyas* belongs, it falls on those counts as below:

Soleares: **12**, 1, 2; **3**, 4, 5; **6**, 7; **8**, 9; **10** 11; ($\times$ 3; $\times$ 3; $\times$ 2; $\times$ 2; $\times$ 2)
Seguiriyas: **8**, 9; **10** 11; ($\times$ 2; $\times$ 2;)
            12, 1, 2; **3**, 4, 5; **6**, 7;   ($\times$ 3; $\times$ 3; $\times$ 2;)

The same could be applied to the other rhythms such as *Peteneras* and *Guajiras* where the count starts on 1, by avoiding the 12-numbered counting and counting **1** 2 3; **1** 2 3; **1** 2; **1** 2; **1** 2.

Classical Composers

In his book *The Music of Spain* Gilbert Chase tells of the foreigners influenced by Spanish music. 'Rossini in part of the variations on Figaro's theme, "De si felice inesto" (Act II), utilises the rhythm of the *Sevillanas*'. Glinka was one of the first foreign composers to use Spanish music. His own country, Russia, has much in common with Spain in semi-oriental exoticism and rich folklores, so it is not surprising that he was attracted to Spain and the Spanish tunes and rhythms which he noted down on his visit in 1845. During his stay in Madrid he heard a muleteer named Zagal singing a *Seguidillas Manchegas*, which inspired his composition 'Spanish Overture No. 2' (Night in Madrid). Bizet, another foreign composer who used Spanish music, used the *Seguidillas* in Act I of *Carmen*, 'Près de Ramparts de Sevilla'. Many Spanish composers used the *Seguidillas* when they wanted to bring in a folk element in the *zarzuelas*, or operettas, in rustic or pastoral scenes such as in *La Rosa del Azafran*, *The Hostess of the Inn* ('La Mesonerilla') by Antonio Palomino, which is said to have six sets of *Seguidillas*.

This use of folk melodies is found in *The Lawyer of Farfulla* by Antonio Rosales (1776), where he includes many folk dances besides the *Seguidillas*, such as *Jácaras* and *Folías* and so on. In Esplá's *Don Quijote's Vigil at Arms*, the final movement is a *Seguidillas Manchegas*. Albéniz stylised guitar versions of

Seguidillas for piano. De Falla used the rhythm of *Sevillanas* for the neighbour's dance in *The Three-Cornered Hat*. In Chile, Peru and Argentina, the *Bolero*, *Fandango* and *Seguidillas* were the most widespread Spanish dances during the colonial period. In other Peruvian native dances (such as *Yaravies*, *Cáchuas*, *Lauchas*), collected by Jimínez de la Espada in the 1880s, there are traces of Spanish dances such as *Sevillanas* and *Jota*. The *Jarabe*, which is the most popular of all Mexican dances, has drawn from the *Seguidillas* and *Fandangos*.

A Note on the Onomatopoeia of Castanets

Usually, castanet rhythms are sounded by teachers of Spanish dancing in the following manner:

Pam	both castanets striking a single beat together.
Ta	single beat on the left castanet.
Pi	a single beat on the right.
Ria	a *caretilla* or 'roll' comprised of 4 beats on the right castanet (Ri-), and finishing with one on the left (-a).

The Pericet family, who preserve the Escuela Bolera, use different sounds to describe the beats. Eloy Pericet says that his sister calls the single beat on the left (the *ta*) an *a*, as that is what the 'a' represents in *ria*, the final single beat on the left at the end of the roll. This is very logical and the train of thought makes sense. However, it may make more sense, as in the use of *ta*, to distinguish between the *ta* as being a single beat on its own, and the *a* being the final single beat on the left hand, at the end of the roll. It is mainly a question of what one is accustomed to.

Castanet Rhythm

The *Seguidillas Manchegas* is placed among the Escuela Bolera dances. For this version, the castanets are worn on the thumb, enabling the right hand to play a roll or *carretilla*. This gives a more elegant line to the arm, greater variation to the rhythms played, and a richer sound. It must be remembered that the roll or *carretilla* on the castanets consists of rolling five beats, four fingers of the right hand and one on the left. The rhythm that is played on the castanets sounds: left (1), roll (and 2), roll (and 3), right (and) – *ta-ria-ria-pi* – which repeats to the end of the verse. The Bolero rhythm is just an extension of this but crosses two bars: both (1), left (2), roll (3), left (4), roll (5), both (6) – *pam, ta-ria, ta-ria, pam*. Onomatopoeically it can be represented as *tran tra-ra-an tr-ra-an tran*. However, when played continuously it sounds like: both, both, L, roll, L, roll – with the sixth beat dominating at the start, because the steps of a *Bolero* start mostly on the sixth beat. In fact, a lazy dancer often omits the double beats using both castanets on (6, 1) and plays the simpler *Seguidillas* rhythm.

The Construction of the Dance

The dance, as is typical of Spanish regional dances, is performed in couples, and can be arranged to be danced in fours, circles, double circles or double lines. There are many *Seguidillas*, but the rhythm remains the same and never varies. It is

complex to dance, as three elements come into play: first, the castanet rhythm goes across the music; second, the footwork comprises complex and constantly changing patterns; while third, the arms individually perform repetitive circular movements. As with the castanets, the arms move ceaselessly, doing a set pattern of outward circles. That is repeated endlessly first by one arm and then by the other, from a position above the centre of the head. Each arm moves across six beats of the music. The castanet rhythm is repeated twice in each arm movement.

Considering that this is a dance composed by the local people, it is most complex. The steps fit the music exactly, and all the combinations are repeatable, to the left and right, and to fit these there are arm movements and castanet rhythms, with a precision that is simply amazing. The correct foot is always left free to continue into the following phrase.

Today there is some confusion in the Manchegan *Seguidillas* regarding the steps that pass the partners across each other to change places. This should be made clear from the start. Some versions of the *Seguidillas Manchegas* are danced with limps passing the partner. The *Seguidillas* from La Mancha has three walks passing the partner, not limps as in the *Verdiales*, which is a *Fandango* (Eloy Pericet, personal communication). A remnant of this walked pass can still be seen in the third verse of *Sevillanas* when correctly danced. The pass after the first verse of this copla should be three walks crossing with left shoulders, not the usual pass on the other side of the partner. The usual pass also has these walks after the lift of the leg, but passing with the right shoulders.

Illustration 1.9
'Two Spanish dancers'.
Allan Österlind (1855–1938)
National Museum, Stockholm

Principles and Rules

In the introductory preamble to his music collection Don Preciso mentioned that in 1740 a certain dance master, called Pedro de la Rosa who, after his travels in Italy, put the *Seguidillas* and *Fandangos* into shape with principles and rules. Don Preciso tried to give a feeling for future reference, of the customs of that century and the national dances of the period that succeeded. He listed the *Galliard*, the *Chacon, Zarabande, Zarambeque* and the *Jacara* as well as the *Cumbé, Zerengue, Canario* and many others of the preceding centuries.

Although Preciso did not notate steps or style, Pablo Minguet did, in his *Breve Tratado de los Passos Del Danzar A La Española*, printed in Madrid in 1764 by the author. He describes the 4th position of the feet as the natural position, *El Bacio, El Rompido, La Carrerilla, Floreta* – natural, passada and en vuelta, *El Salto y Encage* – en vuelta and with *Campanela, La Vuelta Descuydo, La Vuelta de pecho, La Vuelta de Tornillo, El Quatropeado* and others. Amusingly, he often writes that a step should be performed with 'violence'! This term is still used today. In his *Breve Explicacíones de Diferentes Danzas y Contradanzas* he suggests that the short dancers raise their arms to shoulder level. The taller dancers are advised to hold theirs at their sides.

A Means of Teaching Neat Footwork

The *Seguidillas* was used as a means of teaching neat footwork in dance schools, an outdated approach today. José Otero, in his book *Tratado de Bailes* (1912), wrote of how the (*Seguidillas*) *Sevillanas* was the first dance taught to any pupil in a dance studio, but how the teachers then in the second round taught the *Seguidillas*

Illustration 1.10 A short treatise on the steps for dancing in the Spanish way, nowadays used in the *Seguidillas, Fandango,* and other types of music. Which can also be used for the Italian, French and English dances, according to the rhythm of the music and the figures of the dances. Corrected in this second edition by the author Pablo Minguet, engraver of seals, pictures and signs. With license: In Madrid, at the shop of the author. In the year 1764. Resident opposite the Royal Prison, above the store, where one will find all his works, beside the steps of the church of Saint Phelipe.

Manchegas as a way to teach good footwork. He maintained that it taught the use of the tips of the toes, good positions, finesse in joining the steps and the polish that is required when dancing. He wrote of the three verses to the dance, and said that never are the heels placed down on the floor in any part except the two stamps. Here again we see the progression into the *Bolero* of these two stamps. In the *Seguidillas* it ends the introduction or *estribillo* and leads into the verse, as in the *Bolero*, where it also starts the verse (counts 6, 1). Otero mentioned 5th positions (for example, at the start), and 3rd positions of the feet. This is very balletic. In the third verse, which has the chorus or *estribillo* step turning, he maintained that they performed it with two or three pirouettes instead. The two stamps were accompanied by two single beats played by both hands on the castanets.

Otero explained that this dance is far removed from the dance called *Las Manchegas* performed by the people at that time, in 1912. According to him, people complained that the traditional way of dancing it was 'old-fashioned', but he claimed that he would be the first to incorporate something modern if it were better, because he liked civilisation to progress; but to compare the old version with the present-day performance was like comparing a diamond to a fake! Any teacher would sympathise with him. Often the lack of knowledge in pupils causes them to look for superficial effect rather than the best, and they confuse novelty with worth. Otero felt that his pupils lacked the discipline and patience to learn it as it should be danced, and that even though he taught it well, they would dance badly because they had no will to master it. A most perceptive teacher.

Antonio Cairón's book (see bibliography) is mentioned in the foreword of Otero's book. Of the *Seguidillas* Cairón stated very simply that it is similar to the *Bolero*, with the same rules, steps, *estribillos*, *bien parados* and so on, but performed at a faster pace with simpler steps. He went on to say that this is how the Bolero has been danced since its conception. However, it must be remembered that it is the *Bolero* that is derived from the *Seguidillas*.

Today's Seguidillas Manchegas

There are two features to the *Seguidillas Manchegas* that are very typical, which some versions do not have: the three walks passing the partner (also found in the first pass of the third verse of *Sevillanas*, but lost in many of today's versions); and the *estribillo* step, with its three walks around oneself (*vuelta normal* in the classical Pericet version). Angel Pericet Carmona, who wrote down his knowledge of the eighteenth-century classical Spanish dance style, is the source of how the steps should be performed. However, as mentioned earlier, both above-mentioned features are often supplanted by 'limps', as in the *Verdiales*, either turning around oneself or crossing the partner, like a long type of *glissade*. According to Angel Pericet this was never a part of the dance (personal communication). This constitutes a loss in style.

In the Pericet version the *estribillo* or chorus step is executed with a step-turn: after a tip of the toe and a step, the next foot crosses over the other, into a turn. The other versions have a stamp and a stamp stepping and turning, simply moving freely around with two more steps, the second stamp already turning. The precision of the Pericet version is most satisfying. It follows the steps set out in the Escuela Bolera exercises very clearly. At the end of this book, where the dances are codified, it is the version as taught by Eloy Pericet. The little stamps are so typical of some of the Escuela Bolera dances.

Another step found in the Escuela Bolera is the *jeté* and *pas de bourrée* going in a semi-circle around the partner. This is the exercise called, *Pifla y pas de bourrée*. A point to note is the *pas de bourrée* starts stepping to side, then behind, side, front. It resembles the *pas de bourrée courru* of the Cecchetti ballet syllabus, and it was used by Danish ballet-master August Bournonville after a jump. This satisfyingly connects them all to the dancing in the nineteenth century.

The first verse's *Malagueña*-type step in the Pericet version has jumps changing the feet; others do two changes and a jump lifting the leg to the knee at the back. It is more difficult to go from a closed position after a jump to a step back; to go from a lifted leg is much easier. Perhaps this is why this variation evolved; however, the Pericet version is more academic and looks very precise.

Difficulties for Foreigners

What is often difficult for a foreigner studying in Spain is that certain details that would make sense of a step are not explained. For example, the three-beat wait at the start of *Seguidillas Manchegas*, at a moment where you would obviously want the dance to begin, is the same three beats where you pass your partner in subsequent repeats during the pass around the partner to change places. Once you know this you know how long to wait before commencing the dance. It is often a mystery how arms get from one place to another until you work out that they move in circles – these things are taken for granted by a Spaniard, who has absorbed it almost from birth, as it were!

It is a charming dance, whatever the version, with the points of the foot, the little jumps and skips and has an extremely joyous feel about it.

If the dancer loses his or her place in the dance, it is easy to pick it up again on the strummed sections, as they are easy to hear, or see, by watching the strumming movements of the guitarist's hand and the steps are aways the same on that section.

Structural Connections

It is frequently written that the *Fandango* became the *Seguidillas*, but this is not stricly true. The one evolved in Andalusia and the other is so clearly a purely Castillian creation. The Andalusian *Fandango* is, broadly speaking, structurally the same as a *Seguidillas*. *Fandangos* have verses divided by choruses, and start with one of the choruses as an introduction leading into the dance. However, not all *Fandangos* have the same structure in all the regions where they are danced. The *Fandango* is one of the oldest dances in Spain, yet it is difficult to connect its influence to the *Seguidillas*. The *Fandango de Huelva* usually has the same structure as the *Seguidillas Sevillanas*: alternating three *estribillos* (choruses) and three *coplas* (verses), thus: chorus, verse, chorus, verse, chorus, verse and a coda. The difference is, that in the *Sevillanas* these are very concentrated and each of these sequences has come to be known as a *copla*, when in fact each *copla* is actually three of each, as described above. To repeat, once the listener knows this structure, it is easy to pick out the *estribillo* section, as this is the strummed section on the guitar in both these dances.

Types of Seguidillas

Seguidillas abound: in Madrid there is the *Seguidillas del Candil* or *Madrileños*; the *Candil* in Ciudad Real and the *Seguidillas Meloneras*. From Andalusia are the *Espartero*, *Coralleros*, and the *Seguidillas Mollares*, which has nine steps and three verses as opposed to more usual verses with three steps. It is danced by four dancers. In Guadalajara there is the *Seguidillas de Mondejar*; in Valencia it is the *Tarara*; the *Agudo* or *Agudillo* is also a *Seguidillas*, from Burgos. Others are *La Cinta* or *La Peseta*, from Avila in Castile; *Seguidillas de Tarancon* from Cuenca; and the *Murcianas* and *Parrandas* of Murcia. Santander has *Los Passiegos* and in Salamanca there is the *Bolero de Sequeros* and the *Charrada*, which changes its name to *Baile del Pollo* or *Baile de la Rosca* according to the occasion at which it is danced. Caballero Bonald mentions *La Cava Sevillanas* and an interesting early Andalusian version of a *Seguidillas* called *Taberneras*, which flourished at the beginning of the nineteenth century. It is one of the original branches of the *Siguiriya* (*Seguiriya*) *Gitana* with an influence from the folk *Fandango*.

Bailes del Candil

The expression *del candil* or *de candil* arose in Andalusia and refers to organised entertainment by lamplight, in public places such as taverns and also the simple homes of the local people. The entertainers were paid for the performance. The room was lit by oil lamps with wicks, not by candlelight as has been written elsewhere. The lamps were made of metal, usually iron or copper, and were suspended from the ceilings. Some dances retained the word *candil* attached to their name. In Madrid we find the *Seguidillas del Candil*, from the period at the end of the eighteenth century, of the artist Francisco Goya, still performed today by the regional dance companies of the capital. Goya immortalised an era of *majas* and *majos* for posterity, the elegance as well as the horrors of human existence.

Other Names

Josep Criville y Bargalló, in his *El Folklore* no. 7 in the Historia de la Musica Española series, says the *Seguidillas* in Castile are referred to as *Castellanas* and *Manchegas*, and in Murcia he includes *Gitanas*, *Playeras*, *Chambergas*, and *Torras*.

We even find it in the home of the *Jota*, in Aragon, where the *Seguidillas de Leciñena* is danced on 15 March, in homage to the Virgin of Magallón, patron of the village, whose fiesta is the motive of the dance. The music is solemn and men sing the numerous couplets, which refer to the Virgin and her miracles. The musical accompaniment is by *bandurrias*, guitars *a pandareta* and *yerillos* (triangles or bells).

According to the music historian García Matos, in Ciudad Real the *Seguidillas*

◆ See colour plate 8

Illustration 1.11
Music by Manuel Pla – José Subirá
for *Seguidillas Religiosas*
(Religious *Seguidillas*)

Meloneras and *Seguidillas Manchegas* are both danced to the same music performed on *bandurrias*, guitars, *tiplillo* (*guitarillo*), and sometimes with lutes on their own or added to the above group. The *Meloneras* pertains to the festivities in connection with the picking of melons and is danced by any number of couples, who form a circle. The *Seguidillas Manchegas*, on the other hand, is danced by two couples. It is particularly popular in Ciudad Real and is danced at family occasions such as weddings, baptisms and at harvests, at the festivities organised by guilds on 15 and 22 August. It is also performed during rest periods from the harvesting of grapes or olives, particularly during the annual homage to the Patron Saint of Ciudad Real, 'La Santissima Virgen del Prado'; the most important day of these festivities is the last, when it is danced in front of the church door at night. This particular gathering is called *La Pandorga*, a name given in Spain in ancient times to signify strident, noisy music that creates a racket.

In Castilla la Vieja there is the *Jabas Verdes*, which takes its name from a line of a song: 'take the (green) beans, take them away, give them to who you will but not to me'.

The *Seguidillas Boleras y Jota* of El Real de San Vicente, Toledo, is an unusual combination of two dances rolled into one, without a stop in between. Danced in a circle by six, eight or ten couples, according to García Matos, it is accompanied on *bandurrias* and guitars.

Baron Jean-Charles Davillier, in his book *Voyage en Espagne* (1874), mentions that the Andalusians love the *Seguidillas*, which he found depicted on fans called *abanicos de calaña*, sold outside the *plaza de toros* when there is a bullfight: the *Seguidillas* 'was also depicted by some peasant Murillo [the artist Bartolomé Esteban Murillo, 1618–1682], on the box of a carriage, painted in many bright colours on a bright canary-yellow background.'

The Seguidillas in Hispanic America

José Blas Vega, in the interesting chapter, 'Apuntes para un estudio del flamenco hispanoamericano' from his book *Temas Flamencos* (Madrid, 1973), writes that in 1810 Serafín Ramírez had mentioned that in Havana the *Seguidillas*, *Polos* and *Tiranas* were sung as serenades in the early hours. In 1832 the *Seguidillas* was among the dances being taught in a dance academy in Havana. Blas Vega notes that during the colonial period in Peru, Chile and Argentina, the Spanish dances represented were the *Bolero*, *Fandango*, *Seguidillas* and the *Zapateado*. In Peru, traces of *Sevillanas*, the *Seguidillas* from Seville, were to be found. In Chile the *Seguidillas* was known as the *Sirilla*.

Cross-Country Influence

One engraving depicts a long scarf (referred to as a shawl) hanging behind a dancer and attached to her hair, from a nineteenth-century Spanish dance. Today, the shawl does not exist in the Escuela Bolera dances in Spain; but it is to be found in Mexico, where it is a requirement for some dances, and usually worn attached to the wrists. It was also used in some ballet dances in Europe. It played a

◆ See colour plate 16

significant role in *La Sylphide* and can still be seen as performed in Bournonville's version of this ballet at the Royal Danish Ballet in Copenhagen.

Bournonville and the Seguidillas in Denmark

Lucile Grahn, the Danish ballet dancer of the Romantic era, performed several Spanish dances, among them the *Seguidillas*. These she learned abroad. Her teacher, August Bournonville, was influenced by the visiting Spanish dancers Dolores Serral and Mariano Camprubí, who also invited him to perform at their benefit concert in Copenhagen (see Chapter 2).

Amongst Bournonville's ballet choreographies were also two Seguidilla (*Seguidillas*). The Danish musicologist and historian Knud Arne Jürgensen maintains that Bournonville's *Seguidilla* finale in *La Ventana* was based on choreography by Paul Taglioni performed as the finale in Mazilier's ballet *Le Diable à quatre* in 1855 in Vienna. In Bournonville's *Far From Denmark*, first produced in 1860 and still in the repertoire, there is a *Fandango*, and in 1866 Bournonville arranged a divertissement called *Seguidilla* to music by Holger Simon Paulli, with costumes by Edvard Lehmann. From Jürgensen's book *The Bournonville Ballets* we find the following fascinating explanation:

> The *Seguidilla*, Bournonville's last dance in the Spanish genre, was choreographed especially for the two leading dancers of the Royal Danish Ballet during the 1860s and '70s, Betty Schnell and Anna Scholl, serving as a display vehicle for their individual talents. It was presented on the playbill as 'A changing dance in Spanish style' and consisted of a series of short variations for each girl, alternating with each other in a sort of non-stop choreographic contest ending in a roguish joint finale. At each alternation between the girls they performed a few steps together while encircling each other dos a dos; . . . Although the dance was very popular, and was extensively performed for two full seasons, it had a strong competitor in the no less popular *Seguidilla* from La Ventana which had been given as an independent divertissement since October 21, 1866, and thus soon manoeuvred the 1868 *Seguidilla* out of the repertory.

His dance is sometimes spelled *Siguidilla*. (Bournonville could not have known about *Seguidillas* always being mentioned in the plural when it refers to the dance or music, and singular only for the verse.) In 1834 a *Seguidilla* and a *Manchegas* were performed by six dancers, including Bournonville. The first dance was costumed as a Spanish peasant, the second (curiously) as Gypsies. The music seems to have been hand copied scores of Spanish folk music, inserted into the three-Act opera *The Guerilla Band*. The references to the various performances of Bournonville's *Seguidilla* can be found in Jürgensen's two-volume *The Bournonville Tradition*. This dance was also peformed by the Danish dancers in the Norwegian and Swedish capitals as well.

Illustration 1.12
'La Parranda'.
Sketch by Enrique Breytenbach.
Marina Keet archive.

Construction of the Seguidillas Sevillanas

Dancers today add their own personalities to the rigid structure of the *Seguidillas*, but the basic structure for it still remains as it was almost four hundred years ago. García Matos, the Spanish musicologist, explains the construction of the *Seguidillas Sevillanas*, usually just referred to as *Sevillanas*, as follows: Introduction (instrumental), Salida (cantable), Vuelta o Estribillo (instrumental), Copla (cantable). *Vuelta* means turn, and the turn sometimes comes in conjunction with the *salida*. The *vuelta* before the *estribillo* does not always happen before the other repeats of the *estribillos*. For example, the first verse of *Sevillanas* has none in the body of the dance, whereas all the others do.

Structure of Other Seguidillas

For *Seguidillas Manchegas*, *Sevillanas* and *Las Parrandas*, this format is repeated four times to complete the entirety. Each time the dancers come to a complete standstill and then the next 'verse' commences. *Las Parrandas* from Murcia is accompanied by guitars, mandolins and even violins.

This is a popular dance of the Murcia orchard lands. It is elegant, gay and showy, capable of making the most worried man feel an optimist. The fiesta begins with a sort of pantomime or invitation while each man looks for a partner among the women. When all are paired off the parrandas itself begins and with it the hubbub of in which both the dancers and the curious spectators of the introduction take part. (Source unknown.)

As they dance, the performers either play castanets or use *pitos* (snapping the fingers). There are several variations of it, although all are basically the same thing and bear the names: 'del medio', 'del Uno', 'del Tres' and 'del campo'. It ends in a final cadence:

Murcianita totanera,	Sweet Murcian woman from Totana,
eres caida el cielo,	You've fallen from heaven,
y te envidian las estrellas,	And the stars envy you,
por ser tus ojos luceros.	Because your eyes are heavenly.

Totana is a town in Murcia. Generally, *luceros* is just a way of saying *estrellas* (stars), but they are more especially the stars you can see in the morning, so you often get the combination *lucero del alba* (Ralph Pemberton, personal communication).

For any of these dances the same structure occurs. In the Spanish Dance Society Syllabus it is described as 'Three steps, divided by a pass and a chorus step'. I should like to expand that, using terminology for a guitar accompaniment, to explain the structure in more detail for the *Seguidillas* from Seville:

The Four Verses of Sevillanas

A dance in 3/8 time. Usually sung.

Introduction (strummed music of the chorus, for as long as it takes for the dancers to get into their positions opposite their partners).

Salida (entrance into the dance). Nine counts of melody are sung, a turn (*vuelta*) may be executed on (7, 8, 9).

Estribillo (strummed chorus) also nine beats. The basic step is danced on place.

Copla (verse). A short burst of song (ends in a turn and a pass). Here the first combination of steps is performed.

Pass. A step passing to change places with the partner.

Estribillo, as above.

Copla. A second and new combination of steps is performed.

Pass to return to original position.

Estribillo, as above.

Copla. A third sequence of steps ending with a turn and *bien parado*, describing the position the dancer makes to end this dance.

The dance lasts for 4 minutes.

Ana Maria Durand-Viel, in her booklet entitled *Sevillanas*, describes the four verses of *Sevillanas* as:

1. That of the continual passes (referring to the last step or third *copla*).
2. That of a circle (referring to the third step or last *copla* where the partners do *pas de basque* around each other).

Illustration 1.13
Careo del Beso or, the pass with a kiss. A *careo* is a step used when passing a partner in *Seguidillas Sevillanas*

3. That of the *zapateado* (referring to the second step or *copla* which has a *redoble* repeated from side to side).

4. That of the *careos* (referring to the second step or *copla* and the third or last one).

Sevillanas First Verse

As can be seen, the first verse of *Sevillanas* is different from the others, as the first step is the chorus repeated four more times, and the last step is the pass repeated four times. The second step used to be known as the *matalaraña*, as it used to be danced with a little run and point to the side, as in the step in the Escuela Bolera syllabus. Eloy Pericet maintains that his grandfather referred to this step as *batararaña* and that it has nothing to do with the popular concept of 'killing the spider' or *matalaraña* (personal communication). Now this is a very interesting point as in fact it was supposedly a Frenchman, Thoinot Arbeau (Jehan Tabourot, Canon of Langres), who first used this expression (he was the author of *Orchésographie* in 1588, a history of dance in the sixteenth century).

This verse has no stops in between, but moves ceaselessly and is referred to as the verse of continuous passes. These passes are sometimes sacrificed, by the man perhaps holding back a beat or two and with feet together, swivelling as the girl does the passing step to change places. When the man passes the woman the arm makes a figure around the partner, whereas when two women dance together, as is often the case, the arm usually does the circle in front of the body and then up to 5th position. The pass using both arms down and then up, leaning towards one another (used in *Sevillanas Boleras*), is actually referred to as the kiss. A famous lithograph showing it is called 'Careo del Beso'.

Sevillanas Second Verse with Typical Stamps

The *Sevillanas* has four verses of complex stepped (as opposed to jumped) choreography. Through the years it has become more *terre-à-terre* and further removed from its origin as a *Seguidillas*. The first, second and third verses have two stamps, one on either foot, ending the *estribillo*, then a pause on the third beat before starting the 'verse' or *copla* step. The two stamps which occur on one foot in the *Seguidillas Manchegas* became modified in the *Sevillanas* and performed on alternate feet. It is found again in Bolero dances and in the *Sevillanas Boleras*, but as performed in the *Manchegas*, with both stamps occurring on the same foot sequentially.

The first step of the second verse of *Sevillanas* has two steps called *embotados*. The leg extends to the side and closes behind, first one foot then another, into 3rd position. (Traditionally the 3rd position in ballet was called *emboîture*; Richard Glasstone, personal communication). This leads to one way of referring to this verse as the *embotados* verse. The same step occurs in *Sevillanas Boleras* as well.

The second verse consists of *pas de basque* in the second and third steps, and is most commonly known as the *pas de basque* or *paso de vasco* verse. However, modern personal renditions have lost almost entirely the third step of *pas de basque* around the partner. Stamp digs with hip movement or with exaggerated lifts of the knee have come to be substituted.

Third Verse

The third verse has also lost its *batararaña* (*matalaraña*), which used to be a light run *pas de bourrée* to the side and point, for its second step, starting on the left going to the right and repeated alternately four times in all. This showed its *Seguidillas* link, and was very elegant. It has become three walks or a *pas de bourrée* to the side and a basic *redoble* beating the feet. (A basic *redoble* is a stamp with one foot, two with the other at double time, and ending with a single beat.) Others just swivel on place and do the *redoble*. Today the men and women dance it with the same arm positions, but Otero describes and shows in a photograph that in the third and last step, the woman would look under her arm at her partner and has her left arm up the first time, as opposed to his right arm. Obviously, after the pass she would then put up her right arm.

Fourth Verse of Careos
Here we find the first step varied by different teachers and dancers. Again, some people do 'limps' around, as in a *Verdiales*, where a stepped turn is more in character. The two middle sections have the *careos* or long waltzed steps with the character of a bullfighter avoiding a bull! The second one has two *pas de basque* and the *careos*. The third step or *copla* is only four *careos* passing the partner.

All the *careos* are crossed while facing the partner, and thus very intimate, a fitting finale to the other three. Here again the male dancer of today varies these steps and often swivels with his feet together following his partner with his arm, like a bullfighter with his cape, while the girl does the *careos*. Another variation of the last step is for the man to do a kneel crossing as the girl does a *careo* crossing, so that he is at her feet, as it were. It has a theatrical effect. In Spain their culture is very alive. Spanish dancing is very much a part of the people's lives, so it is inevitable that the dancers wish to add, embellish and refresh what they dance, thus change is inevitable. We already see a stamped rather than a stepped *Sevillanas*. Up to now the basic structure has not been tampered with, but as one sees in Saura's film, even that is open to improvisation by the professionals.

Sevillanas Boleras

It is in the three verses of *Sevillanas Boleras* that we find the most direct connection between *Seguidillas* and *Bolero*, these verses, with their short bursts of music and song about 11/2 minutes long, being a *Seguidillas* as well as having the Bolero-type jumped steps. The poet and writer Federico García Lorca saved many of the folk songs and music in his collection, *Canciones Españolas Antiguas*, published by Union Musical Española. *Sevillanas del Siglo XVIII* can be found there. It has an extra repeat of the *estribillo*, so it is difficult to fit in the *Sevillanas Boleras* steps to it without some adjustment to either the music or the dance.

There are various types of *Sevillanas*, apart from the *Boleras*, such as the *Sevillanas Rocieras*, performed at religious pilgrimages.

The 'Feria' and Sevillanas in Andalusia

A form of *Seguidillas* found in Andalusia is the *Sevillanas* from Seville. This is always a favourite, but especially so when it is danced during the week-long Feria, established in 1847, the gayest and best-known fair in Spain, celebrated in April following after the Easter *Semana Santa* or Holy Week. For weeks beforehand the local people brush up on their *Sevillanas* at the local dance studios, so that they can dance it, wearing their traditional costumes. The women dress in their colourful frilled dresses covering their ankles, the men don high-waisted pants and short jackets reaching above the waist with white frilled shirts and the broad-brimmed Cordobés hats. Riding on horseback or in carriages or just strolling, they invade the *casetas*, private or public, set up in the streets, where they go to chat with friends, eat tapas and sip sherry and wine. Similar celebrations take place in all the major

◆ See colour plate 30

centres such as Malaga, the home of the *Malagueña*, Cádiz, and Jerez de la Frontera.

Illustration 1.14
A Spanish dancer with castanets'. Allan Österlind (1855–1938) National Museum, Stockholm.

Sevillanas Rocieras

The town of Almonte in Andalusia, lies on the edge of *las marismas*, the marshes of the river Guadalquivir. It is a reservation for wild birds and animals, a constant source of friction between farmers and environmentalists. The marsh, the dried-out remnants of a lake known as the Lago Lingustino to the ancients, is wet during the rainy season and otherwise dry and cracked. It is also where the cattle are pastured and distinct breeds of domestic animals have resulted.

An annual religious pilgrimage to Almonte takes place at Whitsun. Millions of people journey to the outskirts of the town to celebrate the Virgen del Rocío, the Virgin of the Dew (tears), known as the Queen of the Marshes. Her shrine has a magnificent view over the Mother of the Marsh, or the beginning of the *marismas*. These lie in the municipal boundary of the town. From the Friday the pilgrimage starts and people arrive in covered, decorated wagons, on horseback and on foot. On the Saturday, festivities start in earnest and continue into the night, before the religious ceremonies on the Sunday. Music and singing, flutes, guitars and drums

Illustration 1.15
Carola Goya and Matteo in
Seguidillas.

and the *Sevillanas Rocieras* is danced all night long at the *Rocías*. As the dancing starts, the skirts fly up, and you notice that some of the women are wearing high boots! They are, because they have gone on this pilgrimage, walking the long distance in their boots. That is how they dance, in boots under their colourful, beautiful, frilly dresses.

The *Sevillanas* is most popular in Huelva but also at the spring festivals at the Feria in Jerez de la Frontera, Cádiz and, as mentioned above, Seville. The dance, however, is the same as that of the usual *Sevillanas* with some small differences of minor importance. *Sevillanas Rocieras* is usually performed in lines (*hileras*) of men on one side and women on the other, or sometimes of alternating couples, though that is rarer.

Homage through the Film Sevillanas

In the evocative film *Sevillanas*, made by Carlos Saura, other forms of *Sevillanas* are presented, including improvisations by Matilde Coral, Merche Esmeralda, Manuela Carrasco and the late Lola Flores. Unfortunately, individual identification is not given, so the average viewer cannot know who is on screen. However, they are just improvisations, though inspired ones; but the dress with a train worn by Flores is certainly not the usual costume for *Sevillanas*, nor are the steps. But they are fun, as long as a newcomer to Spanish dancing does not take them to represent the true folk rendition. The classical and other forms of *Sevillanas* are paid homage to from the cradle to the grave and via the biblical word, where they sing verses with reference to the Bible. The film too shows modern guitarists and singers of *Sevillanas* and their new styles. It is the last documentation of the revered gypsy singer Camarón de la Isla.

Recorded through the Eyes of a Visiting Writer

In *Voyage en Espagne: le Tour du Monde*, the author Baron Charles Davillier describes his impression of *Sevillanas* being danced in the nineteenth century. It is almost identical to the description by Don Preciso in 1740, hence is not quoted here in full. The translation is by Marie-Louise Ihre:

> The dancers with extended foot and curved arm only waited for the signal to start; the singers stopped for a moment and the guitarist started to play a melody of an old seguidilla[s]. In the second 'compás' the singers continued the verse and it was possible to hear the 'ripiqueteo' of the castanets and at once all the couples threw themselves into the dance, turning around seeking each other and escaping from each other! . . . Those who were able to hold the (end) position gracefully were cheered with cries of 'bien parado' from the audience.

Common Characteristics

The most common characteristics that are shared by both the Bolero and the *Seguidillas* are: the *paseo* or *paseo de gracia* and the holding of a position called *bien parado*, or well-held; having a particular chorus that repeats at the start of each section; the patterning, where the dancer performs on one side of the partner, then changes sides to repeat or dance another phrase on the other side; and the fact that the dance consists of bursts of dancing, a pause, holding a position before launching off into the next burst of dancing (in *Sevillanas* this happens four times and in the *Bolero*, usually three times). When describing the *Bolero*, Antonio Cairón also calls the complete verse a *copla* but seems to refer to each section within that structure as an *estribillo*. However, they run into each other, and although the pauses between verses may be omitted, the introductions are still danced each time. The *Sevillanas Boleras* sections are danced in soft ballet shoes, beating the legs and jumping. However, the *Sevillanas Boleras* have been known to be danced added to the usual four, as the fifth, sixth and seventh verses in hard shoes, boots and all!

◆ See colour plate 7

2

The Bolero

The Period

From the latter half of the eighteenth century, when the name *Bolero* first started to appear in print, until it was fervently embraced by the Spanish people and Europe's ballet dancers in the nineteenth century, the *Bolero* reigned supreme. Since then it has been ignored until quite recently. Suddenly, a new interest has sprung up, even as far as the USA. However, as a regional dance and offshoot of the *Seguidillas*, the *Bolero* as such seems to have been danced long before the classical dance appeared in Spain. The influences can be seen within dances such as *Seguidillas de Leciñena*, which is clearly a *Bolero*, the *Bolero de L'Alcudia de Carlet*, *Bolero de Algodre* and so on, from the regions of Aragon, Valencia and Zamora. As mentioned in the previous chapter, Blas Vega mentions that the *Bolero* was also to be found in Peru and Cuba.

The Origin of the Name Bolero

In many languages the 'b' and 'v' sounds are closely related, and this is especially so in Spanish, which has a soft 'b'. The word *bolero* is said to be derived from the verb *volar*, to fly. Whether this is in fact the case is not known, and it seems that the soaring or airborne steps were added long after the dance was named. However, some of the early printed *Bolero* scores were titled *Volero* or *Seguidillas Voleras*, and Rodriguez Calderón has said that the dancer must be able to fly through the air. There are many other suggestions regarding the origins of the word, such as the bobbles on Gypsy costumes; but they are vague, and the favoured choice of origin here is *volero*.

Fernando Sor and the Bolero

According to the Spanish guitarist and composer Ferdinand Sor (1784–1839) in his erudite entry 'Le Bolero' written for the *Encyclopédie Pittoresque de la Musique* (Paris, 1835), the word *bolero* was used as an adjective. Modifications in movement and rhythm were made to the Spanish dance called a *Seguidillas*, which was then referred to as the *Seguidilla Bolera*. The music illustrating Sor's article has the correct heading of *Seguidillas Boleras*, with an 's' at the end of each word. Sor says that a male dancer performing this type of dance was called *El Bolero* and his lady partner *La Bolera*.

Illustration 2.1
This cover page shows clearly the title *Seguidillas Voleras*, and the suggeston that it is the origin of the word *bolero*, in other words a flying *Seguidillas*. Later the *Seguidillas* part of the title was dropped and it became *Boleras* or *Bolero*. The Spanish 'b' and 'v' are almost indistinguishable from each other. Biblioteca Nacional, Madrid.

Sor maintains that the word *bolero* refers to the air and not the rhythm, that the rhythm can vary without the *Bolero* losing its distinctive character, and that it is the same as that used to accompany a *Polonaise*. (Both are in 3/4 time, but the *Polonaise* has an accent on the third beat, whereas the *Bolero* rhythm is accented [6, 1], and very constant. The melody or tune varies with each dance.) However, the speed can vary within a dance. For example, the end of *Bolero de Caspe* is much faster than the first part, and *Bolero de Algodre* is certainly more measured than some other *Boleros*. On the whole, *Boleros* are danced at a measured pace, and this seems characteristic.

Sor was a very famous guitarist of his day and spent most of his career in France. He left Spain for France in the wake of the Napoleonic army (he had backed the wrong side). Together with other artists and musicians, he was not welcomed in Spain ever again. However, his association (possibly marriage) with a French dancer makes his observations doubly relevant: his was not just a musician's view, but connected more intimately to dance.

The Bolero Rhythm

The music of the *Bolero* is in 3/4 time, but the castanet rhythm is across two bars, counted (6; 1, 2, 3, 4, 5) and then starting again on the sixth beat. The best way to

describe it is in the phonetic translation of the rhythm on the castanets: *tran, tra, ra-an, tra, ra-an, tran*, counted 'one, two, and three, four, and five, six'. The castanets play this: 'both (1), left (2), roll (and 3), left (4), roll (and 5), both (6). Because the *Bolero* flows on endlessly, the rhythm repeating, it is mistakenly thought that the rhythm is 'both (1), both (2), left (3) roll (4), left (5), roll (6)'. This is because the one rhythm runs into the other. If you were to play it that way, starting on the first beat, the accent would come on the wrong beat. However, the steps start on the sixth beat, thereby making it 'both (6), both (1), left (2), roll (3), left (4), roll (5)'. Because of the six beats it can be counted in three sets of two counts, as Blasis seems to have done. As noted previously, this was the old way the *Seguidillas* from Seville was counted by guitarists. Perhaps this is what influenced Blasis to call the *Bolero* a dance in 2/4 time, although he does state that there are *Boleros* in 3/4 time. None in 2/4 have been found today.

The Pericet family call this rhythm the one for a *Jota* (Eloy Pericet, personal communication). It is, but in that dance the *joteros* wear their castanets on the middle finger. They play them by shaking the hands to produce the sound that is played by the 'roll' or *caretilla*, when worn on the thumb. The Pericet version of a

Illustration 2.2
El Bolero, the title of a male dancer performing theatrical Spanish dances of the *Bolero* style.
Illustration 2.3
La Bolera the title of a female dancer performing theatrical Spanish dances of the *Bolero* style.

SEGUIDILLAS BOLERAS,

DISCRETAS Y DIVERTIDAS

PARA CANTAR LOS MOZOS SOLTERUS,

Jóven la mas amable,
y mas querida,
haz feliz en tus brazos
á quien te estima.
    Siempre seré fiel,
corresponde á mi afecto,
y á tanto querer.

    En la escuela de Venus
soy principiante,
dame una leccion, niña,
para no amarte.
    Que te aseguro,
que como salga de esta
seré buen tuno.

Una preciosa rosa
que yo tenia,
ocultaba entre flores
tanta malicia.
    Yo dije al punto:
esos son los placeres
que yo disfruto.

    El sarmiento en la lumbre
y el que enamora,
por un lado se enciende,
por otro llora.
    Tú eres lo propio,
cuando lloras por verme
te vas por otro.

Illustration 2.4
Seguidillas Boleras, discreet and
diverting. By kind permission
of Carmen García Matos.

Bolero rhythm is: 'both, both, (6; 1) left, roll, (2, 3)', and again repeating across the music 'both, both (4, 5), left; roll (6; 1)' etc. continuously. Or, in the Spanish way: *pam, pam, aria*. The Pericet *Bolero* dances have various rhythms to correspond with each sequence of steps.

The Historical Setting

From 1769 there was an increase in social activities, despite the fact that dancing was being frowned upon. The Count de Aranda, although a detractor of the theatre, presented dances and charged an entrance fee, and these became very popular. He used these occasions to infiltrate spies among the ballgoers to listen to conversations and to report back to him. These balls and gatherings, and the following of French fashions in theatre and in clothes, led to a whole series of imitators by the end of that century. Pejorative names such as *petimetre* and *currataco* were coined for the fops and dandies of the upper middles class, who abounded at the time. The *manolos, manolas, majos* and *majas* were admired and almost revered. The upper classes copied these fun-loving middle and working classes as an escape from their more restricted lifestyle.

Later, there was the inevitable backlash against all things foreign, and a Royal Proclamation, issued on 28 December 1799, banned foreign languages and performers, including dancers, from the stage. Spanish dances and dancers became popular. This national fervour continued to be enforced until 1822, according to Blas Vega. From time to time, in all countries, national pride surfaces to protect indigenous cultures and peoples.

The Theatre Reform Council's efforts from 1799 were also resisted by the Spaniards until the arrival of Romanticism. Throughout the centuries many dances were banned. As early as the fifteenth century the *seises* were banned from performing their religious dances until a papal bull in 1439 gave them leave to perform in the Seville Cathedral on the altar steps, where they can be seen to this day. In the 1600s the *Zarabanda* was considered lascivious and was banned throughout the kingdom. The *Bolero* as a mourner's dance was banned in Valencia on 5 October

1765 by the Bishop of Orihuela. There were also many instances of dances being frowned on for political reasons, but they all survived because the Spaniards are fervent and passionate lovers of their culture. Martínez Ruiz, in his interesting discussion of the Spanish eighteenth century in the book *Carl Linneaus and Enlightened Science in Spain*, writes that there were many conflicts in the seemingly peaceful eighteenth century. The attempt in 1765 to ban the religious plays, the *autos sacramentales*, seems part of the jaundiced view taken by the Bourbon monarchs of the power of the Catholic church.

Dress

The Spaniards were not eager for the innovations of shorter skirts brought in in the early 1700s by Marie Camargo (1710–1770), or of flesh-coloured tights, attributed to Charles-Louis Didelot (1767–1836). However, a glance at Gustave Doré's sketches of La Campanera show that shorter skirts were adopted later.

Ballet and the Bolero

In the nineteenth century a great national fervour built up around this now almost forgotten *Bolero*. In its classical form, the dances were taken up in France by the dancers of the Romantic era, who will be dealt with later. This dance style spread across Europe and as far as the United States of America and Latin America, and the *Bolero* became the known as Spain's 'national dance'.

The French and Italian ballet dancers who came to Spain from the eighteenth century onwards were to influence Spanish dance, just as modern dance is influencing it today. Ballet certainly affected the way in which the *Bolero* was presented in the theatre, augmented by more than two performers. Ballet also enriched the repertoire of steps peformed. In the syllabus of *Bolero* steps preserved by the Pericet family the final course has the balletic elements of *batterie*, (beats of the legs in the air), including complex *batterie* such as *brisé volé*, *entrechat cinq* and complex beaten *échappés*. However, these beaten steps are found in only a few of the Spanish dances of this period, in one or two of the *Boleros* of the Escuela *Bolera* (school of classical *Bolero* dancing), the *Boleras de la Cachucha*, *Bolero de Medio Paso*, and so on. It must not be forgotten that some regional dances, such as the Basque dances, include beaten steps in the air, and thus it is not an exclusively balletic phenomenon.

The other dances of the Escuela Bolera repertoire – the *Olé de la Curra*, *Panaderos de la Flamenca*, *Jaleo de Jerez* and others – do not have these elements. Their influence is from the regional dances, themselves so rich and varied. Folk versions abound, and it is from these that the Escuela Bolera was formed. Steps never seen in ballet are present, such as *punta y talon*, *bordoneos*, *sostenidos* and others. These regional dances also had, for centuries, the *pas de bourrée*, the *ronds de jambe*, and various types of jumps assumed to be the domain of ballet. So the ballet influence is far less than imagined. As we know, the influence also flowed the other way, from Spanish dance to ballet. For example, the arm positions used in ballet are Spanish. Even the way the hair was worn, with a centre parting and a high bun at the back, was the typical Valencian hairstyle (minus side buns).

Illustration 2.5
Federico García Lorca.
Marina Keet archive.

♦ See colour plates 10 and 11

Opposite
Illustrations 2.6, 2.7, 2.8 &
2.9: Steps from the *Seguidillas
Boleras*. Four engravings (of
six) by Marcos Téllez depicting the steps of the *Seguidillas
Boleras* at the end of the
eighteenth century: the
campanelas, *pistolees*,
atabalillos, *embotadas*,
Biblioteca Nacional, Madrid]

In other dances such as *Caracoles*, *Peteneras* and *Alegrias*, as their titles denote, the echo is from flamenco. The influences in Spanish dances are so incestuous that it is difficult to untangle the relationships. Yet all these intricate dances are a joy to learn and perform, and those who limit themselves only to flamenco deny themselves a great pleasure. They also do audiences the world over a great disservice in witholding this rich inheritance from them.

Preservation

Apart from the Pericet family from Seville, who have preserved the Escuela Bolera steps and dances, we owe a great debt to the poet Federico García Lorca (1898–1936). He belonged to the 'Generation of 1927', a group of talented Spanish writers that included Pedro Salinas, Gorge Guillén, Vicente Alexander and Rafael Alberti. Lorca preserved the words and music of many of the folk songs and dances, including the *Sevillanas del Siglo XVIII*, the classical *Sevillanas Boleras* of the nineteenth century. Perhaps he was influenced by the dancer La Argentinita, who was a great friend of his. There are recordings of Argentinita singing, accompanied by Lorca on the piano. One listens to their light-hearted duet with sadness, knowing how history unfolded. One of the great tragedies of the Spanish Civil War was Lorca's execution in Granada in July 1936 at the age of thirty-seven, and his burial in an unmarked grave in the mountains. In Pablo Neruda's words, 'He was a physical flash of lightning, a force in perpetual motion, a jubilation, a splendour, a wholly superhuman charm. His being was magical and golden; happiness poured out of him.' It is intriguing that he is known internationally by the name Lorca and not García (in Spanish, the last name, in his case Lorca, is that of the mother).

The Bolero as the National Dance of Spain

On hearing the word *Bolero* today, the classical form of this dance immediately springs to mind. It was this dance type that spread across the world, danced by the famous dancers of the Romantic era. It has therefore been assumed that it is classical ballet danced in a Spanish way. This is far from the truth. In fact, a ballet dancer would be taxed to sustain the movements in the air while playing complex castanet rhythms. A ballerina at the Rome Opera once said that it was easier to dance *Swan Lake* than the *Boleras de la Cachucha* or *Medio Paso*. This was already maintained by Antonio Cairón, who described the *Bolero* as the most famous, most graceful and most difficult Spanish dance to have been invented.

Cuadro Bolero

The word *cuadro* means picture. It is associated with flamenco scenes onstage, with guitarists, singers and dancers seated in a semi-circle round the back of the

CAMPANELAS E LAS SEGUIDILLAS BOLERAS

PISTOLEES E LAS SEGUIDILLAS BOLERAS

ATABALILLOS E LAS SEGUIDILLAS BOLERAS

EMBOTADAS E LAS SEGUIDILLAS BOLERAS

Illustration 2.10
A typical *cuadro flamenco*
scene in Seville's 'Kuursaal' in
1918. According to D.E.
Pohren, the well-known ladies
from Seville are flanked by the
famous Antonio Ramirez,
'Ramerito' and on the right 'La
Quica' in male attire.

stage and each performer coming forward to perform a solo. It is flamenco that is today considered Spain's national dance. This type of *cuadro* used not to be the sole domain of flamenco. A century or more ago, at the same performance of the *cuadro flamenco*, there would also be the *cuadro bolero*, a group of dancers performing the dances of the classical school, the Escuela Bolera. In fact it has returned and can be seen once more in Seville, where a classical *cuadro* has once more been introduced before the flamenco one in the *tablao* at El Patio Sevillano.

The great Antonio said in the 1960s,

> I do not know why, but the classical *cuadro bolero* seems to have gone out of fashion. When I was a little boy dancing in a *cuadro flamenco* in a café in Seville, there was also a *cuadro bolero*. The two were quite distinct and both equally popular. You never saw regional dancing in the cafés then. The [classical] *bolero* dancers would spend their days caring for their children, doing housework, and then going to the cafés at night to take part in the *cuadro bolero* and earning extra money. Very fine dancers they were too and would dance *Sevillanas a la bolera*, the *Cachucha*, a *Panaderos* or simply a *bolero*.

When the *cuadro flamenco* was over, the dancers and musicians in their classical costumes would enter the stage singing and playing their instruments, and then take their places and perform their various dances. Just such a scene is depicted in

Manet's painting of Dolores Serral and Mariano Camprubí in Paris, dancing in Escuela Bolera costumes before the seated musicians and dancers.

Loas

It is interesting to digress here to an earlier form of theatrical performance of the seventeenth century, called a *loa*, which seems to be a forerunner of this type of entertainment. The production generally began with a tune sung by the musicians of the company, followed by a *loa* (praise) or prologue, which was the entrance of the artists onto the stage. It seems to echo what the dancer Antonio referred to seeing in the *cuadros boleros*, that he watched early in the twentieth century. The *loa* often ended with a dance, for which torches were handed up from beneath the stage. However, the *loa* also served the purpose of asking for a favourable reception for the play. An interlude was given between the first and second acts of the play, and a short ballet between the second and third acts. *Jácaras*, or boasting songs and dances, were included in court plays, which generally ended with the *fin de fiesta* or finale.

Crotology

Crotalum is the Latin word for the castanets and small metal cymbals worn on the thumb and middle finger used by the Romans and the Greeks. A fascinating description of castanets by Federico García Lorca is: 'black beetles clicking in the grip of the spider hand, ruffling the hot air of a Spanish café' (from 'Crotalo', *Poema del Cante Jondo*, Buenos Aires, 1942; this translation by Deborah Jowitt appeared in *Dance Perspectives*, Spring 1968.)

In 1782 (according to José de Udaeta; other editions 1791 and 1792), an Augustinian Monk, Juan Fernandez de Rojas published a treatise on castanets under a pseudonym Francisco Augustín Florencio, *Crotology or the Science of [Playing] Castanets*, with especially the *Bolero* in mind. He maintained that if castanets were to be played at all, it was better to do it well.

Sir Thomas Beecham is reputed to have said 'The English don't like music, but they love the noise it makes'; and the same can be said of castanets. Pupils love the noise they make, and Florencio claimed that youth was attracted to castanets because they were partial to luxury, partying, amusement and noise. He describes how the two castanets, the pair for the right and left hand, differ in tone, the right hand one being higher, which he calls the female and cunningly says it is the subtler tone, and the left, the male, is thicker and thus gives a deeper sound.

This use of calling them male and female persists to the present day. When a *carretilla* or roll is played, it runs from the right and higher tone, down to end on the left or lowest one. I have heard less flattering and undiplomatic ways of

Illustration 2.11
Rosario and Antonio, 'Los Chavalillos Sevillanos'.

♦ See colour plate 23

Illustration 2.12
José de Udaeta with the author
in front of part of his vast
castanet collection housed in his
home, the castle at Sant Pere de
Ribes, Barcelona. The 25th
Anniversary of the Spanish
Dance Society, 1990.

representation nowadays, the four beats on the right, referred to as the chattering of the women and the single sonorous beat of the left, to the monosyllabic male's reply!

A well-known early castanet notation shows the 'roll' played by both hands. It was notated by a Frenchman, Raoul Feuillet (1675-1710), using music notes, above and below a line. The left castanet is represented over the upper line, the right castanet below it. Emma Maleras also favours this method and adds other types of beats of the castanets. Feuillet composed a dance which he called *Folie d'Espagne pour une Dame* and notated the castanets and steps. In it he used both castanets playing the roll simultaneously in that dance. Today, when dancers perform castanet concerts, they use this double roll on both hands as well as the roll played by right on left castanet, as opposed to the normal roll on the right hand only and vice versa.

One of the most exquisite performers of castanets today is Maribel Gallardo of the Ballet Nacional de España. When she performs Victoria Eugenia's *Chacona* to José Nieto's music, a thrill goes through the watching public. Beautiful and bird-like Carola Goya from New York, together with her partner and husband Matteo, made the castanets part of their concert tours. After she passed away Matteo has

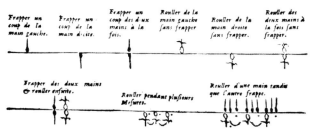

Illustration 2.13
Castanet notation.
Raoul Feuillet (1675–1710).

continued, joined by Jerane Michel and the group of players he and Carola had formed. José de Udaeta is a past master at the art, and Emma Maleras, also a Catalan, has taken it a step further not only with a method of writing down the rhythms but by training a whole 'orchestra' of castanet players who perform concerts with her as conductor.

It was (and still is) customary for a dancer to have several pairs of castanets of varying sizes, and hence of various tones. The material from which they are made also affects the sound. In the last century, ivory (which made a sharp but dead sound) and very small castanets of wood were used to accompany the dances of the Escuela Bolera. It would have been this type that Fanny Elssler, the nineteenth-century Austrian ballerina, would have used for her *Cachucha*. She learned it from Dolores Serral in Paris in 1836, and wore particularly small castanets. This is still the tendency for dancers performing the dances of the Escuela Bolera type. Their castanets are smaller than usual, to suit the delicacy of the dances. Many dancers, such as La Argentina, who pioneered Spanish dancing in the theatre in this century, had similar pairs. Today, dancers prefer heavier and louder sounding instruments for other types of Spanish dancing. Wooden ones tend to break and this, during a performance, spells disaster. So today dancers use *tela* and *fibra* castanets, made of compressed cloth or fibre.

Galiano in Madrid, who for years has made castanets for performing artists all over the world, maintains that it is very costly in time to continue to make the wooden ones, because at the last moment, after hours of work, they can suddenly split in half (personal communication). The results of these new materials on dancers finger-joints is not yet known, because these man-made fibres are relatively new. The resonance that the wood produces – *granadillo* being the best – is most satisfying. The great castanet-maker in Barcelona is Parramon.

Perhaps one should just mention that castanets are not a feature of flamenco dancing in its original solo form. This was a later addition to theatricalise it, as is flamenco as a duet or group dance.

Matteo quotes Francisco Barbieri as saying that 'The custom of dancing with castanets in an impromptu manner in church is of considerable antiquity.' Matteo mentions an old Christmas Carol in Gerona describing Saint Joseph playing castanets in his joy at the birth of Jesus, and the Carmelite nuns playing and dancing round the Christmas crèche. He says that their founder, Saint Teresa of Avila, during her recreation hour, danced while she played a tambourine and the nuns joined in on castanets. The *Seises*, or sixes, of Seville are well known for their dancing on the Cathedral altar steps at religious festivals, such as Corpus Christi. There used to be six young boys performing these dances. Later there were more. The most interesting reference Matteo makes is to Saint Thérèse of Lisieux who 'allowed herself a few moments of speech each day that were interrupted three times by the sound of castanets.' She used them as bells to signify the 'Holy Presence'.

In Ibiza they use oversized castanets worn over the whole hand, which produce a deep sonorous tone during the dance. This is also used to summon the man's partner to him at the start of a dance. He holds out his castanets, and with a loud imperious 'toc' and a shake of his arm he summons her to join him. She obediently runs forward with downcast eyes and gets ready to twirl her way through the dance, as he performs primitive jumping, turning and truly ancient-looking steps before her. She is dressed in a plain-coloured silk dress pleated from the breast and is wearing round her neck all her worldly wealth – a truly splendid sight as the gold chains and coins glisten as she moves.

José de Udaeta describes all the notations used to assist private study (that is, study without a teacher) as 'a risky way' to learn. I concur. The castanet is an instrument, and needs to be approached with great care. There is a definite way to play correctly, and if faults are built up while playing without a teacher, it is nigh on impossible to correct them without much agonising 'undoing'.

Foreign Influences in Spanish Dancing

Spain is unique in the way it transforms foreign influences in dance. Gypsies are found throughout the world, but only in Spain has the vibrant flamenco been created among them. The melody of the *Soleares* is thought of as flamenco, but it was known in Spain for several centuries before the Gypsies arrived there. For

Illustration
2.14
Maribel
Gallardo,
dancing
Chacona.

Illustration 2.15
Emma Maleras in the Teatro
Romea in 1975. Photo: Toni
Catany. Pilar Llorens archive.

example, according to Ivanova, Nos. 13 and 318 of *Las Cantigas de Alfonso El Sabio* (1253–84), a collection of music played by Moorish musicians and assembled by the musicologist Julián Ribera, resemble the *Soleares* of the *Cante Jondo*. In the same way there can be found in some Escuela Bolera Andaluza dances an element of flamenco, not in name only but in the steps as well of the Escuela Bolera dances such as the *Soleares del Maestro Arcas, Fandangos, Alegrias, Caracoles.* The technique of stamping could have been there already, in such towns as Cádiz, Seville, Granada, Córdoba and Jerez de la Frontera, for the Gypsies to pick up. The dance *Canario*, for example, has typical stamps in it, although the feet are used more loosely, and brushed, as in tap rather than Spanish dancing.

Gypsies, Flamenco and the Bolero

Flamenco is derived from the Gypsies' interpretation of what they found in dance forms when they arrived in Spain (more exactly Andalusia) from North India, via Persia and Egypt, whereas the regional dances stem from the local folk themselves. There was already stamping in the local dances, and this the Gypsies added to their Kathak dance heritage, with its rhythmic cycles or measures (counting in 12s and 8s for example), rather than the bars of the Western music.

The folk dances are rich in the variety of costuming, styles and differing techniques of the cultural regions of Spain. They show the influence of Berber, Greek, Celtic and Moorish influx as well as their own local colour. Contrary to the belief that the Gypsies and flamenco are only from Andalusia, it should be noted that another wave of Gypsies came to Barcelona later, and brought different culture, language and customs that they had acquired on their stay in north Europe. They danced differently, jumping and not stamping; this shows how the Andalusian dances influenced the Gypsies of Southern Spain.

We come now to an interesting observation by Pietro Camacho as quoted in the *Encyclopaedia of Flamenco*: that rhythmically the flamenco *Bulerias* is a sung *Bolero*. In fact, although a *Bulerias* is considered to belong to the family of 12-count *compás* or rhythmic cycle, such as the *Alegrias, Soleares, Caña* and *Seguiriyas*, it is counted by guitarists in cycles of 6 beats – just like the *Bolero*. Also, the basic footwork covers cycles of 6 beats. Alberto Lorca considers this an interesting theory, but finds the complexities of rhythms in the *Bulerias* too many to simplify it in this way (personal communication).

No one knows the origin of the word *Bulerias*. Everyone speculates; but could it not be, as Camacho states, a corruption of the word *Bolero* – in the same way that the flamenco *Seguiriyas* is a corruption of *Seguidillas*? The *Bulerias* dance can be considered a flamenco *Bolero*, something the Gypsies picked up on their arrival in Spain. The *Bolero* rhythm is an insidious one and creeps into many forms of Spanish life and customs.

Flamenco as Representative of Spanish Dance

In the nineteenth century the *Bolero* reigned supreme, and became known as Spain's 'national dance'. Yet today the words Spanish dancing have become synonymous with flamenco. This view is especially prevalent abroad. It is a sad view of Spanish dancing, as Spanish folk dances are very much alive, a vibrant, fascinating part of the culture that is rarely seen abroad today. Often the dances are seen only when the Zarzuela Company of singers and dancers go on tour, which is seldom. Luckily, they are then well presented, imaginatively and theatrically choreographed and staged by Alberto Lorca. But these tours are few and far between. Early in the twentieth century, La Argentina, Argentinita, and later the companies of Pilar López, Mariemma, Antonio, Luisillo, Ximinez/Vargas, and José Greco always represented the folk and classical dance in their repertoires. Nowadays the influence on dance companies is mainly that of flamenco, sometimes infiltrated by modern dance, as in the companies of Joaquín Cortés and Sara Baras, and the choreography of José Antonio (Ruiz), José Granero, Javier Latorre, and others.

The Bolero and Classical Composers

Today, because of Maurice Ravel's famous composition, the *Bolero* is universally recognised as a rhythm. Ravel is the first name that comes to mind with the mention of the word *Bolero*. He did not use the form of the Spanish *Bolero*, but experimented with the rhythm. He wove two melodies played alternately, each time by different instruments, ending in a third section for the coda. It was commissioned by Ida Rubinstein, who performed it in Paris on 22 November 1928, with choreography by Bronislava Nijinska and décor by Alexandre Benois. Nijinska arranged it for Ida Rubinstein to perform on a table, an idea later followed up by Maurice Béjart in 1960, who basically ignored the fascinating music and the typical *bolero* rhythm and choreographed across it. According to G.B.L. Wilson, Serge Lifar choreographed Ravel's *Bolero* for the Paris Opera in 1941, as did Anton Dolin for the Sadler's Wells Theatre in 1932. Harald Lander produced a version in 1934 for the Royal Danish Ballet. The music has been used by many choreographers since, including Lavrovsky and the Spanish choreographers La Argentinita, Pilar López, Nacho Duato and José Antonio. José Granero made a version for both the Ballet de Madrid and the Ballet Nacional de España, for whom he did several versions, one with innovative use of mirrors.

During one of Luisillo's tours, his own ballet to Ravel's *Bolero* was accompanied by a local orchestra. The wrong instrument came in for one of these passages. Only disaster could follow. Luisillo had seven women dancers on stage, each with a partner. Each woman's dance with him related in style and feeling to the instru-

Illustration 2.16
Bolero (Ravel)
choreographed by
Luisillo. Luisillo
and Cynthia Rowe,
Alhambra Theatre,
Cape Town.
Photo: Don Bain/
Terence Shean.

ment playing the section of the music, and each dancer would respond to a certain part of the score. Thinking quickly, Luisillo danced to the wings and signalled to his manager, Roberto Zafra, to bring down the curtain. He went in front of it and diplomatically announced, that due to a technical hitch they had had to stop the ballet. He said that he was sure the audience would like to see it as it was supposed to be seen and the company would therefore start it from the beginning again. On his wall at home now hangs a document signed by every member of that orchestra in gratitude to his quick thinking and to saving their reputation. It is headed, 'To a gentleman'.

Each choreographer's approach to the same music is very different. Luisillo works closely to the score, like Balanchine, using the melody line for each woman, who comes from a semi-circle of static couples, to dance with him in the centre of the stage. As each woman returns to her partner, the next joins him; the men keep the rhythm, moving back and forth, each man starting his step as his partner leaves him. The returning girl starts another cross-movement around her partner. So the build-up comes across the semi-circle of dancers from left to right. In the finale, a dramatic addition of castanets, previously hidden in built-in pockets of their costume are used to dramatic effect when added to the dance, moving into a big circle around him.

According to Gilbert Chase in *The Music of Spain*, composers such as Delibes, Auber (in 'Masaniello'), Weber (in 'Preciosa'), and others such as Mehul, have used the *Bolero* dance rhythm in their compositions. He says that there is 'a kind of *bolero*' in Rossini's *The Barber of Seville*, in the chorus *Mille Grazie*. He also quotes de Falla writing of a composition of Debussy, *La Soirée dans Grenade*: 'The work takes us away from the *Serenades . . . Madrilènes* and *Boleros* with which the so-called Spanish music-makers used to regale us'. Chopin's Op. 19 (1833) is also inspired by a Spanish *Bolero*.

In the opinion of Julien Tiersot, the collection most likely to have been consulted by Bizet was one entitled *Échos d'Espagne*, which was published in 1872. It is interesting to see the then current dance trend: *Seguidillas*, *Boleros*, *Tiranas*, *Habañeras*, a *Malagueña*, a *Jota Aragonesa*, and a *Polo*.

The composition *Puerta de Tierra* by Isaac Albéniz is based on the *bolero* rhythm, rather than its structure, and is in the repertoire of the Ballet Nacional de España. Among the great exponents of this dance are Alberto Lorca, who learned it as choreographed by Luisa Pericet in Madrid, and José Antonio Ruiz, who introduced it during his terms as artistic director, dancing it brilliantly with Aida Gómez, the artistic director of the company since 1997. Alberto Lorca later re-

Illustration 2.18
Bolero, (Ravel) choreographed by
Marina Keet for CAPAB Music's
Orchestra, Cape Town 1976.
Hazel Acosta, Gerard Prinsloo,
Glen Lawmon.
Photo: Keith Mackintosh.

choreographed his dance when his technical prowess exceeded the choreographic components of Luisa's. Another composer of a *Bolero* was Pablo Sorazábal (1897–1988), one of Spain's great composers of music for the theatre.

In Rome in 1980, the American Richard Trythall composed a very dramatic percussion *Bolero*, played on many fascinating instruments. He used a form of doubling the rhythm into 12 beats and then played around with combinations of that, 5 plus 7 for example, juxtaposed and alternating with others, lending it a freshness of approach. He later incorporated it into a ballet score leaning more towards Hispanic than Spanish influence. His original *Bolero* was performed in 1983 by the Danza Lorca Company in Cape Town to choreography by Marina Keet. This was again staged for the Spanish Dance Theatre in Washington DC in the USA in 1984.

Gilbert Chase maintains that in Cuba, where Spanish music dominates, the *Bolero* became a dance in 2/4 time, with typically syncopated off-beat accents.

3

Regional Boleros

The dancer Pacita Tomás once said with a sigh, 'Everything in Spain is a *Bolero!*' She has a point, as we see that even the flamenco *Bulerias* could rhythmically be a flamenco *Bolero*.

Other Regions

Although Valencia seems to be the home of *Boleros* most related to the style of the classical form, this dance is found in many regions throughout Spain. In Zamora they know all about the intricacies of the *Bolero*, for the words of the *Bolero de Algodre* say, 'He who dances the *Bolero*, beware!' There is the *Bolero Mallorquin* from the Balearic Isles, where the ancient, stately Parado de Valldemosa is also a *Bolero*. The *Bolero de Caspe* in Aragon is thought to be a court *Jota* in *Bolero* tempo with delicate bobbing step-kicks in a circle for each chorus section. All these will be explored, and they date from well before the 1750s, the generally accepted date for the origin of the *Bolero*.

Moorish Trios

Throughout the history of Spain, when the country was overrun by various peoples, foreign influences have appeared in the dances. These can also be found in the various *Boleros*. The Moorish influence is clearly seen in the *Bolero de Algodre*. Spanish dances are usually couple dances, whether in pairs, quartets, or even lines and circles, where men alternate with women. From notes at the Casa de Zamora in Madrid, we learn that a trio of one man with two women, as in the above-mentioned *Bolero de Algodre*, shows its Moorish heritage. In it one also sees the steps in which the women bow low in obeisance to the man. One also sees this obeiscence to the man in the *Parado de Valldemosa* from Mallorca, another trio. According to the publication *Spanish Songs and Folk Dances*, the *Bolero* from Algodre is dated, by investigators, to the tenth century, in the region of León. The dance only acquired its present form in the twelfth century, becoming smoother in style and settling into its present rhythm and shape. Once the religious Order of St Agatha had been established, the *Bolero of Algodre* was danced before her image at the feast of Saint Agatha. On this occasion the dance is interrupted so that the majordomo may hand a piece of bun, called a *migaja*, to the dancers. The women's costumes, which are almost completely covered by hand-embroidery with a lot of

◆ See colour plate 12

Illustration 3.1
'A *Bolero* in Algeciras' from
the nineteenth century. A
sketch by Wilhelm Gail.

glistening gold thread, are spectacular. Even their shoes have embroidery at the front and round the sides. The blouse is covered by a fichu crossing in front and tied at the back. Both the fichu and the long, broad apron are covered with the same rich embroidery.

Gypsies in Valencia and Catalonia

Concerning the *Bolero de l'Alcudia de Carlet*, mentioned below, which is of Arab-Andalusian origin, there was a connection with a tribe of Gypsies. These were the Sudras, who migrated from the north of India, via the Middle East (and Egypt) and settled in Granada. Others migrated to Spain across Europe to the Barcelona area. Some of these Gypsies passed through Valencia, and one of their songs resembled the *Seguidillas* of Carlet and was incorporated into it. It is also of interest to note that this resembles the type of dancing found among Gypsies in other countries, and differs from flamenco.

In Barcelona, in the region of Catalonia, the Esbart Dansaire de Rubí Company have a ballet in their repertoire based on these Gypsy dances from the area, danced at Christmas. It is jumped, not stamped as in flamenco dances. In Barcelona the *Les Gitanes del Vallès* Gypsy dance, from Tortosa in Tarragona, is also jumped, and was performed by the Esbart Dansaire de Rubí company when Queen Elizabeth II of Great Britain visited Barcelona at the Palacio de Pedralbes in October 1988. It is a stock item performed in Catalonia by folk companies and the local Gypsies. It seems that the flamenco element arrived among those Gypsies when the Amaya family moved there from Andalusia, bringing the stamping with them. Carmen Amaya became an exponent of the Garrotín in its present stamped technique, although it migrated from Asturia and León in a different form. This is why in construction it is not flamenco. There is what seems to be a form of this dance, dating from the beginning of this century (it was first danced by Faíco in Seville in the 1920s), before it was completely flamencoised. In its present form, this version of the Garrotín could possibly have originated from the teacher Realito, or Otero, in Seville.

The Valencian Boleros and the Escuela Bolera

There are many Valencian dances called Escuela. No one knows which way the influence has flowed. Perhaps the influence moved in both directions. Certainly, there are many *Boleros* in Valencia. One of the most beautiful is *Bolero Pla*. *Pla* means smooth in the Valencian dialect. A counterpart is found in the Escuela Bolera's *Bolero Liso*; again *liso* translates as smooth. The music is identical, again showing a strong folk rather than balletic influence.

The Flamenco and Escuela Bolera Connection

Valencia is linked by language with the other regions along the eastern seaboard. Catalonia, the Balearic Isles, Valencia and Murcia all share similar linguistic characteristics. Trade routes of silk, for example, going out from Valencia to other regions, made contacts with surrounding regions such as Murcia, Castile, Catalonia and so on.

To the west, Valencia has connections with Andalusia. The oil route from Andalusia through Valencia was also a means of trading music and dancing. The carriers of olive oil stopped in Valencia on their way to France. They sang their songs, danced their dances and traded cultures. As a result, both the Escuela Bolera Andaluza dances and Valencian dances share names and melodies of Andalusian flamenco.

In both can be found examples of flamenco music and dance titles. Both the Escuela Bolera Andaluza and the Valencian dances are completely different to flamenco, because they are counted in bars, not in rhythmic cycles of twelve beats. The *Peteneras* is a typical example. The flamenco link is not easily recognised in the Escuela version. In Valencia the music is identical in words and reminiscent in melody to its flamenco counterpart. However, the accent is totally different, falling on the first beat of each bar. The Valencians also give a lilt to the music. This gives it a gay, carefree feel, contrary to the tragic story of its verse. The dance has

◆ See colour plates 12 and 13

flamenco beats and is bouncy in interpretation. In the dance are found the typical flamenco *desplantes* as in the *Panaderos de la Flamenca*. The arm movements also move in inward circles as in flamenco in the *Peteneras*.

Valencian Boleros

From the region of Valencia there are the *Bolero de Castellón* and the famous *Bolero de Torrente*. In the 'fantastic pantomime' known as the *Baile de Torrente*, a *Bolero* is sometimes performed – though Enric Marti i Mora disputes this and maintains that there is no *Bolero* in the *Baile de Torrente*. Perhaps someone, some time, performed a *Bolero* during this festival and it has been recorded. This *Baile* from the town of Torrente is really a type of pageant with dancing. In the pageant, the dancing takes place after a group of smugglers arrive on horseback and fight the locals. After the battle their womenfolk arrive dressed (like the horsemen) as Aragonese, Castillians, Manchegans, Valencians or Andalusians. They perform a dance from the region represented by their costumes. The most famous dance performed during the *Baile de Torrente* is a *Bolero*. The dances are performed between a battle scene and a depiction of a grotesque dinner. At the Festival called El Torneo, the residents of Algamesi sometimes perform a *Gallegada y Bolero*, wearing antique costumes from the middle ages. The alternate dance to this is a *Jota Valenciana y Aragonesa*.

The Valencian *Bolero de L'Alcudia de Carlet* is like a jewel in its stylish and glittering period costumes, as performed by Núria Majó and Juan Fosas of the Ballet Folkloric de Esbart Dansaire de Rubí, Barcelona. The introduction for it was choreographed especially for the company by José de Udaeta. It was seen in Dame Margot Fonteyn's BBC television programme 'The Magic of Dance'. In this folk dance it is the intricacy of footwork, combined with the castanets, that makes it a dance more for the professional than for the amateur.

The main centres for dance in Valencia are Xativa and Alzira. According to Enric Marti i Mora, when the *Bolero* was popularised it was festive and alive, and those forms that survived in the towns of Albal, Carlet and Tavernes among others, were called Escuela, and were mounted by dance masters. The nineteenth-century schools of music modified and changed these from the traditional folk influence, creating new forms which in turn influenced the dances. The *U* (meaning 'one') is a form of *Bolero* which followed the rhythm of the *rondalla* or orchestra, while the singing was free. The famous *Valencianas* has the same basic step as the *Sevillanas*, but performed in a slightly different style. The Valencians have wonderful dances of other types, including the *Seguidillas*, *Fandangos* and *Jotas*.

The Bolero as a Mourners' Dance

One of the most dramatic and moving of folk dances is the Valencian *Bolero* called *Danza de Velatori*, a dance of mourning. Danced when a child dies before the age of seven, it celebrates the passing of a pure soul into heaven. It has been staged with great artistry by Albert Sans for the Esbart Dansaire de Rubí, Barcelona, and titled *Mortitxol* (*txol* meaning child in Catalan). The *Bolero* rhythm's relentlessness lends itself to the poignancy of the occasion. José Inzenga, in his book *Cantos*

Illustration 3.2
'Lo Rat Penat' group, led by
Enric Marti i Mora, Valencia.

Populares de España, mentions the gravity of the dances of the Valencians, belying their cheerful dispositions; the stately *Jácara*, called *Xaquera Vella*, is an excellent example of this. He contrasts this with the grave and serious Aragonese, who dance the most spirited dances in Spain!

Baron Charles Davillier, during his famous voyage through Spain in 1862, chanced upon a funeral in the town of Jijona near Valencia. Drawn by the sound of strumming of a guitar as he and his companion walked along a deserted street, they entered the house of a working-class family, where they thought a wedding was in progress. Seeing a child of five or six years of age, crowned with a wreath of orange blossoms and in folk costume lying on a carpet covered table, they assumed him to be asleep. Upon noticing a vessel with holy water nearby, they realised that the table was a bier with candles at the four corners. They had stumbled upon a wake. (see page 10)

He gives a remarkable description of the scene, with the young mother seated beside her child with passionate tears pouring down her cheeks. The rest of the company strongly contrasted her grief with singing, hand-clapping and, to the visitors' astonishment, a young couple were dancing a *Jota*. From the drawing of the scene by Davillier's companion, the artist Gustave Doré, it is possible to ascertain that they were in fact dancing a *Bolero*. It is the dance performed under the title *Mortitxol*, by the Esbart Dansaire de Rubí, and not a *Jota*. The arm movements of the steps opening each verse of this *Bolero* are so distinctive they cannot be mistaken. The Rubí company agree that this assumption is correct.

Albert Sans i Aris's staging of this dance is very moving. The costumes, based on antique clothing from the beginning of this century were designed by Puigserver,

It is now in the repertoire of the Spanish Dance Society in Washington DC as well, staged by Joan Fosas and myself. Sans was the artistic director of the Rubí Esbart for many years. His artistry and talent have turned the folk dances into works of art, lifting the company from folk dance to theatrical presentations. The Esbart Dansaire de Rubí company was founded in 1923 and perform dances from the eastern seaboard of Spain, where Catalan or closely related languages are spoken. The dance of mourning is already dying out and was therefore particularly difficult to reconstruct, and they had to travel and seek out the elderly inhabitants who still remembered the steps.

Enric Marti i Mora, from Valencia, quotes in his paper for the Ministry of Cultural Affairs' symposium Encuentro Escuela Bolera in 1992, that this dance, performed during the wakes of children under the age of seven, was prohibited on 5 October 1765 by Don José Tormo, the Bishop of Orihuela. From then on it was performed only in secret and that is why it was almost lost.

The Bolero de L'Alcudia de Carlet

The *Bolero* is a slower version of the lively *Seguidillas* rhythm. Through research, and again through the Valencian *Bolero* from the town of Carlet, this link is confirmed. In an old programme, seemingly published by the Sección Feminina del Movimiento Nacional, it is stated that the *Bolero* from Carlet is of Arab-Andalusian origin, danced in Carlet at the end of the eighteenth century. It seems that a tribe of Gypsies passed through the area dancing it, and that the local dancers saw 'a certain analogy with the *Seguidillas* that they danced'. After taking it into their repertoire, the process of incorporating their Valencian steps began the evolution that changed its character and technique. It continued to evolve until reaching its present technical standard, almost removing it from the folk dance category and placing it in the realm of professional dance.

Historical Valencia

This region had a chequered existence, successively occupied by Iberians, Greeks, Carthaginians, Romans (138–75 BC), Visigoths in 413 AD, and Moors in 714 AD. It was wrested from the Moors in 1049 by El Cid, only to be retaken in 1101. It was re-established as a kingdom in 1146, then annexed by James I of Aragon in 1238. As late as 1812 it was annexed by the French, who relinquished it again a year later. Throughout this turmoil it seems to have had a wealthy merchant class who survived it all.

Valencia is a rich region on the eastern seaboard. It lies between Catalonia and Murcia, along the Mediterranean sea, facing the Balearic Isles. There are three provinces in Valencia: Castellón de la Plana, Valencia and Alicante. It is a wealthy area of Spain, and the Romans used the sign of the cornucopia on their coinage to symbolise it and the riches that came from this area. Because of its thriving silk industry, the costumes are rich and elegant. The Moorish influence in this area is strong and is reflected in the regional dialect, which 'stems from the Catalan-Valencian-Balearic-Romance spoken at the court of James the Conqueror', according to Ruth Matilde Anderson.

◆ See colour plates 14,15,17 and 18

Costumes

The distinct hairdo of the women, worn in a roll (*caragol* or snail) over the ears (and a bun, high at the back) can be seen in the fifth century BC statue of La Dama de Elche, the lady of Elche, found on an archaeological site near Elche in 1897, according to the *Encyclopaedia Britannica*. Into these buns are stuck gold pins with precious stones. The brocade, mid-calf dresses of the women are gathered at the waist, with a fichu and an apron covering it. These are covered with gold embroidery and sequins and decorated with gold braid. Gold jewellery with precious stones is worn. The men wear breeches tight at the knee, and velvet jackets, a white shirt with a frill down the front, and rope-soled shoes called *alpargatas* or, in Valencian, *espardenyes*. The women's footwear is usually an elegant heeled court shoe, cut round in the front. The peasant dress of the men is a pleated white skirt like long shorts or *caraguells*, thought to be derived from the Moorish dress. However, there is a far greater likeness to the Greek skirt, although it is more bouffant than the Valencian one. There was, after all, a great influence from Greece along that seaboard.

The Bolero in the Balearic Islands

In his book *Bailes Populares Baleares*, Antonio de Galmés mentions the dance *Boleros Nuevos* and says that 'as in most (dances)' it is the woman who directs the steps and variations performed. 'It has, as in all *boleros*, an introduction, which resembles an invitation to dance, which the man performs to the woman.' He says the dance *Boleras* has two tempos, the first being slower and resembling some steps from a minuet, and the second much livelier, the man dancing in front or at the side of his partner. Even the Mallorcan *Bolero*. which shares its music with the classical *Bolero Liso*. is measured and stately. There are mainly two skips – step hop, step hop, step, step – and they seem closer to the old *Seguidillas*, as they have verses and alternating *estribillos*, the two sections mentioned by Antonio de Galmés. Usually danced in couples in a circle, and like the *Seguidillas de Leciñena*, it has sections where the step is danced with

Illustration 3.3
Bolero de l'Alcudia de Carlet. Joan Fosas and Núria Majó of the Esbart Dansaire de Rubí company in Barcelona. Photo: Bohigas. Marina Keet Archive

◆ See colour plate 21

Illustration 3.4
*Parado de
Valldemosa,*
Mallorca. Sección de
Feminina F.E. de la
J.O.N.S.

the dancers following each other in a circle. Each town in Mallorca seems to have a version: *Bolero de la Paloma, Bolero de Sant Pere, Bolero Toni Moreno, Boleres Antigues* are some of them.

Instruments

The *rondallas* accompanying Mallorcan dances have guitars, violins and *guitarrós, bandurrias,* and castanets in the plains and along the coast; in the mountains there are *cornamusas,* a form of bagpipe, called *chirimias* or *xeremies,* and also flutes (*flaviol*) and drums and bombos (*zombombos*). The latter are anything which can make a sound when struck or blown across the opening, such as a bottle or jug (Luisillo, personal communication.)

Parado

From the *Spanish Songs and Folk Dances* of Sección Feminina de la J.O.N.S. we learn that the name *parado* comes from, 'the abrupt ending, which contrasts with the smooth cadence of the rhythm'. It is accompanied by violins, guitars, castanets and the triangle. The *Parado de Selva* is danced with four partners and is very lively. The pattern danced is circular, which is rare in Mallorcan dances. The *bolero* of Valldemosa has a pecululiar lordly air, different from the other *boleros* which are nearer to the popular rhythms.'

George Sand in Mallorca

In her book *Winter in Majorca* (1855), which describes her not very successful stay in Mallorca, George Sand gave excellent descriptions of the dances, costumes, hairstyles and customs. Sand was accompanied by the very ill composer Frédéric Chopin and her two children from a former liaison, Solange and Maurice. Included are sketches of the dancers and local scenes by her fourteen-year old son Maurice. She wrote, 'Their songs are gayer than their dances. We followed them into Maria Antonia's cell across which were draped curved sprays of ivy hung with little paper lanterns. The orchestra of three, consisting of a guitar, a mandoline, a treble violin and three or four pairs of castanets, began to play the native *jotas* and *fandangos*, like those of Spain, but of more original rhythm and bolder pattern.'

Sand, her children and Chopin lived in some cells in a monastry in Valldemosa. The *Parado de Valldemosa* is the best known of the old Mallorcan *Boleros* called *Parados*. It is a stately trio, with delicate arm movements, made in small circular motions.

Sand gave a description of the dances she saw. 'The Majorcan *boleros* have an ancestral gravity, and none of the secular charm one admires in Andalusia. Men and women keep their arms spread out and still, while their fingers rattle the castanets without pause.' (However, one has to disagree with her: the *Parado* is a captivating dance with a nostalgic feeling in the music.) She discussed the singing in general: 'But the musical phrase, though nothing in itself, takes on a greater character when thus sung at long intervals, and by the voices that have a peculiar quality of being, as it were, veiled even when full-throated, and dragging even when brisk. I believe the Moors used to sing like this, and M. Tastu's investigations persuaded him the chief rhythms and favourite grace notes of the Majorcans, their whole style in fact, is of Moorish tradition.' In fact the very fact that the *Parado* is a trio shows this Moorish influence.

The Mallorcan Costumes

Sand continued: 'We were less interested in their carnival disguises than in the traditional Majorcan holiday costumes. These are elegant and graceful. The women wear the *rebozillo*, a white wimple made of lace or muslin, consisting of two parts: one, the *rebozillo en amunt*, fixed rather towards the back of the head, and passing underneath the chin like a nun's coif; and the other the *rebozillo en volant*, flowing loosely like a cape over the shoulders. Their hair is neatly parted in the middle, and caught behind in a long thick plait that emerges from the *rebozillo* and is tucked into the belt at one side. On ordinary days of labour, however, the hair is left unplaited and hangs down the back in the *estufada*, which means loose array. The bodice, made of merino or black silk, low necked with short sleeves, is adorned

Illustration 3.5
Dancing to castanets
(Mallorca), a sketch by 14-
year old Maurice Sand, son
of the author George Sand.

above the elbow and on the back seams, with jewelled buttons through which silver chains are stylishly threaded. These women have slender, well-proportioned figures, and tiny feet which, on holidays, are elegantly shod. Every village girl wears open-work linen stockings, satin shoes, a gold chain around the neck and several yards of silver chains to hang around her corsage and dangle at her belt.'

What Sand neglected to mention is that beneath the chin, fastening the *rebozillo* is a couple of inches of pleated, starched white lace fan-like material pinned with the semi-circle downward. It is very typical and a flattering way to secure the mantilla-like material.

Of the men's 'becoming costume' Sand noted: 'This consists on Sundays and holidays, of a *gipó* or waistcoat, cut heart-shape from some flowered material, and worn wide open, as is also the *sayo*, a short close-fitting, buttonless jacket, like a woman's bodice. A respendently white shirt, caught at the neck and sleeves by embroidered bands, leaves the throat bare and the chest gleaming with fine linen: which always sets off a costume to great advantage. A coloured sash is tied tightly around the waist, over wide, baggy Turkish pantaloons. made from striped cotton or silk of local manufacture, below come white, black or fawn linen stockings and shoes of undressed natural-coloured calf-skin. The wide-brimmed hat made of *maxine*, or wild-cat's fur, with cords and tassels of silk and gold thread, detracts from the oriental character of this attire. At home they tie a silk scarf or a painted calico handkerchief, turban-wise round their heads, which suits them much better. In winter they often wear a black woollen skull-cap over their tonsure, for they shave the crown of their head like priests, whether as a measure of cleanliness . . . or whether for religious reasons, I cannot say. A fringe cut across the forehead completes this mediaeval hair style and gives every face a vigorous look.'

'In the fields, their costume is less formal, but still more picturesque. Their legs are bare, or cased as far as the knees in tan leather gaiters, according to the season. In hot weather they wear only a shirt and pantaloons. In winter they wrap themselves in a grey cloak which suggests a monk's habit, or in a huge African goat's skin, with the hair outside. When they pass in groups, wearing these long fawn-coloured skins, which have a black streak down the spine, they look from the rear just like a herd of goats balancing on their hind legs. Nearly always, when they go out to the fields or come home again, one of them walks ahead playing a guitar or a flute, and the others follow silently at his heels, hanging their heads with a look of guilelessness . . . They are usually tall, and their costume lends an effect of slenderness, which makes them seem taller still. The neck, always uncovered, is fine and strong; the chest, unconfined by tight waistcoats and braces, is open and well-developed.' (See illustration page 74)

Sand was not always flattering in her descriptions and the less complimentary ones have not been included here. Chopin was very ill at the time, she found her life there very hard and she seems to have poured out this frustration onto the Mallorcans. In fact the translation by Robert Graves carries with it a refutation of her criticisms of the Mallorcans, written by a Spaniard, José Quadrado, and very necessary it is too. Sand wrote that the features of the older men 'bore a certain stamp of nobility' and all seemed to resemble the monks. She called the younger ones 'lusty'.

Catalonia

There seem to be no *Boleros* as such in Catalonia. They are found in Castile, its neighbours Valencia, Murcia and Aragon, but it skips Catalonia and is found again

Illustration 3.6
An evening party at Maria Antonia's (Mallorca). A sketch by Maurice Sand, 14-year-old son of the author George Sand.

in the Baleares. However, the Catalonian dances are more *señorial* or regal, and the dance *El Cap del Ball* does have the *Bolero* rhythm in the same way as *Bolero de Algodre* has. It is not a dance of elevation, as in Valencia. It is stepped to the fascinating rhythm of the drum beat that accompanies the melody. The man advances making circular movements with the arms, which are held up, and the woman retreats with the arms low across the body, elbows dropped. It seems ancient and steeped in mystery, with the music supplying the atmosphere.

In Catalonia, dances are often performed in suites. Danzas Tortosinas (dances from Tortosa), including *El Cap del Ball*, *El Punxonet*, *Bolero* and a *Jota* are grouped under the title of *Balls de Dolçaina* (the *dolçaina* is a musical instrument).

One of the folk companies performing in Catalonia is Esbart Verdaguer, which was founded by Manuel Cubeles. The company's choreographer is Salvador Melo. There is also the Esbart de Sant Cugat and the above-mentioned Esbart Dansaire de Rubí, with choreographer Albert Sans and with Joan Fosas as an inspiring former principal dancer and choreographer.

◆ See colour plates 19 and 20

The 'Cobla' or Catalonian Orchestra

Instrumentos Autoctonos

Madera:

1 *flaviol* (*flabiol*), a type of recorder.

2 *tible*, a double reed instrument (like an oboe).

2 *tenora*, a double reed instrument.

Metal:

2 *trompeta*, a trumpet.

1 *trombon*, a trombone and according to Pemberton a valve rather than slide trombone is usually used.

1 *fiscorno*, is a keyless cornet – a bugle.

1 *contrabajo* (3 *cuerdas*), a three-stringed double bass.

Percussion: *timbalas* (triangle) and *caja* (a type of drum).

Illustration 4.1
El Bolero, Lars J. von
Röök (1778–1867),
National Museum,
Stockholm.

4

The Bolero as the National Dance of Spain

Changes in the Bolero

The foundation of a theatre in Madrid in 1787, Los Caños del Peral, brought a new aspect into the dance. The theatre became the home of a small resident dance company of five women and six men. A resident Italian opera company performed there for twelve years. At the instigation of the Marqués de Perales, a dance school was founded in 1807, where the emphasis was on Spanish national dances.

In 1850, on the foundations of the old theatre, the Royal Theatre of Madrid was built, which housed a resident company of 116 dancers and a ballet-master called Enrique Monet. Ballets from well-known choreographers were produced in the theatres. There was a succession of foreign ballet dancers performing in the theatres in Barcelona, Madrid, Cádiz, Malaga and Seville and elsewhere.

The change in the presentation of the *Bolero* is reflected in the *sainete* Matos quotes from 1791, *La Petra y la Juana*, by Ramon de la Cruz, referring to the demise of the *Seguidillas'* structure induced by the *Bolero*:

Vale una seguidilla	A *Seguidillas* from La Mancha
de las Manchegas	Is worth twenty sets of *Boleros*
por veinte pares	Damn all fashion
de las boleras	Because it even gets into things
Mal fuego queme	like this
la moda que hasta en esto	
tambien se mete	Translated by Ralph Pemberton

Because of their special status, the foreign dancers, being under Royal patronage, paid no taxes and lived rent-free. As was mentioned before, this eventually led to discontent and a Royal Proclamation issued 28 December 1799 banned foreign languages and performers, including dancers, from the Spanish stage. This was all part of a national feeling that was to sweep Spain, yet interestingly enough, it does not seem to have affected Barcelona.

The native *Bolero* dances became dramatically changed in structure because of the ballets presented with Italian and French dancers. According to García Matos, the public desired more spectacle in the productions than the *Bolero* could provide

Illustration 4.2
A lithograph of Mariana Márquez depicted dancing a *Zorongo* (in 1793, according to José Blas Vega). Marina Keet archive.

in its form as a couple dance. Thus variations for four, six, eight or more couples were introduced.

Technique in the Bolero

It also meant that a more spectacular technique was sought. Steps from the ballet became incorporated into the Spanish dance of the schools, and also vice versa, especially concerning arms and style. However, as discussed below, the Escuela Bolera, where the arms are used in circular movements, is distinctly different from ballet, where the movement is freer. In the dances especially, its influences coming from the folk tradition, particularly from Valencia, not ballet. The dances that have the most balletic influence are the *Boleros* – such as *Boleras de la Cachucha* and the *Bolero Liso* – and the very classical *Zapateado de Maria Cristina*. Even there, one can probably find the beats in the Basque dances and the other steps also from folk sources. It was more the competition from the ballet companies that had the greatest effect.

Around the mid-1790s Calderón described a dancer called Mariana Márquez, 'despite whose swirlings in the performance of a *Zorongo* at the Theatre Coliseo de Principe, it was clear that [it was] the *bolero* [that] emerged as king, lord and master of Spanish dance.' So, in the end, it was not possible to outstrip the *Bolero* as the national treasure, at that period. The sensual *Zorongo* was supplanted in the public's favour.

According to the Spanish guitarist and composer Ferdinand Sor (Sors in Catalan), writing in 1835, 'The word *bolero*, which in its origin is an adjective, is used today to describe a Spanish dance.' Speaking of its origins, he maintained that the people greeted the *Bolero* with fervour, while it also excited the interest of the upper classes, because it did demand some talent to execute it.

The Bolero in the Theatre

In the theatre the *Bolero* was performed between acts of a play or opera, the usual place for dancing at that time. Dancing was meant to draw the audiences, in the

Illustration 4.3
The arms as held in an eight-
eenth-century *Bolero*. A position
found in regional dances across
Spain, Aragon, Extremadura,
Balearic Isles etc.

stalls or orchestra level and in *la cazuela* (earthenware casserole), a word used in Spain for 'the gods', usually for women only. The *Bolero* was noble and graceful, and no attitudes of abandon had yet been introduced to its perfection, not even in the use of the arms, which resembled the frame of a boat. This could be referring to the circle made by rounding the arms outward to the sides.

Sor writes of the *Bolero* as it was derived directly from the *Seguidillas Manchegas*. It was still a dance of the people and then of the stage, but not yet accepted by the aristocracy. Gradually some of the nobility donned the theatrical costume of the *Bolero* to wear when attending carnivals.

The Technique

The technique of many of the *Boleros* have *batterie* or beaten steps, like the Basque dances or ballet, and they have elevation, where the body is hurtled through the air. A good example of the evolution is to be found in the *Boleras de la Cachucha* and *Boleras de Medio Paso*, and where the *bolero* sections have jumped and beaten steps and balletic pirouettes, whereas the *cachucha* and *jaleo* sections that are interspersed between them are stepped and earthy, like regional dances. The dances differ in their manner of being presented, which is reflected in their titles: the Stolen *Bolero*, where sections are performed alternately by the partners, the Smooth *Bolero*, where it can be danced solo, and the 'Half-Step *Bolero*'. And then again the title sometimes denotes little except a type of dance. An example is the *Bolero del Candil* (a *candil* is an iron lamp), which is performed in Madrid, where the first part is danced by the woman, the next by the man to show off his *entrechats* and scissor jumps, and the third as partners. It is worth looking at the codified notes that are included. One sees the basic steps from the regional dances such as the *Bolero* introduction, the *lazos* and *vuelta fibraltada*, which are typically Spanish. The *grands battements* to the sides with a lean *(cambré)*, are typical of the nineteenth-century ballet found in the Cecchetti school, yet they exist in the Escuela Bolera in smaller versions with less leg height, and in other Spanish dances of the Goya period, such as *Seguidillas Antiguas*.

Agility in Performance

The *Bolero* was treated as a curious *hors d'oeuvre*; at get-togethers in private homes, if the host or hostess knew that one of the guests could dance the *Bolero*, he or she might be asked to dance it, but only as a polite gesture. Sor states that the dancers in the theatre went off too far in a direction contrary to that of the creator of the dance. He mentions no names. He says that they wished to compete with the 'grotesque' Italian dancers, with steps such as *entrechat six*, beating the legs in the air, which they considered the ultimate achievement. They ignored the original artistry and only attached importance to dancing *por alto* or leaping in the air. Sor is very scathing of the young men who followed this trend, calling the group of *aficionados* who adopted this trend, 'consumptives'. He says the idea was no longer to end with a *bien parado*, or well-held position, but to be so breathless by the end of the dance as to be unable to utter a word.

At this time the number of ladies who performed the *Bolero* became fewer; they danced with grace, but the kind of grace 'from which modesty suffered'. The men, on the other hand, were keen to learn this dance, especially the Valencians and the Murcians. These were two regions where the *Bolero* and the *Seguidillas* were danced to local melodies, one Murcian *Seguidillas* being *Las Parrandas*. Sor claims that the Valencians, being natural jumpers, were drawn to the costume of the *Bolero* because of all its decorations. The Murcians, he maintained, liked it because it resembled the music of their *Seguidillas*. It began to die out because men could rarely find a lady who danced it. This meant that when they wanted to show the *Bolero* to visitors, it was necessary to bring in someone from the theatre, or pay a stranger to come and perform it. However, according to Sor, some ladies allowed themselves the luxury of performing the *Bolero* at carnivals, but only with a gentleman of their choice, and with whom the steps were agreed in advance. This is a wonderful glimpse into the life and times of this dance.

Styles of Bolero Dancing

The *Bolero* was put back into shape in the early nineteenth century by the mysterious Requejo. Who he was, no one knows. He wished to bring back the elegant arm movements, restore the steps that could only be performed gracefully, and remove all those unsightly gestures. He also increased the distance between the dancers, to enable them to perform the improved version. Regarding the arms, he felt that the elbows should never be raised higher than shoulder level, and that the hands should not be over the head, indeed rarely be elevated to that height. We see here the style of arms, forward of the head, that can be found in the old engravings, porcelain figures and in the old French school of ballet, still retained today in the Bournonville school in Denmark and the Cecchetti method of ballet. There is a strong connection with ballet and the classical Spanish dancing of the nineteenth century. This style disappeared in the steps taught by the Pericet family at the beginning of this century. They made the posture upright, with the arms held over the head and the use of high extensions of the legs. It is explained in Paula Durbin's article for *Jaleo* magazine (January/February 1984): 'We Pericets have kept our grandfather's style exactly as he gave it to us. We haven't changed a step. What can be changed, yes, is the body expression. Dancers' bodies are very different from the way they were in the nineteenth century. Dancers are more turned out now and they have more elevation, greater extensions. That must be used, but the original technique must not be forgotten. Especially not by the Spanish dancers, when there are foreign soloists who can do a perfect *bolero* or *panaderos*' (Angel Pericet).

Requejo found it necessary to slow down the *Seguidillas*, which is the basis of the *Bolero*, but in doing so discovered that he could not find singers who could also slow down. He also objected to what he considered to be the strumming of the guitar, which he felt sounded harsh in comparison to the instruments one found when attending a ball: two violins, a bass and a flute or flageolet. Therefore he took his idea to a violinist called Cañada, who composed music for a dance called Requejo, after the choreographer, with the flute replacing the voice.

Antonio Cairón discusses the *Bolero* in his book *Compendio de las principales reglas del baile...* – the long title ends with ... *la mayor parte de los bailes conocidos en España, tanto antiguos como modernos*. He calls it the most famous, gracious and the most difficult of dances. He is so correct in his assessment of the difficulty of the *Bolero* lying in the composure of the upper body being retained while dancing the steps both on the ground and in the air, all the while playing the castanets beautifully timed to the music. He also mentions the correct dress, fitting tightly at the waist; the way the feet are used, the way the body is held, the way the arms are used, and that not many people are able to hold the gracious final positions. What is difficult in the *Bolero* is to do all this together with the airborne steps.

The Seguidillas and Bolero in the Era of Goya

From Carmen Gordo in Madrid (personal communication), with comments by the author we know the following that all the following dances are from the period of the artist Goya:

1. *Bailes del Candil*
Bolero del Candil
Fandango del Candil
Seguidillas del Candil

◆ See colour plates 6 and 22

2. Tirana del Zarandillo

Performed at the Carnavales after action of the tossing of the 'straw mannikin' or *pelele* into the air. (It can be seen in Goya's painting titled *El Pelele*.) In the dictionary *zarandillo* is said to be an active, restless or fidgety person.

3. Bailes Antiguos
Bolero de tres
Fandango antiguo
Seguidillas antiguas

The dances in section 2 and 3 were reconstructed (in the 1950s) on the Grupo Provincial de Madrid by García Matos.

4. Bailes de la Pradera
Bolero de la Pradera
Seguidillas de la Pradera
Jota de la Pradera

These are danced at the Fiestas de Madrid de la Pradera de San Isidro or in the Plazas of Madrid (*pradera* means meadow; Saint Isidro is the Patron Saint of Madrid).

5. Other Dances
Researched by García Matos
Tirananueva
Bolero Antiguo
Cachucha
Bolero robao (robado)

Saraos

These dances were also performed at *saraos*, which the English would call soirées, or in France a *salon* – elegant, refined gatherings where some form of entertainment for the guests would be arranged.

Majos and Majas

Madrileños, or the inhabitants of Madrid, had the habit of finding nicknames for the people. As early as the Middle Ages, they were referred to as *gatos* (cats), because of 'the ability of the local troops to scale the walls'. This custom persisted. Then, during the period of the artist Goya at the turn of the eighteenth and nineteenth century, the word *majo* came to be used to describe the middle classes in Madrid, who copied the lower classes in their rather showy apparel. It was also reflected in their manner of speaking, as they affected a specific accent. Their form of dress is actually best described as 'natty', or elegant in a rather showy way. The word was derived from the Arab word for brilliance, *mahar*, as this was rather descriptive of their shiny silks, satins and velvets adorned with shining gold braids.

◆ See colour plate 6

The men and women wore their hair caught back in snoods that hung down behind their backs, but the women also had fantasy headdresses of bows and frills, often of very outsize proportions. The hats of the men varied from a round crown with the brim curled, to tricornes and something that looks like a chimney pot. All to great effect.

Illustrations 4.4, 4.5, 4.6
Majos and *Majas*.

As seen above, several of the dances have the word *pradera* added to describe them, as the people used to meet on Sunday mornings on the meadow outside Madrid. Goya depicted them in their finery, dancing on the meadow, where the Museo del Prado now stands. The low-heeled, often ornate footwear, with buckles as decoration, were very suitable for dancing outdoors, except that they had rather pointed toes. In one of Goya's paintings a woman has a very charming little hat coming to a point on the forehead, with ribbons coiled in loops at the back and side and the ends trailing and hanging down the coiled locks of hair, which are drawn to one side. In another, a woman has only smooth gold surrounding her head behind the bun. The men were often depicted looking mysterious, with capes flung over one shoulder.

In Cádiz the street toughs of the lower classes also took on the name of *majo*.

Manola and Manolo

See *La Manola* (p. 143).

Classical Boleros

The *Seguidillas Boleras* was the first name of the *Bolero*, in the same way that *Seguidillas Sevillanas* was the first name of the *Sevillanas*. In both cases the word

2 Del antiguo *Manolo,*
he aqui un ejemplar solo.

Illustration 4.7
A *manolo* and 4.8 a *manola.*

Seguidillas was later dropped from the title. The theory has been advanced (quoted in Alfonso Puig's *Ballet y Baile Español*) that the ending with the 'o' (*Bolero*) indicated a single couple were dancing, and that the 'as' ending (*Boleras*) indicated more than one couple was performing. The *Boleras de la Cachucha* he calls *Bolero con Cachucha*; the *Bolero de Medio Paso* or 'Half-Step *Bolero*' is called *Boleras* in the Pericet repertoire and in printed music scores, and the *Bolero Liso*, which is usually danced as a solo (*liso* means smooth, plain, simple, straightforward) are all couple dances. It is difficult to find a firm reason why some dances are titled *Bolero* and others *Boleras*, apart from this theory advanced by Puig. As we see below, Davillier describes the *Bolero Robado* as being performed by several couples. The regional influence is to be found in the music of the *Bolero Liso* which is the same as that of the Mallorcan one; the *Bolero del Candil* or *Bolero* of the lamp, or perhaps 'Lamp-light *Bolero*' is more descriptive of dances performed in taverns and private homes by paid performers.

The *Bolero Robado* or Stolen *Bolero* is mentioned by Baron Davillier on his journey through Spain in 1862. He writes about the teacher called Luis Botella of Seville presenting entertainment 'this evening and every following Saturday'. The advertisement for these performances announces extraordinary National and Andalusian dances, including the most celebrated *Boleros* of this capital, to be performed by his pupils and Spain's principal dancer, none other than Doña Amparo Alvarez, otherwise known as La Campanera. Today we have a direct heritage tracing the original steps back to her through her pupil Angel Pericet

♦ See colour plate 24

Carmona and his descendants. Davillier describes the above-mentioned *Bolero* danced lightly and agilely by a couple who are electrified by the enthusiastic exclamations and applause. They double their agile efforts, are supplanted by another couple, and again by another, and then all return to perform a finale together. So much for the theory that the dance with many couples is in the plural.

This exchange of performers is typical – hence the name 'Stolen' *Bolero* – and still performed thus today. This dance is performed by three couples, and as Davillier points out, the one leaves and the next one takes over, three times, one couple after another performing only one verse each and then on the fourth verse, all return and dance together as a grand finale.

Alfonso Puig lists others of the two categories:

1. *Boleros*
Bolero Seco, Popular, de Medio Paso, Bolero con Cachucha, del Zorongo, de la Caleta, Extranjero, Mallorquin, Jarabe, Jarabe Americano, Zapateado. Con Adagio, de Pot Pourri, Piache, de Fray Luis Leon, de los Viejos, de la Civila, de la Fragua del Vulcano, de los Bandos, de los Confitera, de los Fanfarrones, de la Soledad, del Solitario, del Currito, del Canillita, de los Canarios del Café, etc.

2. *Boleras*
Boleras Robadas, del Capricho, a Ocho, Jaleadas, de Madrid, etc.

Illustration 4.9
Baile de Candil.

Today we also have *Boleras de la Cachucha*, not called (as above) *Bolero con Cachucha*. It is said to be the one performed by Mariano Camprubí and Dolores Serral in Paris and in Copenhagen, together with August Bournonville. It is also said to be the one performed by Fanny Elssler, as taught to her by Serral. We will discuss these later under the *Cachucha*, and in connection with Bournonville.

A musical composition (though not a specific dance in the Escuela Bolera repertoire still danced today) is the *Boleras Jaleadas* of the composer Saldoni. According to the *Diccionario Biografico de Elemérides de Musicos Españoles*, Baltzar Saldoni, who became Professor at the Conservatorium in Madrid, was born in Barcelona in 1807. He composed operettas and *zarzuelas*, operas and possibly the *Boleras*.

Alberto Lorca thinks that some *Boleros* such as the ones with names like the Chocolate *Bolero* and the Smugglers *Bolero* (personal communication) could come from the Southern ports, where there was trade. And who knows the origin of the *Bolero* of Liberty?

The *Bolero* of Charles III is thought, by Carmen Gordo, to be a more recent concoction comprising various melodies of *Boleros* (personal communication). Spain experienced a cultural and economic revival from 1759 to 1788, during the reign of Charles III (b. 1716, d. 1788). He was from a branch of the Bourbon family. Here we find a link to Italy, as before becoming King of Spain Charles was Duke of Parma in 1732 and King of Naples and Sicily in 1734. He was said to be a good dancer and during this period dance and theatre were to flourish.

Caballero Bonald's comments on some of these dances mentioned above are interesting. Published in 1959 in 'Andalusian Dances', he says of the *Bolero Seco* ('dry' *bolero*), that it is 'generally danced by a single couple'. Of the *Bolero Robado* he comments that it is 'always a single person who performs the figures whilst the opposite partner simply keeps time on the castanettes'. The 'half-pace and stolen' *Bolero, Boleras Robadas y Liso* (the *Liso* to the same music as the *Bolero Mallorquin*) is 'performed by several couples at a time, changing and altering the tempo in succession.' Here there is a double link with the Balearic Isles. In some Mallorcan dances, one partner (usually the woman) often plays castanets and waits, while the man performs alone. Among the *Bolero* dances codified in this book is the *Bolero del Candil*, believed to be very old and dating from the period of Goya. It is a short dance and each solo danced sequence is brief. The woman waits while the man dances. Then the woman dances and then the man returns very briefly, just to show off with an *entrechat*, scissor jump, *entrechat*, scissor jump. They end by dancing a short sequence of steps together. (notation p. 288)

Some more *Boleros* with strange names can be found in *Historia de la Música Teatral de España* by José Subirá, published in Barcelona in 1945. He mentions some of the ones found in print elsewhere, such as the *Boleras del Chocolate, Robadas* and *Jaleadas*, and others that are self-explanatory such as *Boleras de la Madrileña, Boleras Amanchegadas* (from La Mancha), *Boleras Acuchadas*, but also some strange ones, which in a way show how much a dance of the people it was: *Boleras de la Matraca* (the rattle *bolero*), *Boleras de la Charandel* (a *charranda* is a rascal or villain), *Boleras de la Marica* (the milksop's *bolero*),

Boleras del Escondite (the hide-and-seek bolero), *Orgia* (the orgy), *Tinta* (ink) and *Sereni* (could this be *Bolero Liso* or 'smooth' *Bolero*?). Most of these are not performed any more, apart from *Boleras Robadas*.

A Nineteenth-Century Performance in Seville

Davillier in the nineteenth century described the Salón del Recreo, Botillo's, in Calle de Tarifa, Seville, where performances were held at 8.30 p.m. every Saturday, on the second floor of the building. The rectangular room where the dancing took place was sparsely furnished with simple chairs, despite the protestations on the magnificent advertisements on pink paper to the contrary that no trouble has been spared to make it comfortable. There were chairs for the dancers – and here we note they were called *boleros* – and the spectators, who Davillier describes as being artisans. He mentions that the upper classes would not dignify such a place with a visit. The rest were foreigners, German, French, English and Russian, accompanied by a few ladies. There was a small entrance to another room for the dancers and musicians, to which no one was allowed entry. The spectators surrounded the artists before the performance.

La Campanera took up her pose in the centre of the circle to dance *Jaleo de Jerez*, dancing spiritedly while poorly accompanied by a blind violinist, who did not exactly play in time. After a while there were cries of 'Away with the violin' and 'Bring on the guitar' from some of the spectators. According to Marta Carrasco Benítes in her informative article for the 1992 Encuentro Escuela Bolera in Madrid, the name La Campanera was given to her by her father, who was *el campanero* (bell-ringer) in the Cathedral of Seville.

Illustration 4.10
Amparo Alvarez 'La Campanera', Seville. Sketch by Gustave Doré.

The Cafés Cantantes

The above description comes from the era of the *cafés cantantes*, the many salons where the dances were performed in artistic presentations, between 1847 and

◆ See colour plate 25

CELESTIN PIARD DESSAYS

Melle DOLORES SERRAL

1920, of which above-mentioned Café de Recreo was one of several in Seville. This period is described in detail by José Blas Vega in his book *Los Cafés Cantantes*. He lists the ones in Cádiz, Jerez de la Frontera, Malaga, Granada, Almeria, Córdoba, Madrid and Barcelona.

In Seville he discusses the venues where, as late as 1935, even the famous Carmen Amaya 'La Capitana', appeared in the Salon Variedades. On a poster at the beginning of the twentieth century the name of Don Angel Pericet appeared, with Luisa Fernández, in the Cuadro de Baile Español at the Café Concierto Novedades. In the 1920s is to be found the name of his brother, Rafael Pericet, who presented his choreography and his most accomplished pupils in the venues such as the Kuursaal and Salon Variedades.

The dancer Antonio, as a child, saw some of these *cuadros boleros* performances and later wondered why they had died out. In Elsa Brunelleschi's biography, Antonio mentions how the dancers of *cuadros boleros* entered onto the scene singing and clapping. One wonders just what they chose to sing for their entrance. One also wishes that someone had questioned him about it and written it down for posterity. According to Blas Vega, Antonio and Rosario appeared as 'Los Chavallos Sevillanos' at the Variedades from 1936 until the war, when it was turned into one of the most important prisons. Maybe the interruption of war caused a vacuum that was never again filled by the *boleros* and *boleras*. Much later the prison became the cinema Trajana.

Illustration 4.11
Dolores Serral in her
Cachucha costume.

Accompaniment

It is interesting to note that the dances in the nineteenth century, according to Puig, were accompanied 'without exception' by guitars and *vihuelas*, until the modern musicians were inspired to compose for piano and orchestra. The *vihuela*, according to the *Encyclopaedia Brittanica*, is a stringed instrument of six, sometimes seven, double courses of strings, tuned like a lute. In Spain it held the same popularity accorded elsewhere in Europe to the lute.

Carlo Blasis and the Bolero Dances

The Italian Carlo Blasis (1795–1878) codified his own method of teaching ballet in *Treatise on the Dance* (1820) and *The Code of Terpsichore* (1828). He was a mysterious character and what is written about him is often difficult to verify. Much of what we know about him is not always what it seems. Historian Giannandrea Poesio also echoes this feeling in his articles on mime (*Dancing Times*, September–November 1995). Blasis's Spanish dance connection (mentioned later) is intriguing when discussing the *Cachucha* and the dance he calls *Seguidillas Taleada*.

Amongst the dances Blasis presented on the stage were several of the Spanish *Bolero* style. In his treatise on Blasis for the Encuentro Escuela Bolera in Madrid in 1992, Alfio Agostini listed the Spanish dances staged by Blasis: in France, a *Bolero*, a Gypsy dance, Basque Dance, Spanish Dance; in Milan, a 'Grand Pas' for Seven Spaniards, two 'Tercetos' in a Spanish Style, a Catalonian Dance, an Andalusian Dance; in the 1850s, a *Cachucha*, 'A Spanish Pas de deux', *La Castellana*, a *Bolero* for two ballerinas, a *Sevillana* in London and also a ballet in four acts titled *The Spanish Galentries* which included a *Minue Afandangado*, *Seguidilla Manchega*, a new *Cachucha*, revived in Piacenza as *Hermosa o la Danzatrice Spagnola* in the Fenice in Venice.

If Blasis's Spanish output was so prolific, did he present the original dances or choreograph his own dances to Spanish music, as did Petipa and Bournonville? Blasis went back and forth to Spain quite often. One wonders what was actually produced. A Spaniard from Aragon, writing about *Jotas*, laments in his book that foreigners use the music of Spanish dances and that he would not mind if they only put the correct steps to the parts of the music where they belonged. One can understand his pain.

Illustration 4.12
Dolores Serral and Mariano Camprubí dancing a *Bolero*. Arcadio Carbonell archive.

♦ See also colour plate 26

Dolores Serral and Mariano Camprubí in Paris

Thanks to Ivor Guest's painstaking research published in *Gautier on Dance*, we find out about which Spanish dancers were performing in Paris during the Romantic period, and also where and what they were dancing. When one reads Gautier's assessment of Dolores Serral's performance of the *Cachucha*, it is the Spanishness of her dancing that he admires.

In 1834 Dolores Serral, with her partner Mariano Camprubí together with Manuela Dubinon and Francisco Font, caused a flurry of excitement amongst the Parisian public with their performances. In 1836 Serral was again performing in Paris, at the Opera Balls, partnered by Mariano Camprubí. They made a great impact and were painted by Manet, who immortalised them for posterity.

In 1837, the Spanish couple were re-engaged for these balls as well as performing in the Théâtre du Palais-Royal and Théâtre des Variétés. Gautier waxed lyrical about them, wondering why the management of the Paris Opéra had not engaged them. He claimed that those who had not reserved seats to see them, had 'missed one of the most ravishing and poetic performances in the world'. The very acerbic Gautier praises Camprubí: 'as pleasing a sight as a woman', but says that he 'preserves a heroic and gentlemanly expression in his poses that has nothing in common with the foolish affectation of French male dancers.' After a really cruel attack on the French ballet girls, he says of Serral, 'Dolores has a plump bosom, rounded arms, slender legs and tiny feet, and in addition to being a very good dancer, is very pretty.' He goes on to say that it is an essential requirement for a dancer to be beautiful, and continues, 'Dolores and Camprubí have nothing in common with our own dancers. They have a passion a vitality and an attack of which you can have no idea . . . Their dancing is an expression of temperament rather than a conforming to a set of principles; every gesture is redolent of the fiery Southern blood. For Dolores the *Cachucha* is a faith, a religion. It is obvious that she believes in it, for she performs it with all the emotion, passion, guilelessness and seriousness that it is possible to sum up.'

Gautier discusses why this manner of dancing is not indecent. He decides that this 'is a national dance of primitive character and such barefaced simplicity that it has become chaste. It is so openly sensual, so boldly amorous, and its provocative coquetry and delirious exuberance are so full of the of youth that it is easy to forgive the very Andalusian impetuosity of some of its mannerisms.'

When Gautier speaks of Serral bending back, 'proudly arched, head thrown back, a large red rose unfolding in her beautiful half-loosened black hair, arms dreamily extended and only gently shaking the castanets, smiles over her shoulder at the lover who is approaching to steal a kiss', it could be a movement in one of the *desplantes* to be found in the Pericet version of a *Panaderos*. This gesture happens as well in *La Maja y el Torero*.

In 1840 Serral and Camprubí toured to Copenhagen and had a profound influence there on August Bournonville.

The critics, Gautier in particular, remarked on the impression made by the Spanish dancers. Gautier wrote of the male dancers' 'ferocious grace', insolent stance and of their allure, seeming to be always in love, the languor that is suddenly supplanted by jaguar-like leaps. This contrasted greatly with the male ballet dancers of that period, who seem to have produced only scorn from Gautier. It was also this manner that brought out critical remarks from Bournonville.

Gautier also mentions the movement of the body curving, the dancer bending back her head (a typical *renversée* of the body, circling the arms down to the floor and around, as the picture drawn by Gustave Doré shows, found in Olé de la Curra), brushing the floor with her arms, while still playing castanets. His words describe passion and voluptuousness, as well as alertness.

Gautier remarked that they danced with their whole body, their backs arched and the torso twisting, the arm movements languorous and flexible. He likened it to a loose scarf or a snake. His enthusiasm for Serral led him to sum up his thoughts on the non-Spaniards' performances: 'Fanny Elssler and Mlle Noblet dance it like unbelievers, more to satisfy a whim or cheer up the opera glasses of that bored sultan, the public, than out of any real conviction. Also, they are both spirited flirts, amusing but not erotic, which is an unpardonable sin in a *cachucha* or a *bolero*.'

The Cachucha

Described as a Spanish dance in 3/4 or 3/8 time, the *Cachucha* caused a sensation in the nineteenth century when danced by Fanny Elssler. Dolores Serral and Mariano Camprubí had already started the Spanish fever with their visit in 1834.

Illustration 4.13
Cristl Zimmerl performing the *Cachucha*, as reconstructed by Ann Hutchinson from the Zorn notation, at the 1969 centenary celebration of the Vienna State Opera.

The Austrian dancer Fanny Elssler was the first non-Spaniard to introduce the *Bolero* style into the repertoire of ballerinas in Paris theatres. She was considered a 'pagan dancer', earthy in contrast to the ethereal sylph. She was also very beautiful, and certainly the reception she received from the performances of the *Cachucha* almost forced the dancers such as Marie Taglioni, Fanny Cerrito and Lucile Grahn to dance Spanish dances if they wished to compete for glory. Grahn on more than one occasion was put out by the fuss that was made over Elssler.

Dances such as the *Cachucha* and other Spanish dances became not only part of the dancer's solo repertoire, but were incorporated into ballets by choreographers such as Filippo Taglioni and August Bournonville. We know that they performed these dances, because the critics recorded it in daily papers and books; but which steps they danced remains a mystery.

Friedrich Albert Zorn notated a *Cachucha* and sternly wrote at the start of his manuscript, 'The *Cachucha* is a solo dance.' It was for the ballet dancers in France,

Illustration 4.14
Lola de Valencia painted by
Edouard Manet (1832–1883),
Paris.

but in its native Spain it was and is a part-ner dance of great elegance. It occurs in between the recurring sections of a *Bolero*. The notated Zorn version of Elssler's *Cachucha* in his *Grammatik der Tanzkunst* (1887), bears no resemblance to the Pericet version that survives in Spain today. It is discussed and transcribed in Labanotation and has very clear instructions by Ann Hutchinson. Her beautiful book includes an introduction and a biographical sketch about Zorn by Ivor Guest. Zorn used his own notation, evolved after some discourse with Arthur Saint-Léon about his form of notation. This codifying of the *Cachucha* by Zorn happened some years after he had seen Elssler dance it.

A feverish furore was initiated on 1 June 1836 when Elssler included her version of the *Cachucha*, as a sensational solo, in Jean Coralli's *Le Diable Boîteux* at the Théâtre de l'Académie Royale de Musique in Paris. Burat de Gurgy and Alphonse Nourrit (ac-cording to Cyril Beaumont) were responsi-ble for the libretto, and Casimir Gide com-posed the music. Gautier maintained that Paris had seen, 'Rosita Diaz, Lola, and the finest dancers of Madrid, Seville, Cádiz and Granada; we have seen the *gitanas* in Albaicín, but nothing approaches that *Cachucha* as danced by Elssler.'

Cyril Beaumont, in his *Complete Book of Ballets*, quotes from Charles de Boigne's *Petits Memoires de L'Opéra* of the effect produced on the general public by this dance:

A certain number of performances were required to accustom the real public to the *Cachuca* [*sic*]. Those swaying of the hips . . . those provocative ges-tures, those arms, which seemed to reach out for and embrace an absent being, that mouth which asked to be kissed, the body that thrilled, shud-dered, and twisted that seductive music, those castanets, that unfamiliar costume, that short skirt, that half-opening bodice, all this, and above all, Elssler's sensuous grace, lascivious abandon, and plastic beauty were greatly appreciated by the opera glasses of the stalls and boxes. But the public, the real public, found it difficult to accept such choreographic audacities.

The dances of the Romantic era's ballerinas have been lost to history. However, as consolation, the Escuela Bolera steps that still remain in the Spanish dancers repertoire are being performed today, unchanged, by the descendants of the Pericet family, 160 years later, a heritage from 'La Campanera' and Maestro Faustino Segura. The Spaniards say categorically that Elssler's *Cachucha* is the dance performed as a duet by Serral and Camprubí. It became so popular that other ballerinas of the period vied with Elssler to perform dances of this style. According to José de Udaeta and Eloy Pericet (personal communication), Elssler's *Cachucha* was surely the alternating sections of the *Boleras de la Cachucha*, that she had learned from Dolores Serral. Ivanova, in her book *The Dancing Spaniards*, names, under an illustration, Lola de Valencia as the dancer who taught it to Elssler, but also elsewhere names Serral. Ivanova claims that de Valencia was the first Spanish dancer to bring to Paris the dances of her native Spain. Dolores Serral and her partner Mariano Camprubí appear in Manet's painting, Serral and Camprubí dancing and de Valencia seated at the back with the musicians. Or could the two other dancers be Manuela Dubinon and Francisco Font? The large painting depicting them hangs in the Phillips collection in Washington DC in America.

Blasis makes interesting comments about the *Cachucha*:

> The name of this dance is a word of very general signification, and is applied to an infinite number of articles, by way perhaps of abbreviation, as caps, fans etc. and here is a verse that refers to a ship:

> *Mi cachucha, por la mar,*
> *a todos vientos camina,*
> *pero nunca va mejor*
> *que cuando va de bolina.*

> When my *Cachucha* moves through the waves
> Her sails catch every breeze;
> But she's never more lively
> Than when she sails close to the wind.
> Translated by Ralph Pemberton.

One wonders about Blasis's information after his mention of *Seguidillas Taleadas* (not found mentioned in Spain), when one assumes that it should be *Jaleadas*. *Jaleo* is the noisy cheering-on of the dancers. He writes: 'The *Cachucha* is a solo danced either by a man or a woman alone, though better suited to the latter, and is admirably calculated for and adapted to that melody which it is always accompanied, and which is sometimes calm and graceful, at others sprightly and vivacious, or at times impassioned and expressive.' Of course it became known as a solo dance through Elssler and others outside Spain, but was definitely not so in Spain, where it is a couple dance.

Blasis also writes of the *Bolero* as being danced *terre à terre*, while it was very much *al aire, en l'air*; elsewhere he maintains that the *Bolero* is in 2/4 time, when

♦ See colour plate 26

LA CACHUCHA.

Dansée par

FANNY ELSSLER,

Arrangée pour le Piano
avec accomp.t de Castagnettes ad libitum de Sala

Paris.

chez MEISSONNIER & H.HEUGEL, RueVivienne, N.º 2 bis
près le Passage Colbert.

Lith. de Magnier.

Illustration 4.15
Cover of music for the
Cachucha showing Fanny
Elssler. Royal Ballet
School archive.

it is printed as 3/4. The Pericet castanet rhythm does go across the music, counting it in two counts to the 3/4 timing: both; both, (6; 1), L, Roll (2, 3), and then it repeats both, both, (4, 5), L, roll (6; 1). This may tie in with Blasis's idea of a 2/4. He also claims that the *Seguidillas Manchegas* is of Moorish origin, when it is inherently Spanish . . . and so on. Interestingly, he speaks only of lightness in performance and not of elevation, even though he says that the word *Bolero* is derived from the verb *volar*, to fly.

There is much written information about Elssler's performance. August Bournonville, the great Danish dancer, teacher and choreographer wrote:

The dance begins with a graceful advance, and then a few steps back. She performed the first part as if she meant to say 'be content with a little jest'; but in the second portion a rapturous glow suffused her entire countenance, which radiated a halo of joy. The moment never failed to have its effect, and from then on the whole dance became a frolic in which she drove her audience wild with delight.

Théophile Gautier, critic for *La Presse* in Paris in the 1830s, called Fanny Elssler, 'That German girl who has transformed herself into a Spaniard.' He was totally enamoured with her and thought that she was the *Cachucha* incarnate and that she raised the *Cachucha* of Dolores Serral to the state of a classical model. He claimed that Elssler was 'the most spirited, precise and intelligent dancer who skimmed the boards with the grip of her steely toe'. He stated that the ballet *Le Diable Boîteux* was an excellent vehicle for her talents, and felt that no Spanish dancer in Spain or elsewhere approached Elssler's performance of the *Cachucha*. He wrote, in Cyril Beaumont's translation:

She comes forward in her pink satin basquine trimmed with wide flounces of black lace; her skirt, weighted at the hem, fits tightly over the hips; her slender waist is boldly arched and causes the diamond ornament on her bodice to glitter; her leg, smooth as marble, gleams through the frail mesh of her silk stocking; and her little foot at rest seems but to await the signal of the music. How charming she is with her big comb, the rose behind her ear, her lustrous eyes and her sparkling smile! At the tips of her rosy fingers quiver ebony castanets. Now she darts forward: castanets begin their sonorous chatter. With her hand she shakes down great clusters of rhythm. How she twists, how she bends! What voluptuousness! What precision! What fire! Her swooning arms toss about her drooping head, her body curves backwards, her white shoulders almost graze the ground. What a charming gesture! Would you not say that in that hand, which seems to skim the dazzling barrier of the footlights, she gathers up all the desires and all the enthusiasm of the spectators?

In an American caricature, Elssler is depicted with one foot in the USA and one in Europe. The adoration with which she was showered all over Europe is shown in the many lithographs, porcelain statuettes, casts were made of her feet and her hands; her effigy was put on lamps, beermugs, watches, tobacco pipes and cigarette cases, and etched on glassware in the different countries to which she toured, including Russia where in St Petersburg she was given a diamond brooch by the Empress. In the last photograph of her in 1883, a handsome face and intelligent eyes look out at the viewer, but this time her dress sweeps down to the floor. A hundred years after her birth she was still being celebrated in Vienna and New York. In the press she was called 'the girl of the century' and she had 'the smile of the century'; yet it is written that Elssler performed the *Cachucha* for the last time in Vienna, simply, modestly and without exaggeration in her movements – as she always had.

Gautier says something similar about Dolores Serral and her rendering of the *Cachucha*: 'In the most exaggerated *écarts* of this unrestrained and animated *pas* she was never immodest. She is full of passion and voluptuousness, but true voluptuousness is always chaste . . .'

Marie Taglioni and her Cachucha

Filippo Taglioni staged for his daughter, Marie Taglioni, the ballet *La Gitana* (*The Gypsy*) in St Petersburg on 23 November 1838. The nomadic lives led by dancers, with no affiliation to any particular company, resulted in ballets being lost. Here Bournonville was to benefit from his position in the Royal Danish Ballet, which has retained some of his ballets in the style and choreography of the former era. Taglioni and other choreographers were not so privileged. Thus we have no record of the *Cachucha* as it was staged in *La Gitana*, and only the critics' appreciation as a guide.

The ballet is set in Madrid and the principal role is that of an abandoned non-Gypsy child who grows up with the Gypsies, a role tailored for Marie Taglioni, as her very delicacy makes her unsuitable for the role of a full-blooded Gypsy girl. According to the synopsis in Beaumont's *Complete Book of Ballets*, the *Cachucha* is performed in the final Act III, Scene II, set in a magnificent ballroom. Taglioni had such success that 'all kinds of articles were named after her. There were Taglioni caramels, Taglioni cake, *coiffures à la Taglioni* and so forth.' When it went to London, *The Times* thought it 'one of the most beautiful ballets ever produced.' N.P. Willis ('Famous Persons and Famous Places'), summed up her performance: 'But there is one thing, the *Cachucha*, introduced at the close of the Ballet, in which Taglioni has enchanted the world anew.'

Social Mores

One is inclined to forget the social aspect of the theatre, that women were showing their legs and that the theatre represented immorality to many and that the dancers were being ogled through opera glasses, as we find in this representation from a 'Social Observer' in the *Illustrated London Life* (16 April 1843):

> We perfectly recollect in admiring the emotion of several ancient aristocrats in the stalls, in the recent appearance of the legs of Fanny Elssler. We thought that we observed one aged and respectable virtuoso shedding tears; another fainted in his satin breeks and diamond buckles; one appeared to go mad and bit his neighbour's pigtail in half in sheer ecstasy. Oh! The legs of Fanny displaced a vast deal of propriety, and frightened sober men from their prescribed complacency.

– much as today the young girls quiver and gasp as Joaquín Cortés passes bare-chested through the audience on his way to the stage.

From Ivor Guest we know that Mrs Harriet Grote, in a letter from London, called Elssler, 'the demented Fanny' and tried to help her by looking after her daughter and freeing her to continue to perform.

Elssler's Cachucha Compared to Other Dances

The descriptions of Elssler dancing the *Cachucha* seem to represent more the steps of the Olé de a Curra than the traditional *Cachucha*. No one, other than Zorn, tells us about steps of the dance.

In Copenhagen, Kirsten Ralov believed that some steps from Elssler's *Cachucha* were incorporated in the little solo for her role in Bournonville's *Konservatoriet*, taught to her by Valborg Borchsenius, who had probably learned it from Hans Beck. Ralov was seven years old at the time. The steps are very simple, but Bournonville had just seen Elssler perform in Paris and it was probably fresh in his mind. She said that the tune that is played is certainly the traditional *Cachucha* of Spain. The scene in the ballet is where a violist arrives with his daughter to audition for her entrance into the Conservatorium. Ralov felt that the couple represent Elssler and her father and that these were the last representations, however simple, of some of the steps that Elssler had danced (personal communication). This scene was later removed from the ballet and has luckily been returned to it, taught by Ralov, to the newest generation of children in the Royal Danish Ballet School in the production in 1995. It could so easily have been lost forever.

Various Cachuchas

In all balletic historic references the *Cachucha* is referred to as a solo dance. Yet Eloy Pericet says that there is only one basic *Cachucha*, that of the central *Cachucha* sections of the alternating *Boleros* and *Cachuchas* in *Boleras de la Cachucha*, which is a couple dance (see p.319), and seems to be the Double *Cachucha* danced by Duvernay and Perrot. Eloy Pericet and José de Udaeta are convinced that it was the extracts of the *Cachucha* that were taught to Fanny Elssler by Dolores Serral in Paris. The descriptions, however vague, by critics and fellow dancers who saw Elssler perform it, describe something different. They write about different movements, such as her shoulders almost touching the ground, whereas the Pericets' is very upright. The *Cachucha* that Eloy performed with his sister Carmelita in Margot Fonteyn's *The Magic of Dance* television programme, is again different. It is a *Cachucha* adapted by their brother, Angel Pericet 'El Jefe', which contains choreography with steps from the *Cachucha* sections of the *Boleras de la Cachucha*. There is also the *Cachucha* performed during the period of the artist Goya called *Cachucha y Bolero* Robado.

Carmen Gordo, a fountain of knowledge about Spanish regional dances, refers to the *Cachucha* danced in Madrid as a solo, but often performed today as a group dance. She also points out the very different *Cachucha* danced by the Gypsies of Sacromonte, Granada, with the words, '*La Cachucha de mi madre*'. It is a very simple dance of mainly *pas de basques*. She demonstrated the steps, dancing the *pas de basques* on place, explained that the partners then crossed each other, still doing *pas de basques*; one kneels while the other goes around in a circle. When the dance is repeated it is the other partner's turn to circle while her partner kneels. José Luis Navarro García writes in his article on the *Cachucha* that a Russian traveller, Vassili Botkine, had mentioned the *Cachucha* and *Fandango* being danced in Triana, the Gypsy

Illustration 4.16
Pauline Duvernay performing the *Cachucha* in London, 16 March 1836.
Marina Keet archive.

Illustration 4.17
Lucile Grahn in the *Cachucha* in 1838.

◆ See colour plate 27

quarter of Seville in 1845. The Swedish writer Selma Lagerlof, in her book *Gösta Berling's Saga* (1891), wrote about the eternally young Gypsies of Granada performing the *Cachucha*. Bournonville's little dance to *Cachucha* music seems very much like the dance of the Granada Gypsies as demonstrated by Carmen Gordo (personal communication).

Pauline Duvernay also performed the *Cachucha* with great success. It was she who danced it in London on 16 March 1836 at the King's Theatre, in the production of *The Devil on Two Sticks*, the English title of Coralli's ballet *Le Diable Boîteux*. The critic of *The Times* apologised for the lack of space and concluded, 'We cannot, however, omit to notice the admirable dancing of Mademoiselle Duvernay in the *Cachucha* dance, one of the celebrated dances of Spain, which was executed by her with as much spirit as grace.'

Captain Scott, writing in 1838 in *Excursions in the Mountains of Ronda and Granada*, points out that a Spanish lady considers it necessary to avert her eyes when the dancer of the *Cachucha* raises her skirts.

The *Cachucha* continued its success with Elssler during 1837 through to 1846, when Gautier called Adelina Plunkett and Elssler 'The most authentic Andalusians we have ever come across'!

The *Cachucha* was parodied by Tom Mathew. Another foreign dancer in Paris was Bournonville's pupil Lucile Grahn, who was also to include the *Cachucha* in her repertoire. Beaumont discusses the popularity of this dance and that it was being included in other ballets such as *Beniowsky*, revived in 1837 on 16 March. Ivor Guest writes that the ballet was choreographed by André Jean-Jacques Deshayes and performed in the Kings Theatre in April 1836 by Pauline Dauvernay. It had a Russian theme; how this Spanish dance came to be incorporated is a mystery. Deshayes was a French dancer (1776–1846) whose father was in charge of the Paris Opera Ballet school. According to G.B.L. Wilson, he had danced in nearly every season at the King's Theatre between 1840 and 1846. He also choreographed several other ballets, and produced *Giselle* together with Jules Perrot.

The Double Cachucha

This dance was performed in its intended form, as a *pas de deux*, by Fanny Cerrito and Jules Perrot on 14 July 1842 at Her Majesty's Theatre in London. The *Times* critic was carried away and wrote of not remembering seeing anything as beautiful as this: 'it is an inspiration; she is a creature of fire. It is in the Spanish spirit of defiance that she and Perrot dance at each other. The fury, as it were, of this part of the dance is beautifully relieved by those exquisite attitudes, where Cerrito falls on one knee and leans back with languishing expression, while Perrot stands over her.'

Cachucha and Escuela Bolera Dance in Mexico and Cuba

José Blas Vega in his book *Temas Flamencos* quotes Vicente T. Mendoza, the Mexican folklorist, as saying that the *Cachucha* plays a major role in Mexican folklore and is one of the Andalusian melodies most often to be heard in the music of Hispanic America, which extends as far as the Antilles, Peru and Chile. In 1810 a Spanish company went to Havana, Cuba, and performed there for more than 22 years, according to Alejo Carpentier in his *La Musica En Cuba* (Mexico 1946). In theatres, societies and other public performances, the Cubans popularised Spanish songs and dances, and the *Cachucha* was to be found among the *Fandangos*, the *Minuet*, the *Caballito Jaleada* and the *Jarabe*, the fandangoised *Minuet* – many of the same dances as those in Mexico, according to Blas Vega. In 1832 the *Cachucha* was among the dances listed as being taught by the company in a studio in Havana, amongst others such as the *Panaderos* and the *Bolero*.

Illustration 4.18
The Mexican shawl worn in various ways (in dances from Jalisco) by the group 'Des Colores' in Washington DC. In a vigorous dance it is tied to the wrists or wrapped twice around them, otherwise it is draped over the arm. Photo: Nancy Sedgwick.

The Scarf or Shawl in Escuela Bolera and Mexican Dances

In the archives of the Theatre Institute in Barcelona there is a picture of a Spanish dancer with a long scarf stretched behind her, draped forward over her arms. It is in colour and it is called a dance with a shawl or the *Bolero* of Seville. In Spanish dance this custom has seemingly disappeared, but one is reminded of the role the shawl plays in the ballet *La Sylphide*. Fanny Cerrito in *Lalla Rookh*, Fanny Elssler in *La Volière*, Carolina Rosati, Augusta Maywood and Louise Fitzjames with castanets in her hands in a *Pas Venetien* are all depicted with such shawls. These instances all stem from the same period. However, in Mexico, it is a requirement to have a shawl worn behind the dancer, attached to the wrists, falling under the frill on the dress. Originally the frill was a crossed fichu.

Other Foreigners Performing Spanish Dances

Marie Taglioni performed *La Gitana* in St Petersburg in 1838; Carlotta Grisi, Fanny Cerrito, Arthur Saint-Léon and Jules Perrot, Pauline Duvernay, Bournonville's pupil Lucile Grahn and many others all danced in the *Bolero* style. So much has been published about these dancers that we need not concern ourselves further with them here. Fanny Elssler also performed the *Jaleo de Jerez* in Vienna, 1842, and Lucile Grahn included the *Jaleo de Jerez* in her repertoire. Bournonville was to stage his version (spelling it *Jaleo de Xerez*) in 1840.

From Ivor Guest we find out what the dancers were performing in and around the early 1880s. In 1838 Lise Noblet and Mme Alexis Dupont were dancing *El Jaleo de Jerez* 'with furious attack, much bold arching of the back, and unbelievable exuberance'. In 1839, in a performance of *Don Juan*, Noblet and Dupont repeated the *Jaleo*; Nathalie Fitzjames danced a *Bolero* and Manuela Dubinon performed their arrangement of *Las Seguidillas de Andalucia*. Taglioni was appearing in *La Gitana*. There is an amusing reference to a Spanish dancer, Lola Montez, who appeared in March 1844 in *Las Boleras de Cádiz*. Ivor Guest translates Gautier's feelings about this lady from Limerick: 'There is nothing Andalusian about Mlle Lola Montez except a pair of magnificent dark eyes. She "habla" very mediocre Spanish, and speaks hardly any French and only passable English. So from what country does she really come?' After her brush with the police and attacking a Prussian gendarme with a riding crop, Gautier felt she was 'more at home on a horse than on the boards.' Charlotte Christensen, in *O! Pepita!* (see page 106), mentions that Montez was a protégée of Louis of Bavaria; following in his father's footsteps as regards interest in dancers, his son Duke Maximilian became involved with Pepita de Oliva, who claimed that she had a son by him and that he became the child's godfather.

In 1851 Marie Guy-Stephan danced two Spanish dances, *Las Boleras de Madrid* and *Jaleo de Jerez*. Fanny Cerrito performed with Petipa in 1854 and also with Saint-Léon. Matteo says, 'Since few ballet dancers today can play castanets, the Spanish dance in "Swan Lake" is generally performed without them. In the original production of the standard Petipa-Ivanov choreography, however, they were used. A photograph of this 1895 St Petersburg production shows Maria Skorsiuk and Alexandre Shirayev with castanets in their hands. It also shows, however, that they were not played in the classic style, for they were worn on the third finger of each hand, rather than on the thumb' ('Woods that Dance', *Dance Perspectives*, Spring 1968). This is the rustic form of castanet playing, by shaking them rather than using the fingers to play them.

Copenhagen and August Bournonville

The Danish choreographer August Bournonville came up against Spanish dancers more than once in his career. In his autobiography *Mit Theaterliv* we read about these clashes. For him it was difficult to accept the adulation – of press and public alike – for dancers in whom he discerned a distinct lack of training and finesse. It irritated him that passion and excitement overrode this lack of polish and was accepted in Copenhagen without constructive criticism. He wrote, 'but no one has

◆ See colour plate 28

drawn our attention to the fact that the Spaniards, when they bring their romantic dances to the north, give them an addition of crudeness in the same way that for our spoiled palates they mix their noble wines with aquavit.'

Bournonville carried the Spanish dances a step further, choreographing his ballets set in Spain, *La Ventana* and *Toreadoren*, using the Spanish style, technique and most interestingly the actual Spanish dances. Like Marius Petipa, he also used other types of folk dances in this way, for example Italian dances in *Napoli*, Norwegian in *Brudefaerden i Hardanger*, and Flemish in *Kermesse i Brugge*. His first ballet in a Spanish vein was *Don Quixote ved Camacho's Bryllup* (*Don Quijote at Camacho's Wedding*) in 1837, which did not succeed and had only two performances. This was followed by the tremendously successful *Toreadoren* on 27 November 1840. He was probably very stimulated by the visit of Dolores Serral and Mariano Camprubí, because he incorporated the *Bolero à Quatre* and a *Zapateado* duet in this ballet.

The Royal Danish ballet company included dancers from the Price family (pronounced 'Preesuh' in Denmark). Juliette Price was Bournonville's favourite dancer and a memorable Sylphide; her brother Waldemar (Valdemar) was a very good-looking young man and their cousins were Ellen and Sophie. According to historian Svend Kragh-Jacobsen, the Price family were 'jugglers, ropewalkers and circus riders who originally had come from England and, settling in Denmark, were recruited into the Bournonville company'. They became a dancing dynasty in Denmark. For the three cousins Bournonville choreographed a divertissement from *Toreadoren* entitled *Las Hermanas de Sevilla* (*The Sisters from Seville*). Ellen Price was the model for the famous Little Mermaid statue, so admired by all the tourists to Copenhagen. (In recent years she has been beheaded at least twice by vandals.)

Bournonville evidently detested what he called 'the flood of lascivious Spanish "bailadores".' On the other hand he admitted to learning a lot from the visiting Spanish dancers Mariano Camprubí and his partner Dolores Serral. They were invited to Copenhagen in June 1840, to be part of the celebrations for the Coronation of Christian VIII. They had danced to much acclaim in Paris in 1834 and had created a great interest in Spanish dancing in Europe. Thomas Overskou reported in his book *Den Danske Skueplads* (1864) that they performed in Copenhagen on 12, 17, 22 and 26 June as well as on 6 July, and that Serral was exceedingly graceful, while Camprubí dominated and the public were jubilant. They had lively expressive faces and an interesting southern appearance, which was winning. He says that they performed their national dances so uniquely, with such charm and expressiveness, that the audience responded with resounding applause, amongst them such eminent Danes as the writer Hans Christian Andersen, the sculptor Thorvaldsen and the artist Edvard Lehmann.

Of course the Spanish dancers came into contact with August Bournonville. He felt slighted that he had not been included to take part in, nor had been asked to choreograph a new ballet to celebrate the Coronation. He had been supplanted instead by these two foreigners and his comments must be seen in this light. He claimed that their reception from the audience was lukewarm and mentioned that the press overpraised them, running down the 'school of Vestris' with derogatory

Illustration 4.19
August
Bournonville
dancing *Jaleo de
Xeres* (Jerez),
with one of his
pupils, in his
ballet,
Toreadoren, music
Edvard Helsted
(1840), immortal-
ised in a sketch
by Edvard
Lehman in 1847.
Teatermuseet,
Copenhagen.

words and claiming that this national dancing was the stuff that dance was made of and that ballet could not hold a candle to it.

However, Bournonville was invited to join the Spanish couple in a *pas de quatre* at a benefit performance for them before they departed. Perhaps this took place on 6 July. To the audience's astonishment, Bournonville performed with much tossing of his head and body and the public reacted with laughter and applause. His exaggerated manner of dancing created doubts as to whether he was serious or sending them up. He noted that the audience and critics would have to wait for his answer until he choreographed his ballet *Toreadoren*. He did not stint on self-praise. Apart from imitating carefully what the dancers did, Bournonville said that he was able to add his own touch to this because of his training and artistry! This may well be true.

Bournonville studied their dancing with interest and found it different to that of his classical studies; which of course it is. He mentions the *Bolero* and the *Jaleo* that he learned. In Spain the alternating *Cachucha* sections of the *Bolero* are referred to as *Jaleos*. Thus the dance he performed with them can be identified as the *Boleras de la Cachucha*, or because of the description of it, more like *Bolero de Medio Paso*, part of which is danced to the same music.

Of course, as he states, they were folk dancers and as such he found them quite extraordinary. The new material which they presented to him provided inspiration for his future ballets with the national character of Spain. He maintained that it had opened up a new world for him, which he had realised existed but had not fully understood the extent of the material awaiting him.

However, the public was angry with Bournonville because through him they had lost their ballerina Lucile Grahn. Grahn explained her reason for leaving the Royal Danish Ballet in a letter to her friend Augusta Nielsen, another Bournonville pupil. She insinuated that Bournonville had propositioned her, and this after her family had almost impoverished themselves through the years by giving him expensive gifts. After Grahn's departure, Bournonville was angrily shouted at by the public as he made his first entrance in the ballet *Toreadoren*. He stopped dancing, walked up to face the royal box, and appealed to the king to tell him whether he should continue the ballet. This was considered *lèse majesté*. The stunned monarch told him to remain and continue. Bournonville claimed that he immersed himself in any part that he performed, taking on the character and nationality of that role. In the case of *The Toreador*, he was over-emotional, like a Spaniard would be. However, reading his diaries gives one an understanding that

Illustration 4.20 Grete Ditlevsen, Richard Jensen, Elna Lauesgaard and Gustav Uhlendorff in August Bournonville's '*Bolero à Quatre*' from his ballet *Toreadoren* (performed 1840–1929 and now lost).

Illustration 4.21
Hans Beck as Alonzo in
Bournonville's *Toreadoren*.

he himself was an emotional person. He could have faced imprisonment or worse, but was placed under house arrest instead. His friends persuaded him to go abroad to Italy for six months to allow tempers to calm down. This turned an embarrassing experience into a triumph, as he returned to choreograph *Napoli*, based on his Italian experience. It delights audiences to this day.

More can be read about this incident concerning Grahn in Robert Neiiendam's biography of Nielsen *En Danserinde*, published in Copenhagen in 1965. Patricia McAndrew also touches on this matter in her excellent translation of Bournonville's autobiographies. Bournonville maintained that Grahn had left to seek more fame than she could get in Copenhagen, and that he felt let down. He writes in his biography that teachers must not expect gratitude from a pupil!

In the 1980s Danish television filmed a programme on the Bournonville Spanish dances at the Royal Danish Ballet. Flemming Ryberg and Eva Kloborg danced two of Bournonville's dances from *Toreadoren* that they had learned from Hans Brenaa (Ryberg, personal communication). They performed *Jaleo de Jerez* and *Zapateado* to the music of Ferdinand Sor. The original music for the ballet was by Edvard Helsted. According to Knud Arne Jürgensen, the costumes for the ballet were assembled by Bournonville himself, taken from existing ones in the costume cupboard. These few dances seem to be all that remains of Bournonville's ballet *Toreadoren*, first performed on 27 November 1840 and last performed in its original version in 1927. Thus Ryberg performed a great service, saving these for posterity, whereas the *Bolero à Quatre* has been lost forever.

We are given a glimpse of the historic succession of these dances in the Danish dancer and ballet-master Hans Beck's autobiography *Fra Livet og Dansen* (*From [my] Life in Dance*). He refutes the idea that he was August Bournonville's last pupil. He wrote that he entered the Royal Danish Ballet School in 1869 at the age of six, when Ferdinand Hoppe took over at the time of Bournonville's retirement. Very soon he was put on the stage as an extra in *Toreadoren*, absorbing the ballet through the years until his own debut in the leading role of Alonzo on 13 February 1884. On 13 May 1911 Gustav Uhlendorff made his debut in this role, and it is probably from his knowledge that Hans Brenaa's version came. The others who danced these roles after Uhlendorff were Richard Jensen (1911), John Anderson (1920), Harald Lander and Kaj Smith (both in 1929).

Beck's performance, when he took over the role from Valdemar Price, drew

Illustration 4.22 *(top left)*
Mirror scene with Marie Guy-
Stephan.
Illustration 4.23 *(left)*
La Ventana with Flemming
Ryberg, Inge Jensen and Linda
Hindberg. Royal Danish Ballet.
Photo: Rigmor Mydtskov.
Illustration 4.24 *(above)*
Mirror scene from *La Ventana*
with choreography by
Bournonville. A sketch by Edvard
Lehman, from Helena
Bournonville's 'Stambok'. Royal
Danish Library.

Illustration 4.25
O! Pepita! Lithograph by an
unknown artist. Owned by
Charlotte Christensen.

critical comment from Edvard Brandes for the way he handled his cape, but he was praised for his dancing. A visiting guest singer, Marguerite van Zandt, was entranced. She could not get enough of it, especially of the *Bolero à Quatre,* in which he participated as part of the leading role that he was dancing. 'You I love,' she said to him in Danish, after a flood of French words. He was chosen to be painted by the artist P.S. Krøyer and he wrote that the finished picture was hung in the Theatre Museum's ballet division, over a bust of him by Helen Schou.

There has been a reconstruction of *Toreadoren* by Flemming Flindt in 1978, but that was with his own choreography, using Bournonville's libretto. The dances such as a *Fandango, Bolero,* a *Danza Castellana y Jota, Jaleo,* and the *Bolero* for four dancers were choreographed by José de Udaeta (Flemming Ryberg, personal communication). The Danish critic Sven Kragh-Jacobsen disapproved of it as a venture in recreating a Bournonville ballet in a modern way. De Udaeta had come from Barcelona to add the dances. Barbro Thiel-Cramer in Stockholm had been asked to come to Copenhagen to choreograph them, but had referred them to Udaeta, saying that he was a specialist on that subject.

The *Bolero* was perhaps the very one Bournonville performed with Camprubí and Serral, and this represents a doubly great loss to both ballet and Spanish dance worlds. Bournonville's *Jaleo de Jerez* could have been inspired by the one his pupil Lucile Grahn performed on 29 November 1838. She had returned from a second visit to Paris during the summer of 1838 and had probably learned it from the Noblet sisters. It was to be the last dance that she performed in Copenhagen, on 23 February 1839, before her final departure from the Royal Danish Ballet (Knud Arne

Jürgensen, personal communication). The *Cachucha* had been performed after her first visit to Paris in May 1837. She had studied for two hours daily in the Paris Opera foyer with the French teacher M. Barrez. The Danish author Robert Neiiendam believes that Grahn had learned that dance from Barrez. It was featured in her performance on 13 February 1838, inserted into D. F. E. Auber's *Fiorella*. Grahn also danced a *Seguidillas*, which may have influenced Bournonville's *Seguidilla*.

Of the two dances from *The Toreador* of the Bournonville version, one dance, performed by Ryberg and Kloborg for the Danish Television, is called *Zapateado*, and the other *Jaleo de Xerez*. The latter is not recognisable as the one performed in Spain, one reason being that the music for it was by the famous guitarist/composer of the nineteenth century Ferdinand Sor, rather than the folk music. In Argentina, Flemming Flindt's version of Bournonville's ballet *Toreadoren* was staged in Buenos Aires in the 1970s (Eloy Pericet, personal communication).

Looking at these Spanish dances in the Bournonville repertoire, it is interesting that Bournonville had not quite grasped the concept of circular arm movements in Spanish dancing. He used an opening out of the arms to the front or from side to side that is not typically Spanish. This is if one accepts that Brenaa's interpretation was faithful to the original. We can assume this as he would have learned it from Gustav Uhlendorff via Hans Beck, who would have been taught by Bournonville himself. The steps where the legs extend to the side and close in fifth are done with both knees bent, which they would not be in Spanish dancing. The use of toe heel would be at the side (*punta y talon*); this is done with the toe tipped on the floor turned in at the side, then the heel dug, again at the side but turned out. In the Bournonville version there is a step that is between that and a *bordoneo:* the foot is lifted off the floor, turned in and doing a dig on the floor with the toe, and the foot is stamped at the side of the other foot (not turned out on the heel). This does not make ballets such as *La Ventana* and *The Toreador* any less charming. After all, Petipa took greater theatrical licence, and he spent four years in Spain.

Illustration 4.26
Pepita de Oliva. Lithograph by Edvard Lehmann. Theatre Museum, Copenhagen. Photo Niels Elswing.

Udaeta lists all the Spanish dancers known for dancing the *Bolero* style at that time, and amongst them is that of Pepita de Oliva. She performed in Copenhagen in the Casini Theatre in 1858, and was dancing an Olé to the public's delight and the disapproval of Bournonville. Now we do not know which version of this dance she performed, but it overshadowed a production of Bournonville's ballet to a Norwegian theme and his bitterness overflowed. He lashed out over the 'Pepita craze' produced by her visit (see above on Bournonville and Spanish dancers). His opinion of Pepita was upheld by a Spaniard, Manuel Guerrero, who was dancing in Copenhagen at the same time that she was. He considered Pepita very beautiful but not talented. He thought that she might have been good enough for performances in Germany, but that she would never be accepted in Spain. She was the great-grandmother of the writer Vita Sackville-West and it is in her book *Pepita* that we find out about her life and career.

5

The Escuela Bolera

From the second half of the eighteenth century a whole school of classical dance developed in Spain. It flourished during the nineteenth century in dance academies and in the theatres of Spain, where dancers were employed to perform in this particular style. They were termed *boleros* or *boleras* to distinguish them from those dancers who performed ballet.

There was also a category for those persons who performed 'grotesque' dances. Often dancers were able to dance the styles of both ballet and the Escuela Bolera dances. Eventually the *Bolero* dances spread across Europe and as far as America, through the popularisation of choreographed dances in this style. The dances and steps were choreographed and taught by teachers in schools and it came to be called the Escuela Bolera, or the *Bolero* school of dance. This created a distinctive new tradition. It was this formal tuition that was influenced by ballet, through the progression of exercises taught in daily classes with choreographed dances arranged from a specific range of steps. Dances had previously developed amongst the people, and were handed down from generation to generation. The new dance style comprised dances that needed a specific training and technique. This required a teacher and daily classes, a special 'school' of teaching exercises and steps as separate from set dances. This was unlike anything known before in Spanish dancing. No longer was the *Seguidillas* to be used to teach good footwork and agility. Dances in this style were also being created by the teachers in their schools.

It can never be stated enough that Escuela Bolera is not ballet with castanets. Any ballet dancer would be hard pressed to dance one of the Spanish dances from this 'school'. There are many very special steps that simply do not exist in ballet. Angel Pericet Blanco is also very concerned about this confusion of the Escuela Bolera with ballet. It is discussed in this book in several places, including the section under Angel Pericet Blanco.

Style

There is a strong connection with the origin of the Escuela Bolera style and the dancing in Valencia, and a cross-fusion with that in Andalusia. The use of the arms and the arm positions can be linked with those used in Valencian dances and the Castillian *Seguidillas*. The *Bolero* style resembles the old French style still found in

Illustration 5.1
The *Bolero* dance with Dolores Serral and Mariano Camprubí, and *Corraleras* with Manuela Dubinon and Francisco Font.

the Danish Bournonville school and the method of the famous Italian teacher Enrico Cecchetti.

Requejo's reforms from the end of the 1700s and beginning of 1800s in putting back into the *Bolero* the style of arms from earlier times can very clearly be found echoed in Pierre Rameau's statement that 'The arms should be like a frame to the body', in his book *Le Maître à Danser* (1725). Rameau was the dance instructor to Philip V's second wife, Isabel Farnese.

Changes in Style

There are two distinct styles of using the arms in the dances of the Escuela Bolera school: one with the arms very well rounded and forward of the head, and the other upright, as in the present-day ballet, as changed by Angel Pericet Jiménez.

The *rodazánes* or 'rounds of the leg' were performed in front, as in Basque dancing. These Pericet changed to the side in a very high second.

Social Dances

Mention should be made that the social dances were also taught in the Spanish dance schools and Otero transcribed some of these dances of the period together with those of the Escuela Bolera. He also noted how the then popular waltz was incorporated into the *Panaderos de la Flamenca* by way of an added introduction. The original *Panaderos* certainly did not have that section of music or introduction with it. An early play, *The Dancing School* by Navarrete y Ribera from the early 1600s, was a satire dealing with a local dance master and included dances of that era such as the *Canario, Villano, Zarabanda* and *Folía*, and these were both social and for performance.

Types of Escuela Bolera Dances

There are two distinct types of dances, one danced in *zapatillas*, or soft ballet slippers, the other in heeled shoes used in dances with flamenco names in their titles, such as *Peteneras* and *Soleares*. Sor laments the addition of stamps to the *Bolero* dances.

When Napoleon invaded Spain in 1808 and the court fled to Cádiz, they came upon the classical dances with stamped steps incorporated into the repertoire by the teachers of the classical school of Bolera Spanish dance (José de Udaeta, personal communication). Referred to as Escuela Bolera Andaluza, this is a flamenco-type of dancing performed in heeled shoes, called *chapines*, with castanet accompaniment (there is no use of castanets in the true flamenco), but with a more classical style. The dances represented are the well-known flamenco names such as *Caracoles, Peteneras, Alegrias, Soleares* (*del Maestro Arcas*), *La Flor de la Maravilla, Olé de la Curra, El Olé Gaditano,* and the regional *Fandango*, and so on, danced in this style. The local dance masters seem to have created these dances for their studios from the street forms. There were, after all, thriving schools in Cádiz, Seville and Jerez through the centuries. Cádiz has the oldest and most revered history in Spain's dance annals. The *chapines* are not, however, ballet shoes with small heels. Their heels are slightly higher than those and the shoe firmer than a ballet slipper. They often have ribbons attached, like ballet shoes. These are sometimes not only tied around the ankle, but with the ribbon laced up the leg.

Illustration 5.2
Angel Pericet Blanco performing *Bolero Liso*. Photo: Armand La Habana. Eloy Pericet Blanco archive.

Bolerologia

Juan Jacinto Rodríguez Calderón dedicated his book *Bolerologia* to dance masters and their 'knowledgeable pupils of the bolerological academies in Madrid, Seville, Cádiz, Murcia and all the other towns where *bolero* schools exist'. It was published in 1807 in the USA, by a Zacharias Poulson (a Danish name) in Chestnut Street, Philadelphia. Poulson apologises for any errors and says it was the best he can do in a country where mainly English is spoken. After a flowery dedication, Rodríguez retitles the 'Bolerology, Picture of the Bolero Dance, as they were in the Court of Spain 1794–1795' as *Antibolerologia o La Total Ruina del Baile* (Anti-Bolerology, or The Total Ruin of Dance).

Baile and Danza

Let us digress a moment on the words *baile* and *danza*. *Baile* was used to describe the folk dances which were jumped and used arm movements, whereas *danzas* were more measured, with little or no use of arms, such as the court dances, which required technique and style and therefore needed tuition. Ivanova points out the social significance of this difference in the categorising of the dances. This meaning was to alter with time, so that *danzas* came to be used to describe any dance, and *baile* for anything balletic or athletic, allowing freer movements of the arms and feet. But there is still a mixed use of these two words for many dances.

Bailadora and Bailarina

A *bailador/a* (or in the corrupted form, *bailaor/a*) is the term used to describe flamenco dancers, who perform in heeled shoes without jumping, and moving *terre-à-terre*. The exponents of classical ballet are called *bailarin/a*.

Steps and Contributors to the Bolero

As noted earlier, during the height of its popularity the *Bolero* was considered the national dance of Spain. The *Bolero* is 'the most aristocratic dance', according to C. Gascuoine Hartley in *Things Seen in Spain*, published in London in 1912. The dance as such is truly a dance of the people who, as can be seen in the examples given earlier, weave it into their daily lives at all social levels. They have also added to the steps and the style.

José de Udaeta says that the *Bolero* moved into the salons in about 1840, and in his writing mentions Antonio Boliche from La Mancha and Sebastián Cerezo from Seville. Everyone credits Cerezo with setting the norms of the *Bolero* and creating brilliant sections of jumps, beats and turns. However, Carlos José Gosálvez Lara refers to Cerezo as the 'Gaditano' (coming from Cádiz) in his booklet *La Danza Cortesana en la Biblioteca Nacional*. Meanwhile, Ivanova seems to have them confused: she claims that Boliche was from Seville and writes that Cereza(o) was from La Mancha and that he returned to his native village and saw the 'lads of the village dancing with such ease and elevation that they appeared to fly'. In his *Escenas Andaluzas* Serafín Estébanes Calderón says that a certain D. Preciso (Juan Antonio de Iza Zamácola) at that time referred to Cerezo as a *hidalgo*, or personage of some importance. La Meri refers to the Cerezo *Bolero*, which was in every company's repertoire in the 1940s. In her book *Spanish Dancing* she maintains that he was a dancer at the court of Charles III who, coming from the court of Naples, Italianised the form of the *Bolero*, introducing steps from the ballet repertoires.

Boliche, in Rodríguez Calderón's *Bolerologia*, is referred to as having died (in 1794) – dancing – 'like a soldier at war or a torero in the plaza'. Rodríguez Calderón also refers to another dancer involved in the steps of the *Bolero*, Chinchilla from Cádiz and an innkeeper Juanillo of Chiclana. These were ordinary folk shaping the *Bolero*; Boliche was supposed to have earned his living driving a chaise.

Before we examine the steps of the period as described satirically by Rodríguez Calderón in *Bolerologia*, 'as they were in the court of Spain' in 1794 and 1795, let us just note the earlier steps in 1642 as written down by a dance master, Ivan de

Illustration 5.3
'Dancing
couple' by
Egron Lundgren
(1815–1875).
National
Museum,
Stockholm.

Illustration 5.4
Conchita del Campo,
Spanish Dance Society,
London.
Photo: Elaine Mayson.
Marina Keet archive.

Esquivel de Navarro of Seville in *Discursos Sobre El Arte del Dançado*: *Floretas, saltos al lado y en buelta, encaxes, campanela, campanela breve, de compas mayor, y por dentro, bacios, cabriolas enteras, cabriolas atravesadas, medias cabriolas, sacudidos, quatropeados, quatropeados atras, vuelta de pecho, vuelta de folias, vuelta de descuydo, giradas, sustenido, cruzado, reverencia cortado, floreo, carrerillas, cargados, retiradas, boleo, dobles, rompidos*, and also discussed are the *passos, con que pie se comiencan las dancas, composturas de cuerpo, planta* (the steps, with which foot to start on, posture and placement).

In Rodríguez Calderón's *Bolerologia* we come across satirical references to dancers and steps, here roughly translated.

Glisos

The 'not difficult to execute' *glisos* are attributed to 'a certain adjutant of the Engineering Corps known by the name of D. Lazaro Chinchilla', from the 'illustrious city of Cádiz'. He is supposed to have named it for posterity after a type of fortification, an earth ramp leading to a wall, called a *glasis*.

Small runs ending with one foot extended in a point

'*Mata La Araña* ("kill the spider") was attributed to a medical assistant in the hospital in Burgos. It was carelessly written in a manuscript containing various thoughts and notes, and spotted by the oil of sweet almonds and syrupy cordial. The Collins Concise Spanish Dictionary describes this term as an idiomatic one of 'taking the edge off one's appetite'. (Note: there was no such name amongst the notes of Angel Pericet Jiménez, nor did he ever refer to the step by that name. It was called *batararaña* and had nothing whatever to do with the killing of a spider. Was this heritage of 'killing a spider' derived from the above tongue-in-cheek description, to be handed on to posterity in this way?). The step is still danced this way in the *Seguidillas Manchegas*: a free *glissade* travelling to a corner, bringing the second foot over and releasing the first foot to point in front, with the supporting leg on a *fondu*. It was one of the steps of *Sevillanas* which has changed unrecognisably today, becoming a *pas de bourrée* (placing the feet behind, side, front) and then placing the foot on a dig in front, with the supporting leg straight.

Laberinto

This, he said, was 'to be accredited to Juanillo the innkeeper from Chiclana. According to some, people recalled that it was called Macarena during his lifetime.

Pito-coloni is said to have discussed it knowledge-
ably in his dissertation *Bolerologicas.*

Pasure

'*Pasure* encompasses two steps in one, because there
is *pasure cruzado sin cruzar* (crossed and not
crossed). This discovery is attributed to Perete
Zarazas of Ceuta, who was one of the victims of the
Bolero fever. He was to die peacefully in hospital
after breaking his leg practising his *Bolerologico* exercises, mourned by his compatriots.' (Note: according to Ana Ivanova, the *pasure* – written *pasura* in
her book *The Dancing Spaniards* – is like a *pas de
bourrée* and is a much-used step. I have come across
them in *Boleros*, used to close the feet at the end of a
verse, or to lead into a jump, also done turning on
oneself.)

Beats of the heels

'El Taconeo was performed principally in Cartagena,
according to Rodríguez Calderón. A Mallorcan shoe-
maker was credited with introducing this step into
Spain, to boost his sales of heels, according to "our
secretary Pito-coloni". "The heel(work) shines in this, and the ballerino and ballerina earn loud applause – even though the salon is filled with ignoramuses. What a
noise is heard when performing this movement".'

Illustration 5.5
El Bolero. A sketch by Francisco
Lamayer for Serafín Estébanes
Calderón's *Escenas Andaluzas*
(1847).

Paso Marcial

In Ivanova's translation: 'Ye gods! You mean to say that there are military evolutions
in the *bolero?*' 'Yes, sir, there are, and this is not the only one, for you see something
of all the others is embraced in our bolerological science.' 'The Paso marcial is the
work of Rudolfo Engama [read Esgarra], sergeant of pensioners from Almeria. This
good man, having developed a cough, continued to practise *bolerologia* too much
and found it necessary to apply for retirement. In view of his uselessness this was
easily obtained. God bless my soul! the *bolero* was even useful to a blue cap and a
white belt.' (I believe the cap and belt were standard equipment of the military).

Abanze con Retirada

'. . . this word is purely and simply military. In this the dancers advance and retreat
determinedly and the good professor of *Bolerologico*, if he is quick about it, can
brush his lips across his partner's cheeks. No one knows who invented it, and it
was attributed to the most outstanding exponent, Alfares of the Infantry of Lucena,
young and applauded and with infinitely great aspirations.'

◆ See colour plate 29

Puntas
'Some grotesque positions, well-executed, that deserve not only general applause, but to be appraised in the annals of the *bolero*; because the placing of the feet give the impression that the dancers intended to fly. Moreno, that famous professor who reached the pinnacle of *Bolerological* science invented this, and his name should be etched in bronze to his eternal memory.'

On the subject of turns
'Vuelta de Pecho. Here you get to know the agility and skill of a good dancer, because, certainly, it needs an inexplicable swiftness to perform it. Its author, called Eusebio Morales, a *pasamanero* [lacemaker or staircase-maker], although he left his job to embrace this admirable science, died after a few months of a haemorrhage, which originated from his invention. Many followed in his steps, and according to the latest piece of news, this has launched more people into the next world than the Lisbon earthquake.'

'Vuelta Perdida. The name given to a movement that ended with a turn, and the most commendable is, that there is nothing difficult or dangerous about it. On only one occasion did the certain professor dislocate his right foot doing it, and it is unnecessary to publish his name, but that of the inventor, who executed with the best success the *bolerologia*, in Madrid for three consecutive years, until the jealousy of his contemporaries obliged him to seek refuge in Cordova, where he expired in a drawing-room as the result of a stamp (of his foot). He was called Don Ciriaco Galludo, native of Valladolid in Castile, and his main profession was doctor, or butcher.'

On batterie or beating of the legs in the air
'Trenzados con sus Terceras, Quartas, Quintas, y Sextas. In one fell swoop one understands many things, as can be seen by the word *trenzado*. In these steps the skill of good dancers of both sexes shine, and where the women can show off the most, it's indispensable that they wear pantaloons and short skirts; because if their calves can't be seen, there is no point in their performing these beats. Some *bolerologias*, if he is allowed to refer the young students thus, discover the use of their legs . . . The *Bolero* has its own special suitable attire, which has been, and is for all time, that of the *maja*. The supreme bolerological assembly forbids, on pain of notorious impropriety, that individuals, either male or female, should appear in long skirts, either in theatres or on stages in European territory or the colonies. The inventor, now a "figurant" [a rank] at the Barcelona Opera, a studious man, although a Venetian, idolised Spanish dancing. He published a catalogue of *Seguidillas* that many people claim not to be his . . . In any case, Lazaroni, as this Venetian was called, became immortal through his *trenzados*.'

The crux of the *Bolero* was the holding of a final position to end the dance. This was inherited from the *Seguidillas* and was called *bien parado*. 'The whole science of the art of Bolerologia is embodied in the *bien parado*. Yes sir! The best dancer

who does not stop in time, gracefully, cleanly and rhythmically, although skilfully, does not deserve the smallest applause. Daily debates are provoked, by representationes from the ballet masters to the board, about *bien parado*. Today there is one decision, tomorrow another; today one is allowed to stop in the third position with the feet placed together; tomorrow it's decreed that the left foot remains in the air in preparation for the jump. An edict is published that the arms are lowered to their natural position when stopping, when already there is another proclamation allowing the arms to be raised symmetrically. Ultimately in the *bien parado* is embodied all the grace of the dance; it is the touchstone of all *bolerologico*, and regularly they impress the importance of this on all who execute it. The same happened to the *paseo*, also varying daily, and before he died Antonio Boliche stylised it in twenty or thirty different ways. However, going here, or going there, almost always it is the same, and only the name varies. There are many steps, positions and differences . . .'

During the height of its popularity, the *Bolero* came to be called the national dance of Spain. It can be seen from the next paragraph from *Bolerologia*, although tongue-in-cheek, that this is maintained by the author.

Illustration 5.6 *Baile del Candil* in Triana, Seville. A sketch by Gustave Doré for *Voyage en España*, a journey that he undertook with Baron Davillier in 1862, to illustrate his book.

Tipos Andaluces

Illustration 5.7
José Otero Aranda with his pupils in Seville. They are wearing *chapines* on their feet, the one on the left shows the sculptured heel, the one on the right the ribbons tied around the ankle. Seville early twentieth century.
Marina Keet archive.

He says that, 'The *bolero* has now spread through the universe and there are few countries that do not know and admire it. Sweden is one of the principal addicts of this dance, and in Stockholm it was deemed essential in a cold climate. The Russians, following the good taste of their neighbours, the Swedes, have founded in St Petersburg the first school in the North, there are actually Lapps, Tartars, Poles and other types of "birds". [Ivanova notes that the word is sometimes used in Spanish to denote an effeminate man.] Not to mention France and Italy! In those two most beautiful parts of Europe you will come across the most expert professors. Solely for reasons of language, foreigners give the *bolero* a different name, but there is only one dance called *bolero*, and Spain boasts, and with reason, that she is the true mother, and that the Spaniards are the finest *bolerologicos* in the world. Throughout the peninsula, whether in both Castiles, Aragon, Valencia, Murcia, or Andalusia, a young person's education can be gauged at once by what he knows about bolerology. We believe that in order to be a useful member of society, every citizen should not be without some knowledge of that which is *bolero*.'

Rodríguez Calderón also gives a wickedly humorous, tongue-in-cheek parody of a typical class in a Madrid academy of *Bolero* dancing of 1794/95. A smoke-filled room, with an odour that would make even a hardened grave-digger reel, with blackened pictures on the walls depicting the 'science' taught there, is complete with applauding, cigar-smoking spectators, a ballet mother with contempt for the Fandango and aspirations for her daughter dancing the more elegant *Bolero*, without which no one's education was considered complete. Together with French and piano lessons she hoped this would equip her daughter for life in society.'

She would never be expected to go on the stage; this was merely considered part of the education of a young girl going into society. Even today, studios receive the daughters of aristocratic families who have no intention of appearing on stage, but consider it essential to dance a *Seguidillas Sevillanas*. In *Bolerologia*, the seventeen-year-old daughter, Doña Clara, is to break a leg in the attempts to dance this fatal, popular dance style, clattering her castanets opposite a 'doughnut-seller'. Other aspiring pupils hang from ropes to practise beaten steps and, immodestly, ladies lift their skirts, so that their steps can be seen, exposing tight pantaloons.

The teacher starts to teach – a *Seguidillas*! He accompanies the students on his guitar, just as the early teachers of ballet did with their violins. Most studios in Madrid or elsewhere in Spain have the roles of teacher and guitarist separated.

6

Main Centres of the Escuela Bolera

Cádiz

Three main centres of Escuela Bolera are Barcelona, Seville and Madrid, and the eternal city of dance, Cádiz, must not be forgotten. Maestro Otero considered that dances such as *Olé*, *Jaleo* and *Panaderos* all originated in Cádiz. The composer Jerónimo Giménez used the dance school of a supposedly famous teacher, Luis Alonso, in Cádiz, as the setting for his Zarzuela in two parts, the first part 'El Baile de Luis Alonso', with choreography in the style of the Escuela Bolera around 1840, and 'La Boda de Luis Alonso' as the second part.

Cádiz has the oldest history of dance in Spain. Gadir ('enclosure') was the name given to the city by the Phoenicians in 1100 BC. Romans wrote about the *puellae gaditanae* (dancing girls) of Gadir when they conquered the city from the Carthaginians. The *Andaluces delicias*, with their *crotalos* or finger cymbals, danced their way into the hearts of the Roman society of the conquerors. *Crotalum* was the word for the castanets and small metal cymbals worn on the thumb and middle finger, used by the Romans and Greeks. The dancers were even transported to Rome and caused a fashion in small cymbals worn as earrings. Telathusa, the dancer praised by Martial in epigrams, was from Gadir. La Meri says that the famous statue Venus Callipyge is of her.

Juvenal (Decimus Junius Juvenalis), thought to be the most powerful of all the Roman satiric poets, wrote that he hoped to see the girls of Cádiz taking provocative postures and, animated by the applause, bend backwards and rotate the top of their bodies in a circular movement.

A manuscript tells of the Greek, Eudoxio de Cizico who, 'one hundred years ago', carried a strange cargo of dancers from Baética (the Roman name for Andalusia), to exhibit them on the coast of Africa.

Seville

One of the earliest dance treatise was from Esquivel Navarro of Seville, 1642.

A beautifully descriptive poem by Manuel Machado, quoted in a programme, sums up the cities of Andalusia, leaving the poet speechless to describe Seville:

Cádiz, witty clarity; Granada,
Hidden water that weeps,

◆ See colour plate 31

Roman and Moorish, silent Córdoba;
Singing Malaga;
Golden Almeria;
Silver Jaén; Huelva on the bank of the three caravels,
And Seville.

The translator cannot be acknowledged as there are no sources.

'Seville is the repository of the universal memory of this type, the workshop where is founded, modified and recomposed in other new ones the old dances,' says Estébanes Calderón. It is a veritable cradle of dances, dancers and dance masters. It is from here that we inherit the style most dancers performed in classical dance of the *Andaluza* type.

From Antonio Alvarez Cañibano's manuscripts produced for the 1992 Encuentro Escuela Bolera, we know about the *Bolero* dancers under the direction of José Rojo. They interspersed the programmes performed in the Teatro Cómico by the French family called Lefebre (written without the accent in all sources). The Lefebres arrived in 1810 to perform ballets in Seville after Napoleon's troops, led by his brother, moved in. The *Boleros* presented there were for two, four, six or eight dancers. This and other Spanish dances were interspersed among the many ballets presented there. In 1813, according to Alvarez Cañibano, Spanish dances were presented almost daily, including a *Bolero* as danced by Rita Oliver and José Rojo. The Lefebres and the French troops departed when the French occupation ended.

In the nineteenth century, Manuel and Miguel Barrera were two of the city's dance masters. They had a well-known academy in the Calle Tarifa in Seville's City Centre, teaching the Escuela Bolera and folk dances. Their most famous pupil was Amparo Alvarez, better known as La Campanera. After studying with Amparo Alvarez and with Maestro Segura, Angel Pericet Carmona opened his studio in Seville. Seville had important teachers of every type from a very early time and onwards. Today it is the Pericet family from Seville who, in Madrid and also Buenos Aires in Argentina, hold the torch of the classical dance form. However, it was in Seville and Barcelona that dancers had theatres with companies to perform the Escuela Bolera. It was from Seville that the Pericets provided the heritage for many of the modern exponents of today.

In Seville, the teacher who was considered at the beginning of the twentieth century to be able to imbue the true pure Andalusian style, was Realito. For forty years he taught the Sevillanas and other Andalusian dances to all comers, in his studio at the corner of Alameda and Calle Trajano. He was also the teacher of the famous couple from Seville, Los Chavalillos, later known as Antonio and Rosario, of Pacita Tomás and Carmen Sevilla. Realito, 'the diminutive', as Elsa Brunelleschi described him, was called Manuel Real Montoya, a pupil of La Campanera. He was evidently also a student of Rafael Pericet, who was rather critical of him, calling him a craftsman rather than an artist. Despite this, senior teachers of today, such as Carmen Gordo, consider that he had an amazing gift of imparting the true elegance and style of Andalusia, and of being able to get the dancers to perform, rather than

Illustration 6.1
The studio of Rafael
Pericet in Seville. Eloy
Pericet Blanco archive.
Illustration 6.2
'Don Angel' Pericet
Carmona. Eloy Pericet
Blanco archive.
Illustration 6.3
Luisa Pericet Jiménez.
Eloy Pericet Blanco
archive.

Illustration 6.4
'Realito', Manuel Real,
posing in Seville in 1955.

just go through the movements. His *Olé de la Curra, Sevillanas* and other dances of that era are considered to be the true choreographic style and elegance of that period.

Apart from the remarkable teacher Realito, there was also José Otero de Aranda (1860–1934), who was a well known and a greatly respected teacher. He left us the legacy of the written word about the dances, *Tratado de Bailes*, published in Seville in 1912. Unfortunately, he devotes half the book to social dances of the day, but the descriptions of the period, costumes and Spanish dances are invaluable. He was a pupil of La Campanera and Maestro Alonso. In his book Maestro Otero retained for posterity some of the dances of this period as well as his thoughts on a variety of subjects and people. As a sort of Sevillian Bournonville, he seems to have raised the status of dancers, and was often performing with his pupils before the King and Queen when they came to Seville.

The Spanish dances he wrote down in words and not notation were *Sevillanas, Las Peteneras, Las Manchegas, Soleares de Arcas, El Olé Bujaque, La Gracia de Sevilla, El Vito, Los Panaderos, El Garrotín, La Farruca, El Tango, Las Marianas, Las Guajiras*. The social dances were, among others: the Waltz in various forms (in 3/4 and 2/4 time!), Polka, Polka Mazurka, Lancers, Schottische (Scottish and American types), Parisian Cuadrille, Minuet, Cotillon, Pavane, two types of Rigodon, then dances such as the York, Ostende, La Berlina, Virginia, El Huracán, La Redowa and El Pas de Cuatro.

He mentions other teachers as well, including his partner in his studio. I point this out in connection with steps and dances and their execution varying from teacher to teacher. He maintained that he and his partner could have their pupils dancing together, with only minor differences. However, it would have been impossible with pupils from different academies doing the same dance. He taught social dancing as well as classical Spanish and regional dances. He also had in his repertoire his flamenco *Garrotíns, Farrucas* and others.

There was also, from 1894, the dancer and teacher Fernandillo el del Baratillo. Frasquillo and his wife La Quica were also two famous dancers and teachers from Seville. In Madrid, until 1999, their daughter and son-in-law, Mercedes and Albano, had neighbouring studios with their daughter Maria Mercedes León, who is La Quica and Frasquillo's granddaughter. Angel Pericet Jiménez went to study with Frasquillo, and from Barcelona Juan Magriña also studied further with Angel Pericet Carmona and continued the classical tradition in Barcelona.

Antonio Gades considers that Pilar López is, in the theatre, the one who was imbued with this particular style of the south. Thus all the dancers trained by her – such as Alberto Lorca, Antonio Gades, Roberto Ximinez, Manolo Vargas and many others – inherited this. Seville was also the city to which travellers gravitated, and that is why we know more about it than other places from the journals and books of people like Baron Davillier and Théophile Gautier.

Illustration 6.5
The studio of Realito on the corner of Calle Trajano and Alameda, Seville.
Illustration 6.6
Inside the studio of Realito on the corner of Calle Trajano and Alameda, Seville.

Illustration 6.7
Maestro Otero with his pupils,
Seville, early twentieth century.
Marina Keet archive.

A dancer and teacher of renown is Matilde Coral. She is known for teaching beautiful arm movements and for her method of working with the *bata de cola* or tailfrock. For her it is almost a science. She can be seen in Saura's films *Sevillanas*, with her sister and husband, and *Flamenco*, in which her pupils also perform.

Malaga and Granada

Two cities have much dance history, and dance also flourished in their theatres. At the end of nineteenth to the beginning of the twentieth century in Malaga there were also excellent teachers mentioned by José Otero: Juan Manuel Reguero, Carlos Galán, Antonio Recio and Carmen Parejo. In Granada there was Maestro Vásquez, who was the first to dance his piano version of *Soleares del Maestro Arcas* in Seville. He had also taught in Seville and from 1909 in Barcelona. Afterwards he went to Granada. These cities are the home of the *Malagueña* and the *Granadína*, of the *Fandangos* family.

Barcelona

Many world-famous dancers of the Romantic era came from Barcelona in the region of Catalonia, such as Mariano Camprubí (who worked with Marie Taglioni and Jules Perrot in Paris in 1830), Francisco Font, Juan Camprubí, Dolores Serral (partner of Mariano Camprubí) and Manuela Dubinon. They all went to Paris in 1834, although still in the employ of the Queen of Spain, who had given them leave from the two theatres in Madrid, the Teatro del Principe and Teatro de la Cruz. Mariano Camprubí had transferred to Madrid from Barcelona. In France they were able to get away from the chaotic conditions in Spain.

Another dancer from the Gran Teatro del Liceo in Barcelona, from Reus in Catalonia, was Rosita Mauri (Roseta in Catalan) who not only danced her native Spanish dances, but also became the star of the Opera Ballet in Paris. Her father, Pedro, also a dancer, worked closely with the choreographer Mérante on the dances for *Le Cid*, in which Rosita won great acclaim in Paris, according to Roger Salas (Madrid). Pilar Llorens lists *La Tertulia*, *La Flor de Maravilla* and *La Torera* among the Spanish dances in Rosita Mauri's repertoire.

From Pilar Llorens's valuable research one finds information about the Escuela Bolera in Barcelona. The town of Reus supplied another dancer to the Catalonian capital's Liceo theatre, Juan Camprubí, born in Reus in 1825. He was the son of famous dancer Mariano Camprubí. Both he and his future partner, Manuela García, made childhood debuts. At the age of eleven Juan Camprubí was already dancing in Madrid, Granada and Seville. Juan partnered Manuela García, herself a pupil of José Cañete, and who had learned her flamenco in Andalusia from the Gypsies in the caves of Sacramonte in Granada. Her dance debut was made in Madrid, aged six. According to Pilar Llorens, they toured the capitals of Germany, Austria, France, Hungary, Switzerland and Russia. In Paris they were described as the principal dancers of their epoch by the Académie Royale de Musique. Together with his partner Manuela García, Camprubí danced his choreography of *La Rondeña* to music by José Lund, on 4 April 1847, at the inauguration of the Liceo Theatre in Barcelona.

Illustration 6.8
Maestro Coronas (Carlos Pérez), dancer and teacher, Barcelona, with his wife Elvira Sevilla.

One teacher who had much influence was Ricardo Moragas (1827–1899). He arrived as a child in Barcelona in 1837. After his training and touring abroad he returned to the Liceo Theatre in 1859 as principal dancer 'of all types', partnering Manuela Perea, 'La Nena'. He was also director at the Liceo in 1859. Among his pupils were Maestro Coronas, Juan Magriña, Emma Maleras, Paulita Pamies.

Maestro Coronas (Carlos Pérez Carillo) came from Jaén. Pilar Llorens gives him the title of a *Bailarin Bolero*. Although a thoroughly theatrical and very good-looking man, dancing in the theatre and opera, he decided to specialise in teaching dance and especially the Escuela Bolera dances. His own teachers were Maestro Tarrida, Miguel Salud and Ricardo Moragas. He became the dance master at the Liceo and was revered by the dancers he trained, among them Teresina Boronat, Emma Maleras and the well-known Barcelona dancer Juan Magriña.

Among the more recent descendants of these teachers is Aurora Pons, a former co-artistic director of the Ballet Nacional from 1993 to 1997.

Illustration 6.9
El Baile de Luis Alonso, with choreography by Alberto Lorca, performed by España Danza, directed by Felípe Sanchez. Photo: Antonio Villanueva.

Madrid

This city became the home of Angel Pericet Carmona. The Pericet family, who transferred from Seville, taught a whole generation of Spanish dancers. Angel's studio was in the street Encomienda No. 10. At present it is Eloy Pericet Blanco who teaches in Madrid, at Relatores No. 20 on the second floor. He is the grandson of 'Don Angel' and the studio where he teaches is that of the granddaughter of 'La Quica', Maria Mercedes León.

Another teacher, Julia Castelao, taught in Aduana No. 15. The dancer Elvira Lucena studied with her and 'Don Angel'. There are several other lines of inheritance, apart from the Pericet family, such as the teaching of La Quica, in Madrid, but who was also from Seville; her daughter and son-in-law Mercedes and Albano; Mariemma and also Maestro Roy. La Quica's granddaughter, Maria Mercedes León, had studied with his daughter, Rocio Aragon. Rocio in turn had studied with Castelao. From Rocio, Maria Mercedes learned many other Escuela Bolera steps to those in the Pericet syllabus, which she had also studied. She remembered learning different beats and turns (personal communication).

Valencia

In this region there were dances called Escuela and two distinct styles of dancing, steps, arms and footwork developed there in Xativa and Alzira (Enric Marti i Mora, personal communication). Many of the Escuela Bolera steps of the classical school can be traced to Valencia. One example is the famous pose in which Fanny Elssler was sketched, called the Valencian position; Elssler is depicted with one arm raised and the other slightly behind her (Eloy Pericet, personal communication).

Illustration 6.10
Eloy Pericet Blanco.
Eloy Pericet Blanco archive.

7

Dances and Dancers of the Escuela Bolera

Dances from the Escuela Bolera can be found in A.S. Arista's *Colección de Bailes Populares Españoles* published by Union Musical Española. Included are some regional items such as a *Jota Aragonesa* and Galician, but it is the classical dances which are of interest here. There is also the music of F. García Navas, again printed by Union Musical.

There are the two types of Escuela dances, the classical Bolera dances performed wearing ballet pumps (*zapatillas*), or soft shoes, and the *Andaluza* danced with heeled shoes (*zapatos*) called *chapines*. The dances are listed as found in the music book of Arista and the shoes worn for them as advised by Aurora Pons:

Panaderos de la Tertulia, soft ballet shoes (*zapatillas*): Udaeta maintains that this dance can be performed in heeled shoes.
Panaderos de la Flamenca: soft ballet shoes (*zapatillas*) or heeled shoes (*chapines*).
Seguidillas Manchegas: soft ballet shoes (*zapatillas*).
Jaleo de Jerez: heeled shoes (*chapines*).
Ocho Sevillanas Escogidas: (selected) heeled, (*chapines*) for four verses, the
Sevillanas Boleras: in ballet shoes, (*zapatillas*).
La Macarena: soft ballet shoes (*zapatillas*).
Peteneras: heeled shoes (*chapines*).
Boleras de la Cachucha: soft ballet shoes (*zapatillas*).
Bolero Liso: soft ballet shoes (*zapatillas*).
Bolero (Boleras) de Medio Paso, soft ballet shoes (*zapatillas*).
Soleares de Arcas: heeled shoes (*chapines*).
Olé de la Curra: (classical), soft ballet shoes *(zapatillas)*; (regional), heeled shoes (*chapines*).
Malagueña: soft ballet shoes (*zapatillas*).
El Vito: heeled shoes (*chapines*).
La Maja y el Torero, Pericet version: (soft ballet shoes) (*zapatillas*).
Manchegas Pias: ballet shoes (*zapatillas*).
Los Caracoles: heeled shoes (*chapines*).
Soleares Granadinos: heeled shoes (*chapines*).
La Perla del Guadalquivir: heeled shoes (*chapines*).

Illustration 7.1
Sheet music
for *Boleras de
la Cachucha*
by F. García
Navas. Marina
Keet archive.

La Maja Jerezana: heeled shoes (*chapines*).
Olé Andaluz: heeled shoes (*chapines*).
La Sal de Andalucia: heeled shoes (*chapines*).
La Bella Española: heeled shoes (*chapines*).

Not included in this music book are the beautiful *Zapateado de Maria Cristina* and *Panaderos de la Vuelta de la Corrida, Panaderos de la Juerga*. The *Soleares del Maestro Arcas* is there as the *Soleares de Arcas*.

Recorded Music

Until very recently no good recorded music has existed of this repertoire. The musicians of the dance group called Francisco de Goya in Madrid have recently recorded music of the dances performed in Madrid from the past centuries. They include some of the Escuela Bolera dances in two volumes on compact discs and cassettes. In the first volume the *Boleras de la Cachucha* is incorrect for dancing to in the *Cachucha* section. This has been rectified in volume 2. They have worked with Eloy Pericet on these dances. Escuela Bolera dances in the first volume are: *Bolero Liso*, *Jaleo de Jerez*, and on the CD but not the cassette, *Seguidillas Manchegas* and *Olé de la Curra*. The Pericet repertoire presented in the second volume is: *La Maja y el Torero*, *Zapateado de Maria Cristina*, *Olé de la Curra*, *Panaderos de la Tertulia*, *Malagueñas*, *El Vito*, and the correct version of *Boleras de la Cachucha*. Also included, and of interest to the readers of this book, is the music of two early *Bolero*s mentioned here, that of Requejo and the other of Sors. This is a valuable addition to the Spanish dance repertoire. The address where this can be obtained is La Asociación de Coros y Danzas Francisco de Goya, Calle Valencia, 5 1 piso, 28012 Madrid, Spain, tel/fax: 34-91-527-61-81.

Illustration 7.2
Panaderos. Sketch by Doré.

The Titles of Dances

It is not easy to find answers to the origins of the names of the various dances. Some are obvious and some pose a problem. It has taken much searching to arrive at these following conclusions.

'What's in a Name?' The *Bolero* Dances

Within the school of Spanish classical dancing there have always existed dances with flamenco names, such as *Peteneras*, *Soleares*, *Caracoles*, and so on. These are performed in heeled shoes, not soft ballet shoes. Classical arm positions are used and also castanets are played, something alien to true flamenco. It is also of interest that the soft shoe dances (*zapatillas*), such as *Boleras de la Cachucha*, the two *Panaderos* and *Seguidillas Manchegas* amongst others, share the time signature of 3/4, whereas *Caracoles*, *Peteneras*, *Soleares* and *El Vito* are in 3/8 time and are danced in heeled shoes called *chapines*. The exception is *La Maja y el Torero*, which shows its folk roots in a 3/8 tempo with the more flamenco-type dances, but is usually danced in ballet slippers. (Illustration page 135)

◆ See colour plate 32

Boleras de la Cachucha

A dance in 3/4 time performed in ballet shoes, *zapatillas*. One could call this dance an extended structure of the *Seguidillas*. *Boleras de la Cachucha* has the entrance introduction, a typical remainder from the *Seguidillas*. Still following the *Seguidillas* format is the pause in a position and the danced introduction *Salida* leading into each *Bolero* section, as seen in *Sevillanas Boleras*. The *Bolero* sections are divided by a *Cachucha* or *Jaleo*, as that section is called, following the sequence: big entrance introduction to enter onto the stage, introduction, *Bolero*, *Cachucha* (which has two sections), *Bolero*. This too is an extended form of the *Seguidillas* which has alternating sections of verses and choruses. Again, like *Seguidillas*, it ends with a *bien parado*, or well-held position, before recommencing the next short introduction and *Bolero*, *Cachucha*, *Bolero* sections, and so on. Each *Cachucha* starts with the same steps, a sequence of *sostenidos* or dig steps, each time progressing into a second part, when the melody changes slightly. The second section passes the partner back and forth. This is different each time. There are theatrical adaptations of this dance cutting out the lead into each *Bolero* section and combining it into one flowing dance. The *Cachuchas* are delightful, in that the passes are hopped, and the third section, like the last verse of *Seguidillas Manchegas* or *Seguidillas Sevillanas*, is all passes and very intricate to perform.

A theatrical version can be seen in the BBC's *Magic of Dance* programme with the dancers Eloy Pericet and his sister Carmelita.

This dance shows the origin of flying or *voleras* in the *Bolero* name. Of the Escuela Bolera dances, it has this in common with *Zapateado* de Maria Cristina. There is also the *Bolero de Medio Paso*, which shares the music of the *Boleras de la Cachucha*, *Bolero Liso*, which has the same music as the folk *Bolero Mallorquin*, and there are many others in Zarzuelas and folk dances.

Bolero Carlos III

Soft shoes called *zapatillas* are worn. The *Bolero Carlos III* seems to refer to the king who ruled from 1759 until 1788. However, it also seems to be a more modern combination of dances such as *Bolero de Medio Paso* and others (Carmen Gordo, personal communication).

Soleares de Arcas

A dance in 3/8 time. *Chapines*, small-heeled shoes, are worn. We know that the *Soleares de Arcas* should really be *Soleares del Maestro Arcas*, because the composer of the music was the celebrated guitarist, from the province of Almeria, known as D. Julián Arcas. He was born on 25 October 1832 and died in Ronda in 1878. This gives us the period of this dance.

From Eusebio Rioja we learn that the *Soleá* (*Soleares*, corrupted from the word *soledad*, meaning solitude) has been dated in a popular, folk and danced form, by

Illustration 7.4
Dudley Tomlinson and Lorna Levy dancing *Boleras de la Cachucha* in Cape Town, South Africa. Photo: Keith Mackintosh. Marina Keet archive.

the authors Molina y Mairena, García Matos and Blas Vega, as existing from the first half of the nineteenth century. Ivanova, in *The Dancing Spaniards*, maintains that a similar melody is to be found in the thirteenth-century collection of music of Alfonso X, the Wise, of Castile. It therefore could have been played long before coming to the attention of the scribes. Rioja says that it assumed its flamenco danced and sung form towards the latter part of that century, greatly influenced by Arcas. So, contrary to popular belief, it came from folk before flamenco, and from there transposed to its classical form for guitar by Julián Arcas.

As noted above, it is a dance in 3/8 time, and from Maestro Otero we understand that it has eight *compáses* which are repeated so that the steps can start on the other foot in the repetition. He considered it the most beautiful Andalusian dance, the most graceful and most celebrated in all concepts, as performed by artists of repute. At some stage he comments critically that both Seville and Malaga have produced good dancers but that in his day dancers were not conscientious about what they are doing, and were unable to explain the smallest detail, or why, for example, something is done on the one foot and not on the other.

'La Cuenca' (Manuela García) was the first person to perform *Soleares de Arcas* as a flamenco *zapateado* – dressed as a man in *traje corto* and wearing boots – in the Cafés Silverio and Burrero in Seville. It is easier to dance in boots than in shoes, as they hold the ankle firmly and have a broad sole as a base. A piano version was arranged and this version was first taught, with the use of castanets, to dancers in Malaga by Eduardo Vásquez. He was born on 13 October 1839 in Granada. From the age of eight he had studied with Antonio Badillo and afterwards with Petra Cámara, Juanito Alonso, Antonio Olivar and lastly Marcos Diaz. He travelled widely, performing in Spain, Portugal, Uruguay, Brazil the Azores and Canary Islands. He performed the *Soleares de Arcas* for the first time in the famous *cafés cantantes* of the time, the Filharmonico and then the Centro Theatre, before going on to the others at the Silverio and the Burrero. Once retired from performing, he directed dance in Seville, Barcelona and Granada, where he had an academy of dance. Otero states that he trained many dancers, amongst others Paco Ramos and Juana Ruiz, both from Malaga, who were the first, after Vásquez, to perform this *Soleares* in Malaga. They also performed it in Seville. Among others from Malaga performing it in Seville were: La Cándida, La Isabel Espinosa, and María Píteri. The Pericets' teacher from Seville, Maestro Segura, taught it as well. It is this piano version that has been passed on by that family, from their grandfather 'Don Angel' Pericet to the present day.

Otero says that two *coplas* of this *Soleares* may be rather lengthy to perform, and could be danced alternately by two dancers, performing the first together and sharing the second for variation and also in order for it to be less tiring.

Foreigners who also danced it included, amongst others, Lise Noblet, Alexis Dupont, Lucile Grahn, Fanny Elssler and Marie Guy-Stephan.

Olé de la Curra
A dance in 3/4 time. Ballet shoes, *zapatillas*, are worn. There is a folk Andaluza version, utilising shoes with small heels, *chapines*. The two versions vary only

Illustration 7.5
Susana and José dancing
Panaderos de la Tertulia.
Comet-Photo. José de
Udaeta archive.
(see p.142)

slightly. At a certain point in the coda of the folk dance, the shout of *olé* is appropriate. In the classical version, it features as well, after the second small jump to point the foot in front. However, in a recording of the folk version it comes later, in the coda, after the *rodazánes* and small steps back into a position. It comes only once. It may be appropriate here to mention the difference in accent when the word is used in other circumstances. At a dance performance it is on the last syllable (*olé*); at a bullfight it is on the first syllable (*óle*).

The *Olé* was a type of dance from Jerez de la Frontera, in Andalusia. It was taken into the repertoire of the Escuela Bolera. Carmen la Cigarrera created a furore when she danced *Olé Antiguo*, a dance that required a particular unaffected grace when performed. According to Carmen Gordo, Cigarrera was a famous singer, of the type of Lola Flores, who both sang and danced. In Seville in 1840 the dance masters decided that the dancer called 'La Curra', who was known for her grace and beauty, was the best exponent of this dance called *Olé Antiguo* and it was renamed *El Olé de la Curra* in her honour. There is also the *Olé Andaluz*. Other examples of this type of dance are *Olé Gaditano* (from Gadir, the Roman name for Cádiz), and *Olé de Bujaque*.

A significant feature of *Olé de la Curra* is the kneel, when the dancer does a *renversé*, bending forward and doing a complete circular rotation of the upper body

Illustration 7.6 (left)
Trini Borrull in *Olé de la Curra*.
Illustration 7.7 (right)
Marina Lorca from Cape Town in *Olé de la Curra*, danced in the Andalusian style in London 1998. Photo: Elaine Mayson, Marina Keet archive.

and arms. This movement was, together with the rotation of the hips, much appreciated by the Romans when they came into contact with the *puellae*, girls with 'honey in their hips', the dancing girls of Gadir. Cervantes thought that the Andalusians were 'born to dance', and certainly these women's dancing was so admired that they were transported to Rome to be shown off and admired there at feasts.

Davillier writes of the performance of La Nena, when he saw her dance *Olé de la Curra* in the *barrio* of La Viña in Cádiz. He mentions that she had acquired that nickname because of her short stature. Curra, he writes, is a word that is difficult to explain and give it a meaning; however, as we see above, according to Maestro Otero it is the name of a dancer.

Davillier explains in his book that *Olé de la Curra* is usually a solo dance and he writes how there is, more than in any other Spanish dance, the need for flexibility, fluidity – ease of movement. La Nena possessed this ability more than any other dancer of her day. According to Davillier, she had no rival for her marvellous performance of it. Her waist had the flexibility of a cane as she arched enchantingly and languidly. As in the days of the Roman occupation, she almost touched the

floor as she bent her arms and shoulders smoothly, and held the position for some moments, neck stretched and head inclined in a sort of ecstasy. Then suddenly, as though she had received an electric shock, she jumped to her feet and resumed rhythmically playing her ivory castanets, starting to dance with the same animation as at its commencement. Thus she built up excitement for the finale.

It is this kneeling and body roll and ecstasy that is recalled when Elssler danced her *Cachucha*, the same movement described above being a feature of her dance. However, it is not found in the genuine *Cachucha*, and thus one can only arrive at the conclusion that Dolores Serral must have cleverly choreographed a dance especially for herself and Elssler, using the best moments from several Spanish dances, including this movement from *Olé de la Curra*. Or else, Elssler cleverly copied them into her solo, after seeing them performed by Serral.

Olé de la Curra has produced two markedly different reactions from dancers at either end of the world. The former Royal Ballet soloist, South African David Poole, exclaimed when he saw *Olé de la Curra* performed for the first time, 'If I had choreographed that dance I would die happy!' (personal communication). However, in 1858 when Pepita de Oliva performed *Olé* in Copenhagen, she was rapturously received by the press and public, but it rightly produced a furious outburst

Illustration 7.8 (left)
El Olé.
Illustration 7.9 (right)
Customs of Andalusia, El Olé.

◆ See colour plate 33

Illustration 7.10
Olé Gaditano.
Sketch by Gustave Doré.

from August Bournonville. He was mainly disturbed that her poor dancing received such adulation, but he also called it a choreographic 'horror'. Perhaps the fault lay with the dancer. Manuel Guerrero, a Spaniard who happened to be in Copenhagen at the same time as Pepita, was asked by her for his opinion of her performance of *Olé*. It was certainly not flattering, as he set it out in a letter to his family.

Once again one experiences a Spanish dance through a French writer's prose: Alexandre Dumas mentions the voluptuousness of the *Olé* and revelled in its sensuousness. His and the dancers' mutual enjoyment of the ebullience that they displayed is testament to the temperament and style displayed in the folk versions of this dance type. Choreographically, the *Olé* danced by La Curra remains masterful in its construction, even in the cooler, more refined version that remains in the Escuela Bolera repertoire.

Zapateado de Maria Cristina

A dance in 3/4 time. Ballet shoes, called *zapatillas*, are worn. The *Zapateado* part of the title is not flamenco. It refers to the dance type. In August Bournonville's ballet *Toreadoren*, there is a *Zapateado* of this genre, and Arthur Saint-Léon also danced a *Zapateado* with Marie Guy-Stephan.

This dance, the *Zapateado de Maria Cristina*, seems to have been named after the Queen with that name, as no dancer by that name is found during that period (there may have been one of course; but we just do not know, because, sadly, so little has trickled down to us about the ethereal art of dance in Spain). Maria Cristina was a forceful Queen Regent during the latter part of the nineteenth century, exactly at this period when these dances were so popular. George Sand mentions meeting the Queen's forbidding troops patrolling Barcelona's streets. Maria Cristina continued to reign after her husband's death and it was she who founded Madrid's Conservatoire of Music, so her interest in the arts was perhaps rewarded in this music and dance.

Peteneras

A dance in 3/8 time performed with small-heeled shoes, *chapines*. From Maestro José Otero's (de Aranda) book *Tratado de Bailes* (1912) we can trace the present dance to approximately 1888. The book is interesting because Otero says that he

wrote so as not to lose the refined and artistic dances, the social as well as the folk ones. He mentions that it was impossible to write down all the dances taught in his studio, which would have resulted in a volume of extraordinary proportions. However, it *is* regrettable that he did not continue with the Spanish dances instead of including the foreign 'social' dances of his day, the waltz, the lancers, and so on, which comprise two thirds of the book.

Illustration 7.11 Arthur Saint-Léon and Marie Guy Stephan performing *El Zapateado* in Paris, 1850. A dance type in the Escuela Bolera repertoire. Sketch by Bertraux Cadet.

Our gratitude should go to the 'multitude of foreign ladies' for whom he included the Spanish dances – the ladies who, on a brief visits to Seville, tried to learn what is almost impossible to do in a short time, and who kept asking him whether there was a book describing the technical requisites of the *Sevillanas* and the *Peteneras*. Otero said that it was also written for teachers and dancers to appreciate the difference in those dances from thirty years previously, when he started teaching them; and for those who constantly learn new dances without being able to have a proper schooling and the knowledge of how to use their feet. Also he wished to preserve the structure of the dances from when he started learning them, forty years earlier, to his most recent dance, choreographed in 1912, 'in which we find everything – the old and the new.' His final note in the book gives his address as San Vicente 67, in Seville, and says that anyone needing the music for the above-mentioned dances could buy them from him in Seville, for about two pesetas. Would that we could today!

The music for *Peteneras* was known for a long time and played at parties and *fiestas* in Seville, and became so popular that the teacher Don Paulino Ruiz, in collaboration with the dancers El Chivo and Emilio el Tuerto, made a dance of it at his studio situated in the street Universidad, later called Laraña. An academy was inaugurated under their ownership in 1882 and lasted until 1892. All the great masters of the time taught there, the last of these being Faustino Segura and Otero himself, together with Pepe el del Coliseo, who became very popular as a result of owning a number of taverns. In 1894 Otero asked to use the hall belonging to Don Matias to organise an Andalusian entertainment for about a hundred foreign tourists. No further dance performances were given there after that concert, at which the *Peteneras*, taught by Don Paulino, was premiered. He demonstrated the dance to all the other teachers and enthusiasts and, as always happens, these teachers developed their own individual versions, so that the only ones who could dance it together were Don Paulino's own students. This was no longer the case afterwards, as the *Peteneras* danced in the early 1900s was the version choreographed by Faustino Segura and Otero, today taught by the Pericet family, whose grandfather was a pupil of Maestro Segura. This version was choreographed jointly by Faustino Segura and Otero since they were great friends and always in each other's company, and their pupils were often required to dance together. However, at first they could not combine their versions because Segura's had been developed by Amparo Alvarez, 'La Campanera', and Otero's by Juanito Brenes. They therefore decided to produce a single version that their students could dance together without any problems. At a *fiesta Andaluza* which Otero organised for tourists in 1894 (in the Salón de D. Matias in Seville), he and Segura therefore had to reformulate the *Peteneras*. Otero believed that the dance handed down and performed today is the one choreographed by Faustino Segura and himself. As Segura was one of the teachers of Angel Pericet Blanco, I assume this is the same version of the dance passed on by that family today. Otero felt that their version of *Peteneras*, choreographed 25 years before, was taught everywhere, even though that may not have seemed to be the case, because arm positions had been changed and the various postures were not performed as they had set them and as he continued to teach them. The *Peteneras* had become as popular as the *Sevillanas*, because all students wanted to learn *Peteneras* after mastering the *Seguidillas*.

The *Peteneras* was supposedly named after a woman of doubtful reputation, according to the words of a song, a beautiful Jewess on her way to look for Rebeco, who was in the synagogue. The town of Paterna has a statue of a dancer called Petenera. Some think there is a corruption of this word Paterna into Petenera. At any rate, of interest is the fact that Paterna is near to Jerez de la Frontera, which is known for its Bulerias. Historian José Blas Vega considers this a likely origin. When teaching me the style of this dance, Eloy Pericet told me to 'think of *Bulerias*'. So that is something to be kept in mind when performing it. The dance itself has *desplantes* which are found in the *Bulerias* rhythm. The flamenco rhythm and tune were taken up by the dancing masters in a classical Andalusian style, performed in heeled shoes. Unlike flamenco, it has castanet rhythms added to it.

As noted in the section on the regional *Bolero*s, the melody was also picked up, through travellers transporting oil and silks between Andalusia and Valencia, and it became a jolly dance in the latter region of Valencia. Originally the flamenco

Illustration 7.12
Andalusian-style dress
suitable for *Peteneras* of the
Escuela Bolera.
Marina Keet archive.

Peteneras was much more cheerful and light than the dance of today. Perhaps it was at this stage that it was picked up in Valencia and that the Valencian version is our legacy of that period today. The Gypsies may then have taken it and moulded it to their own mood, and the original was lost. In flamenco it is of a sombre character. The accent is on the first beat of each of the phrases of (**1**, 2, 3; **1**, 2, 3; **1**, 2; **1**, 2; **1**, 2;), not with accents on the counts 3, 6, 8, 10 and 12 in the usual flamenco way. The words of the Valencian and flamenco song are identical:

¿Donde vas, bella judía,	Where are you going, beautiful Jewess,
tan compuesto y a deshora?	so elegant at such a time?
Voy en busca de Rebeco	I am looking for Rebeco
que está en una sinagoga	who is in the synagogue

The expulsion of Jews from Spain happened in 1492. The Spanish language of that period, known as Ladino and spoken by those Jews who left, has remained with them as it was spoken in the fifteenth century, whereas the language in Spain continued to evolve. So, historically, we are going back a long time. If you hear Spanish spoken in Yugoslavia, you know that the person is Jewish, according to Flory Jagoda (personal communication). Richard Glasstone maintains that the same can be said of the Belgian Congo, where the Sephardic Jews emigrated from the Mediterranean. Jagoda performs in Washington DC, singing in Ladino, the songs she learned from her grandmother in Yugoslavia. D.E. Pohren mentions that the same applies to the Sephardic Jews in Turkey where the old Spanish customs and traditions survive, and that they still sing *Peteneras* there.

Serafín Estébanes Calderón speaks of the *coplas* of the *Perteneras* (note the extra 'r') in his *Fiesta in Triana*. He says that the song is reminiscent of a *Seguidillas*, only the penetrating voice gives it an inexplicable melancholia. It has inspired both singers and writers: Federico García Lorca wrote the poem 'Gráfico del Petenera', and the dramatists Serrano Anguito and Manuel de Góngora wrote the drama *La Petenera*. According to Blas Vega, the height of its popularity was in the eighteenth and late nineteenth century. In Seville, the young Andalusians favoured it in 1879 and in 1881 it caused a furore. They sang, 'Del Año de las *Peteneras*, nos tenemos de acordar, que andura la Pura y Limpia, y el canasto de pan.' The singer of that time, Medino el Viejo, developed a style that was very difficult, with a change of voice, enriching it melodically. The dancers of this century to interpret it were Rosita Durán in the theatre and the Zambra and Soledad Miralles. The classical version has no song.

Panaderos (illustration on page 135)
Zapatillas or *chapines* can be worn. According to José Otero, *Los Panaderos* is a dance quite distinct from the dances called *Panaderos de la Flamenca* and *Panaderos de la Tertulia*. The allusion to bread (*pan*) in the word is thought to be an allusion to bread in the cries and songs of street vendors. Both dances are from the Escuela Bolera, performed in soft ballet slippers. *Panaderos de la Flamenca* can have shoes with a small heel, but the *Panaderos de la Tertulia* is very much more balletic than the *Panaderos de la Flamenca*. The latter is also performed by such regional companies as the Coros y Danzas de Madrid and the Grupo Francisco de Goya, with steps varying in the folk versions choreographies. There are more types, such as *Panaderos de la Flor*.

In the *Panaderos de la Flamenca*, the waltz section belongs to a period when it was a popular social dance and was added to the older original *Panaderos*. Otero mentions that the woman is wearing a mantilla and that the man carries his jacket over his arm and the hat in his hand. (See also 'Mantillas and Fans', p. 146) The pass of the *Seguidillas* is incorporated in both dances, but performed with a different arm position. In *Seguidillas Sevillanas* the arms make outward circles, in *Panaderos* inward ones, giving it a distinct look as the position, with the leading arm up, is made at the start of each of the passes. (see illustrations pp.131 and 135)

Tiranas
A dance in a moderate 3/8 or 6/8 time. These are 'sung dances', such as the *Tirana*

del Zarandillo, which today have no song. Don Preciso describes the *Tiranas* of the eighteenth century as having, together with *La Polaca* (also a sung dance), replaced the *Seguidillas* in popularity. He found the songs firmly Spanish in origin, then the dance fell into disuse and only remained in a song as a word here and there, such as with the *Tirana del Caramba* and *Tirana del Contrabandista*, in the chorus or *estribillo*. The verses consist of four lines of eight syllables. The Tiranas sounds charming, in Don Preciso's description of ladies marking time with graceful movements of their aprons while the men make gestures with their hats and kercheifs in the style of the old dances of the Gaditanes. The dancers moved from one side to another with steps clearly defined. He claims that there are many compositions of songs in this style that travelled as far afield as St Petersburg and Vienna. (Eduardo Huertas, in his book *Teatro Musical Español*, cites this from F. Pedrell's *Dictionario Técnico*.) Subirá describes the words as slightly malicious in intent, picaresque and satirical.

Huertas states that the *Tirana* evolved from a dance-song into a song or dance, then became a loose item in the *saraos* or soirées, to guitar or piano accompaniment, before ending the *Tonadillas Escenicas*. He claims they attained a great popularity for some years, in all social spheres, precisely because of the erotic spiciness and maliciousness of the words.

La Manola

This is not in the Escuela Bolera repertoire of dances. Madrid was divided into different areas referred to as 'Los Madriles'. The names not only signified the geographical terrain, but a social significance as well. The quarters or *barrios*, as they were called, were divided into the *barrios altos*, or upper quarter, *barrios centrales* in the middle, and the *barrios bajos*, the lower area from Puerta del Sol and through Plaza Santa Ana that spilled over towards the river, where the most picturesque *barrio*, Lavapies, is found. Meaning literally 'wash feet', Lavapies was formerly the old Jewish quarter. When the Jews were asked either to convert to Catholicism or to leave, those that chose to convert and were baptised often took the name Emmanuel, which was used in its diminutive form of Manolo – hence the *manolos* and the *manolas* came into being. It is of interest to note that the Gypsies in the south refer to Christ as Emmanuel. (Some of this information is from the *Encyclopaedia Britannica* but also from Ralph Pemberton, personal communication.)

The word *manola* also signified, for the women, a specific attire with a dress with lace, frills and a mantilla being worn. Therefore, dances called *La Manola* must have been special choreographies in the style of the Escuela dances. Another example is *La Macarena* (Eloy Pericet, personal communication).

The dancer Adelina Plunkett is depicted dancing *La Manola de la Favorite* in Paris, as are Fanny Cerrito and Arthur Saint-Léon at Her Majesty's Theatre in London. Plunkett, a Belgian dancer, and Elssler were written about in the press as 'the most authentic Andalusians we have ever come across'!

We know from Vita Sackville-West's family research that Pepita de Oliva summoned a young dancer called Raffael Guerrero to her room at 2 a.m. to teach her *La*

◆ See colour plate 34

Illustration 7.13
La Manolla (*Manola*). Fanny
Cerrito and her husband Arthur
Saint-Léon 'of Her Majesty's
Theatre, Drawn from the Life by
Monsr. Numa Blanc.' London
1844. Royal Ballet School
archive

Manola. She rehearsed with Guerrero for six hours. (One wonders about her neighbours, as Guerrero brought musicians with him!) It is from his brother's letters that one learns that Pepita had no talent. This information is also to be found in *O! Pepita!* by Charlotte Christensen (Copenhagen).

La Maja y el Torero, or La Malagueña y el Torero

A dance in 3/8 time danced with *zapatillas*, ballet slippers, or in some cases the shoes with a small heel called *chapines*. In his book about his 'Voyage en Espagne' (1840), Théophile Gautier tells about *La Malagueña*, which he calls the local dance of Malaga. However, his description of it sounds like the dance *La Maja y el Torero*. A *Malagueña* is a *Fandango* from Malaga, which does not resemble his description.

1. *Bolero de L'Alcudia de Carlet,* Joan Fosas, Guest artist (1990) with the Spanish Dance Theatre, Washington D.C. and Nancy Sedgwick showing the typical Valencian arm position used by Fanny Elssler in her Cachucha and Carlos Blasis in his 'attitude'. Photo: Victor Cohen. Marina Keet archive. (see p.5 and p.179)

2. The arm poised on the shoulder – the male dancer showing his fatigue! Marina Keet archive. (see p.6)

3. The Spanish Dance Theatre of Washington D.C., performing the Mourners Dance from Valencia in 1990. Albert Sans' choreography for Esbart Dansaire de Rubí, is called *Mortitxol*. Staged by Marina Keet, lighting by Carl Gudenius. Dancers: Jaime Coronado, Lourdes Elias, Ziva Cohen, Joan Fosas (Guest Artist from Barcelona), Mary Ann Shelton, Nelson Sitton, Danielle Polen and Orlando Vargas. Photo Bill O'Leary, *The Washington Post*. (see p.9)

4. Two Manchegans dancing Seguidillas.
Print from the eighteenth century.
By kind permission of Carmen García Matos.
(see p.13)

5. The Fandango.
Biblioteca Nacional, Madrid.
(see p.13)

LE FANDANGO

6. Oil painting by Francisco Goya (1746–1828), Dancing on the banks of the Manzanares river, Madrid, 'El Baile de San Isidro', showing the *majos* and *majas* of the city. Note the arm positions. (see p.14 and p.82)

7. Provinces of Spain, Sevilla, The Dance. Oil painting by Joaquin Sorolla y Bastida.
Courtesy of the Hispanic Society of America, New York. (see p.20 and p.43)

8. Baile del Candil. Garcia Matos archive. By kind permission of Carmen García Matos. (see p.32)

(see p.32)

9. Dancing the Sevillanas. Marina Keet archive.

47139 EDITION PHOTOGLOB CO., ZÜRICH

Sevilla - Bailando las sevillanas

UN PASAR DE LAS SEGUIDILLAS BOLERAS

10. Engraving by Marcos Téllez depicting *Un Pasar* of the Seguidillas Boleras at the end of the eighteenth century. Marina Keet archive. (see p.50)

nº 6.

PASEO DELAS SIGUIDILLAS BOLERAS.

11. Engraving by Marcos Téllez depicting the *Paseo* of the Seguidillas Boleras at the end of the
eighteenth century. Marina Keet archive. (see p.50)

12. Bolero de Algodre, Zamora.
Marina Keet Archive (Gift from
the Casa de Zamora, Madrid)
(see p.63)

13. 'Les Gitanes del Vallès', with Carmen Pous, Joan Fosas, Rosa Julià Fosas and Pedro Julià.
Esbart Dansaire de Rubí. Marina Keet archive. (see p.65)

BOLERO D'ALCUDIA

15. Design for the Esbart Dansaire de Rubí, Barcelona, of the Bolero D'Alcudia de Carlet (lady) by Fabià Puigserver. (see p.68)

BOLERO D'ALCUDIA

14. Design for the Esbart Dansaire de Rubí, Barcelona, of the Bolero D'Alcudia de Carlet (man) by Fabià Puigserver. (see p.68)

16. 'A shawl dance.' (see p.34 and p.212)

17. A Valencian Scene. Marina Keet archive. (see p.68)

18. The Provinces of Spain, Valencia. Oil painting by Joaquin Sorolla y Bastida.
Courtesy of the Hispanic Society of America, New York. (see p.68)

19. El Cap del Ball as performed by the Esbart Dansaire de Rubí. (see p.74)

20. Lourdes Elias from the Spanish Dance Theatre of Washington D.C. and guest artist Joan Fosas from the Esbart Dansaire de Rubí, Barcelona, dancing a Catalonian Seguidillas at the Smithsonian Institute in Washington D.C. (see p.74)

21. A dancer from the studio of Maria Jesús Garcia de Bayarri, Valencia. (see p.69)

22. Dancers of
the Coros y
Danzas de
Madrid,
founded in
1949, in
costumes from
the period of
the artist Goya.
(see p.81)

What he is describing is the dance known as *La Maja y el Torero*. The *maja* part denotes a lady from Madrid in the era of the artist Goya, her male counterpart being a *majo*. The several versions of this music actually have these two names of *Maja* and *Malagueña* (Eloy Pericet Blanco, personal communication). It is difficult after so much time has lapsed to find out where this distinction of titles originates. It probably originated in Andalusia, like the other Escuela Bolera dances, and the title changing when danced in Madrid. The dance remains today known as *La Maja y El Torero*.

Gautier describes the dance as 'really an enchanting poem'. He says that the man appears first, with a hat worn rakishly over one eye. He is muffled in a red cloak, like a *hidalgo* strolling in search of adventure. (A *hidalgo* is a contraction of *hijo de alguno*, meaning son of someone of importance.) The lady then appears, adorned in a mantilla, with a fan in her hand, as though going for a stroll along the Alameda. The 'gallant', intent on seeing her face, is thwarted by the excellent manipulation of the fan by the lady, who rhythmically opens and closes it, raising and lowering it expertly up to and from her face. The 'gallant', discouraged, retires a few steps and resorts to another strategy. He plays his castanets beneath the cape. This produces instant attention from the lady, who smiles and her bosom throbs and she marks time on place, on the tips of her toes. She throws away the fan and the mantilla, and reveals that she is dressed for dancing, with dazzling sequins and tinsel, a rose in her hair and a large comb of tortoiseshell on her head. The gentleman removes his mask and his cape, and both execute a dance of 'delicious originality'. This is still its form today, with the slower, mimed section leading into the dance. It is a favourite in the Pericet repertoire.

Jaleo de Jerez (Illustration page 149)
Jaleo is the shouting and clapping that accompanies Spanish dancing. José Blas Vega, in the *Diccionario Enciclopedia Illustrado del Flamenco* (1988), says as his third suggestion of the meaning of *jaleo*, 'An Andalusian dance, with a passionate rhythm, voluptuous and, at times, provocative, which seems to be close to flamenco and which towards the middle of the nineteenth century became a mixed theatrical dance.' The sections of the *Cachucha* in the *Boleras de la Cachucha* are also referred to as *Jaleos*.

As the name denotes, the *Jaleo de Jerez* came from the town of Jerez de la Frontera, the home of the *Bulerias*. It was performed by Lucile Grahn on 29 November 1838 in Copenhagen when she returned to the city in 1838, and two years later, on 27 November 1840, Bournonville added his version to his ballet *Toreadoren*, which is very different to the one danced in Spain,. It was also in the repertoires of other dancers such as Dolores Serral and Josepha Soto in 1840. In 1851 Marie Guy-Stephan included it in her repertoire, and Fanny Elssler danced it with great success, especially in Havana, Cuba. The Bournonville version of it in *Toreadoren* was reconstructed for Danish Television, with the help of Hans Brenaa, by Flemming Ryberg. He danced it together with Eva Kloborg, but to music by Sor,

Illustration 7.14
La Malagueña y el Torero,
sketch by Gustave Doré.

not the original music by Edvard Helsted. Sadly, this is now all that remains of the choreography of that ballet.

Two French travellers in Spain, the author Baron Charles Davillier and the famous artist Gustave Doré, saw La Campanera perform this dance in the studio of Don Luis Botella in the Calle Tarifa in Seville. Elsewhere are described their experiences during the subsequent performance. Strangely, the artist Doré took over the accompaniment on the violin of *Jaleo de Jerez* for La Campanera. Because the blind musician accompanying her had been performing poorly, sometimes forgetting to play at all, the audience grew restive, shouting for him to leave. The search for the official guitarist gave negative results and the audience was voicing their discontent. The violin was handed to an *aficionado* and then to Doré, who played in an inspired way, inflaming La Campanera. The composer Rossini had given written testimony to the talent of Doré, not only as an artist, but also as a musician.

However, nowhere is there a mention of sheet music. How could Doré have known what accompaniment to play? Davillier does mention Doré as playing *Jaleo de Jerez* in an inspired, improvised way. La Campanera, who was described as performing as though electrified, must have improvised as well. Surpassing herself, she used to her advantage the enthusiasm and applause. She danced some steps in front of a foreigner in the audience, who sported large red whiskers and was assumed to be English. She then gave him her small embroidered shawl – as was the custom, according to Davillier, in the manner of the *bayadères* of India. Thus flattered, a spectator usually handed over some money (in a secluded corner). The gentleman in question gazed with a sombre mien at the object and responded likewise. Having secreted the gold coin, La Campanera thanked him by dancing once more, especially for him. All ended well when the truant guitarist, Enrique Prado from Seville, finally appeared richly attired in Andalusian dress. A singer sang, a *bolero*, danced a solo. Together singers and dancers performed with the audience who, being true Andalusians, had brought their own guitars and castanets. Everyone gave vent to *Bolero*s and *Jaleo*s as well as *Mollares*, *Panaderos* and other dances of that genre. These could be heard, with their obligatory accompaniment, echoing throughout the entire night. Davillier does complain of the nasality of the singing in Andalusia.

Mantillas and Fans

It is of interest to note, in *La Malagueña y el Torero*, the removal of the mantilla by the woman before the dance starts, as mentioned by Gautier in his visit to Malaga in 1840. The fact that this reveals her attire shows that it must have been a very large and enveloping mantilla. In the region of Valencia such large mantillas are also worn, and removed before dancing. The same removal of mantilla and throwing away of the fan also occurs in the dance *La Macarena*, with choreography by

Rafael Pericet Jiménez. In *Panaderos de la Flamenca* the fan is thrown away to allow the playing of castanets, but only after dancing with it and manipulating it during the waltz introduction.

Naming of Other Types of Dances

Bailes del Candil

The *candil* was a lamp of a specific shape, made of iron or brass. *Bailes del Candil*, as mentioned in the section on the *Seguidillas*, were danced at organised entertainment in lamplit taverns and houses. There were paid entertainers, but at times the people themselves danced the dances. There are *Seguidillas*, *Fandangos*, *Jotas* and *Bolero*s all with the words *del Candil* attached to them.

Corraleras

A dance in 3/4 time. Heeled shoes and boots are worn. *Sevillanas Corraleras* was called after the *corral* or sandy plazas of the towns and cities, which were often markets and places for horse trading. It is one of the forms of *Seguidillas Sevillanas*, a regional couple dance from Seville.

Fandangos

Other dances, such as the *Fandangos*, adapt the city's name for their titles, such as the

Illustration 7.15
Marina Keet
Photo: Duncan Melvin

Malagueña, which is a *Fandango* from Malaga, the one from Ronda is a *Rondeña*, the one from Granada the *Granadina* (*Granaína*). However, these *Malagueñas*, *Rondeñas* and so on can often be found in their purest form in other areas such as Castile and the Canary Islands, because the ones in Malaga, Ronda and Granada have undergone changes locally, adaptations having been infiltrated into them through the years.

Tertulias (see also Appendix II)

The *Tertulia* of *Panaderos de la Tertulia*, a much more balletic dance than *Panaderos de la Flamenca*, seems to have derived its title from the popular name for gatherings or *tertulias* in Andalusia, where people came to entertain themselves with dance, song and music. However, it seems that the name was actually coined in Madrid at the end of the eighteenth century, where meetings of a totally different kind – literary gatherings – were held at an inn. For some reason these gatherings

Illustration 7.16
Carmelita and Angel Pericet Blanco.
Photo: J. Castañar.
Eloy PericetBlanco archive.

were called after a doctor of theology called Tertulian, who they say was much quoted at these informal get-togethers (José Blas Vega, personal communication). There was, however, yet another *tertulia*, that in the theatre. It was the section where only men congregated (the section for women was called the *cazuela*, earthenware casserole). The men also had standing room directly in front of the stage, the amphitheatre. The *cazuela* could also be used to designate 'the gods', where they were crowded together in close intimacy, high up in the theatre. The public were admonished to behave with decorum at all times. These people had to remain in their seats throughout the performance unless they went out to eat. They were also forbidden to wear hats or caps in the theatre or during intermission, by written decree. In the eighteenth century no encores were allowed. (In Denmark until recently, it was also the tradition for the dancers to take no curtain calls. The audience clapped, rose and went home.)

Tertulias were also the highest stories of the *corrales*, where the performances could be watched from rather cramped and dark positions. These were again the male domain and used by clerics and students, for probably very little payment or even free.

Illustration 7.17
Lise Noblet and Mme Alexis Dupont in *Jaleo de Jerez*.
(See page 145)

Théophile Gautier and Tertulias

Théophile Gautier, in his book *Voyage en Espagne* (1862), did not think very highly of the gatherings or *tertulias* which he attended, as described in a section where he discusses Madrid. It seems that this form of social gathering was popular, and was often a form of benefit for charities. One of these was for the benefit of orphans and took place at the palace of Villahermosa, where the Queen mother and the socialites of Madrid assisted.

Even today, this form of entertainment for charity, with reversal of roles of the aristocracy, is still organised. I attended one with Carola Goya and Matteo where the people who served were members of the aristocracy, countesses and baronesses. There was much good humour as they walked around taking orders for food and drink, wearing pretty little aprons, sometimes over flamenco dresses. Every now and then they would join in a *Sevillanas* or two. Tables and chairs were

◆ See colour plate 35

Illustration 7.18
'*La Cazuela*' or 'stewpot' at the
Corral del Principe Theatre,
reserved for the use of women
in the seventeenth century.

arranged in front of a constructed temporary stage. An orchestra played social dances and the audience participated. In between there were organised items to guitar. One such was a group of dancers from Cádiz, who had come specially for this occasion. We were the guests of their teacher Carmen Tejada. The youngest dancer was a boy of seven, who gave a stunning portrayal of a *Farruca*, and sat on the sidelines doing *jaleo* and *palmas* with an intensity that would have worn out an older performer. It was amazing, considering that their performance slot came at long past midnight. Carmen explained which gestures performed during the dances were typical of Cádiz. The occasion was also attended by local well-known performers, who good-naturedly rose to sing or dance at the bidding of the crowd.

The organisers in Gautier's day did not spend much money on the refreshments, offering neither tea nor ices, but merely placing clear water on a tray with sugar sticks, *azucarillos*, which were used with abandon to oversweeten the water. Gautier mentions several matters of interest, one being that at the *tertulias* the dances were performed to piano, 'as in Paris', but in a much more modern way. The other is that the ladies were required to have a *decolleté* neckline, and were dressed in a French style, excepting for one woman. She was wearing a dress with six lace frills like the dress worn by Fanny Elssler in the Cachucha from *Le Diable Boîteux*. Gautier claims that she had been to Paris, where she learned how to dress in a Spanish way! The women's clothes in Madrid were simpler than the fashionable ones of the men.

Why, Gautier asked, do people who dance badly, and why do those who are untalented dance at all? Women were frozen rigid with dread when faced with dancing a *Bolero*, *Fandango* or *Cachucha*. When he was in Burgos, Vitoria and Valladolid, Gautier was told all the good dancers were in Madrid. Yet when he was in Madrid, he was told they were in Andalusia. After seeing a horrendous couple going through the motions without even looking at one another, he despaired of seeing the true dance of Spain for which he was searching, in Spain. He decided that just as seashells are never found at the sea but only as curios in shops, so Spanish dance can only be seen in Paris! He mourned Elssler who, he said, was among the savages in America, and was convinced that it was she who had invented the *Cachucha* even before coming to Spain! It must be said that Gautier vacillates in his writings, praising the Spaniards and running down the local French ballet dancers when the Spaniards first arrived in Paris, but then being critical when he saw them in Spain and praising foreign dancers. To give him his due, the best dancers were probably performing abroad.

Zambra

The word *zambra* can mean three things: an entertainment, a dance and the group of musicians who play together. As a form of entertainment in which the local people participated, it originated after one of the Muslim invasions. In the beginning of the eleventh century, the former Caliphate of Córdoba was riven by civil strife. The easy-going court life in Córdoba was supplanted by that in Seville, which became the cultural centre. There were open-air revelries and feasting, where all inhabitants, regardless of race, religion or creed, danced and sang until the early hours of the morning. Everyone mixed freely, whether they were slaves or masters. They all imbibed the good wine for which the area was known. Jews, Christians and even the Moorish tribes, to whom alcohol was forbidden, partook of the alcohol (the early tribes were often Berbers and they were much more lax about their rules).

The word *zambra* was also used to describe the musicians who thrived in this relaxed atmosphere when lutes and drums throbbed for the dancing. The Moors brought their own dancing girls with them, and the *Zambra* is also a specific dance. The sensuous swaying of the hips while dancing brought it under the censure of the clergy and, like the Sarabande, it was later banned.

Tonadilla, Sainete and Entremeses

The *tonadillas* (from *tonada*, meaning song) were a form of musical entertainment found in the middle or end of plays in the seventeenth century. These had interspersed, or coming after them, the *jácara*, *entremeses* or the *sainete*. The dances often included the *Zarabanda* and *Chacona*. The *entremeses* were originally interludes introducing courses at a banquet and arrived in Spain through Catalonia from France. In Barcelona in 1440 and in 1453 the guilds entertained King John II and his queen with *entremeses* and dancing. The plays of that era were usually four acts, with interludes including dance, and were performed in public theatres, which were usually patios, inn yards and public squares called *corrales*.

Spanish Dancers of the Bolero Style

In his book *La Castañuela Española*, José de Udaeta lists all the Spanish dancers known for dancing the *Bolero* style in the early nineteenth century: Dolores Serral,

◆ See colour plate 36

Illustration 7.19
Manuela Perea and Felix García

Dolores Grande, Pepa Gallardo, Manuela Valle, Paula Lenguo, Amparo Alvarez (La Campanera). Between 1840 and 1870: Josefa Vargas, Lola Montes, Dolores Montero, Mariquita Edo, Manuela Perea (known as 'La Nena', because of her diminutive stature, according to Puig), Amparo Alvares (called 'La Campanera', because she was the daughter of bell ringer of the Seville Cathedral), Petra Cámara, Manuela García (La Cuenca), and from the Barcelona Liceo; Lola de Valencia, Elvira Coronas and Rosita Mauri. The most famous male dancers between 1820 and 1850 were Mariano Camprubí, his son Juan Camprubí, Gorito, Miguel Salud, Sandalia Luengo, Manuel León, Antonio Ruiz and Manuel Guerrero. During the second half of the nineteenth century there were Eduardo Torres, Carlos Pérez, Manuel Casas y Juanito Alonso, Ricardo Moragas, José Otero, Realito, Coronas and Angel Pericet Carmona. Next to Angel should be other members of their family, all dancers and teachers, Rafael and José, who died young and later the Pericet Jiménez family. Also amongst the listed names are two foreigners Pepita de Oliva and Lola Montes.

Spanish Dancers Abroad

Gautier was right when he said that the best Spanish dancers were to be found in Paris. As is often the case, they were less highly thought of at home in Madrid. It was not yet fashionable. Even today, all over the world, a dancer often goes abroad to 'polish his halo' in order to be better appreciated at home. Distance often does lend enchantment. Dolores Serral noted that in Paris the audiences appreciated the passion and voluptuousness of the Spanish dances she performed. In Madrid, when someone commenced dancing a *Jota Aragonesa* or *Bolero* the 'distinguished' members of the audience departed and the others and foreigners remained.

Today it is very different and Spanish dance of every type has had a renaissance in Spain. They have an excellent National Ballet as well as many regional groups that perform regularly. The good dancers now all perform in Spain as well as touring abroad in smaller or larger companies such as those of Luisillo, José Antonio and Antonio Gades. As late as the 1950s and 1960s another reason for touring abroad, apart from reaching new audiences, was that better money was to be earned abroad. Now that has changed.

Spanish Dancers in Paris

In the Phillips Gallery in Washington DC hangs a painting by Manet of Dolores Serral and Mariano Camprubí. Seated in the background, according to Puig, is Lola de Valencia. However, dancing in Paris at that time were also Manuela Dubinon and Francisco Font, depicted elsewhere in a lithograph dancing a *Bolero*. Serral, Camprubí, Dubinon and Font are also depicted in a *Corraleras Sevillana(s)*.

Thanks to the painstaking research by Ivor Guest published in *Gautier on Dance*, we find out which Spanish dancers were performing in Paris during Gautier's time, and also where and what they were dancing. It must be mentioned that Gautier was querulous. As was noted earlier, when the Spaniards came to Paris, he praised them and ridiculed the poor ballet dancers, and when he himself was in Spain, he could only think back on the French dancers in Paris, saying that there,

◆ See colour plates 23 and 36

dancing could be found. (In the latter case he may have had a point, as Spanish dancers are often on tour to earn good money, because at home there are so many of them competing for the same audiences.) In Spain Gautier found the Spanish women very beautiful and surpassing the French in gracefulness and charm. Although he thought that they lacked the finish and polish of the French, who he unfortunately describes as having the leanness of a horse in training after doing their torture-like exercises for limbering.

In Paris in 1836 Fanny Elssler performed the *Cachucha* that Dolores Serral had taught her. In that same year Dolores Serral was performing in Paris at the Opera Balls, partnered by Mariano Camprubí. In 1837, the Spanish couple were re-engaged for these balls as well as performing in the Théâtre du Palais-Royal and Théâtre des Variétés. Gautier discusses why this manner of dancing is not indecent: it 'is a national dance of primitive character and such barefaced simplicity that it has become chaste. It is so openly sensual, so boldly amorous, and its provocative coquetry and delirious exuberance are so full of the of youth that it is easy to forgive the very Andalusian impetuosity of some of its mannerisms.' When he speaks of Serral bending back, 'proudly arched, head thrown back, a large red rose unfolding in her beautiful half-loosened black hair, arms dreamily extended and only gently shaking the castanets, smiles over her shoulder at the lover who is approaching to steal a kiss', it could be a movement in one of the *desplantes* to be found in the Pericet version of *Panaderos de la Flamenca*. This gesture happens as well in *La Maja y el Torero* and one wonders to which dance he was referring.

These two dancers were not the only ones from Barcelona. Francisco Font and Manuela Dubinon were also dancing in Paris and being immortalised by artists. Lola de Valencia was another Spanish dancer to be painted by a French artist Manet. He also painted the Spanish ballerina at the Opera, Rosita Mauri, from Reus.

Mariano Camprubí was from Catalonia, and his famous partner was Dolores Serral. The language, Catalan, is related to the south French Languedoc. There is a strong connection between Catalonia and France, making it easy for these dancers to cross the border and feel at home there. Camprubí and Serral's success was repeated in 1838 with the dancers Piatoli and García. A dance mentioned at this time is called *Las Seguidillas de Andalucia*, obviously the *Seguidillas Sevillanas*, which is the *Seguidillas* of Andalusia. Later the dance became known simply as *Sevillanas*, and today many dancers do not even realise that it is a *Seguidillas*.

Ivor Guest quotes that in 1839 in Paris, Serral was dancing better than before, and again in 1843 at the Variété with Manuela García, Juan, and a singer called Cáceres, and yet again in 1847 in January at the Vaudeville theatre. Other Spaniards also appeared in Paris, such as Escudero and Marianna in 1838 at the Palais Royale. In 1846 Josefa Soto danced *Jaleo de Jerez* in *La Muette de Portici*. This *Jaleo* is still being performed today and also in Bournonville's *Toreador*, though it is not recognisably the same dance. In 1851 a troupe of dancers was led by Petra Cámara. In 1854, Manuela Perea, known as 'La Nena' (a baby or little child) because of small her stature, and her company performed at the Gymnase, and Concepción Ruiz performed a Galician Gallegada with Maldonado. Petra Cámara was to return

◆ See colour plate 33

to perform at the Variété in 1865 'more buxom than before'. In Guest's *Gautier on Dance* there is a lithograph of Josefa Vargas by August Off.

Alfonso Puig Aclaramunt wrote about Paris in 1859 when Petra Cámara inspired Gautier with her *Bolero* and Granadina, and of Josefa Vargas's *Olé de Cádiz*, as well as the Fabianos with their *Jaleo de Jerez*.

Roseta Mauri from the Liceo in Barcelona became one of the greatest stars of the Paris Opera and was immortalised in paintings by Dégas and Manet. These can be seen at the Louvre in Paris and the Phillips Gallery in Washington DC in the USA. She was also painted by Lépic, Bonnat and others and sculpted by several sculptors. She appeared in the Gran Teatro del Liceo in Barcelona in 1866 with her father, Pedro Mauri (1830–1906), a compatriot of Juan Camprubí. Her father and mother, Carmen Amanda Segura, were her teachers. Because of birth records in Palma de Mallorca stating one date and her own claim of being born in Reus, the Teatro Principal has her down as aged seventeen at this time, whereas she might have been as young as fifteen. She was given the title of *primera bailarina*. There, apart from many dances simply called Spanish dances, she also appeared, according to Roger Salas, in the following Spanish items: *La Feria de Sevilla, La Aldeana, La Rosa de la Macarena, La Flor de la Maravilla, La Tertulia, La Perla de Sevilla*, as well as many other national dances. She studied, at great sacrifice to the family, with Mme Dominique, to whom Salas referred to in a lecture he gave on this subject as 'the famous teacher at the Opéra (Paris)'. Mauri returned to the Liceo and performed *La Torera* with the dancer Soria, and then travelled to Trieste, Vienna, Rome and Berlin, and was acclaimed as the successor to Elssler and Cerrito. In 1877 she returned to Barcelona where Ricardo Moragas choreographed *El Pont de Diable* for her.

Illustration 7.20
Mariano Camprubí in *Cachucha* costume.

The composer Gounod saw Mauri perform in Milan and contacted the director of the Paris Opera, who sent the French dancer and choreographer, Louis Mérante to see her dance. He engaged her for the Paris Opera. Salas says that after her first Paris performance, she was emotionally received by her teacher, Mme Dominique, and the exiled Spanish Queen, Isabel II, from whom she received flowers.

Dancers from Reus

Reus achieved the status of a city in 1840. Important for its wines and textiles in the last century, it also produced ballet dancers of note. They also danced Spanish dances. One such dancer was Roseta Mauri who made her fame in Paris. From the book by Ferran Canyamares i Josep Iglesias, *La Dansarina Roseta Mauri (1850–1923)*, we learn that it is she in Edgar Dégas' *Fin d'Arabesque* in an *attitude penchée* with a bouquet of flowers in her right hand. In *Danseuse sur la Scène* she is seen during a performance at the Paris Opera where she became a star, dancing not only ballet but also *Boleros*, *Jotas* and *Fandangos* of her native Spain. Roseta is the Catalonian for Rosita, the name by which she was generally known abroad.

She was taught by her parents, her father dancing at the Liceo in Barcelona in 1848, when another product of Reus, Juan Camprubí was *primo ballerino* there. Both her parents were dancers, and they named her Isabel Amanda Rosa Mauri, but she became famous as Roseta Mauri. She was born on 15 September 1849 and always claimed that she was from Reus in the province of Tarragona, Catalonia. Her father, Pedro, was from Catalonia and her mother, Carmen, from Mallorca. There, in the Parish of St Nicolau in Mallorca, ecclesiastic documents between the years 1841 and 1851 show evidence that a child was born to them in 1850 in Palma de Mallorca and the birth attended by the grandparents. She had brothers and sisters, Francese, Pere, and Carolina born in 1861, who was also a dancer.

Mauri's father had been taught by the dancer-choreographer Henri Devine, while he, Devine, was dancing at the Liceo around 1862. Roseta's name appears for the first time on a programme of the drama company at the Teatro Principe in 1865. The principal dancers at the time were Dolores Montero and Manuel Perez. Roseta also appeared in that same year in the L'Esterpe Theatre in Reus and the Tivoli de Vilanova in Geltru.

Mariano Camprubí's son, Juan Camprubí, was also born in Reus in 1825. He was a pupil of the Italian dancer Antonio Fabiani from the age of eleven. In Spain he performed in the cities of Barcelona (on his doorstep next to Reus), Madrid, Granada and Seville. According to Pilar Llorens, he toured with his partner Manuela García to Germany, Austria, Hungary, Switzerland, Russia and France, where he was described by the Académie Royale de Music as 'one of the principal dancers of the epoch'.

Campubrí and García were lured back from these foreign shores to become the principal dancers of the inauguration of the Liceo Theatre in Barcelona in *La Rondeña*, which Campubrí choreographed to music by José Lurch. They also danced traditional *Boleros Robados, Mollares, Zapateado, Boleras a Ocho*. Other dances they performed were from Catalonia, *Ball Pla, Ball Rodó*. They also danced the famous *La Cachucha* and *Los Majos del Puerto* among other regional dances such as a *Jota* from Aragon and a *Seguidillas* from la Mancha, Castile.

Some Other Foreigners Dancing Spanish Dance

The Cachucha continued its success with Fanny Elssler during 1837 through to 1846, Gautier calling Adelina Plunkett and Elssler 'the most authentic Andalusians we have ever come across'.

Bournonville's pupil Lucile Grahn was also to include the *Cachucha* and the *Jaleo de Jerez* in her repertoire. The latter Bournonville was also to stage in 1840 in Copenhagen.

The 'much appreciated Pepita de Oliva' travelled throughout Europe and was found dancing everywhere to much acclaim and criticism. She was in Paris in the late 1850s. Also worth mentioning is the extraordinarily beautiful, Irish-English Eliza Gilbert, who called herself Lola Montez. She led a tempestuous life, causing fights and disruptions wherever she went, including being responsible for the abdication of King Ludwig I of Bavaria. Her life has been painstakingly traced by Bruce Seymour in *Lola Montez: A Life*. Although she was definitely not a notable dancer, she performed the typical dances of the era, such as the *Cachucha*, *El Oleana* (*El Olé*), *Jaleo de Jerez* and *Zapateado* among others. Her escapades were written about in the press in Europe and America, where she died.

Matteo (in 'Woods that Dance', *Dance Perspectives* Spring 1968) says, 'Since few ballet dancers today can play castanets, the Spanish dance in *Swan Lake* is generally performed without them. In the original production of the standard Petipa-Ivanov choreography, however, they were used. As mentioned before, a photograph of the 1895 St Petersburg production shows Maria Skorsiuk and Alexandre Shirayev with castanets in their hands. It also shows, however, that they were not played in the classic style, for they were worn on the third finger of each hand, rather than on the thumb. This is the rustic form of castanet playing, by shaking them rather than using the fingers to play them. Anna Pavlova used castanets worn on the thumb.

Illustration 7.21
Anna Pavlova with castanets.
Drottingholm Theatre Library.

Bailarina or Bailadora?

Baile clásico is the classical ballet as we know it today. The National Ballet of Spain has two companies, the classical Ballet Nacional Lírico, and the Ballet Nacional de España. In Spain they use the classical term *bailarina* for their classical dancers, and it is a paid professional's title. However, for the flamenco equivalent the word is *bailadora* or *bailaora*, the corrupted form of the word.

Considering the number of teachers in each centre, it is not surprising that there are differences in style and technique in the performance of the dances of the Escuela Bolera today. The technique has been polished and brought to a high standard. Bent knees are no longer acceptable to the eye of an audience accustomed to the full extension of ballet, hence the Pericet family's adoption of the extension of arm and leg. In the Bournonville school of ballet this was always present, and the style of the rounded arms can be compared to the Escuela Bolera.

The Romantic style was typical of the time of the Danish choreographer August Bournonville, with rounded arms, held slightly forward from the head when held up in fifth position, and the body slightly forward. This is seen in engravings from that period, and was the style of Spanish dance first known throughout Europe.

Illustration 7.22
Rosita Mauri, from Reus, Catalonia. Ballerina at the Paris Opera.

Harald Lander is said to have polished up the Bournonville ballets and one hopes nothing was lost to history; perhaps the style was retained in the Bournonville classroom exercises. With the intake of so many dancers from other backgrounds nowadays, one wonders how the style will be affected. Certainly the Escuela Bolera style changed in the first half of the twentieth century when Angel Pericet Jiménez influenced the way it was interpreted.

The Pericet Dynasty
The Change in Style of the Escuela Bolera
There are unique differences between the *Bolero* style and ballet (this has been discussed in earlier chapters as well). The style has changed, as it has in ballet. To study the progression into its present accepted style, one has to go back in time to find it.

In Madrid in 1992 there was a very important symposium called the Encuentro Escuela Bolera, organised by Roger Salas of the Ministry for Cultural Affairs. At this gathering of scholars and dance critics, José de Udaeta again confirmed the stylistic change from the forward held arms to the upright position used in ballet today. This I knew, because Eloy Pericet, during my studies with him in Madrid, had answered my question as to how the style had changed. However, Udaeta had studied with Rafael Pericet, the brother, in Seville and learned to dance with the forward pitch of body and arms. This is a very important point. Many people only consider the Pericet version of upright closer arm positions and high elevation *à la seconde* correct. This has now been accepted into the Spanish Dance Society's international syllabus. However, when the dances are performed in the forward style, with the arms held wider apart, they are perfectly correct, and in fact showing the period style of the era in which they were created.

If you study the pictures of dancers and figurines of that era, the arms are held in a very open position, almost at the side of the head rather than over or in front of it. In fact that is what Requejo was setting out to reform. If only a few of these pictures had represented the position one could interpret it as a faulty depiction, but they all seem to be depicted in these open positions.

In Spanish dance the arms move in circles, whereas in ballet they are freer, although the positions are derived from Spanish dance. Certain steps are shared by both, but Spanish classical Escuela Bolera school dances have very unique features. For example, the *jerezana*, or step from Jerez, as it is called, has three walks, the foot points in front and then kicks backward. This form is called *alta* (high). In the *jerezana baja* (low) there are three walks, the foot points in front and then to the back, a step similar to one found in a flamenco *Farruca*. This type of step does not exist in the classical ballet repertoire. There is a toe, stamp of the foot at the start of the verse of *Sevillanas Boleras*, that is typical and is referred to in the notations of the *Cachucha*, by Zorn, as is the *retortille*, a step where the toe and heel form a small beat ending with a stamp on the other foot. A *pas de chat* does not exist in the Escuela Bolera syllabus of steps, nor does it appear in the dances. A *tijeras* is the closest to it, like a turned-in *pas de chat*, with the legs kicking to the sides with bent knees. These above steps are not found in the classical ballet repertoire.

Angel Pericet Blanco maintains, and correctly so, that today the Escuela Bolera is confused with ballet and thought of as an extension of it. He deplores the additions of ballet steps, that have nothing to do with it, such as *arabesques* and *grands jetés*. He goes as far as feeling it wrong to insist on a ballet training, because it produces a different 'look' to the dances.

The eye of today's spectator is ballet-trained and one is inclined to equate the one style with the other. Style is elusive and not easy to define, but in the steps such as the *glissades* and the *pas de basque* one sees a distinct difference to those of ballet. The *glissades* of the Escuela Bolera are stepped, and they glide along the floor. The *pas de basque* are also performed in distinct ways during the different dances of the Escuela Bolera. Sometimes there is a drop onto the foot, at other times a step – but it is not *sauté* as in ballet.

Angel Pericet was invited to join the Ballet Nacional de España as assistant director to Maria de Ávila. This was a great chance to put into place the actual style of the Escuela Bolera on the company's dancers. However, he felt that between 1983 to 1985 he was merely as a spectator. All he managed to do was mount one

Illustration 7.23
Fanny Elssler in the *Cachucha* costume of Florinde in the ballet *Le Diable Boîteux*.
Arcadio Carbonell archive.

Illustration 7.24
Seis Sonatas por la Reina de
España by Angel Pericet,
1985. Ballet Nacional de
España.

choreography for the company, *Seis Sonatas por la Reina de España*, to music by Scarlatti. He feels that although the presentations under Ávila and her successor, José Antonio, have achieved much success, the Spanish side of the company does not advance because the line followed is that of introducing ballet choreographies.

Suffice to say that it is through the Pericet family that this classical syllabus of steps and dances has survived and been handed down to us in a very well documented and pure Spanish classical style today.

8

The Pericet Family

The Pericet Family Heritage

The First Generation: Angel Pericet Carmona
The first generation of Pericet dancers studied with the teachers Amparo Alvares, known as 'La Campanera', and her partner Faustino Segura. (La Campanera was a dancer from the studio of Manuel and Miguel Barrera in Seville.) Angel Pericet Carmona (the First) (1877–1944), known as 'Don Angel', taught in Seville and Madrid. His brother Rafael Pericet Carmona taught in Seville. Another brother, José, taught in the Academy with Angel, but died young. His brother Salvador, with delicate health, did not dance.

The Second Generation: Angel Pericet Jiménez
These were Angel Pericet Jiménez (1899–1973), and his sisters Luisa Pericet Jiménez and Concepción Pericet Jiménes (Concha, Conchita), who danced as 'Las Hermanas Pericet'.

The Third and Present Generation: Angel Pericet Blanco
These are Concepción Pericet Blanco, who is not a dancer, the dancers Angel Pericet Blanco ('El Jefe'), Carmelita Pericet Blanco, Amparo Pericet Blanco, the dancer and teacher Eloy Pericet Blanco, and the teacher Luisa Pericet Blanco (in Beunos Aries, Argentina).

Angel Pericet Blanco, the present patriarch of the family, is affectionately called El Jefe (the chief), by his fellow siblings. He comments on the fact that this Escuela Bolera heritage has been handed down in his family through the male lineage, in a dance form usually associated with (and made internationally famous by) women. His father and grandfather were both married to non-dancers. This tradition, of the inheritance through the male lineage, comes to an end with the present generation. Angel has no descendants and Eloy has two daughters. They have so many pupils now carrying on the tradition, in Spain and Argentina, as well as those who are spread out over the world, that this has less importance today than formerly. Angel maintains that the Escuela Bolera is not dead, but needs reawakening. It is some-how symptomatic of the times and tastes that at present no Pericets teach in Seville, whereas at one stage, in 1927, there were three family members with

Illustration 8.1
La Campanera.

studios in that city. Of interest is that both Don Angel Pericet Carmona and his son Angel Pericet Jiménez stopped dancing at the early age of twenty-six. They were married, and family responsibilities made it easier to teach than to tour the world dancing.

The Pericet Carmona Family

Angel Pericet Carmona

Angel Pericet Carmona (b. Aguilar de la Frontera, 22 February 1877, d. Madrid, 7 October 1944) is known in the family as 'Don Angel'. He became famous as a dancer and teacher, teaching his own brother Rafael, amongst others. He and his and brothers José and Salvador were all Sevillanos, born in Seville, and it was in this city that their careers were nurtured.

Angel studied from the age of five, when his grandmother took him to the classes of Amparo Alvarez, known as 'La Campanera'. She was the daughter of the bell-ringer at the cathedral (*campana* means bell). She taught in the studio of Manuel and Miguel Barrera in Calle Tarifa 1, in Seville. She has been immortalised by the writings of the French author Baron Charles Davillier in his book on his travels in Spain in the 1860s. The sketches of her in the book, by the famous artist Gustave Doré, have recorded her for posterity in a very striking manner. It has given flavour to the whole period in a very distinctive way. Don Angel also studied with Maestro Faustino Segura. Segura was a partner in the studio of José Otero. According to his grandson, Angel Pericet Blanco, 'Don Angel' specialised in the Escuela Bolera, but had also studied regional dances as well with 'La Campanera'.

'Don Angel' is thought of more as a dancer than teacher. His grandson Angel (Blanco) holds him in great esteem as both dancer and innovator. One must remember that he was at the edge of the epoch where the Escuela Bolera had been at its height. Later it was to disappear almost completely.

In 1897 the Grand Café El Teatro el Suizo had its name changed to become El Teatro Palacio Edén. It was situated in the walking street of Seville called Calle Sierpes. Don Angel staged there *El Baile Inglés*, *La Sal de Andalucia*, *La Flamenca* and *Petenera*, amongst all sorts of other presentations that were performed there.

In September 1902, in the Café Concierto Novedades, with dancer Luisa Fernández, he presented in a programme of *Bailes Boleros, Zambra de Gitanos, De Vueltas de la Corrida, En la Playas de Windsor* (a fantasy of English dances) and *Velada de San Juan*. Later that same year he presented at the Salón Concierto

Illustration 8.2
'Don Angel' Pericet Carmona.
José de Udaeta archive.

Illustration 8.3
The partner of 'Don Angel'
Pericet Carmona, 'La Lolita'.
José de Udaeta archive.

Filarmónico y Oriente a new programme of more *Bolero* type dances with his pupil Amalia Molina as principal dancer. She was later to continue her career in the theatre, but as a singer.

Don Angel began his teaching career practising on his younger family members, and opened his first studio at the tender age of seventeen, in Calle Espíritu Santo. This was in 1905. He gradually extended his teaching and soon the 'Académia Pericet' was swamped with pupils wanting to study with him. He therefore moved to larger premises, la Casa de los Artistas in the Plaza de San Juan de la Palma.

In 1905 he formed a *cuadro de baile* when he was asked to perform at the inauguration of the Teatro Nacional in Caracas. He left the teaching of the Escuela Bolera in Seville to his pupil and brother, Rafael. His partner La Lolita is immortal-

ised in a photo, with the ribbons of her shoes tightly tied round her ankles. He also toured throughout Spain. When 'Don Angel' Carmona returned to Seville he resumed his teaching. Rafael Pericet Carmona was also teaching and thus Seville had acquired two studios and teachers from the Pericet family.

According to Marta Carrasco Benítez, several of the pupils went on to a career as dancers and all the children of the well-to-do families in Seville entered his academy. This is still typical today. Children study dancing but may not necessarily pursue the profession on stage. As in the former era, and still today, it is considered a necessary part of the child's education to be able to dance. Teachers like José Otero taught social dances as well in their dance academies.

In 1932 'Don Angel' went to further his career by moving to Madrid. Maestro Cansino left Madrid for America and offered his studio to Angel Pericet Carmona. Cansino's niece was to become famous in Hollywood first as a dancer, and then in an acting career, as Rita Hayworth. At the end of the war, in 1943, 'Don Angel' was joined by his son Angel Pericet Jiménez. It was then that they wrote down all the steps of the Escuela Bolera. The Pericet sisters, Concha and Luisa, decided to move to Madrid to be with Don Angel, and joined him in the studio in Calle Encomienda 10. On 7 October 1944 'Don Angel' died of pneumonia, in Madrid. His son was to continue the Pericet Saga.

Salvador and José
Don Angel's brother Salvador never danced, and José taught in Angel Carmona's studio, but passed away at an early age, dying of dysentery in Tangier, so it seems, while on military service.

Illustration 8.4
Rafael Pericet and his wife and partner La Martinez. José de Udaeta archive.

Rafael Pericet
Rafael (b. Seville, 1875, d. Seville 1956) studied with his brother Angel and also with Maestro Faustino Segura. The latter was a partner in José Otero's studio. Rafael was considered a very strict taskmaster and had very high ideals. This is interesting on two counts. He must have been very successful to be financially secure enough not to be forced to teach other dance forms, as the other dance masters seemed to do. Secondly, in refusing to present the more popular forms of Spanish dancing, he reflects his times. For example, it took a long time for flamenco to be socially acceptable. As we saw with Baron Davillier, the local people often did not stay to see Spanish dances at performances. It was the foreigners who stayed.

So Rafael stood his ground for very good reasons for that period, as his studio had to be refined enough for all the gentry to allow their children to attend it.

According to the research of Marta Carrasco, he considered only the Escuela Bolera good enough to be staged. He refused to consider anything other than that as something to be danced during the *Feria* festivities. He taught barre-work as in a ballet class – and his theatrical performances were presented without any flamenco, only such classical Spanish dances such as *Panaderos de la Flamenca, El Vito, Boleras de Medio Paso* and *Panaderos de la Flor de Maravilla*. This whole period in Spanish dance history was when the *cafés cantantes* reigned supreme and Seville had its dance performances presented in these venues.

Rafael never made dancing his main career, although married to a dancer, 'La Martinez', who gazes lovingly at him in one of the photos. The couple did perform together, but he concentrated mainly on teaching in his own school in Calle Amistad 2. Eloy Pericet thinks that it was he who accompanied his own classes on the violin, like the old ballet-masters used to do.

Illustration 8.5
Luisa Pericet Jiménez. José de Udaeta archive.

Illustration 8.6
Angel Pericet Jiménez. (1899–1973). Eloy Pericet Blanco archive.

He continued to teach Escuela Bolera in the *barrio* of San Juan de Palma in Seville, which he took over when his brother Angel left for Madrid. One of his pupils was José de Udaeta, who learned, amongst others, the dance *La Macarena* from him. After Rafael's death his son continued in the studio with his wife Mercedes Masot and taught their daughter Conchita, who had received her first lessons from her grandfather, Angel.

The Pericet Jiménez Family

Luisa Pericet Jiménez

The sisters Luisa and Concha danced as 'Las Hermanas Pericet' (The Pericet Sisters) until Concha got married. Luisa then added teaching to her career and became established in Madrid, where she taught almost all the great dancers of the era, imparting her choreography to the folklorists of this period. One of her illustrious pupils was Alberto Lorca.

Angel Pericet Jiménez

Although Angel Pericet Jiménez (b. Valencia, 9 April 1899, d. Buenos Aires, Argentina, 23 May 1973) was a very elegant dancer and pianist, he was also to dedicate his life to teaching. He performed with his sisters Luisa and Concha as the 'Trio Pericet', and with a small company in Buenos Aires. His son, Angel Pericet Blanco, the grandson of Pericet Carmona, considers him more of an organiser and maintainer of the heritage rather than an artist and innovator, as his grandfather was. Eloy, his other son, is very proud that his father was not only a pianist, but also a composer, with published music to his credit.

Illustration 8.7
'Trio Pericet', Angel Pericet Jiménez and his sisters Luisa and Concepción, dancing a *Jota Valenciana*, circa 1920. Eloy Pericet Blanco archive.

Angel Jiménez was born in Valencia while his father, 'Don Angel', was there for performances. However, the baptism took place in Seville, the domain of the Pericet family. He received his training from his father, in Seville, and participated from the age of eight in his father's performances together with his sister Concha. Later they were joined by their sister Luisa and they performed as the 'Trio Pericet' between 1922 and 1932. From an early age, he was also teaching his sisters.

His music studies at the Seville Conservatorium commenced when he was ten, with the teachers Font de Anta and Quiroja, after receiving a piano as a gift from his family. This piano is still a proud possession of the family. He also studied at the conservatorium of Madrid and became the composer of the family, who have his published music to prove his prowess. He was co-founder of the Sociedad de Autores, the SGAE. He married Amparo Blanco in Seville on 26 April 1923. Their progeny are the dancers Angel, Carmelita and Amparo and the teachers Eloy and Luisa. Their daughter Concepción did not dance but has always supported the artistic endeavours of her siblings in every way.

He toured throughout Spain and Portugal, and later made a decision that would influence the future of his family: he went to Buenos Aires in 1926, with the Alegría Enhart Company. Once there, with his sisters, the Trio Pericet, he formed his own group of eight performers. He was the sole choreographer and male dancer, performing with them for an extended period in the Teatro Casino in Buenos Aires. Argentina was thriving during this period and had one of the highest standards of living in the world. It thus provided excellent audiences for Spanish dancing. Argentina was also to prove a great attraction for the family, some of whom were later to emigrate there. He returned to Seville to open his own studio in Plaza Zurbaran, but war intervened and he was conscripted into the army in 1936, where he was in the musical corps of his battalion. After being wounded in battle, he was sent home and was able to return to his dance classes.

After his father, 'Don Angel', moved to Madrid, Angel Pericet Jiménez remained in Plaza Zurbarán in Seville until 1942. Amongst his pupils were Rosario and Antonio, who at that time were known as 'Los Chavalillos Sevillanos'. Then he too moved to Madrid from 1943, joining his father in the studio in Calle Encomiendo 10.

Angel Pericet Blanco speaks about the period immediately after the Civil War, when there was a need to go back to the past and preserve what could be lost of Spanish culture. It was during this period that the regional groups were started called 'Coros y Danzas', and it was also at this time that their grandfather 'Don Angel' Pericet Carmona and his son Angel Pericet Jiménez wrote down and grouped the exercises that they remembered of the Escuela Bolera, in a certain way, collected under headings in a manual, 'Tecnicas, pasos y aprendizase de la Escuela Bolera Andaluza', with ten different *vueltas* or turns, and 39 different steps grouped in three courses, each with three sections. There he made notes of the steps in his father's repertoire. He thus transcribed what had been passed on orally by his father and systematised and organised the vocabulary, as well as the practical components. Eloy Pericet and his siblings have further refined the form by setting the exercises to music, with castanet rhythms to accompany them. The steps are usually taught without musical accompaniment.

Angel Pericet Jiménez declined the offer of the position of director of the Conservatorium in Madrid in 1948, preferring to remain in his own studio, which he shared with his sisters Concha and Luisa. Among the many dancers who were trained by him in the Escuela Bolera style were Juan Magriña from Barcelona, Pilar López, Elvira Real and Roberto Ximénez from her company, Carmen Sevilla, Pacita Tomás and her husband Joaquín Villa and many more than one can mention here.

Illustration 8.8   Angel Pericet Blanco.
Illustration 8.9   Luisa Pericet with her award from the Province of Buenos Aires. Pericet family archives.

Angel tried to discourage his children from following such an insecure profession, urging them to take up individual and different careers. His son Angel attended the conservatorium of music and Eloy studied electrical engineering. However, growing up as they did surrounded by dancing from morning to night, this was difficult to impose on them. Although they complied with their father's wishes regarding their studies, they gravitated back to dancing once their studies were completed.

In 1956 Angel decided to join his sister, Concepción, who had married and settled in Buenos Aires. According to his son Angel 'El Jefe' Blanco, this visit became permanent and he started anew to impart his knowledge to the Argentinians together with his sister Luisa. He was teaching until the day before he died in 1973.

The Present Generation: Pericet Blanco

Angel, Carmelita, Eloy and Amparo all performed at the Encuentro Escuela Bolera in 1992. It was a very historic occasion that brought the four present members of the family together to dance in Madrid. Watching them were the most important personalities in the Spanish dance world. In the audience were Pacita Tomás and her husband Joaquin Villa, Victoria Eugenia, Aurora Pons, Alberto Lorca, Mercedes y Albano and their daughter Maria Mercedes León, Luisillo, Pilar López, Nana Lorca and many others including the historian José Blas Vega. From the USA came Carola Goya and Matteo, from Russia, Italy, France, Denmark and elsewhere were all the historians who had presented their papers the week before, including from London, Ivor Guest and his wife Ann Hutchinson Guest, who had reconstructed and notated in Labanotation the Zorn *Cachucha* danced that night by Margaret Barbieri, former ballerina of the Sadler's Wells Royal Ballet in London. On stage were also the performers José Antonio, Aida Gómez and the entire National Ballet of Spain led by Maribel Gallardo, Ana González and Juan Mata; Peter Schaufuss from Denmark came to perform dances from Bournonville's *Toreador*. His partner was Arantxa Argüelles from Zaragoza, and they were accompanied by the pianist Pablo López; also from abroad came Rosario Sárez and Lienz Chang from Cuba.

Angel and Carmelita danced La Maja y el Torero from c. 1850, reconstructed by Angel Pericet to traditional music, which was orchestrated by Juan José García Caffi. The dance was also immortalised in the last century by Gustav Doré. Eloy Pericet and Maria de Amparo performed *Panaderos de la Flamenca* (c. 1870). They all danced *Sevillanas Boleras* (c.1880) reconstructed by the Pericet family and also orchestrated by García Caffi. The evening closed with more Escuela Bolera represented in the first part of

Mariemma's impressive *Danza y Tronio*. The other part of the programme comprised dances from foreign choreographers such as Bournonville, who had been influenced by Spanish dancing of the Bolero type; and Petipa's *Paquita* and *Don Quijote* stunningly danced by Peter Schaufuss. The orchestra was conducted by the well-known Enrique García Asensio.

Angel Pericet Blanco

The eldest son, Angel Pericet Blanco (b. Seville, 28 February 1932), is known fondly by his siblings as El Jefe, the 'boss'. He was urged to study seriously to become a pianist, and attended the conservatoriums in Seville and Madrid. Then one day, in 1947, he was asked to partner a dancer, Elvira Lucena, in the Escuela Bolera style in the Teatro Español in Madrid. After that experience he felt he wanted to spend the rest of his life dancing. He had not found anything that he wished to do more than to dance in public. He persuaded his father that he could practise his piano in each theatre when on tour, and travelled with his music in his luggage, but in fact the dancing took preference. Obviously his training in music has stood him in good stead during his career as a dancer.

He and his sister were the first to leave for South America in 1950 to tour in Argentina, Brazil, Chile, Uruguay, Cuba and Mexico, with a company called Romeria. They moved with the family to Buenos Aires in Argentina, where he and his sister Carmelita perform.

From 1983 to 1985 he was assistant director of the Ballet Nacional de España, during the directorship of Maria de Ávila. He was in charge of their tour to the USA during that period. His sister Concepción, although retired and committed to looking after the family, is not averse to joining in to help Angel with his company every now and again. He has been dancing at the Teatro Nacional Cervantes in Buenos Aires since 1990.

On 14 May 2000, the four dancers of the family, Angel, Carmelita, Eloy and Amparo joined with José Hartmann to give an historic performance in Barcelona's Cultural Centre. *El Vito* was danced by Angel; he and Carmelita were together in *La Maja y el Torero*; *Seguidillas Manchegas* was danced together with Carmelita, Amparo and José Zartmann. All these dances are from the Escuela Bolera, as also are *Soleares de Arcas*, danced by Angel, and *Sevillanas del Siglo XVIII*. The latter two, however, appeared with a group of other dances under the title of *Solera y Duende*. That suite represented the progression of Spanish dancing, starting with the song (*tonadilla*) called *Tirana del Tripili* which he performed with Carmelita, and two

Illustration 8.10 Carmelita Pericet Blanco. Eloy Pericet Blanco archive.
Illustration 8.11 Eloy Pericet Blanco.

solos *Soleares de Arcas* and *Zapateado*. The *Sevillanas* showed the classical one and the folk verses, the *Corraleras*. He also performed a solo to *Triana* and the finale *El Albaicín* in *Suite Albéniz*.

Luisa Pericet Blanco
Luisa Pericet is teaching in Buenos Aires and has been well established there since 1952. She teaches other types of dancing as well as the Pericet style of the Escuela Bolera. She is director of the Grupo de Danza de la Casa de Galicia, one of the most important cultural institutions in Buenos Aires. Under the Cultural Secretariat of the Ministry for Culture, it forms part of the tribunal of the dance examinations in Argentina. In 1993 she was awarded the Premio Manuel de Falla and in 1994 she was honoured by the Argentinian Ministry of UNESCO for her teaching and training of generations of dancers in that country.

Carmelita Pericet Blanco
She is the fifth of the six children, the most beautiful and vibrant member of the Pericet family. Her performance of the *Cachucha* with her brother Eloy in BBC TV's 'The Magic of Dance' bears witness to this. It is very satisfying that this historic talent has been captured for posterity. As with all the Pericet children, Carmelita started to dance from an early age. Her debut, at fifteen, was at the Palacio de la Musica in Madrid in the Imperio Argentina Company, together with her brother Angel and Eloy. Together with her brother Eloy as a partner, they went in 1957 to perform in the Teatro Avenida in Buenos Aires. Angel states that she later joined his company and together they toured the world – to the Opera House in Alexandria, the Kirov in St Petersburg, Carnegie Hall in New York, the Zarzuela Theatre in

Illustration 8.12
The siblings Maria del Amparo Pericet Blanco and Eloy Pericet Blanco. José de Udaeta archive.

Madrid and the Belles Artes in Mexico. The Compañia Nacional de Teatro Clásico and director Miguel Narros commissioned Carmelita to choreograph *Danzas Cortezanas Francesas del Siglo XVII*. The first performance was held in the Teatro

de la Comedia in 1993. She has danced as guest artist in many gala performances in the USA, Canada, Italy, Russia and elsewhere.

On 14 May 2000 she performed with her siblings at the Centro Cultural in Barcelona the dances: *Olé de la Curra* with Amparo, *La Maja y el Torero* with Ángel, *Seguidillas Manchegas* with Angel, Amparo and José Zartmann, all from the Escuela Bolera. In a suite tracing the evolution of Spanish dance she performed the *Tientos* as a solo and *Sevillanas del Siglo XVIII* with the others under the title of *Solera y Duende*. In *Suite Albéniz* she danced in *Puerta de Tierra (Bolero)*, *Triana* and the finale *El Albaicín* with the other three dancers.

Eloy Pericet Blanco

Eloy Pericet, like most of his siblings, was born in Seville and moved with his father to Madrid. He was the principal dancer of the Palacio de la Musica de Madrid. He has also taught at the Málaga Escuela Superior de Arte Dramático y Danza. He and his brother Angel revised all the dances of their grandfather's legacy of the Escuela Bolera for the conservatoires in Andalusia. In 1957, together with his sister Carmelita, Eloy went to perform in the Teatro Avenida in Buenos Aires.

The future of this dance form lies with Eloy, who teaches it in Madrid to the present generation of Spaniards and foreigners, and with his sister Luisa in Buenos

Illustration 8.13
Carmelita Pericet Blanco, Angel Pericet Blanco ('El Jefe'), Lupe Gómez, soloist of the Ballet Nacional de España, Maria del Amparo Pericet Blanco and Eloy Pericet Blanco at the performance at the Ministry of Culture's Encuentro Internacional, 'Le Escuela Bolera', in Madrid, Spain, November 1992.

Aires, Argentina. Because of them, the future of this precious heritage is secure. It will survive as it was taught in the last century in Seville, by his family. Eloy is married to Mercedes Rodríguez and they have two children, Isabel Maria and Esperanza.

On 14 May 2000, the four dancers of the family, Angel, Carmelita, Eloy and Amparo joined with José Zartmann to give an historic performance in Barcelona's Cultural Centre. He and his sister Amparo danced *Panaderos de la Flamenca* in the section in the Escuela Bolera item titled *Cinque Danzas de l'Escuela Bolera*. He joined his siblings in the *Sevillanas del Siglo XVIII* in the *Solera y Duende* suite.

Maria del Amparo Pericet Blanco
Maria, or Amparo as she is known, was born in Madrid when her parents returned there from Argentina. She too joined her brother Angel's company, but first she had performed in the Teatro Odeon in Buenos Aires. She was invited to dance for the Ballet Nacional Festivales España, touring for six months. She was also the prima ballerina in the Zarzuela *Doña Francisquita* at the Colón Theatre. The fifth Biennale in Lyon was dedicated to Spain and she performed there in 1992. She also continues her career as an interpreter. In May 2000 she performed with her siblings at the Centro Cultural in Barcelona dancing, *Olé de la Curra* with her sister Carmelita, *Panaderos de la Flamenca* with her brother Eloy, *Seguidillas Manchegas* with Carmelita, Angel and José Zartmann, they all danced *Sevillanas del Siglo XVIII*, she performed *Lavapies* as a duet with José, *Puerta de Tierra* as a trio with Carmelita and José and in *El Albaicín* they were joined by Angel and Carmelita.

9

Biographical Information

Antonio and Rosario

Antonio Ruiz Soler (b. Seville, 1921, d. Madrid 1996), known as 'Antonio', was probably the most charismatic and famous Spanish dancer of this century. His tuition came from another legendary figure in Seville, Maestro Manuel Real, known as 'Realito'. In his miniature studio on the corners of Alameda and Calle Trajano in Seville, Antonio received dance lessons from the age of six, performing at the Leija International Festival in Seville two years later. Also in the studios was another child, Florencia Pérez Padilla (b. Seville, 1918; d. Madrid, 2000), two years older than he was, who would also become a star. She was later to take the stage name of Rosario. He studied flamenco and *zapateado* with Frasquillo, and Escuela Bolera with Angel Pericet. They first performed outside Spain in Belgium. Together they were to become famous as 'Los Chavalillos Sevillanos', named thus to avoid an earlier title given to them by their French impresario when they performed in the south of France in 1936. For fourteen years they were not to see Spain again, because from there they were hired to tour to Argentina, where they not only became famous, but were seen by the conductor Arturo Toscanini, who arranged their appearances in the USA in 1940.

When they returned it was to the Fontalba Theatre in Madrid in 1949, and from there they toured throughout Europe. Their partnership ended in 1952 after Antonio received the medal of Isabella La Católica. There were many awards to him, such as gold medals from the Circulo de Bellas Artes and the Swedish Royal Academy of Dance, the New York World Fair and the Scala of Milan. He was also awarded the French Legion of Honour, the International 'Vicente Escudero' award of Valladolid, the Spanish National Theatre Prize for best ballet, the key to the City of San Francisco and many others..

Antonio set about forming a company with regular ballet classes, engaging Ivanova as the ballet mistress. His home had a studio and a theatre where the company could rehearse under actual stage conditions before going out on tour. Much attention was paid to the Escuela Bolera style of dance. He himself excelled in all the different styles of Spanish dancing, but he was most famous for his performances of flamenco. The famous *Martinete* solo, captured for posterity in the film *Duende y Misterio del Flamenco*, came from an idea conceived after his return

Illustration 9.1
Rosario and Antonio.
Photo: Roger Wood

to Spain, when he became fascinated by the Coros y Danzas regional groups, and their recuperation of dances lost in the mists of time. He went on a quest for old flamenco singers and musicians and was brimming with new ideas, such as dancing to the beat of a hammer on an anvil, with only a song as accompaniment. He seems to have been the first to do this dance, a *Martinete*.

During his career he appeared in 16 films and choreographed the ballets *El Amor Brujo* and *Tricorne* (also among the many performances filmed for television). His choreography also including his classical *Sonatas*, to music by Padre Soler, and many ballets with regional themes such as *Fantasía Galaica*. He died in 1996 in Madrid after a long illness.

After parting from Antonio, Rosario did solo performances, danced with her own group, or as guest artist with other companies. She also opened a studio in Madrid together with Gloria Librán y Victoria. She was honoured by José de Udaeta at his summer school in Sitges, Barcelona. There she spoke privately of her disappointment at the loss of feminine style and finesse in the dancing of women of the present day. Coming from the school of Realito, which is recognised for precisely those attributes, her voice should be heard and listened to.

In the illustrated *Diccionario Flamenco* of José Blas Vega and Manuel Rios Ruiz, her main awards listed include: La Copa de Plata, New York, 1946; Medalla de Oro from the Circulo de Belles Artes de Madrid; Lazo de Isabel la Católica; Primer Premio Internacional de Interpretación Coreográfica, 1955; Premio de Castanuelas de Plata de la Asociación de Amigos del Arte, 1956; Medalla de Oro de los Festivales Internacionales de Danza, 1958.

La Argentina

La Argentina was born Antonia Mercé y Luque in Buenos Aires, Argentina in 1896, to Spanish parents. She was fated also to die outside Spain. Her parents were both principal dancers at the Teatro Real in Madrid. She lived in Madrid as a child and was taught by her parents. According to Blas Vega, she made her debut at the age of fourteen in the Teatro Romea in Madrid. She was to popularise a specific form of theatrical dance throughout the world, bringing the regional, classical and flamenco styles to audiences with her charismatic presentations. Among her presentations were the classical *Olé de la Curra* and *La Maja y el Torero*. Vicente Escudero said that Pavlova was without doubt the dancer of the century, but La Argentina the dancer of all the centuries, and he devoted an entire chapter to her in his autobiography *Mi Vida*.

In her time La Argentina was considered the Queen of Castanets, and certainly her recordings show her creative sensitivity of interpretation and technical prowess. She had a remarkable charisma and won over audiences in Madrid and abroad. Her first Paris visit in 1905 was an instant success, and she was to divide her time between Paris and London. She performed with the legendary figures Faíco, Antonio el de Bilbao and Realito. She toured the Americas in 1915, making her debut in New York in the Maxine Elliott Theatre. Her repertoire included composers such as Halffter, Esplá, Turina, de Falla, Albéniz and Granados; she also danced to Grieg, Massenet and Valverde. The critic André Levinson said that through her the Iberian dance was elevated to a great art.

Féderico García Lorca introduced her to New York at the Cosmopolitan Club. He called her 'a creator, inventor, indigenous and universal'. In 1925 she was to create with Manuel de Falla *El Amor Brujo* in Paris. In 1928 she staged *La Vida Breve, El Amor Brujo* and *El Retablo de Maese Pedro*. Her death in Bayonne, France, in 1936, was in character because she was constantly on the move.

Illustration 9.2
Antonia Mercé y Luque, 'La Argentina'. Museo del Teatro, Barcelona.

La Argentinita

Encarnación López Julvez, known as 'La Argentinita', was posthumously awarded the medals of Alfonso the Wise and Isabel la Católica for her immense contribution to Spanish dance. She was another great Spanish dancer to be born in Buenos Aires – in 1895, of Spanish parents. She died in New York on 24 September 1945, after a performance. She returned to Spain at the age of six, where her sister Pilar López was born. She danced in Madrid from a very early age. Argentinita was great friends with the poet Federico García Lorca.

Illustration 9.3
'La Argentinita'. By kind
permission of Pilar López.

The sisters Argentinita and Pilar danced together with Vicente Escudero, and a performance of theirs exists on film. It includes a charming trio which they sang and danced, *Lagarterana*, later to be José Greco's great success. La Argentinita toured to Argentina in 1920 and then continued to dance in Paris, London, New York, Milan, Berlin and elsewhere, dancing with several partners – Antonio de Triana, Féderico Rey, José Greco. She was considered to impart dignity and artistry to her dancing. The type of programmes they performed included dances such as *Malagueña, Mallorca, Triana, Jota Alcañiz* and *Farruca Torera* and dances from the Spanish Zarzuelas. She fell ill during a tour of Argentina and Rio de Janeiro. Argentinita continued to the USA and Canada and later Mexico, but her health was clearly failing. After Argentinita passed away, her sister, Pilar López, was to continue to keep her memory alive by choreographing the dance *Pepita Jiménez* (to music by Albéniz), which she performed with two superb male dancers, Antonio Vargas and Alejandro Vega, on tours throughout the world. The dedication on the programme was to the memory of her sister.

María de Ávila

Former director of the Ballet Nacional Español (1983–1986), María de Ávila has been the recipient of countless awards and honours, among them the Premio de Santa Isabel from Zaragoza in 1965 and the San Jorge in 1974, and the Gold Medal from the City of Zaragoza in 1982. An exceptional personality as a teacher and director of several companies, she is also the first dancer to have obtained membership to the Royal Academy of Spain, when she became a member of the Real Academia de Nobles y Belles Artes de San Luis.

In Barcelona, her birthplace in 1920, she studied at the Danza Académica with the Liceo Theatre's famous teacher, Pauleta Pamies. After the death of Pamies, de Ávila continued her ballet studies with Alexander Godinov, a pupil of Cecchetti, giving her the foundation that made her so respected as a teacher of ballet. She also studied Spanish dancing with Antonio Bautista and Antonio Alcarez.

Her career as a dancer started with recitals on her own and with Juan Magriña. At the age of nineteen she became *prima ballerina assoluta* at the Teatro del Liceo. Even then her recitals with Magriña continued. Her teaching career began with the opening of her own school, Estudio de Danza Académica in the capital city of Zaragoza in 1954. Their official inauguration performance took place two years later and from the school have come many of Spain's principal dancers and soloists in companies at home and abroad, among them Trinidad Sevillano, formerly of London Festival Ballet, Arantxa Argüelles and Antonio Castillo, principal dancers

Illustration 9.4
María de Ávila, artistic director of the Ballet Nacional
de Español (1983–1986)

Illustration 9.5
Trini Borrull.

of the Ballet Nacional de España and winners of the gold medal at the Paris competition in 1986, Victor Ullate, Carmen Roche and Ana Laguna who joined the Cullberg Ballet in Sweden. She also opened a school in Madrid, while continuing the one in Zaragoza.

She has been the director of several companies, Compañas de Españolas de Ballet and Ballet de Barcelona as well as the Ballet Nacional Español. It was formed into two companies, dividing the Spanish dance from the ballet. The latter, of exceptionally high standard, was known as the Lírico section of the national ballet company.

Trini Borrull

Trini Borrull was a Spanish dancer, of the type of La Argentina, who danced all the Spanish dance genres, including flamenco. She also wrote a book, *La Danza*

Illustration 9.6
Matilde Coral

Española, published in Barcelona in 1965, in which she described the steps of regional and Escuela Bolera dances, with sketches to show their positions.

She was born in Barcelona, started dancing at the age of ten with Pauleta Pamies and Maestro Coronas (Carlos Pérez Carillo), studying first ballet, and five years later, Escuela Bolera. When she moved to Madrid, she furthered her studies with Julia Castelau and Escuela Bolera with Angel and Luisa Pericet. She became the *prima ballerina* and also choreographer at the Gran Teatro del Liceo there from 1937 to 1947. She toured with Juan Magriña throughout Spain and abroad in Europe. Now living in Las Palmas, she is assessor for the Instituto de la Escuela de Folklore de Las Palmas. At the Encuentro Escuela Bolera in Madrid in 1992, she was on the round table discussion panel and spoke of the dancers' hard lives at the beginning of this century, having to eke out a living dancing at all occasions and under difficult circumstances, especially when touring. Her sense of humour delighted the audience. Alfonso Puig singled out her performance of *Paya y calé* – signifying the two types of dancing in one dance, the aristocratic *paya* (non-gypsy), and the *calé* (gypsy) of which she was master. She was written about with much enthusiasm and appreciation for her star quality and charisma, when performing.

Matilde Coral

Matilde Corrales Gonzáles, known in the theatre as Matilde Coral, was born in Seville in 1935. She is considered an expert on the use of the *bata de cola* or tailfrock, and the style of arm and hand movements. A pupil of Adelita Domingo, she started dancing locally and then danced with Pepe Pinto and Pastora Imperio. She then performed in Madrid at the *tablaos* as well as in Seville.

According to Blas Vega, in the 1960s she formed a group called Los Bolecos with El Farruco and Rafael el Negro, winning the Premio Nacional de Baile de la Cátedra de Flamencologia y Estudios Folkfolklóricos Andaluces de Jerez de la Frontera in 1970 and 1979. She became the main exponent at Andalusian festivals, creating in 1976 for the twenty-first Festival Internacional in Seville a performance she called Flamenco de Matilde Coral. She was honoured by the Conservatorio Dramático y Danza of Córdoba and has won the Juana la Macarrona of Mairena del Alcalor, the Premio de Honor La Argentinita in Córdoba as well as the Pilar López at the

Concours in Córdoba, the Llave del Baile in Seville and many more. In the *Diccionario Enciclopedico Illustrado del Flamenco*, much is written about her way of dancing, quoting many writers who admire her artistry. Today she is also known as a teacher, sharing a studio with her sister Pepa. She is married to Rafael el Negro. Her students can be seen dancing an Alegrias with her in Carlos Saura's film *Flamenco*. It is a dance for which she is particularly famous.

Joan Fosas

Recipient of the Chevalier de l' Olivade from the French city of Nyons in 1969, Joan Fosas was former principal dancer and director of the Esbart Dansaire de Rubí, in Barcelona. He was born in Rubí on 11 April 1938 and at seven years of age he entered the school of the Esbart. He became director of the junior section of this company, the Esbart Infantil, at the age of seventeen, a position he retained for eight years. From 1955 until 1990 he was the pupil of Albert Sans, director of the Esbart Dansaire de Rubí. In 1964 he preceded to study with Juan Magriña, collaborating in several productions at the Gran Teatro del Liceo in Barcelona. He was also studying with Alicia Calado, Sabina Rocamor and Pastora Martos (Pilar Llorens). From 1960 until 1965 he was a member of the Esbart Verdaguer de Barcelona and thereafter again with the Esbart Dansaire de Rubí.

As principal dancer of the Rubí Esbart, he performed throughout Europe at International Festivals in the Palacio de UNESCO in Paris, at the Opera in Modena and Ferrara in Italy, Palacio de Bellas Artes in Mexico, the Music Auditorium in Tunis, in the Liceo, Palacio de la Música and Teatro Romea in Barcelona as well as in Cuba at the Gran Teatro de Habana. He also performed at their official appearances at the Gran Teatro del Liceo in Barcelona in 1980, 1982, 1988 and 1992, and in a performance for the state visit of the British Queen Elizabeth, in the presence of Queen Sofia of Spain, in October 1988.

In 1978 he worked on reconstructing the dances from one of the oldest books on religious dance, dating from the fourteenth century, known as the *Libro Vermell* (The Red Book), together with Padre Gregori Estrada of the monastery of Montserrat and Albert Sans. These were performed later in Berlin, Paris, Andorra and Barcelona as Danses del Libre Vermel de Montserrat. The following year he performed the dance Bolero de l'Alcudia de Carlet in the BBC television series *The Magic of Dance*, by Margot Fonteyn. In 1989 he also choreographed for the first time a ballet, called *Disfressades*, and in 1993 he choreographed *Castellterçol*.

In 1990 and 1992 he was guest artist with the Spanish Dance Theatre of the Spanish Dance Society, in Washington DC, performing with them at sold-out performances at the Kennedy Centre and the Smithsonian Institute, and in New York at the Juilliard School of Music. The performance included *Bolero de l'Alcudia de Carlet* and *Bolero de Torrent* with Nancy Sedgwick, *Seguidillas* with Lourdes Elias and Albert Sans' *Mortitxol*, with Lourdes Elias, Ziva Cohen, Mary Anne Shelton, Paula Durbin, Nacny Heller, Jaime Coronado, Antonio Saldaña, Nelson Sittón and Robert Teri.

From 1996 he became director of choreography of the Esbart Santa Anna of Andorra and collaborated with José de Udaeta in perfecting castanet playing and

♦ See colour plate 1

Illustration 9.6
Maribel Gallardo, *prima ballerina*
of the Ballet Nacional de España.

performing with them. An invitation in 1998 from the Ballet Español in Havana, Cuba, to teach classes in Catalonian dance also led to the staging of the *Bolero de l'Alcudia de Carlet* for them. He also worked on the staging of dances from Villafranca for the Esbart Dansaire de Rubí for their 1999 season.

Maribel Gallardo

Maribel Gallardo was born in Cádiz and trained there with Maria Montes from the age of six. She joined the Escuela de Coros y Danzas, and at the age of fourteen finished her studies at the Conservatorio in Madrid. She is the product of the teaching of Maria Magdalena, Victoria Eugenia, Juana Taft, Pedro Azorín, Juanjo Linares, Aurora Pons, Ana Baselga, Aurora Bosch and Mirta Plá. From the Ballet Folklórico Español, which she joined in 1975, she went on to join the company of Maria Rosa as well as working in companies such as those of Luisillo, and Rafael de Córdoba, as well as Alberto Lorca's Ballet Antologia de Zarzuela (1978) as their ballerina in a series of television programmes.

In 1981 she joined the Ballet Nacional de España, becoming *prima ballerina* in 1985. Ballets performed include *Doña Francisquita* (Alberto Lorca), *Homenaje* (Felipe Sánchez), *Castilla* (José Antonio), *Bolero* (José Granero), *Medea* (José Granero), *Ritmos* (Alberto Lorca), *Danza y Tronio* (Mariemma), *El Sombrero de Tres Picos* (José Antonio), *Bodas de Sangre (Blood Wedding)* (Antonio Gades), *Don Juan* (José Antonio), *La Chacona* (Victoria Eugenia), *Los Tarantos* (Felipe Sánchez) and *Leyenda* (José Granero). She was a guest performer in *En Clave Flamenca*, a performance staged in Paris by the Adrián Galía in 1996.

Aida Gómez

The dancing career of Aida Gómez has been spectacular and she became artistic director of the Ballet Nacional de España in 1997 at the age of thirty. She was born in 1967 in Madrid, and studied ballet and Spanish dancing from the age of seven with many teachers, including Juana Taft, Maestro Ontin, Pilar de Oro, Aurora Pons, Merche Esmeralda, Juanjo Linares, Paco Fernández, Carmina Ocaña, Maria Magdalena, Ciro, La Tati, Manolete, Lola de Ávila, Luis Fuentes, Victoria Eugenia and Aurora Bosch. She attended the Madrid Conservatorium, finishing with honours at the age of twelve. In 1981 she joined the Ballet Nacional de España and was promoted to soloist by Maria de Ávila. Her debut was in soloist roles in ballets choreographed by Antonio, *Sonatas de Padre Soler, Puerta de Tierra* and *Corpus*. Her roles included *Danza y Tronio* (Mariemma), *Ritmos* (Alberto Lorca) and *Medea* (José Granero). After being made *prima ballerina* in 1985, she danced *Sonatas* (Antonio), *Laberinto* (José Antonio), *Los Tarantos* (Felipe Sánchez), and several other ballets by José Antonio, *Soleá, The Three-Cornered Hat* and *Zarabanda*, the last choreographed specially for her.

For the company's tenth anniversary, Antonio Gades came to perform and stage his ballet *Blood Wedding*. She danced the leading role opposite Gades. In José Antonio's ballet *Don Juan* she performed the role of Doña Inéz in 1989. During 1990 the company toured to Russia, where she not only performed La Cachucha and Zarabanda in a gala at the Kirov in St Petersburg, but also performed in other theatres there and in Moscow. She had also toured with the company to the Santander Festival in Spain.

In 1990 she danced in a gala in honour of the memory of La Argentina, and other such galas in Carcasonne and Trieste. In 1992 the Ministerio de Cultura arranged a symposium called Encuentro Escuela Bolera. Once again she appeared at the Zarzuela Theatre to celebrate this occasion, dancing with José Antonio in his arrangement of the classical *Puerta de Tierra*. She left the Ballet Nacional de España to dance with the company of Joaquín Cortés, a former member of the National Ballet. When she returned it was to accept the post as artistic director of the company in 1997.

Illustration 9.7
Aida Gómez, artistic director of the Ballet Nacional de España from 1997.

Ana González

From programmes of the Ballet Nacional one finds out that this elegant dancer was born of Andalusian parents, in Sens, France. She received her classical ballet training there under Latosti and Lucien Legrand, joining the *petits rats* at the Paris Opera school. She furthered her studies at the Paris National Music Conservatoire under Solange Schwartz. In Spain she studied with Nina Parra, Karen Taft, José Granero, Aurora Pons, Vicoria Eugenia, Paco Fernández and Ciro.

Her career was varied, dancing with the Ballets Russes de Monte Carlo, Antonio, Maria Rosa and Pilar López companies. She joined the Ballet Antologia and was a founder member of Alberto Lorca's Festival of Spain company, also performing in Antonio's ballet *Eterna Castilla*. While she collaborated in forming a company with Ciro and Juan Manuel, she performed in BBC television programmes as well as at international festivals.

When Gades directed the Ballet Nacional Español she became a member of the company, dancing in ballets by Antonio, Pilar López, Mariemma, Rafael Aguilar and Gades. She danced in the ballets of Antonio under his directorship and in Luisillo's *Don Quijote*. She represented the company at the Gala of Stars in Helsinki

Illustration 9.8
Ana González, former *prima ballerina* of the Ballet Nacional de España.

during the company's period under Maria de Ávila and excelled in Mariemma's *Danza y Tronio*, Alberto Lorca's *Ritmos*, *Doña Francisquita* and in Victoria Eugenia's *Danza IX*. She danced in the first performance of *Medea* in 1985 with the choreographer José Granero, when it was performed at the Spoleto Festival, in the USA in New York, Washington and Charleston, and in Russia, Australia, Greece and Colombia. She performed in Gades' *Blood Wedding* to celebrate Ballet Nacional's tenth anniversary and remained with them until her retirement, performing in many of José Antonio's ballets when he was the director.

Carmen Gordo

Carmen Gordo Sobrino, born in Paracuelles del Jarama, is the recipient of the award of the Folklore Hidalguía of the Casa de Castilla la Mancha of Madrid. It is the first such award and she was unanimously voted for the honour, as 'professor', a title bestowed on her by the Royal Conservatory of Madrid. Gordo is deserving of this honour. It recognises her research and preservation of the music, dances, folklore of Spain, as well as the teaching to which she has dedicated her life. She has taught the Coros y Danzas of Madrid their entire repertoire of dances of the Goya period in Madrid. During her travels throughout the 1960, collecting the dances, she also included the dances from two Manchegan towns, Malagón and Fuente del Fresno.

A fiery, enthusiastic exponent of her country's regional dances, she worked closely with the musicologist García Matos and Maria Esparza during the 1950s, the period when the Coros y Danzas of Sección Feminina de la FET y JONS was founded to preserve the folklore of Spain. She has directed many of these folk dance groups and imbued them with her lively temperament. Her main contribution has been to the Coros y Danzas of Madrid, where she now directs their school.

In the 1960s she formed a group of dancers in Santa Cruz, Tenerife, both directing and teaching them, and collaborating with Maestro Rosén in the reconstruction of dances. More recently she has been teaching children for performances on television programmes, and has taught classes to the Grupo de Francisco de Goya in Madrid. She is also recipient of the Llave de los Martínez of the TVE, and was honoured in New Orleans at the ASTA convention.

Her parents and grandparent are from Santa Cruz de Mudela in the province of Ciudad Real. She is married and has a daughter, Aurora, who also is a dancer, though not by profession.

José Granero

Granero is a choreographer who moved from Argentina to the USA and then to Spain. He was part of the Ballet de Madrid company with José Antonio in the

1980s. His most famous ballets are for the Ballet Nacional de España: *Medea* (1984), with script (based on Seneca's text) and designs by Miguel Narros and music by guitarist and composer Manolo Sanlúcar, premiered at the Metropolitan Opera in New York; and *La Gitanilla* (1996), to music by Antón García Abril. He choreographed, to Ravel, *Alborada del Gracioso* (1985) and *Bolero* (1987; he has done several versions of this ballet). To music by Isaac Albéniz and José Luis Greco he choreographed *Leyenda* in 1994. *Cuentos del Guadalquivir* was to the music of Joaquin Turina, also in 1994. For the Ballet Nacional's company called the Lírico he choreographed *Maria Estuardo*.

Granero experimented fusing Spanish dance with his modern dance experience in his ballet *Don Giovanni*, for Antonio Gades' company, with the theme by Alfredo Mañas. This created a trend in Spanish dance – and not necessarily in its best interests, according to some of the older dance teachers, as it was the first time the folk traditions were not drawn from. But Granero felt it was a fusion with rather than a departure from Spanish dance. He choreographed for several films and television programmes about *zarzuelas*, also choreographing for *zarzuelas* for the

Illustration 9.9
Bolero, choreography by José Granero. Ballet Nacional de España.

♦ See also colour plate 37

Illustration 9.10
Ballet Nacional de España:
two guest stars, Antonio
Márquez and Lola Greco in
Danza y Tronio with
choreography by
Mariemma and music by
Soler, Boccherini and
Garcia Abril. Photo Paco
Ruiz. Marina Keet archive

company that was forerunner of the National Ballet, where he was both ballet master and choreographer.

Ballet Español de Madrid was the co-operative company he founded with members of the Gades company. For this company he choreographed *El Jaleo*, *Diágolo del Amargo*, *Albaicín*, *Homenaje a Albéniz* and *Hamlet*. For Manuela Vargas he staged two ballets, *La Petenera* and *El Sur*. Merche Esmeralda formed the Ballet de Murcia for which company he choreographed *Sinfonia Española* and *Triana*. His ballet *Las Furias* was for the Festival de Mérida.

His dance training was in the school of the Teatro Colón in Buenos Aires, where he also performed in ballets and operas. He won a grant to study in the USA from whence he went to Les Ballets Russes de Monte Carlo, New York City Ballet, American Ballet Theatre, and the Contemporary Ballet Theatre under Hanya Holm and Martha Graham. As principal dancer he performed in many companies: Ballet Teatro Argentino in Ciudad de la Plata, Renata Shotelius Ballet de Danza Moderna, Bashkar Indian Dance Company (at the Brooklyn Academy Theatre in New York) and with the Ximenez/Vargas Ballet Español, preferring to dance with them rather than joining the first performance of *West Side Story*. It was this move that decided his career in Spanish dance. After this he danced in the companies of Luisillo, Mariemma and Pilar López, the last profoundly influencing his style.

Lola Greco

Greco is the daughter of the dancers José Greco and Lola de Ronda, and was born in Madrid. Greco was a late starter and at fourteen years of age enrolled at the National Ballet School in Madrid, where she received her training for three years. She was immediately cast as the younger sister in *Rango* based on Lorca's play *La*

Casa de Bernarda Alba. The choreography was by Rafael Aguilar. Her next important role was Candela in *El Amor Brujo*, choreographed by Antonio. At nineteen
she was made *prima ballerina* at the Ballet Nacional de España. She has performed
in many places in Europe: in Paris with choreographer van Hoecke, at La Fenice in
Venice, La Scala in Milan and other French and Italian cities. She has toured widely
in the United States with her father José Greco and his company, including at the
Kennedy Center in Washington DC and the Joyce Theater in New York. She has
also performed in many galas and homages to such dancers as Mariemma (*Las
Divinas de Pisa* by Aguilar) and La Argentina (*Danza de los Ojos Verdes* to Granados,
and *La Cariñosa* to music compiled by Didi Aguinaldo).

Choreographers have created roles for her such as Julieta in Felipe Sánchez's
Los Tarantos, and in Victoria Eugenia's *Danza IX*. José Antonio created the role
'lechery' for her in *Laberinto*, and the ballets *Yerma, Rango, La Noche de San Juan
de la Cruz* with Rafael Aguilar.

Illustration 9.11
José Antonio (Ruiz), artistic
director of the Ballet
Nacional de España, 1986–
1992.

José Antonio (Ruiz)

José Antonio was director of the Ballet Nacional de España from 1986 to 1993, and
their principal dancer from 1985 until his departure in 1993. He brought a contemporary mode to Spanish dancing in the Ballet Nacional. A child prodigy, he was

born in Madrid in 1951 and his dance training started at the early age of four. When he performed at the age of eight years in Buenos Aires, he was regarded as a phenomenon. His diverse studies in all forms of Spanish dance came from the teaching of Victoria Eugenia, Alberto Lorca, Héctor Zaraspe, José Granero and, amongst others, Pedro Azorín (*Jota Aragonesa*), and ballet with the Danish teacher in Madrid, Karen Taft.

He was to dance professionally for the first time in the company of Maria Rosa and thereafter as principal dancer with the great Antonio. Although not related, they shared the same surname of Ruiz, leading to much confusion and also some amusement with Antonio calling him 'my son' in public.

Together with his wife Luisa Aranda, he started his own company in 1972, Ballet Silhouetas, also beginning a choreographic career with *Pepita Jiménez* and *Pas de Quatre* to Pablo Sorazábal's music. In 1978 he became the leading dancer of Spain's newly founded Ballet Nacional under the directorship of Antonio Gades. There he remained until 1980, when Gades departed. In 1982 he founded his second company, Ballet de Madrid, for which he created, amongst others, *Variaciones Flamencas* and, to the music of guitarist/composer Emilio de Diego, *Desenlace*. Diego is the composer of the ballet *Blood Wedding* (Antonio Gades).

He returned to the Ballet Nacional under María de Ávila in 1985 as their star performer, and became director the following year, combining it with the post of principal male dancer. To date his is the longest directorship of the company, which has grown in strength and numbers. He invited the choreographer José Granero to stage several ballets, Ravel's *Bolero* (in several versions), *Medea* with music by Manolo Sanlúcar, and in 1988 he performed together with Gades in his ballet *Blood Wedding* with music by de Diego. This was also the year in which the company was awarded, by the Association of Entertainment Critics, the prize for the Best Artistic Performance at the Metropolitan Opera House in New York.

His own creations for the company were many: Manuel de Falla's *The Three-Cornered Hat* with the original Picasso designs, *Laberinto* with an original score by Xavier Montsalvatge, *Con mi Soledad* with accompaniment by ultra-modern Valencian musician Carlos Santos, *Soleá* with music by Manolo Sanlúcar. He used the music of José Nieto for his *Don Juan* with a script by Miguel Narros. Other creations for the company were *Alborada del Gracioso* with music by Ravel, *Zarabanda* (Nieto) and *Romance de Luna* (Nieto).

His career included choreography for foreign ballet companies, in operas and performing in films, for Antonio amongst others. In 1967, together with Luisa Aranda, he appeared in *Fantasía Galaica* at La Scala in Milan. In 1975 he choreographed for the opera *Carmen* in Bologna. In 1981 he returned to La Scala to stage the dances in Mozart's *Marriage of Figaro*. He appeared in the film *The Ballerina* with Carla Fracci and Peter Ustinov. In 1988, Alicia Alonso requested that he stage his choreography of *The Three-Cornered Hat* for the Cuban National Ballet in Havana. He also used the music of Nieto for his ballet for the Kirov with Natalia Makarova, *Romance de Luna*, performed in Leningrad on 20 December 1990. His performance was said to be the first of any Spanish dancer on the Kirov stage. The Kirov also took into their repertoire his choreography *Zarabanda*.

Currently he is once again director of a company, Compañia Andaluza de Danza, in Seville, each member the calibre of a soloist, bringing to the performances a unique quality of freshness and a new period of creativity in his career. His programme at the end of 1998 included two works by the flamenco dancer and teacher Manolete: *Latido Flamenco*, with the singer Enrique Morente, and Javier Latorres' *Cosas de Payos*, to illustrate the two ends of the scale between the Gypsies and the non-Gypsies. Both had a favourable reception from the critics, appreciating the beauty and sensitivity of themes and dancers. He also has the responsibility of directing the Arts School (Programa Cultural) of Andalusia, situated in an old convent in Seville where, in large airy studios, the dancers are trained in all forms of dancing, including Spanish dancing.

'La Quica'

'La Quica' (b. Seville, 1905, d. Madrid, 1967) was another exponent of Escuela Bolera who taught in Madrid from 1932. She was artistic director of El Arco de Cuchilleros from its inauguration in 1961 until 1967. She was born Francisca González Martínez and she married the well-known flamenco dancer Frasquillo. They were the parents of Mercedes León and grandparents of Maria Mercedes León. According to Blas Vega, 'La Quica' danced at the Kursaal with Antonio de Triana in 1927. She formed a partnership with her husband in 1928, touring throughout Spain with Antonio Chacón. She and her husband performed in London in 1951, and in 1953 returned there for a presentation by the Royal Academy of Dancing at the Albert Hall. She was highly thought of as a dancer and artist, and toured internationally with José Greco's company in 1953, her repertoire encompassing not only flamenco, but other styles such as Escuela Bolera as well. Her ability as a teacher was held in high esteem.

Pilar Llorens

Llorens, who performed under the name of Pastora Martos, commenced her ballet studies at the age of twelve in Barcelona. She continued with Phyllis Bedells in London, as well as studying Spanish dancing there with Elsa Brunelleschi. Her professional career as a dancer was from 1954 to 1968. She then pursued her interest in dance in diverse ways by teaching, writing and choreographing and she has also become a respected dance historian. Until its

Illustration 9.12
'La Quica' and José de Udaeta.
José de Udaeta archive.
Illustration 9.13 Pilar Llorens.

Illustration 9.14
Pilar López.
Pilar López archive.

dissolution, she was the editor of *Montsalvat*, until recently the only dance and opera magazine in Spain. She was a member of the UNESCO International Theatre Institute, the International Institute of Choreographic Arts in Paris and the International Dance Alliance in New York. Her daughter, Gala, was a member of the Ballet Nacional de España for many years. Pilar Llorens died in 1998.

Pilar López

Her choreographic career has gained her many prizes and medals. According to José Blas Vega they are: Premio Nacional Coreográfico Amadeo Vives (1947), in New York two silver cups for the best choreography of Spanish dances, the gold medal of the Círculo de Belles Artes de Madrid (1954), the cross and the ribbon of Dame of the Order of Isabel La Católica, the key and a plaque of her city of birth, San Sebastian (1965), a figure of a bull from '*el gremio de hostelería le otorgo*', the Saggitario D'Oro from Italy, and the Cruz de Oro del Instituto Internacional de Cultura. She was an artist of rare stature, pure style and elegance as a dancer, and had a great influence on many dancers.

Pilar López was born Pilar López Julvez in San Sebastian in 1912. She started her professional career at the age of fifteen by giving concerts in which she not only danced but also played the piano and sang. She wanted her own career separate from that of her sister, La Argentinita, according to José Blas Vega. In 1934 she joined with her sister to dance together. She stylised flamenco, and together with Rafael Ortega danced recital programmes. This was in 1934. They toured Europe and the Americas, and after the death of her sister in 1945, she formed her own company, the Ballet Español de Pilar López.

She certainly had an aura of elegance and distinction, and brought her own style to the dancing. Everything she presented was in the best taste. Her success with her own company, after the death of her sister, was witness to this unique talent. She influenced many male dancers who all started out as her partners. Among them were Alejandro Vega, Roberto Ximénez, Manolo Vargas – who can all be seen dancing with her in the film made in the 1960s called *Duende y Misterio del Flamenco*. In her programmes, as in those she danced with her sister, she produced all forms of Spanish dancing, including the Escuela Bolera. In the above-mentioned film is another of her partners, Alberto Lorca, seen in *Panaderos de la Flamenca* with members of the company.

López was deeply affected by her sister's death, and created the dance *Pepita Jiménez* (Albéniz) in her memory. She danced this choreography with Vega and Vargas. José Blas Vega lists her choreographies in his excellent *Encyclopaedia of Flamenco*. Her ballet *Concierto de Aranjuez* was placed into the repertoire of the

Ballet Nacional Español in 1979, but has not been performed for many years. Antonio Gades, another of her protegés, considers her to have the purest Andalusian style. She is elegance personified on and off the stage.

Alberto Lorca

In 1974 Lorca was awarded the Vicente Escudero gold medal. He was a latecomer to dance, starting at the age of twenty, studying Escuela Bolera from 1947. He laughs at the very idea of starting so late, and yet nothing seemed difficult to him. At the Teatro Español during the 1940s, children's shows were presented every two weeks by the second director, Roberto Carpio. Lorca saw these afternoon performances and was completely enraptured by the magic and beauty of it all. The director noticed him and asked him to do a *jeté*, which he did; and then he was given another step to perform and then another – and he could do them all. Before long, to his surprise, he was performing a polka in the Sunday performance the following week. For six months this continued and suddenly he was enrolled in the classes of Luisa Pericet and his formal dance studies of the Escuela Bolera began. He also studied

Illustration 9.15
Alberto Lorca.
Alberto Lorca archive.

with Angel Pericet Carmona. Within six months he was again plunged into performing. This time it was in the opera *Aida*, with choreography by José de Udaeta. From there he graduated as leading dancer in a German revue, Berlin Scala, presented by Duisberg, who regularly brought such shows to Barcelona and Madrid. He also studied classical ballet with Karen Taft, the Danish teacher who laid such good foundations for Spanish dancers. His repertoire of classical dances was the *Panaderos de la Flamenca* (seen in the film *Duende y Misterio del Flamenco*) and *Panaderos Tertulia, La Maja y el Torero, Bolero Liso, Bolero de Medio Paso, Boleras con Cachucha, Malagueñas* and *Seguidillas Boleras*.

After this flurry into the lighter side of dance he once again pursued formal studies, this time in the classes of El Estampío in the studios in Relatores 20, two floors up a broad staircase. Estampío taught in bedroom slippers, but Lorca managed to absorb it all. These were the studios where all the companies came to rehearse their touring programmes. He was called in to be introduced to Pilar López. A month later she called on him to replace a dancer, and he found himself performing in the ballet *Los Cabales*. He also danced the classical *Bolero Liso*. With him in the company were seasoned performers like José Greco and Manolo Vargas.

During the mid-1950s and 1960s the performances of the Spanish dance companies represented regional and classical dancing as well as flamenco. In 1947

Illustration 9.16
Nana Lorca, co-director of
the Ballet Nacional de
España, 1993–1997.

Lorca joined Pilar López's company where he and others danced in all these styles. He danced the classical *Panaderos*, and for years performed the highly exciting *Puerta de Tierra* choreographed by Luisa Pericet to music by Isaac Albéniz. Lorca toured with the López company to Buenos Aires and Mexico, and then in Argentina fell ill with debilitating asthma. In those days it was untreatable, thus he retired from performing but remained with her as artistic adviser and ballet master until ill-health forced him to return to Madrid.

It proved to be the start of a new career as an inventive and theatrical choreographer. José Tamayo, the director of the Zarzuela Theatre, recruited Lorca in 1956 to choreograph the dances in the *zarzuelas* that were presented in his theatre. It has been a lasting partnership. The *zarzuelas* are a unique Spanish form of musical theatre, falling between opera and operettas and representing every region of Spain. They often require a special way of singing. Often set in the various regions of Spain, they require specialised choreography. This venture has shown Lorca at his most inventive, and he has audiences riveted with *Jotas* from Aragon or Navarra, *Charradas* from Salamanca, Andalusian *Tangos* or the thrilling dance from *La Boda de Luis Alonso* that builds to a climax with the audience clamouring for more, as well as the *Boleros* of Ravel and Sorazábal. He also choreographed for their outdoor performances such as *La Destrucción de Sagunto*, *Romeo and Juliet* (after Shakespeare, and J.M. Pemán and Lope de Vega's famous play Fuenteovejuna). While choreographing for films he worked with stars such as Sara Montiel, Raphael, Rocío Durcal and Ava Gardner. For Spanish television he was head of choreography for their Antologia de la Zarzuela programmes as well as Divertido Siglo.

In 1960 he formed a company, Lorquiana, and performed at the New York World Fair in 1964. Together with Maria del Sol and Mario de la Vega he founded, in 1973, the Antología Company and toured it throughout the world. He formed the Ballet Nacional Festivales de España in 1975 and this became the Ballet Nacional de España. For them he choreographed *Ritmos* (1984) and *Doña Francisquita* (1985). His ballets for the Ballet Nacional de España are still in the repertoire.

Nana Lorca

Nana Lorca was born in the town of Lorca in Murcia, and studied at the Royal Conservatory in Madrid. Her teachers included many famous names such as Alberto Lorca, Pedro Azorín (*Jota Aragonesa*), Mariemma, Paco Fernández, Juanjo Linares, Enrique 'El Cojo', Maria Magdalena, and Karen Taft, José Granero and

Héctor Zaraspe (ballet). In 1950 she began studying
Escuela Bolera with Luisa Pericet Jiménez.

She is a very positive person and considers that
she was very blessed in everything she undertook to
do, and has achieved much success. From 1951 her
professional career as a dancer started, and she went
on tour for four years in Spain and the USA, as
partner to Jesús Sevilla. Pilar López engaged her as
prima ballerina in 1956; she remained until 1960,
when she joined the Compañia Folías directed by
Roberto Carpio, to perform in New York as their
star. Next she joined the company of José Greco,
soon becoming co-star and choreographer. They performed together on television in the USA's *Ed
Sullivan Show*, and with famous stars such as
Donald O'Connor, Abbe Lane, Tony Martin and
Frank Sinatra. She was also to marry Greco.

For a while she joined Alberto Lorca's company,
Lorquiana, performing at the New York International
Festival and at the Gran Teatro de Liceo in Barcelona. She even formed her own company. She had
much success everywhere. In 1985 she was invited
as guest artist to the Ballet Español de Madrid, directed by José Antonio and worked closely with
José Granero.

In Spain she was invited to collaborate in courses
with Maria de Ávila and Caracolillo and she also
gave more dance courses at the universities in Chi-
cago, Boston, Los Angeles and New York. When

Illustration 9.17
Luisillo.
Luis Pérez Davila archive.

José Antonio became director of the Ballet Nacional de España and he found
dancing and directing too much of a burden, she was offered, in 1987, the post of
vice director. She accepted and in 1993 she became one of the three directors who
took over after his contract expired. The three women were very organised. They
divided the work so that Nana Lorca took charge of the artistic direction, Victoria
Eugenia was the dance director and Aurora Pons was in charge of the management.
The ballet company achieved much financial success during their term and toured
internationally. The three directors remained in office until 1997.

Luisillo

A choreographer of rare theatrical talent, Luis Pérez Dávila, otherwise known as
Luisillo, was born in Mexico in 1927. His choreography is musically sensitive in the
way that Balanchine's is. His version of Ravel's *Bolero* is masterful. His awards and
honours include the Ben Meritate medal from the Secretary of State of the Vatican
for his production during a reunion of Gypsies from all over the world. From Spain
his recognition came in the Cross of Isabella la Católica; and from Italy, La Rosa de

Illustration 9.18
Arcadio Carbonell of the Madrid
Conservatoire, and former
member of Antonio's company,
with Juan Magriña.
Arcadio Carbonell archive.

Garda from Verona, Medaglia de Oro di Teatro La Fenice, Golden Archer of RAI in Rome, Sagitario de Oro of Fuggi, the Medal of the Order of San Ambrosio in Milan. The Eurovision Prize was awarded for his ballet *Don Quijote*, when it was televised; he also won the Gold Medal of the International Dance Festival in Wales, the Gold Aztec of Teatro de Belles Artes (Cultural Olympiad) in Mexico, the Silver Giraldas for the best choreography and best programme at the Festival Internacional in Seville.

His company Luisillo y su Teatro de Danza Española was founded on 1 September 1956. They have toured many times to Australia, New Zealand, South Africa, the Philippines, Thailand, Japan, Malaysia, the USA, where he premiered Turina's *Sinfonia Sevillana*. The Ballet Nacional Español presented his ballet *Don Quijote* during their 1983/84 season and also on their tour throughout Europe. His theatrical experiences have been varied. In the presence of Pope Paul IV he premiered *El Hijo Pródigo* in the Vatican's Clementine Room, and later *Cristo Luz del Mundo* in the Basílico de Mazencio. Many of his ballets have appeared on foreign television programmes.

He had wanted to be a bullfighter, but after seeing Carmen Amaya dance he followed her to the USA, where she trained him as a flamenco dancer. He had had some dance training in Mexico. He danced in her company and finally arrived in Spain via Argentina. He danced for the first time in the Teatro de Madrid in 1948. In 1949 he and Teresa Viera Romero, who had also been in Amaya's company, teamed as a couple to perform as Teresa y Luisillo. Their picture was used on the cover of the printed music of the *Zorongo*. Together with Teresa he formed his own company in 1950, and toured in Europe and England. The following year he extended his tours to North Africa and the year after that as far as the United States and Argentina. From then on he steadily built on the enormously enthusiastic reception he received everywhere, extending his tours to include Australia from 1962, Japan and the Far East and other outlying countries such as South Africa, where he took his company seven times within ten years.

Because of his extensive touring, he has had an enormous influence on foreigners and their perception of Spanish dancing. His programmes were an excellent mix of classical, regional and flamenco, all beautifully costumed, staged and professionally presented with orchestras and flamenco guitarists and singers. His music master was Maestra J. Ruiz Azagra, who composed and orchestrated the music. In South Africa the enthusiasm reached such a peak that it led to the formation of the Spanish Dance Society, a group of teachers codifying the steps of Spanish dancing into a method and examination system with a syllabus. This has now spread worldwide and their method is also taught in Spain. Luisillo was invited to be Patron of the Society. The enthusiasm he engendered in Japan has led to Japanese guitarists and dancers flocking to Spain to study. In Belgium the performances led to an open-ended invitation to return to a particular theatre annually. He also performed in Madrid in between touring, something his company still does.

In 1963 the company performed at the Festivale de España, and produced a record, 'Luisillo y su Teatro de Danza Española', which has his ballets, *Sanlúcar de Barrameda*, *Rias Baixas* (Galicia), the moving *Romance Cordobés*, beautifully sung by his wife Maria Vivo and the flamenco *Alegrias Romeras*. In the company at that stage were Conchita Antón, Carmen Aracena, Nuria Ranz, Angeles Tirado, Juan Ortega, Antonio Salas, Enrique Segovia and Antonio Vega. The *cantaor* was José Salazar and guitarists Antonio Zori 'Muñeco', Antioco Moracho and Manuel Sisón. Azagra was the music master, and through the years his best friend, Roberto Zafra, was his manager, confidant and friend. Their humour was legendary. Zafra was to become the superintendent of the Ballet Nacional de España.

In 1964 Luisillo produced his ballet about *Don Quijote*, to music by Moreno Torroba and songs by Juaquin Calvo Sotelo, which he was able to draw on when asked in 1981, by Antonio, to produce it for the Ballet Nacional de España. He inaugurated the fifth Festival de Musica, Danza y Teatro in 1966, going on to Russia and finding it emotionally draining experience. He was also to visit China in 1984/85. He has toured to Hungary, Estonia, Budapest and many times to Italy to direct performances or dances in Operas.

Since 1996 he has again presented masterful choreographies such as *La Malquerida*, based on Benavente's play of that name, using regional dances and customs; *Carmen*, a ballet about Carmen Amaya; and *Romeo and Juliet*. Luisillo now oversees the dance schools in Madrid as well as touring with his company. For some years he had his own *tablao*, which he named Los Cabales.

Juan Magriña

Juan Magriña Sanroma (b. 1903, d. 1995) was a pupil of Carlos Llongueras. Magriña's partner, Maria de Ávila from Zaragoza, studied the Escuela Bolera

Illustration 9.19
Mariemma.
Mariemma archive.

dances in Madrid with Luisa Pericet. Together they performed recitals and tours. He also toured with Trini Borrull, from Madrid. With these dancers and Rosita Segovia and Maria Luisa Nogues, Magriña took Spanish dancing to the Spanish towns. In 1951 he founded Los Ballets de Barcelona, touring Spain and abroad to Paris. The company was incorporated into that of the beautiful, old, historic Liceo Theatre in Barcelona, which tragically burned down in 1994. He was choreographer, director and principal dancer. He also formed a cultural association, Cultural del Ballet, to promote ballet. He retired as a dancer in 1957, but programmes of classical ballet and Spanish dancing continued to be performed under his direction. He was the recipient of many medals and honours, and was the teacher of many generations of Spanish ballet dancers. His legacy is continued by his many pupils and in Madrid by his pupil Aurora Pons, who was principal dancer of the Ballet Nacional de España and later a co-director of the company.

Mariemma

Mariemma, honoured in 1987 with the medal Lazo de Dama de Isabel la Católica, is also an exponent of the Escuela Bolera style and teaches it in Madrid in her own school. A strange turn of fate caused Mariemma (Guillermina Martínez Cabrejas, born in Iscar, Valladolid in 1917), to study her native dances in Paris, where she moved with her parents from the age of four. She was enrolled at the age of ten for dance classes at the Théâtre Châtelet. She studied the Escuela Bolera with Francisco de Millares, who had been principal dancer in St Petersburg. Later she studied with another exponent of the Escuela Bolera, Juan Martínez.

She returned to Spain in 1943, and performed in the Teatro Español. Because of the Second World War, touring possibilities were confined to Spain, Portugal and Morocco. In 1947 her home town of Iscar, in Valladolid, honoured her by naming a street after her (Valladolid itself was to name a street after her in 1973). The following year she went on an extended tour of Latin America and in 1949 went to North America under the auspices of Sol Hurok. Her second tour there followed in 1950 and included Canada, and Hispanic countries. It was then that she was awarded the Premio Nacional de Danza. In 1949 she performed in England and then in 1951 presented a recital programme throughout Europe and Central America. She performed *The Three-Cornered Hat* and *Capricho Español* at La Scala, Milan, and was honoured with the Medalla de Oro of the Bellas Artes. (She was to return in 1954 as guest artist.)

Recital tours and performances with Léonide Massine in Santander, and Holland followed in 1953. In 1955 she formed her own company called Mariemma Ballet de España, and was awarded the Premio Nacional de Coreografía after her Madrid performance. Her touring continued in 1957 as far as the World Fair in Thailand, and the Marquis de Cuevas invited her to choreograph a ballet for his company, to which she returned in 1959 as guest artist.

Her touring continued unabated and she also started her own school in 1960, and created a series of television programmes over a period of five months. By 1964 she had enlarged her company to 45 members, performing at festivals and at the World Fair in New York, where she was awarded the Gold Medal at the Spanish Pavilion. She was also given the Vicente Escudero medal for the best ballet. The next highlight for her company was performing with Herbert von Karajan in Salzburg in *Carmen*. In 1967 at La Scala she presented the dances for *La Vida Breve* and her ballet *Iberica*. The following year she was awarded the Medalla de Plata al Mérito Turistico. She was asked to direct the teaching, in 1969, of the Real Escuela Superior de Arte Dramatico y Danza de Madrid. In 1970 she produced an interesting programme on her thoughts on dance for television.

Her choreography has also been staged for the Ballet de Wallonie in 1973. In 1976 she produced three de Falla ballets to commemorate his birth: *El Amor Brujo*, *Sombrero de Tres Picos* and the dances from *La Vida Breve*. This was followed by another TV ballet, on Ravel's *Bolero*. In Rome she was awarded the Sagitario de Oro, Premio Internationale dell'Arte given to international artists of merit, and she was named President of the Spanish Committee of Conseille Internationale de la Danse (CIDD) of UNESCO, and made an honorary member. In 1979 she created two ballets for the Ballet Nacional de España, *Ballet Vasco* and *Fandango*. She became director of the Real Escuela Superior de Arte Dramatico y Danza de Madrid in 1980. She also went to Paris to perform in *Carmen* at the Opéra.

What concerns us is her specialisation of Escuela Bolera steps and style explained in her book *Tratado de Danza Española, Mariemma, Mis caminos a travé de la danza*, published in 1997. She was awarded the Premio Nacional Coreográfico and later the Premio Certamen de Danza Española for her ballet based on Ravel's *Bolero*. In 1981 the King bestowed on her the Medalla de Oro al Mérito de Belles Artes and in 1995 the above-mentioned Lazo de Dama de Isabella la Católica. In 1995 she was awarded the Chevalier de L'Ordre des Arts y Lettres by the Ministry of Culture in France.

In 1982, she performed at the Kennedy Center in Washington DC, and Marina

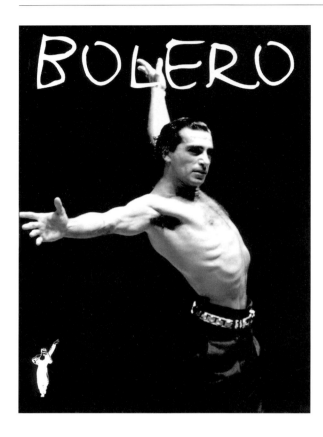

Keet, artistic director of the Spanish Dance Theatre of the Spanish Dance Society, presented her and her company in a lecture/demonstration at George Washington University. She included dances from the Escuela Bolera repertoire and regional dances. She went on to perform for the Casa de España and the Kennedy Center. Other performances of her company in the 1980s included Genoa, Madrid's 'Homage to La Argentina' for the Ministry of Culture, and touring to the cities of Barcelona and Zaragoza. She has been asked to participate in numerous conferences at the Sorbonne in Paris, in New York, and for UNESCO amongst others.

Her fascinating ballet *Danza y Tronio*, to music by Boccherini, Padre Soler and Antón Garcia Abril, was commissioned by Maria de Ávila for the Ballet Nacional de España in 1984. It is most theatrical in its mysterious and vibrant second part, with the opening section in a lighter mood devoted to the Escuela Bolera style and technique. The performers in the ballet, Maribel Gallardo, Antonio Márquez and the members of Spain's Ballet Nacional are all exquisite performers of this style today, as was Ana González, who has now retired. Mariemma herself is most satisfied with her ballet *Iberica: de lo Arcaico a la Actualidad* staged in Spain in the name of UNESCO's Colloquio Internacional called 'La danza y lo sagrado' and staged with her company at the Teatro Calderón in Valladolid.

Illustration 9.20
Antonio Márquez in his ballet
Bolero.

Antonio Márquez

Márquez is probably one of Spain's most charismatic dancers. During his period with the Ballet Nacional de España from 1982 until 1987 he progressed from soloist in 1985 during the directorship of Maria de Ávila, to principal dancer under José Antonio, to guest principal dancer in 1993. In May 1995 he founded his own company, Compañia de Antonio Márquez.

He was born in Seville in 1963. At the age of twelve years he began his dance training with Maria Martín and Paco Torres in Ibiza. After moving to Madrid at the age of eighteen he studied with Victoria Eugenia, Maria Magdalena, Aurora Pons, José Granero, Juana Taft, Merche Esmeralda, Ciro, Paco Romero, Pedro Azorín and Victor Ullate. Later he had further tuition from Aurora Bosch, Maria Pia and Manolete.

Before joining the Ballet Nacional he danced, in 1991, with the companies of Paco Ruiz and Rafael Aguilar. His roles in the National Ballet included ballets by José Antonio (*Soleá*, *The Three-Cornered Hat*, *Don Juan*), by José Granero (*Medea*, *La Gitanilla*, *Bolero*), by Felipe Sánchez (*Los Tarantos*, *Zapateado*), and by Mariemma (*Danza y Tronio*).

He toured to Japan, to Kobe, Osaka, Nagoya, Kyoto and Tokyo, in 1989 and 1990, where Yoko Seanai created for him *The Foreigner From Santiago*, then performed in several galas in Reggio Emilia, Trieste, Paris, Leningrad and at the inauguration of the Biennale in Lyon. He was also in Madrid's Gala of Duos. In 1990 he performed in the Madrid en Danza Festival with Manuela Rodríguez, and then the following year took a year's sabbatical to be the lead dancer with Ballet Español de Madrid and to dance in Granero's *Hamlet* and *Camino sin Retorno*, *Estamos Solos* and *Reencuentros*. In 1992 he was with Merche Esmeralda in her company Murcia Ballet, performing Jason in Granero's *Medea* and *El Cielo Protector*.

He then returned to the Ballet Nacional as guest principal dancer in 1993, and Victoria Eugenia created for him *La Oración del Torero*. He performed with the company at the opening of Madrid's Teatro Real in the presence of the royal family. Victor Ullate invited him to dance the role of Carmelo in his *El Amor Brujo* in 1994, performed at the Teatro del Maestranza in Seville. His own company's repertoire includes Antonio's *El Sombrero de Tres Picos*, *Zapateado de Sarasate* and *La Oración del Torero* (adapted by him from Antonio's choreography), as well as *Solo de Antonio* and his own version of Ravel's *Bolero*, three ballets by José Granero (*Variaciones Románticas*, *Reencuentros*, *Movimiento Perpetuo*) and *Alborada del Gracioso*. The dancers are Trini Artiguez, Ana Moya, Eva Boucherite, Cristina Casanova, Maite Chico, Javier Palacios, Fernando Solano, José Maria Buzón and Jesus Fuentes.

Juan Mata

For years Juan Mata, from Granada, has been a stabilising force in the National Ballet, rehearsing, performing and perfecting their ballets in rehearsals. He studied with Yoscu, Dimitri, Mercedes y Albano, Jota with Pedro Azorín and with the maestros Granero, Pons and Ciro, covering many facets of Spanish dance styles.

Illustration 9.21
Juan Mata, principal dancer and *répétiteur* of the Ballet Nacional de España.

At the age of fourteen he joined the José Greco company. After receiving a study grant from the Harkness Ballet he became a soloist and leading dancer with many others – Pilar López, Maria Rosa, Luisillo, and in Alberto Lorca's National Festivals of Spain – before forming his own company. He toured Europe and the USA and danced for BBC television before he joined the Ballet Nacional de España under the directorship of Antonio Gades. Since that time he has performed the male leads in almost all its repertoire. He has toured world-wide with the company and has represented them at the Helsinki Star Gala performance. At the Vienna Opera he has also performed with Placido Domingo.

Illustration 9.22
Mercedes and Albano.
Marina Keet archive.

Mercedes y Albano

Mercedes and her husband Albano, with their daughter Maria Mercedes León, have lived all their lives in Madrid. A *homenaje* (homage) to them was presented by the Asociación de Profesionales de la Danza de la Comunidad de Madrid on 29 April 1998 at the Teatro Albéniz, Calle Paz. Mercedes is a small fiery woman and her career is inextricably combined with that of Albano de Zúñiga, still at her side after a sixty-year partnership. However, they finally retired from teaching in 1999. Maximo Diaz de Quijano wrote in praise of their dancing and the range they spanned, covering dances with castanets, Escuela Bolera, regional and performing to classical composers such as Albéniz and de Falla as well as flamenco. He called them 'the most extraordinary couple in Spanish dance'.

As dancers they received accolades in Europe as well as in the Americas. Later, their teaching and choreography had incalculable influence on dancers all over the world. The Spanish Dance Society, of which they are patrons, and whose founders were all pupils of theirs, recognises their influence on Spanish dancing. Teachers worldwide sent pupils to study with them, knowing that they would get excellent tuition and personal care.

Mercedes León is the daughter of two famous dancers from Seville, 'La Quica' and 'Frasquillo' (Francisco León, 1898–1940). Her first dance studies were with her parents. She was born in Malaga, where her parents were dancing in the Café de Chinitas. Albano de Zúñiga, who maintains that 'dance is life', was born in Madrid in 1923. He is a Madrileño from Calle Oliver in the *barrio* of Lavapies, just around the corner from where they would later have their own studio in Plaza Tirso de Molina. He was enrolled in the studio of the legendary Antonio de Bilbao in Calle Relatores. He also studied Escuela Bolera with Angel Pericet. Mercedes parents had moved from Seville to Madrid in 1932. There she met Albano in 1934. Albano was performing in Teatro Calderón. Both he and Mercedes were very young, fourteen or fifteen years old. The dancer Del Rio engaged them to tour Europe. This was the beginning of a famous partnership. Later they married.

Together they toured Spain and South America, including Argentina, Chile, Brazil, Uruguay and Cuba. Their daughter Maria Mercedes León was born in Buenos Aires. She was to spend her childhood touring in America and Canada with her parents for the next seven years. Watching every rehearsal and performance, she learned their and the other dancers' repertoires. From 1953 onwards, Mercedes and Albano performed in many venues in New York. In 1956/57 they danced at the World Fair in New York and throughout USA and Canada with Icecapades in *Carmen on Ice.* On a specially built stage, wheeled onto the ice each night, they performed to rapturous applause. Finally, they returned to teach in Madrid. Annually from 1941 they, and later their daughter Maria Mercedes, also taught in Sitges, Barcelona, at the summer course organised by José de Udaeta.

Their historic studio in Madrid, in Plaza Tirso de Molina 20, was the last studio of its kind. Teachers usually rent impersonal rooms from establishments for their classes, but this was their own personal studio, resembling the ones in Seville of a bygone era. It was full of atmosphere and scrupulously tidy. At the entrance to the studio was a small passage with a built-in glass case, filled with small figurines, gifts from pupils from all over the world. A small room was to the right of the passage, with a table and chairs. The walls of the small studio were covered with photos of Mercedes and Albano in dance poses, and others of their famous compatriots. A piano stood directly to the right, and next to that was a room where they changed for teaching. There were benches round the room where spectators could sit to watch classes, and one entire wall was mirrors. At the back were the changing rooms. It was situated next to a small bar from which food and refreshments could be delivered to the studio, and across the square from it is the Teatro Calderón. The studio was in a historic area: around the corner, in Calle Relatores, was the studio where La Quica had taught and where her granddaughter, Maria Mercedes León, opened studios in the 1990s, the Escuela de Actividades Artisticas, 'Relatores'. To Mercedes and Albano, all this is very important as it is a link with the past. Students came from all over the world to study with them and to benefit from the legacy of La Quica, Frasquillo, Antonio de Bilbao and Angel Pericet.

Frasquillo was famous for his *Zapateado* and *Alegrias*, which was danced by his grandchild, Maria Mercedes, in a private showing for Carola Goya, Matteo and Keet in 1992. She also danced her grandmother's and mother's choreography and it was an emotional, historic afternoon. Mercedes was born on 3 June 1923, Madrid, and died there on 17 June 2000.

Illustration 9.23
Maria Mercedes León.
Maria Mercedes León archive.

Illustration 9.24
Aurora Pons, co-director of the
Ballet Nacional de España,
1993–1997.

Aurora Pons

Aurora Pons was trained in classical ballet and Escuela Bolera by Juan Magriña at the Theatre Institute in Barcelona, the city where she was born and where she was given the Premio Extraordinario Antonia Merce prize upon graduating from the Institute. She danced all the major Escuela Bolera dances, but one stands out that most dancers have not studied, *La Tirana del Tripili.*

Pons performed for French Television. A fully-trained ballet dancer, she joined the Liceo ballet company in Barcelona in 1952. As their *prima ballerina* for three years, she danced with Joan Magriña as her partner. Then she became guest ballerina with Antonio. While dancing for the Teatro de la Zarzuela, she also choreographed for them. For a further three years Pons toured with the Ballet of Bulgaria and throughout the USA and South America as *prima ballerina* and ballet mistress of Ballet de Festivales de España.

Moving to Madrid, as *prima ballerina*, Aurora Pons performed with Luisillo and his Spanish Dance Theatre and the Pilar López company. She also appeared in the role of Death, in Luisillo's ballet for Spanish television about a matador who returns to the empty bullring to fight his last fight against death. She also has to her credit many choreographies in ballets and operas. Her role as ballet mistress includes with the Escuela de Arte Dramático y Danza in Madrid and with the Spanish National Ballet under the directorship of Antonio Gades. She was then made acting director during the transition, until Antonio took up the directorship. Although she remained at her post during the directorships of Antonio and Maria de Ávila, she asked to be relieved of her position as ballet mistress to become vice-director of the above-mentioned School of Drama and Dance in 1990. She was voted into this position by an absolute majority.

In an interview for the Encuentro Escuela Bolera in 1992, she lists her own choreographic output in the Escuela Bolera style: *Rumores de la Caleta, Puerta de Tierra, El Baile de Luis Alonso, Concierto para Clavinchenvallo* (de Falla), *Paso de Cuatro* (Sorazabál), *Tapices de Goya, Diablo Cojuelo, Fandango del Candil, Bolero* (Ravel), *Paso a Cuatro* (Pittalugo), *Café de Chinitas, Estampas del Siglo XIX, Sonatas* (Padre Soler), *Intermedio* from Granados's *Goyescas* in a 'Homenage a Granados' (for French television), *Bolero* (in the opera *La Traviata*), and the Spanish dance in Act III of *Swan Lake*, as well as *Malagueña*.

The recipient of many prizes, from Círcolo de Bellas Artes in Madrid to Diputación de Barcelona, she was also awarded the Gold Medal of the Liceo, an honour usually reserved for opera singers, and in 1992 the Medal of Merit of Fine Arts. During her appointment as co-ordinator to the artistic direction of the Ballet

Nacional Español she was to lead the company to prosperity with her wise management. Together with two other women, Victoria Eugenia, known as 'Beti', and Nana Lorca, they had their contracts renewed twice, a rare occurrence.

Albert Sans i Aris

Albert Sans i Aris is a talented choreographer with many honours bestowed on him, including the Chevalier d'Or of Nyons (France, 1964), La Creu de Sant Jordi (1992) from the Consejeria de Cultura de la Generalitat of Catalonia, and the Siver Medal of the Bella Artes (1993) from the Ministry of Cultural Affairs, for his presentation of the dances of Catalonia, especially internationally. He was born in Rubí, Barcelona, on 10 May 1932. He was enrolled in the Esbart Dansaire de Rubí Infantil section in 1940 and made his debut in *Galop de Cortesia*, one of the dances reconstructed by Aurelio Capmany and Joan Amades. He was expected to join in the family business and worked there from the age of fourteen, but his interest lay in dance and all his spare time was devoted to it.

In 1955, under the tutelage of Daniel Bas, an ex-dancer from the Esbart Verdaguer, he became director of the Esbart of Rubí. He was to change the way folk dance was presented in the theatre. He had a theatrical flair and his investigations revitalised the choreography of Catalonian and other dances along the eastern seaboard with his vision and artistry. He was able to do this with no loss of the dances' native origin. As a young choreographer, he was spurred on to greater achievements when seeing, at the Gran Teatro del Liceo, companies such as the Marquis de Cuevas, Jerome Robbins, Maurice Béjart, Paul Taylor, Antonio and José Greco.

Illustration 9.25
Albert Sans i Aris.

From *Danzas d'Artesa de Leida* in 1955 until the ballet *Pasqua* in 1995, he created 56 works including ballets in the operas *Marina* (1968) and *Canigó* (1968); his own ballets *Les Gitanes del Vallès* (1970), *Mortitxol* (1976), *El Sarau* (1977), *El Compte Arnau* (1982), *Carnestoltes* (1982) and *Rapsòdia per a piano i cobla* (1992). Also worth mentioning is his work for the Enric Majó company, *Setmana Santa* inspired by Salvador Espriu, as well as the adaptation of the 'Danzas del Codice', known as the Libro Vermell de Montserrat (the fourteenth-century Red Book of Montserrat Monastery), produced in 1978 in collaboration with Padre Gregori Estrada and the artist/designer Fabià Puigserver, and with a written commentary name by Xavier Benguerel in 1988.

In the 1970s, the Esbart Dansaire was the most popular group in Catalonia and presented their performances on the most prestigious stages such as the Palau de la Musica and the Gran Teatro del Liceo in Barcelona. The company also made numerous performance tours abroad as well as being invited by Margot Fonteyn to participate in the BBC series *The Magic of Dance*. Sans himself gave dance courses at the Institut del Teatro in Barcelona and annual summer schools with José de

Illustration 9.26
Pacita Tomás

Udaeta in Sitges. In 1985 the group was awarded the National Dance Prize by the Diputación de Barcelona and the Generalitat de Barcelona.

In 1990 Sans retired from directing the company, not without a certain sense of frustration at not having achieved his dream of forming a professional folklore company, something very lacking to show Spain's rich dance world. He continues to choreograph for various groups and companies, and to do research on the folklore and dances of Spain.

Pacita Tomás

A recipient of the Medallo de Oro del Circulo de Bellas Artes of Madrid, Pacita Tomás is from Madrid. She and her husband Joaquín Villa have a studio of their own in the city, and she is known to the present generation through her teaching in Madrid. Foreign students enjoyed her vibrant personality and exciting dancing during her classes at the summer schools arranged by José de Udaeta at Sitges, Barcelona. There, she was teaching the choreography of her husband with great energy and enthusiasm. Of late she has been known as a flamenco dancer, but she was also an exponent of dances to classical composers and the Escuela Bolera. She can be seen dancing a Bolero in the film that has recorded for us so many dancers of the early twentieth century, *Duende y Misterio del Flamenco*.

She was born Maria de la Paz Tomás Llory in Madrid in 1928. Her studies were from the great masters Estampio and the brother and sister Angel and Luisa Pericet. She was already performing while still a child. According to José Blas Vega, her debut was during a festival at the Teatro Monumental in Madrid, dancing a *Zapateado*. Her career began as a performer in companies of other dancers, then developed into touring on her own in Northern Europe until she formed her own company in 1951, which performed throughout Spain and Europe, and in 1952 performed with the great flamenco singer Manolo Caracol. Her performances during the following years brought her in contact with her future husband, Joaquín Villa. From 1955 her touring spread from Paris, throughout Europe and as far as London, according to Blas Vega. She reappeared in Madrid in 1959 to perform from then on in local performances and in films (such as *Padre Pitillo y Maria de los Reyes*), make a record, and teach.

José de Udaeta

In 1987 Udaeta was awarded the German Dance Prize in recognition of his dance teaching and presentations in that country. In 1989 he was honoured with the Medalla de Oro of the Belles Artes in Madrid. Udaeta was born on 17 May 1919 in Barcelona, into an aristocratic family of Catalan and Basque descent. In 1941 he began studying medicine, while at the same time studying dance with Juan Magriña. At other times he took classes with Olga Preobrajenska, Alexander Volinine and Boris Kniaseff. In 1945 he decide to concentrate on dance and went to Madrid where he studied with La Quica, El Estampio, Luisa Pericet Jiménez and Regla Ortega, and in Seville with and Rafael Pericet and Enrique 'El Cojo'. He also performed with La Quica. He studied drama and acted and danced in plays, operas and films. It was also in 1945, on 3 October, that he married Marta Font. They have two sons, Alberto and Santiago.

He formed a partnership Susana de Audeoud, a Swiss national, who matched his tall stature of over six foot. They toured as Susana y José from 1948 until 1970. Their performances were of the recital variety with duets interspersed with solos, and took them all over Europe. All types of Spanish dance were represented in their repertoire. His presentations were theatrical and explored themes as well as dances, such as *La Celestina* (1966), *La Centaura* (1963), *Romance de Carmen* (1958), *Orfeo Gitana* (1951). Other presentations included classical historic dances such as *Pavane* (1948), *Folías* (1951), *Capricho de Goya Nr. 75* (1967). By the very nature of their careers, touring ceaselessly to 112 towns in 23 countries, these 46 dances in their repertoire were presented for the first time in such diverse centres as Madrid, Hamburg, Barcelona, Mannheim, Hilversum, Zürich, Bern, Lucerne and Vienna, and performed in other Spanish towns such as Bilbao, Córdoba, Zaragoza and Lérida.

His later career has largely been in Germany, where he started by presenting summer schools in Krefeld and Cologne from 1958 to 1979, as well as teaching regularly in Stuttgart. He has, from 1973 to 1989, presented a summer course in Sitges, on the coast near Barcelona, where he lives in an historic old fort, referred to as 'El Castillo de Sotarribas', in San Pedro de Ribas, near Barcelona. His vast castanet collection is housed there. It was also there, in 1979, for her BBC film *The Magic of Dance*, that Margot Fonteyn filmed him doing Zapateado and, on the grass verge outside, the lovely old *Bolero de l'Alcudia de Carlet*, danced by Joan Fosas and Núria Majó of the Esbart Dansaire de Rubi. In his kitchen is a brass plaque that says, 'Here Margot Fonteyn washed her hair.'

After studying castanet playing and notation with Emma Maleras in Barcelona, he has given castanet concerts in Spain, Austria, London (Covent Garden), Munich, Hawaii, Australia, USA and also played castanets to accompany the Catalan singer Montserrat Caballé, in venues that included New York. Beyond his own partnership, he has choreographed for the Harkness Ballet in New York (*Albaicín*, *Suite Española*, *Bolero*); for the Royal Danish Ballet, helping Flemming Flindt reconstruct the Escuela Bolera dances for Bournonville's ballet *Toreadoren*; with Herbert von Karajan at the Salzburg Festival to produce dances for the opera *Carmen*; *Carmen* in Barcelona; and *Fandango* for the Berlin Opera. In 1998 he was still performing castanet concerts with Joan Fosas and others in Barcelona, Andorra and elsewhere.

At the Government's 'Encuentro Escuela Bolera' Symposium, everyone connected with Spanish Dancing and interested musicians and authors were there to

Illustration 9.27
José de Udaeta performing with the Spanish Dance Society at the Smithsonian Institute in Washington DC, 1985.
Marina Keet archive.

present a paper, to listen to the discussions or to take part in the round table discussions. One of these was José de Udaeta. He has had an amazingly long performing career, first as a dancer, performing in the duo Susana y José from 1948 to 1970, then until the present day presenting castanet concerts. A Catalan, he has performed concerts with the famous Catalonian singer, Montserrat Caballé, including one at the Carnegie Hall in New York. Susana and José included in their repertoire the dances of the Escuela Bolera, *Panaderos de la Tertulia, Bolero con Cachucha, Malagueñas* and *Seguidillas Manchegas*. Both were born in 1919, he in Barcelona and she, Susana Audeoud, in Switzerland. He had studied with La Quica in Madrid and the Escuela Bolera dances with Rafael Pericet in Seville. They toured prodigiously throughout Europe. Both became teachers, Susana settling in Canada and José presenting annual summer schools in Sitges, outside Barcelona, where Eloy Pericet taught the dances of the Escuela Bolera preserved by his family. He was part of the course celebrating the Spanish Dance Society's 25th anniversary celebrations, to whom the course that year was dedicated. There Eloy Pericet taught his great-uncle Rafael's choreography for La Macarena.

Illustration 9.28
Victoria Eugenia, 'Beti',
co-director of the Ballet
Nacional de España, 1993–1997.

Victoria Eugenia ('Beti')

Victoria Eugenia was co-artistic director of the Ballet Nacional de España from 1993 to 1997, together with Aurora Pons and Nana Lorca. Before that she was ballet mistress to the company from 1980 through to 1997, continuing with this work of teaching while a director. Born in Madrid, she was a pupil of Laura Santelmo at the Madrid Royal Conservatory of Music. She also continued to study with other teachers such as Paquita Pagán, the Escuela Bolera from members of the Pericet family, ballet with Karen Taft, Leif Ibars and Maria Ibars. Her gift for choreography was recognised and encouraged by Alberto Lorca when he was teaching her.

At the age of twenty she became one of the founder members of the company of Antonio. She was a very musical and expressive dancer and for five years performed in his company in ballets such as the classical *Allegro de Concierto* and *Sonatas de Padre Soler* and the regional *Jota, Viva Navarra*.

She is a very talented and dedicated teacher, a career begun at an early age in an amateur capacity and ending in 1980 as the ballet mistress of Spanish dance for the Ballet Nacional de España. Under her eagle eye and constructive, inspiring tuition the company were well served. She has also conducted courses in other countries such as Sweden, Israel, France, Germany and Japan.

She took Alberto Lorca's advice and started to do choreography for dancers such as Maria Rosa, but also Lola Flores, Rocio Jurado, Paquita Rico, Antoñita Moreno, Rocío Durcal and other famous Spanish artists. Her other major choreographies are *Benamor*, *El Barberillo de Lavapies*, *Pasión Gitana*, *Tres Danzas*, *Rondeña* and include several dances for the Yoko Komatsubara Ballet in Japan and for Merche Esmeralda's Ballet de Murcia company. In 1990 she staged her ballet *Variaciones* at the Teatro de la Zarzuela. Her output for the Ballet Nacional is prolific: *Solo* (music Adela Mascaraque, 1984), *Danza IX* (E. Granados and E. Halffter, 1985), *Chacona* (José Nieto, 1990), *La Oración del Torero* (Joaquín Turina, 1994), *A Mi Aire* (Granados and Halffter, 1994), and *Goyescas* (Granados, 1996).

Directors of the Ballet Nacional de España

Antonio Gades, 1978–1980
Antonio (Ruiz Soler), 1980–1983
María de Ávila, 1983–1986
José Antonio (Ruiz), 1986–1992
Aurora Pons, Nana Lorca and Victoria Eugenia, 1993–1997
Aida Gómez, 1997–2001
Elvira Andrés, 2001–

The Ballet Nacional de España

This article was commissioned by Mary Clarke and is reprinted by kind permission of The Dancing Times.

The Spanish Directorate-General of Theatre and Entertainment, a department of the Ministry of Culture, at the end of 1997 appointed a very young dancer, Aida Gómez, as artistic director of the Ballet Nacional of Spain. Needless to say it has caused much discussion within the Spanish dance world. *Prima ballerina* of the company since 1985, and still very much a performer, she follows in the footsteps of revered personalities such as Antonio Gades (1978), Antonio (1980), María de Ávila (1983–Sept. 1986), José Antonio (1986), and from 1993–1997 the trio of women co-directors, Aurora Pons, 'Beti' and Nana Lorca. At the age of thirty-one, Gómez takes on the enormous responsibility of running the national company, while in the wings other contenders for the throne, with great stage and choreographic experience behind them, look on.

Spanish Dance's Theatrical Progression in Spain

One needs to understand what came before the founding of the National Ballet in 1978, and also the focus of each of the directors since then, to understand what is meant by a National Spanish Ballet Company.

During the Franco era it was the regional companies that were being fostered. Regional folklore groups were funded under the Sección Feminina de FET y JONS. This support was to encourage the preservation of the nation's culture, music, dance, costumes and the written word – poetry, song and prose. Musicologist García Matos's research of the folklore during this period is a rich legacy, published in three volumes (now out of print): Castile, Extremadura and Andalusia. Unfortunately he died before completing his research on the other regions.

At the beginning of this century soloists such as Vicente Escudero and La Argentina were popularising Spanish dance outside Spain. The latter was perhaps the best publicised. At the same time, in Spain dancers such as Pastora Imperio, Estampio, Antonio de Bilbao, La Quica, her husband Frasquillo (parents of Mercedes León), Realito, and Angel Pericet Jiménez, reigned supreme. In the USA was Carola Goya. The flamenco scene had dancers such as El Farruco (Antonio Montoya), Rosita Durán, Blanca del Rey, and Lucero Tena, amongst many others.

La Argentinita, together with her sister Pilar López, continued the trend of touring abroad, extending the ideas by adding the male dancer Escudero, and performing trios. It was still a concert-type programme that was performed. La Argentinita was a great friend of the poet Federico García Lorca and perhaps this led to his saving the most well-known music and words of folk dances of that period.

Then came the era of the large companies touring the world. The famous duo of Antonio and Rosario, stars since their childhood, ended their partnership and the revered Antonio started his own company. Luisillo, trained by Carmen Amaya, toured his Spanish Dance Theatre and built up tremendous worldwide audiences. José Greco gained a spectacular following in the USA, where Carmen Amaya had held court before. These large companies had a most satisfying blend of programming. Apart from the usual flamenco cuadros (pictures), they presented Spanish dance in ballets and also presented charming regional or classical dances, each in a concept of the well-balanced whole, with scenes based in one particular region and using the music, dancing and rich costumes of that area. The dancer Mariemma also formed her own company, and talented Rafael Aguilar based his company permanently in Paris.

After her sister passed away, Pilar López had started her own company. Later a succession of male dancers from her company followed suit, such as Ximenez/Vargas and Antonio Gades, while Alberto Lorca enriched the Madrid Zarzuela Opera Company with his inventive choreography. From the Antonio Company was to emerge the highly talented young José Antonio, a star from the age of eight years, who was to form the Ballet de Madrid together with José Granero. However, touring such large companies eventually became prohibitively expensive, as costs of hotels and airfares rose. The golden era of the large companies was over.

At the same time, South America and the USA were conquered by individual dancers and smaller companies such as Mercedes y Albano, and the Pericet Blanco family of Angel, Eloy and their sisters Carmelita and Maria del Amparo. The American Spanish dancer Carola Goya was also touring the world, as far afield as South Africa already in 1939. She was later joined by Matteo, another American. José de Udaeta danced with his protegée as Susana and José, throughout Europe and elsewhere. These are a chosen few names from the galaxy of Spanish dancers.

After Franco's death in 1975 many regional companies were disbanded and Spaniards preferred to project an image as a modern industrial nation. They have, since then, regained many of the regional groups.

Amongst the more recent flamenco dancers one finds the names of La Tati, Mila de Vargas, Milagros Mengíbar, Farruco's daughters 'La Farruquita' and 'La Faraona', Manuela Carrasco, Angelita Vargas and 'El Güito' (Eduardo Serrano), Manolo Marin, the son and daughter of Greco, José Greco II and Lola Greco, to mention only a few. The most charismatic performer in Spain today is perhaps the principal dancer of the National Ballet, Antonio Márquez. Dancers such as Mario Maya and more recently Joaquín Cortés formed their own flamenco companies. The guitarist Paco Peña toured the world, first as an individual and then with a company, and built up much following in Britain and America.

From Ballet Nacional Español to Ballet Nacional de España

In 1978 the Ministry of Culture created the Ballet Nacional Español with Antonio Gades as artistic director. The dancers of the Zarzuela Opera Company, founded by Alberto Lorca, were the basis of this new company. Members of Gades's own flamenco troupe followed him into the company, and two years later were to depart with him. Among them was José Antonio, a later director.

Gades wanted a repertoire representative of Spain's rich dance heritage and used other leading choreographers such as Mariemma, Antonio (regional), Pilar López (classical) and Rafael de Aguilar. Except for Aguilar, who used Gregorian chant, the music was of Spanish composers such as Guridi, Halffter, Rodrigo, and the composer/guitarist Emilio de Diego for Gades's own ballet *Blood Wedding*.

When Gades left the Ballet Nacional, Antonio was appointed as the director in 1980. He staged his own ballets, *Three-Cornered Hat*, *El Amor Brujo*, *Sonatas* to Padre Soler's music, and *Estampas Flamencas*. He also invited Luisillo to choreograph the full-length *Don Quijote*, to music by Federico Moreno Torroba.

Another company, a classical one, existed side by side with the Spanish dance company. It was titled Ballet Nacional Lírico. In 1983 the two were united under the directorship of Maria Ávila, who came from her well-known ballet school and company in Zaragoza. She was trained in ballet in Barcelona, and was *prima ballerina assoluta* of the Liceo Theatre there, from the age of nineteen. As director, she invited choreographers to mount new works: Alberto Lorca's *Ritmos*, to music by José Nieto; José Granero's *Medea* to scenario by Miguel Narros and music by guitarist Manolo Sanlúcar; a vibrant flamenco ballet, *Los Tarantos*, choreographed by Felipe Sánchez and set to guitar compositions of Paco de Lucia; José Antonio's *Laberinto* to Montsalvatge's music; Mariemma used music by Boccherini, Soler and García Abril for her evocative *Danza y Tronio*; Angel Pericet (Blanco) who arranged *Six Sonatas for the Queen of Spain* to Scarlatti was among several others who also staged their work. He became assistant director for a short period and toured with the company to the USA.

From 1986 to 1992 the company, now renamed Ballet Nacional de España, came under the directorship of José Antonio, who was also the principal dancer. The six years were the longest directorship to date. Amongst others he rechoreographed *The Three-Cornered Hat* with the original Picasso designs, and *Don Juan* to a script by Miguel Narros and music by José Nieto. Granero was commissioned to choreograph Ravel's *Bolero*. The remarkable conductor Enrique García Asensio was conducting their orchestra. Under José Antonio the company toured worldwide and invited dancers such as Merche Esmeralda and Lola Greco as guest artists. The strong company had Antonio Alonso, Juan Mata, Ana González, Conchita Zerezo, Aida Gómez and Maribel Gallardo among their principal dancers. They performed to over 15,000 people in their 1987 tours of Spain, Soviet Union, Norway, Italy, France and the USA. The following year they won the Critics Prize for the best foreign performance at the 'Met'.

In 1996 Aurora Pons, Nana Lorca and Victoria Eugenia (Beti) presented Granero's magnum opus *La Gitanilla*, regional dances, *Romance* staged by Juanjo Linares, and two other dances, Victoria Eugenia's *Intermedio de Goya*, and *Concierto de Málaga* by Manolo Marín. Under their directorship the company became a profit-making enterprise and their contracts were renewed for a further year.

Luisillo says that the future of Spanish dance does not lie in solo flamenco performances but in bringing it into the theatre in the form of ballets. Similarly, in José Antonio's own words, the aim of the company during his directorship was 'to find a way of being in touch with our times without any loss of identity'. In other words, they were bringing Spanish dance into the twentieth century through the theatre, in a balletic approach, and away from the image of solo flamenco perform-ances and regional duets and groups. A way of expanding the language of Spanish dance. Unfortunately it is not always what public and critics desire. It also does not satisfy the Spaniards who preserve the folk dances. But Spanish dance must be allowed to expand theatrically, and in the inspired hands of artists like Antonio, Luisillo and Gades it does. Luisillo's latest dramatic ballet, *La Malquerida* (The Outcast) with regional dancing, and Granero's *Medea* are examples of what can be acheived.

Ballets in the Repertoire of the Ballet Nacional de España

Antonio Gades: *Bodas de Sangre*, m. Emilio de Diego (1978).

Pilár López: *Concierto de Aranjuez*, m. Joaquín Rodrigo (1978)

Antonio: *Fantasía Galaica*, m. Ernesto Halffter (1978); *Estampas Flamencas*, m. traditional (1980); *Puerta de Tierra*, m. Isaac Albéniz (1980); *La Casada Infiel*, m. Emilio de Diego (1980); *Asturias*, m. Isaac Albéniz (1980); *Zapateado*, m. Pablo Sarasate (1980); *Allegro de Concierto*, m. Enrique Granados (1980); *El Sombrero de Tres Picos*, m. Manuel de Falla (1981); *El Amor Brujo*, m. Manuel de Falla (1981); *Sonatas*, m. Padre Soler (1982).

Rafael Aguilar: *Rango*, m. traditional and Gregorian chant (1979); *Retrato de Mujer*, m. C. Halffter, Bizet and traditional (1981).

Mariemma: *Diez Melodias Vascas*, m. Guridi (1979); *Fandango*, m. Padre Soler (1979); *Danza y Tronio*, m. Boccherini, Padre Soler and García Abril (1985).

Luisillo: *Don Quijote*, m. Federico Moreno Torroba (1981).

José Granero: *Medea*, m: Manolo Sanlúcar (1984); *Alborada del Gracioso*, m. Maurice Ravel (1985); *Bolero*, m: Maurice Ravel (1987); *Leyenda*, m. Isaac Albéniz and José Luis Greco (1994); *Cuentos del Guadalquivir*, m. Joaquín Turina (1994); *La Gitanilla*, m. Antón Garcia Abríl (1996).

Alberto Lorca: *Ritmos*, m. José Nieto (1984); *Doña Francisquita*, m. Amadeo Vives (1985).

Juan Quintero: *Alegrias, Bulerias, Farruca*, m. traditional (1984).

Felipe Sánchez: *Zapateado*, m. Pablo Sarasate, (1984); *Rondeña*, m. traditional (1985); *Los Tarantos*, m. Paco de Lucía (1986); *Homenaje*, m. José Nieto (1988).

23. Dolores Serral and Mariano Camprubí (seated is Lola de Valencia).
Manet, Edouard
Spanish Ballet, 1862
Oil on canvas
24 x 35 5/8 in.
Acquired 1928
The Phillips Collection, Washington, D.C.
(see p. 53 and p.153)

Anda chiquillo

Bolera del Teatro.

24. *Anda Chiquillo*,
Bolero del Teatro.
Arcadio Carbonell
archive. (see p.84)

25. Anders Zorn, (1860–1920),
Café Cantante in Madrid, study,
1884, watercolour.
Zornsamlingarna, Mora,
Sweden.
Photo Lars Berglund. (see p.87)

26. Dolores Serral and Mariano Camprubí dancing a Bolero. Arcadio Carbonell archive. (see p. 89 and p.93)

27. Fanny Elssler (1810–1884) in the Cachucha from the ballet *Le Diable Boîteux*, Paris 1836,
with choreography by Jean Coralli. G.B.L. Wilson Collection, Royal Ballet School archive. (see p.98)

28. Marie Taglioni (1804–1884) in *La Gitana* (*The Gypsy*), where she danced a Cachucha at the close of the ballet. Choreography by her father Filippo Taglioni (23 November 1838). Arcadio Carbonell archive. (see p.100)

29. Couple dancing a Bolero. (see p.115)

30. 1911 Poster advertising the 'Feria'. (see pp. 20 and 40)

31. A Moorish Dancer in a position still used today in Spanish dancing. (see p.121)

32. Baile el Vito. By kind permission of Carmen García Matos. (see p.131)

33. Manuela Perea (known as La Nena, because of her small stature). (see p.154)

34. Adelina Plunkett in 'La Manola' from the opera *La Favorite*. Arcadio Carbonell archive. (see p.143)

35. Corraleras Francisco Font and Manuela Dubinon. Arcadio Carbonell archive. (see pp.90 and 93)

36. Petra Cámara.
(see p.151)

37. *Bolero*, choreographed by José Granero. Ballet Nacional de España. Photo: Paco Ruiz. (see p.183)

38. *La Boda de Luis Alonso*, choreographed by Albert Lorca for the Zarzuela Company in Madrid. (see 121 and p.219)

Victoria Eugenia (Beti): *Solo*, m. Adela Mascaraque (1984); *Danza IX*, m. E. Granados and E. Halffter (1985); *Chacona*, m. José Nieto (1990); *La Oración del Torero*, m. Joaquín Turina (1994); *A Mi Aire*, m. E. Granados and E. Halffter (1994); *Intermedio de Goyescas*, m. Enrique Granados (1996).

Angel Pericet: *Seis Sonatas por la Reina de España*, m. D. Scarlatti (1985).

Martín Vargas: *Caracoles*, m. traditional (1985).

José Antonio: *Laberinto*, m. Xavier Montsalvatge (1985); *Con mi Soledad*, m. Carlos Santos, (1985); *Romeras*, m. traditional (1985); *Martinete*, m. traditional (1985); *Castilla*, m. Isaac Albéniz (1986); *El Sombrero de Tres Picos*, m. Manuel de Falla (1986); *Fandango de Soler*, m. Claudio Prieto (1988); *Zarabanda*, m. José Nieto (1988); *Soleá*, m. Manolo Sanlúcar (1988); *Don Juan*, m. José Nieto (1990); *Romance de Luna*, m. José Nieto (1990); *Soleá por Bulerias*, m. traditional (1991); *La Vida Breve*, m. Manuel de Falla (1992).

Adoración Carpio: *Alegrias*, m. José Maria Bandera and José Carlos Gómez (1993).

Curillo: *A Ritmo y Compás*, m. José Maria Banderas, José Carlos Gómez (1994).

Lola Greco: *Antar*, m. Rimsky-Korsakov, José Carlos Gómez (1994).

Mila de Vargas: *Alegrias*, m. traditional (1994).

Manolo Marín: *Conciertio de Málaga (Tientos and Tangos)*, m. Federico Moreno Torroba (1996).

Juanjo Linares and Pedro Azorín: *Romance*, regional dances (1996).

The Spanish Dance Society

A teacher's examination was in existence in Spain in the fifteenth century, when the dance masters belonged to a guild and had to pass a test to prove not only that they could dance, but that they could teach the dances and impart their knowledge. Somehow this idea got lost.

Then in the late nineteenth century, the organisation of the steps into a system for the Escuela Bolera set a trend in Spain for that type of Spanish dance, surpassing the old-fashioned way of only entire dances being passed on. In modern Spain there has long been an examination certification for those who wish to teach in Spain, comprising ballet and Spanish dances.

In 1965 in South Africa, Spanish dance as a whole was eventually refined, for the first time ever, into a teaching method, graded for age and ability. The Spanish Dance Society was formed by senior teachers from Johannesburg, Cape Town and Durban. At the suggestion of Ivy Conmee, an examiner for the Royal Academy of Dancing, a syllabus was created by founding members Mercedes Molina and Rhoda Rivkind with Madame Gitanilla, from Johannesburg, Mavis Becker, Deanna Blacher and Marina Keet from Cape Town, and Theo Dantes and Bernie Lyle from Durban. Later, others contributed. Enrique Segovia set the male syllabus. They arranged the basic components of Spanish dances, including the existing Escuela Bolera, into a method to teach the technique of Spanish dancing, instead of the old way of only passing on the dances in their entirety.

They had all studied with reputable Spanish teachers and/or performed with well-known Spanish dance companies. They based the exercises on the work of these teachers and set the standard as that needed in a Spanish dance company.

Spanish Dance Society

Illustration 9.29
Spanish Dance Society

Thus the pupil is prepared with basic components that comprise the dances. The technique is broken down into castanet playing, steps, footwork, arm movements and types of turns, which are taught progressively in a series of seven graded junior levels and three senior levels, each examination culminating in the presentation of two or three dances of regional, classical or flamenco styles. The ensuing three examinations for training a teacher comprises knowledge of all the prior work, the theory and historical background plus an understanding of the music, of child psychology, physiology and a course in first-aid. The final examination for teachers also comprises the Pericet Escuela Bolera syllabus as codified by myself after classes with Eloy Pericet in Madrid.

There is also a flamenco line, if the dancer wishes to study that exclusively. Most students follow both lines. This Spanish Dance Society syllabus is spreading worldwide, and at present is taught in Australia, Cyprus, Great Britain, Greece, Italy, Malta, the Netherlands, New Zealand, Sicily, South Africa and the USA, and although it started outside Spain, it is now enthusiastically taught there as well. New centres are starting in Sri Lanka, Bangkok and Mexico.

The aim of the society, which has charitable, not-for-profit status, is to promote interest in the art of Spanish dance, pursuing excellence in presentation, execution and instruction. The society provides free revision classes for the teachers after each examination session, of which there are often two per year in some countries. The society syllabus is used in degree courses in South Africa and the USA, and the society is working towards this in the United Kingdom.

Each year an international summer school is held in London, with guest teachers from Spain and other countries. All types of Spanish dance are offered and lecture/demonstrations with guest artists are included. At the end of this period of study the teachers of the Spanish Dance Society stay on to participate in stimulating course of sessions, to revise the syllabus and learn new material. These summer schools are organised by the executive administrator, Sherrill Wexler, 1 Blackett Close, Staines, Middlesex TW18 3NW, tel/fax 01784 460419.

Appendix I

The Escuela Bolera in London
in the Nineteenth Century

Ivor Guest

Between the Escuela Bolera and the great flowering of ballet throughout Europe under the influence of Romanticism there exists a strong and clearly discernible bond. The branch of Spanish dance which is today termed classical was developed as a distinct form in the latter half of the eighteenth century, almost simultaneously in fact with the advances in technique that led to the popularisation of ballet in the nineteenth and twentieth centuries. Little is known of the early dance academies where the Escuela was danced and taught, but from the dances which it produced, many of which survive today, the two main sources can be recognised. First regional dances clearly gave it a distinctive national style, but these were overlaid with a veneer of technique taken from the classical ballet. Elevation, *batterie*, *pirouettes*, *pas de bourrée*, and other borrowings from the ballet stage were to be moulded into this new form to give Spanish dance a more diverse vocabulary and a sophistication which the dances of no other nation posess.

This new school of dance was too remarkable to remain confined to Spain, and it was soon being displayed by French dancers who had crossed the Pyrenees. The earliest of these appears to have been Charles Le Picq, one of the finest dancers of his time and the favourite pupil of the celebrated Noverre. Le Picq was ballet-master at the San Carlo in Naples from 1773 to 1782, and since Naples was then a Spanish dependency, he would conceivably have had an opportunity of discovering Spanish dancing there if he had not actually visited Spain. Very shortly afterwards, in 1783, he was engaged in London as the ballet-master for the opera season at the King's Theatre, where he produced a very successful ballet, *Le Tuteur trompé*, based on Beaumarchais' comedy, *Le Barbier de Seville*. This provided a natural frame for two Spanish dances, a *Seguidillas* which he performed with the ballerina, Geltruda Rossi, and a *Fandango* which Mme Rossi danced solo in male attire. The ballet was revived in London in later seasons, the two dances being eventually merged into a *pas de trois* known as *Les Folies d'Espagne*, in which three of the most celebrated dancers of the day appeared in the years ahead: Charles Didelot and Madeline Guimard in 1789, and Auguste Vestris in 1791.

During the Napoleonic wars the management of the London opera house had great difficulty in securing the services of foreign dancers. Many of those who succeeded in reaching England arrived by way of Lisbon. It was from there that Armand Vestris, son of Auguste, and Fortunata Angiolini came to make their debut in 1809, and what was obviously first-hand experience of Spanish dancing was soon put to use when they danced a *Bolero*. In later London seasons Armand Vestris continued to perform Spanish dances, and even produced Spanish divertissements which were a constant source of delight.

This couple even taught the elements of the Escuela Bolera to others, and in 1811 one of their pupils, Mlle Mori performed a *Guaracha*, which evoked a glowing description from the critic of *The Times*, who described her as wearing a 'long light scarf with the centre fastened to her hair behind, and the ends to her wrists. The tune was melancholy and slow, sometimes accompanied by the castanets; and the dance mainly consisted of attitudes. There were some periods at which the feet scarcely moved at all, and the effect was in waving the figure, and wreathing the scarf around the head and arms. We never felt the beauty of motion more deeply.'

Armand Vestris was also the teacher of Spanish-born Maria Mercandotti, who made a single appearance in a *Cachucha* in at the age of thirteen. Seven years passed before she was seen again, making her formal debut as a ballerina in the making, but sad to relate, she squandered her promise by eloping with a wealthy admirer.

When Napoleon was finally defeated there was no sudden inflow of Spanish dancers on the London stage. Ballet's monopoly in the theatre was unshakeable in the area of dance, and at the opera house the star dancers were invariably French or Italian. Although what little had been seen of the Escuela Bolera had been found charming it had been a passing novelty for want of exponents to exploit it. In 1816 a Señor Luengo and the Señoras Ramos briefly danced at Covent Garden, but it would be nearly twenty years before the first Spanish dancers of real distinction arrived on English shores.

In 1834 four renowned Spanish dancers, Dolores Serral, Mariano Camprubí, Francisco Font and Manuela Dubinon, arrived in Paris to perform at balls given at the Opera during Carnival. A theatrical paper revealed that they alternately served the two royal theatres in Madrid, the Teatro del Principe and the Teatro de la Cruz. They were still in the employ of the Queen of Spain, but the mounting political crisis – Spain was on the verge of the First Carlist Wars – resulted in the closure of the theatres, and the Queen Regent had placed her actors on half-pay and given special permission to these four dancers to travel abroad. Their triumph in Paris was repeated in London, where they were seen first in a *Bolero* and a *Zapateado*, and a few days later, in *Las Boleras del Tripoli* and *Corraleros de Sevilla*. Dolores Serral was soon to make a significant contribution to the development of the Romantic ballet by providing the model if not actually teaching Fanny Elssler the *Cachucha*, thereby providing a counterweight to the ethereal vision presented by Marie Taglioni. Elssler's *Cachucha* fired the enthusiasm of the London public, as it had done in Paris and was to do in many cities in the Old World and the New. It broadened immeasurably the scope of ballet by introducing a rich new source in

◆ See colour plate 16

the exotic regional dances of Europe, and most significantly it drew attention to the wealth of Spanish dancing and in particular the Escuela Bolera.

The 1840s marked the golden age of Romantic ballet, and many of the great ballerinas of that era followed Elssler's example and appeared in balleticised versions of Spanish dances. Elssler followed her *Cachucha* with a *Zapateado de Cádiz*; Cerrito added to her repertory a Double *Cachucha*, partnered by her husband, Saint-Léon; Grahn and Perrot danced a *Castilliana Bolero*; Marie Guy-Stéphan, who for several years was to be the leading ballerina in Madrid, was much applauded in *Las Boleras de Cádiz*.

These dancers prepared the way for native Spanish dancers who began touring outside Spain from the mid-1840s. The first of these – if we ignore, as we must, the notorious Lola Montez – was Manuela Perea, known as La Nena. When she was first engaged in London in 1845, *The Times* perceived in her performance the authentic Spanish quality that was inevitably diluted to various degrees by the great ballerinas. La Nena's *Bolero Cachucha*, he wrote, 'is not like the idealised versions of Fanny Elssler or Taglioni, but a much more native affair, and it is the native *gusto* with which it is danced that is its recommendation. The intricate steps are given with a sort of bustling rapidity, and with a pretty appearance of decision . . . La Nena bounds through her intricacies with the greatest possible good humour, and with the swiftness of a flash of lightning . . . Also, she has the

Manuela Perea, known as 'La Nena' performing at the Haymarket Theatre in London and sketched for the *London Illustrated News*, 4 November 1854, Ivor Guest Archive.

advantage of a very pretty face, and elicits from castanets a sonorous music, such as is seldom produced by that national instrument.' She became a great favourite in London in the 1850s, giving several seasons at the Theatre Royal, Haymarket. Her *Jaleo de Cádiz* never failed to arouse enthusiasm, and, as it appeared to a contemporary, had all London humming the melody.

La Nena was not the only Spanish dancer to bring a company to London. In the year of the Great Exhibition, 1851, Petra Cámara brought a group of no less than twenty-eight dancers to give a whole evening's performance at the opera house. Again we are indebted to the critic of *The Times* for a vivid description. 'Her suppleness of limb is astounding,' he wrote. 'Those bold gestures which the French and Italian *danseuses* seem to have acquired by art have apparently been bestowed upon her by some peculiar nature. The dance, moreover, is not only remarkable for its vigour, but for its strange eloquence. The artiste seems restless with an inspiring passion, to which her movements, hurried as they are, can scarcely give an adequate expression. Now she will snatch a hat, and, dashing it on the ground, execute her *pas* around it, as if it were a fallen enemy; now she will do the same kind of office for a cloak; now she will execute the boldest steps upon a small table, regardless of the chance of tumbling. These evolutions are effected not only with the legs, but with the arms, the bust, the head – every muscle of the artiste will be dancing.'

By the mid-1850s the ballet boom, if I may use a modern phrase, was beginning to burn itself out. The place of ballet in the opera house was shrinking year by year, and dancers were beginning to find a new focus for their talents in the music halls that were springing up in their capital. But the days of the large touring Spanish companies were over, and only an occasional Spanish dancer was featured on the bill at the Alhambra in Leicester Square. The Casonobas from Madrid were seen there in 1876, and in 1879 Maria Fuensanta and the Royal Spanish Ballet appeared in two numbers, *La Torera* and *The Costumes of Murcia*. Another Spanish element was provided by no less than three ballets on the theme of *Carmen*, which featured two dramatic Spanish actress-dancers in the title role, Maria Guerrero and Maria la Bella. For the last of these *Carmen* ballets, in 1912, two celebrated dancers from Spain were engaged, La Malgueñita and Antonio de Bilbao. These, however, were exponents of flamenco, and here we have an early indication that the Escuela Bolera was being superseded in popular appeal by a more earthy form which, alas, has become the obligatory fare for the masses in search of Spanish culture.

In more recent times the elegance and brio of the Escuela Bolera has brought enchantment to several generations of English dance-lovers through the artistry of La Argentina, La Argentinita and her sister Pilar López, Antonio and Rosario and others, and I am sure that London's *aficionados* of the dance would welcome the opportunity of seeing a broadly-based repertoire of Spanish dancing that would give due prominence, in my personal view, to its most appealing form, the Escuela Bolera.

Manuela Perea (La
Nena) in London.
*London Illustrated
News*, 4 November
1854. Arcadio
Carbonell archive.

Appendix II

Some Theatres in Spain

The Theatres

Most of the early theatrical performances were supported by the hospitals, usually of religious orders, which were were responsible for all the performances and the rules that governed them. They also benefited from the revenue they brought in.

According to Alfonso Puig, the most important theatres were: the Caridad in Malaga, built in 1490; the Hospital de la (Santa) Cruz in Barcelona, built in 1560, which became the Teatro Principal on the Ramblas in 1847; Masón de la Fruta in Toledo, in 1576; the Cruz and Principe in 1579 in Madrid; the Gracia of Zaragoza of 1669; and Los Caños del Peral of Madrid, which in 1787 was constructed where the old Teatro Real had been, and in 1807 housed the first school for dance, mime and theatrical gesture. This school was proposed by the Marquis of Perales; sixteen boys and girls were enrolled to study the national dancing of Spain, a welcome attempt to counteract foreign influence and protect local folklore, as well as to encourage professional Spanish performers.

Habsburg Influence

To go back in time, in Madrid, the Buen Retiro Palace was built in 1630 and the theatre the Coliseo del Buen Retiro in 1639 by Philip IV, the Habsburg monarch. It opened on 4 February 1640, and lavish ballets were presented there. Surrounded by splendour, it became the home of the Italian opera under the two Bourbon monarchs, Philip V and Ferdinand VI. It was a royal theatre with a difference: when the king was not in residence, the paying public could watch performances there, unlike at other royal theatres. Amongst the splendour there were performed the *danzas habladas* with allegorical and mythological themes.

The theatre seems to have been constructed along the lines of the Swedish theatres of Drottningholm and Confidencen, with only benches for seats and no distinctions between who sat where. Like Drottningholm, it had every conceivable mechanical device known at that time. Scenes could be changed in record time and all types of dances could be presented.

The stage opened out at the back, into the garden, where open-air scenes could take place. Later, when elegant restraint was the keynote at court, it became fashionable to have *fiestas* in the countryside to enable the ladies and gentlemen of the court to perform the peasant dances such as the *Fandango* and the *Bolero*.

A model of the Buen Retiro Court Theatre.

Perhaps this was the idea behind the Buen Retiro stage, where the *Seguidillas d'Eco, Matachin, Canario,* as well as the stately *Jácara, Passacalle* and *Menuetto* were danced.

In 1703, by royal command of the Bourbon monarch Philip V, a ballet company was brought to the Buen Retiro Palace in Madrid. A Spanish composer of the time, Sebastian Durón, introduced native elements into the mainly Italian-influenced style of the *zarzuelas* by including dances such as the *Seguidillas* and *Villancicos* in rustic scenes, according to Gilbert Chase.

The Duchess d'Aulnoy wrote about the theatre in her book *Lady's Travels in Spain* (1708). She thought it a lovely theatre with paintings, statues, gilt decoration and curtains for the boxes. (In Sweden, Gustav III had wooden trellis screens to hide behind in his box in the Drottingholm court theatre.)

The artist Diego Rodríguez de Silva Velásquez (baptised 6 June 1599, died 6 August 1660), was appointed to the court in 1623, and was granted the sole right to paint the king. His depictions of the court at the time of Philip IV are masterful and his most famous painting is *Las Meninas*. This Buen Retiro theatre was surrounded by splendour and became the home of the Italian Opera under the two Bourbon monarchs Philip V and Ferdinand VI.

The theatre was substantially enlarged in 1738, and was under the direction of the Italian singer Farinelli. On the accession of Charles III, however, it ceased to be used; the new king disliked it and would not patronise it. It fell into disuse and was abandoned in the nineteenth century, together with the palace.

The Bourbon Monarchy

In 1700, the Duc d'Anjou, grandson of Louis XIV of France, became Philip V, the first Bourbon monarch to become King of Spain. Charles II of Spain, the last Habsburg monarch there, had died without leaving an heir, and bequeathed all his posessions to Philip V. Philip brought with him the influence of French classical culture, and through his two wives, Maria Luisa of Savoy and Elizabeth Farnese of Parma, an Italian influence. In other words, he brought a foreign culture to Spain. He also brought a war with him, the War of Spanish Succession. When Louis XIV refused to cut him out of the succession to the French throne, it led to war, and he lost the Spanish Netherlands and his Italian inheritance, retaining only Spain and the Spanish Americas.

The Zarzuela

The king's hunting lodge in the countryside outside Madrid was called after the brambles, *zarzas*, that grew around it. Today Madrid has grown up around it and the Palacio de la Zarzuelas is the home of the present royal family. The name of the entertainments that were performed there, *zarzuelas*, was thus also derived from these brambles and the palace. *Zarzuelas* are light operas or operettas, usually containing dance. A *loa* preceded the librettist Calderón de la Barca's one-act *zarzuela*, *El Golfo de las Sirenas*. It was performed 17 January 1657 at the Zarzuela Palace. It also ended with an epilogue called a *mojiganga*. This form of entertainment, with words, music and dance, was first called *fiestas de zarzuela*.

There were two phases of *zarzuelas*. Those of the first period, from the seventeenth until the mid-eighteenth century, had classical myths and legends for themes, with a strong Italian musical influence. These themes changed in the middle of the eighteenth century, and instead of entertaining the court the *zarzuelas* were now intended to entertain the people of Madrid. Structures were retained, but the form had moved on, with librettos by Ramón de la Cruz, known for his reforms of the *Sainete*, and with musical influence from Antonio Rodríguez de Hita. The new influence of realism showed in the inclusion of various regional dances. Usually the *zarzuelas* included dances of a traditional folk nature, as they were often set in one or another region. The first era of the *zarzuelas* also at times included the folk dance, but not to the extent of the later period. There is a Bolero in the *zarzuela* by Jerónimo Giménez called *El Baile de Luis Alonso*, which was first performed in Madrid in 1897. It is set in a dance academy of the era of the Escuela Bolera academies. Usually performed at the same time is another short *zarzuela*, *La Boda de Luis Alonso*.

Madrid's Teatro del Circo in the 1840s.

See colour plate 38

Teatro Real:
the exterior.

The *zarzuela* is a popular entertainment at the Zarzuela Theatre in Madrid, where the productions are conceived and directed by José Tamayo, with inspired and inventive choreography by Alberto Lorca. A touring programme is sometimes devised, showing the main attractions in these *zarzuelas* and this is the only time recently that the rich heritage of Spanish regional dances has been seen abroad.

Other Madrid Theatres

From 1842 the Teatro del Circo functioned for four years in Madrid under the Marquis of Salamanca, who founded a ballet company. Later, in 1850, Madrid's Teatro Real was inaugurated. In a lecture in London in 1961, Anna Ivanova said that, 'Ever since the civil war, for the past 20 years, the Teatro Real was standing empty opposite the Royal Palace. It was in the hands of workmen, but the last time they opened it an underground river had overflowed and spurted down the aisles over the feet of the occupants of the stalls.' At that time, there was still no national ballet or Spanish dance company to make its home there. It was later opened to performances and housed the National Ballet's two companies. Then it was closed once more and renovated, and reopened in the 1990s.

Madrid has many other theatres such as the Albéniz, the Calderón, the Zarzuela and the Teatro Español, placed where the old Corral del Principe used to be; it was a roofless theatre like the Corral de la Cruz. This was a typical feature of the sixteenth and seventeenth-century theatres, before they moved indoors.

The Council of Castile forbade dancing in the theatres, but happily this order was not obeyed.

Teatro Real: interior 1898 (left); the gods, 1895 (right).

Cazuela

An interesting feature of the theatres in the early centuries was something which could be a left-over from the Moorish days: the division of the men and women. The section reserved for women only was called the *cazuela*, or stewpot. It was where the dress circle would be today, raised, across from and facing the stage. It was a place where women went to be sociable and have fun; but the theatre was stricly regulated and all regulations were stricly enforced and they could be expelled for unfitting behaviour. (Illustration page 150)

Tertulia

Here we find yet another use of the word *tertulia*, discussed elsewhere. The area where the men sat in the theatre was called the *tertulia*. This was separated from the women by a balustrade. This type of separation of men and women can be observed in a Jewish synagogue. The men could not leave their hats on and they were not allowed to smoke. The rules of the theatres were in the hands of the Hospitals, who managed the municipal theatres. This was an old tradition referred to above.

Seville

According to Antonio Alvarez Cañibano, the Teatro Cómico in Seville, which opened in 1795, had been built by two Italian singers. It was closed in 1808, because of the war with France, and especially opened again in February 1810 for a performance for Joseph Bonaparte, to celebrate the arrival of the French troops in the city.

Barcelona

Performances of opera had reached Barcelona at the end of the seventeenth cen-

Teatro Principal, Barcelona.

tury with the arrival of the Archduke Carlos of Austria. The Liceu Filarmónico-Dramático Barcelonés was formed in 1837, with performances in the Liceu de Montesión, built in 1837 on the ruins of the Predicadores Monastry. It opened for the first time with the opera *Norma*, by Bellini. The director of the Liceu acquired the property of the Convent de Trinitaris de la Rambla in Las Ramblas, a walking street in a desirable situation in the city centre. This beautiful theatre was inaugurated 4 April 1947. It was twice destroyed by fire. The first fire, in 1861, started in the tailoring workroom, and the second, in 1995, began when a workman's blowtorch ignited the scenery backstage. After each disaster it was quickly rebuilt, more splendid that before. During the 1850s there was much rivalry between the Liceu and the old Santa Cruz Theatre, especially after an official decree gave the Liceu the sole right to present lyrical performances. The public was divided between *liceístas* who supported the Italian Opera at the Liceu, and *cruzados* who supported the traditional local productions at the Cruz theatre. The feuding even carried into their private lives, when friends cut each other dead during the traditional Sunday promenades on the Ramblas. In 1893 the theatre was attacked with two bombs in row 13, thrown by Santiago Salvador to protest the execution of the anarchist Pauli Pallás. This was at a time when Europe was swept by a wave of terrorism, according to the book, *Gran Teatre de Liceu.*

Habsburg monarchs (1516-1700): Charles I (reigned 1516-56), Philip II (1556-98), Philip III (1598-1621), Philip IV (1621-65), Charles II (1665-1700).
Bourbon monarchs (1700-1868): Philip V (1700-1746), Ferdinand VI (1746-59), Charles III (1759-88), Charles V (1788-1808), Ferdinand VII (1808-33), Isabella II (1833-68).

Part II
The Pericet Syllabus

Codified Steps of the Escuela Bolera

Compiled by Angel Pericet Carmona (1877–1944)
Codified by Marina Keet, after classes with Eloy Pericet in Spain.

These are my personal notes of the exercises of the Escuela Bolera, the school of classical Spanish dance of the nineteenth century. They are my understanding of this syllabus after study with Eloy Pericet in Madrid. I make these notes available to all dancers who are searching vainly for that elusive subject, the clarification of Spanish dance. To my knowledge it is the first time it has been done, certainly in English and in such detail.

The spelling of the steps is taken firstly as written down by Angel Pericet Carmona, with some suggestions and explanations of other Spanish spelling. The sources have been traced, wherever possible, to French or Italian steps.

It is not easy to notate and describe steps so that other people can understand them. It has been a most gruelling task. Some timing is elusive as the arms move across music and steps. The steps often have complications when being described, such as a preparation of a bend in the knees or a beat in the air that needs to be accounted for. Many teachers have their own way of counting when they teach. I hope that at least this book can be used as a basis when studying these steps and the accompanying dances. The individual dancer can modify the notes according to their liking. Even if it only acts as a stepping stone I shall be happy. These notes have already been used for some years by the Spanish Dance Society, but have been developed after more study.

In Seville in February 2000 I had a very interesting conversation with director and dancer José Antonio and choreographer Alberto Lorca. They decided that because Spanish dance is a living entity, and because teachers and dancers have their own personalities, the Escuela Bolera has and will evolve and change from teacher to teacher. I feel strongly that what matters is that one knows the roots and that important aspects are not lost to posterity, as has happened in Denmark, where August Bournonville's Spanish ballet *Toreadoren* is totally lost, except for two dances saved by Flemming Ryberg, the 'Jaleo de Jerez' and the 'Zapateado', in the style of Zapateado de Maria Cristina.

The Escuela Bolera or Spanish classical school is a very Spanish way of dancing, and the steps often have movements that do not exist in ballet. The Spanish classical dance arm movements are circular. They are moved from a position above the head in inward or outward circles, singly or together. It is from Spain that ballet has taken the arm positions, but in ballet the arms are much freer. During my studies, I have come across old regional dances that have steps which are generally considered the domain of ballet. So perhaps they existed long before ballet. Valencian and Basque dancing in particular have much to offer the researcher. Regarding steps and style between the Valencian dances and the Escuela Bolera, no one knows which way the connection flowed. Some Valencian dances are called Escuela or school dances. Two schools with different styles of steps, arms and footwork came from Xativa and Alzira (Enric Marti i Mora, personal communication). The disappearance of this knowledge with the passing years is a great loss; it is a great strength to know the roots. Perhaps most fascinating of all is the strong connection with ballet, the similarities with the steps taught by Enrico Cecchetti and with some of those found in the Danish ballet.

The exercises were put to music for the Spanish Dance Society with castanets arranged by Eloy Pericet. Washington DC, USA (June 1992), and London (June 1999).

Some Terminology and Abbreviations

(–)	Shows absence of any castanet rhythm
,	Used after a beat
;	Used at the end of a bar or musical cycle of 6 beats
R	Right
L	Left
both	Together: simultaneous R & L castanets
Choque (*posticeo*)	Right and left castanets struck against each other
Pos.	Position
Rodazán	*Rond de jambe* in the air
Escobilla	*Rond de jambe* or *rodazán* on the floor
Escobilla entera	Step L (or R as the case may be), swish leg forward, just off the ground to a point in front or dig at instep, repeat with other leg, step forward on L, lift R in front or do two stamps at the back (depending on which dance is being performed), and a *pas de bourrée* over or under as required. This step is usually danced to a corner on the diagonal. It is found in dances such as Fandangos and Peteneras Boleras (Andaluzas).
Sostenido	A dig in next to the instep on the ball of the foot, then
	Either: Dig the toe in at the instep and extend the foot to 2nd at side (first step of Olé de la Curra).
	Or (as in Olé de la Curra when using the skirt): Step R, dig L, step across with L, (or starting L). The digs can be firmly with ball of foot in front or tipping the toe to instep.
	Or: Ball of the toe in front or at the back – whatever is used is followed by a step onto that foot.
	(Note: in Spanish dance the word *sostenido* is often used for a variety of steps performing the same function initially – digging the foot in and extending it out – but it can be done in various ways.)
Estep or *esté*	A step to the side lifting the other foot in *attitude* in front (e.g. in Peteneras). It can be on a jump – *jeté* to side. Not used in these notes.

Arm Positions

3rd position of the arms, with one arm up and one arm across in front of the body, is called 4th in Spain. In the Spanish Dance Society the arms are numbered according to the first *brazeo* exercise in the syllabus. Our position with one arm across front and one across behind is called 4th. Our 6th, with arms out to the sides, is the Spanish 2nd. The corners and walls are the same as in the terminology of the Cecchetti method.

The eight positions of the arms

Sketches of feet
and arm positions
are by Enrique
Breytenbach

The five positions of the feet

The directions of the room

CORNER 2	WALL 5	CORNER 1
WALL 6		WALL 7
CORNER 3	WALL 8	CORNER 4

ESCUELA BOLERA EXERCISES
Compiled by Angel Pericet Carmona (1877-1944)(original orthography)
Codified by Marina Keet
After classes with Eloy Pericet in Spain

The exercises were put to music for the Spanish Dance Society with castanets arranged by Eloy
Pericet
Washington D.C. USA, June 1992, London June 1999

Contents
1. Grupo de Vueltas
    1. Normal
    2. Con destaque
    3. Girada
    4. Volada o Saltada
    5. De Vals
    6. Fibraltada
    7. De Pecho
    8. Quebrada
    9. Pirueta
    10. Tordin o Salta Tordo

2. Primer Curso
    Grupo Primero
    Abrir y Cerrar
    Tres Cambiamentos Bajos y Tres Altos
    Golpe Punta y Talon Tres Embotados Step y Vuelta
    Fibraltada
    Sease Contra Sease y Vuelta de Pecho

    Grupo Segundo
    Lisada por Delante
    Lisada por Atras
    Retortille Dos Pase de Vasque y Vuelta Fibraltada
    Escobilla Hacia Delante Tres Destaques y Vuelta Quebrada

    Grupo Tercero
    Pifla y Padebure
    Sobresu y Bodorneo (Bordoneo)
    Vuelta de Vals Batararana y Vuelta con Destaque
    Sisol Dos Jerezanas Bajas y Dos Altas

3. Segundo Curso
    Grupo Primero
    Echape y Tercera
    Rodazánes en Vuelta
    Rodazán Hacia Adentro Rodazán Hacia Afuera Asamble y Foete

Rodazán Hacia Adentro Destaque y Cuna

Grupo Segundo
Hecho y Deshecho
Lazos dos Bodorneos y Dos Cambiamentos Bajos
Tres Pase de Vasque Echape y Dos Step
Cuatro Balones Dos Pase de Vasque y Vuelta Fibraltada

Grupo Tercero
Asamble Tres Cuartas y Cambiamento Alto
Tamdecuip
Tijera
Gorgollata

4. Tercer Curso
   Grupo Primero
   1. Rodazán Hacia Adentro Destaque Asemble y Cuarta Volada
   2. Cuatro Asambles con Padebures y Cuatro Sostenidos en Vuelta
   3. Lisada con Tercera por Delante
   4. Lisada con Tercera por Atras

   Grupo Segundo
   1. Asamble y Batuda (French: assemblé)
   2. Espacada Punta y Talon
   3. Balone y Piroueta (French: ballonné)
   4. Espacada Doble y Tordin

   Grupo Tercero (Superior)
   1. Tercera y Cuarta Volada
   2. Rodazán Hacia Afuera Tercera y Cuarta Normal
   3. Briseles Sencillos
   4. Briseles Dobles
   5. Briseles Del Susu (French: sus-sous. G.B.L. Wilson suggests two sources: 'dessus-dessous'
      - over-under from the French, and 'su e giu' from the Italian)
   6. Cuarta Italiana
   7. Quinta

Classical Pas De Basques

A Typical Escuela Bolera Barre

Grupo de Vueltas
(Preparatorio)

1. Vuelta Normal
2. Vuelta Con Destaque
3. Vuelta Girada
4. Vuelta Volada o Saltada
5. Vuelta De Vals
6. Vuelta Fibraltada
7. Vuelta De Pecho
8. Vuelta Quebrada
9. Pirueta
10. Vuelta Tordin o Salto Tordo

GRUPO DE VUELTAS: Preparatorio

Unless otherwise indicated the arms move in outward circles in front of the body.
(*Note*: at end of a beat of music a comma is used, at end of a bar a semi-colon is used).

1. VUELTA NORMAL (normal turn)

To Start
Arms: 5th position over head. Move in outward circle and up front.
Feet: 5th position, R foot front.
Castanets: both (1), L (2), roll (3); both (1), pause (2, 3);

The Step
Place L foot (the back foot) across R and turn to R, continue alternately but subsequent turns start front, not back foot, each time.

The Detail
Start placing L (back foot), across front, arms circle down on count of 1 playing both;
Turn on *demi-pointes* to R taking arms up front to 5th playing L, roll on counts (2, 3);
Settle in 5th (R in front) with arms and feet playing both on count (1),
Hold for (2, 3);
Start next turn with R foot going to left, continue alternately starting front foot each time.

2. VUELTA CON DESTAQUE (turn with a kick; *destaque* means to detach)

To Start
Arms: as above.
Feet: as above.
Castanets: as above.

The Step

Wait for 2 notes.

Grand battement (kick) L (back) leg to side, place across right, turn to R.

The Detail

Kick L (back) leg to side (2nd) playing both while arms held in 5th overhead on count (1),
Place it across R, arms down, turn on *demi-pointe* to R playing L, roll; (2, 3);
Finish with arms and feet in 5th play both (1), and hold for counts (2, 3);
Repeat to left.

Do not circle the arms down until the leg has reached its top height at the side in the *grand battement*. Thus the accent is with arms up in 5th.

2a. VUELTA DOBLADA

The previous step can also be done with a *développé* and is called *vuelta doblada*, but it is not in the Pericet Syllabus, although they do perform it. It is executed with the leg lifted to the side of the supporting knee, while arms are held in 5th. As the leg is extended to a high second, the arm comes swiftly down (same arm as lifted leg) in order to perform the turn, while the leg is placed across the supporting foot to turn, taking that arm up the front to 5th on the turn.

2b. VUELTA CON DESTAQUE AND VUELTA DOBLADA 'LIGADA' (joined)

To Start

Stand in 5th R foot in front.
Arms: 5th.
Castanets: both, L, roll (1, 2, 3); both (1), pause (2, 3);

The Step

Destaque: kick R (front) foot to high second at the side, place across and turn using both arms.
Doblada: lift R (now at the back) to side of knee, arms 5th, kick it high to side and place across and turn to L, bringing R arm down (when leg has reached highest point) into the turn.

Note: the arm is used for the turn, not the kick.

Using the back foot for the *doblada* makes the exercises repeatable to the other side without needing a point to the side and close to change the feet (Eloy Pericet, personal communication).

The Detail

Kick R (front) foot, place it across and turn using both arms as above,
Retiré (lift) R (back) foot to the side of the knee, *développé*, or unfold it to the side, dropping the R arm as you place the foot across and start to turn, after the leg has reached its highest point, taking the R arm up the front to 5th. This brings the L foot in front to repeat the two turns to the R.

3. VUELTA GIRADA (revolving turn)

To Start
Wait for 2 notes.
Arms: as above in 5th over head.
Starting position: R leg raised in *attitude* to corner 2.
Supporting leg straight.
Head: look to corner 2, face in profile to front.
Weight: leaning over the lifted leg and slightly back.
Castanets: both (1), L, roll (2, 3); both (1), pause (2, 3);
Close feet after the music.

The Step
Start on a straight L leg, with R leg in *attitude* in front to corner 2, and arms 5th.
Step to R and turn to R placing L across, step R to side and raise L in *attitude* in front to corner 1, R supporting leg straight. (It can also be stepped back in 4th instead of side; Eloy Pericet, personal communication.)

The Detail
Wait for 2 notes.
Start with R leg in *attitude* in front to corner 2, lean away, and slightly back, from raised leg, looking at corner 2 in profile to front wall.
Step to side with R leg playing both (1),
Place L leg across to turn to R, playing L (2),
Turn to R, playing roll (3);
Step to R sweeping L into *attitude devant* facing corner 1, playing both (1), lean away from lifted leg.
Pause (2, 3);
Repeat to left. Close after the music.

4. VUELTA VOLADA O SALTADA (turn flying and jumping)
I was taught to end stepping to the side and lifting the leg in front, but it is also done stepping behind before raising the leg in *attitude* in front (Eloy Pericet, personal communication). The first is preferred.

To Start
Arms: In 5th overhead.
Starting position: R leg raised in *attitude* in front to corner 2 leaning away, and back, from raised leg.
Castanets: as above both (1), L, roll (2, 3); both (1), pause (2, 3);

The Step
Wait for 2 notes.
From *attitude devant* with R leg, step *grand jeté en tournant* to R with R, step to side on R lift L *attitude devant*.

The Detail

Wait for 2 notes.

Start as described above.

Step to side on R, L starts to move through to wall 8, *grand battement* (kick) L in front to wall 8, taking arms open and down, castanets: both (1).

Keeping arms down: jump turning and changing the legs in the air at the back, landing on L leg, R in *arabesque* facing wall 6 (R leg at back to wall 8), castanets L, roll (2, 3);

Step to side (facing front), arms go up front to 5th as you lift the L leg in *attitude* in front facing corner 1, castanets: both (1), pause (2, 3); lean away from lifted leg.

Repeat to left.

5. VUELTA DE VALS (waltz turn)

To Start

Arms: in 5th overhead.

Feet: in 5th, with R foot front.

Castanets: L,   roll,   roll;   R L,   roll,   roll;   R L,   L,   roll;   both,   hold;
             1,   2,   3;   & 1,   2,   3;   & 1,   2,   3;   1,   2,   3;

The Step

Using 2 alternate arm circles meeting briefly in 5th on count 3 as one arm displaces the next, when the next arm circles down on the turn. Once up on toes remain there for the turn.

Wait for 2 notes.

To R: long *pas de basque* or *careo* for two beats, step to R on *demi-pointe* turn placing L foot over R foot up on *demi-pointes*,

Step to the R, point L to side, close in front.

The Detail

Wait for 2 notes.

Rise up to *demi-pointe* on L, step to side on R, L arm circles down, castanet: L (1),

Step L behind playing roll taking arm up front to 5th (2),

Step to side on R on *demi-pointe*, roll, R arm circles out, (3);

Place L across on *demi-pointe* and turn to R, R arm down on the turn, castanets: R L, roll, roll; (1, 2, 3);

Taking R arm to 5th position:

Step to side on R, and up to 5th playing R L, (1),

Pointing L to side playing L, roll; (2, 3);

Close L in 5th in front castanets: both (1), pause for (2, 3); head can be ready to move to R on the repeat.

Repeat to left.

6. VUELTA FIBRALTADA (turn with vigour)

To Start

Arms: 5th overhead.
Feet: R foot front.
Castanets: both, L,   roll;   both, pause, pause;
               1,   2,   3;   1,   2,   3;

The Step
Wait for 2 notes.
A *vuelta fibraltada*, three times to R, point L (back foot) to the side and close in front, head faces to front on the point. Eloy Pericet also teaches it with the front foot pointing to the side and closing behind. Repeat on the L to the L.

The Detail
Wait for 2 notes.
Lift R foot forward, jump onto it changing foot in front, arms open outwards and down, playing both (1), arms should remain up on the jump and not begin moving until count of (& 2),
Place L foot across and turn to R, take arms down and up front to 5th, playing L, roll (2, 3);
Finish in 5th position, foot and arms; play both (1), pause (2, 3);
Repeat turn to R.
Repeat turn to R.
Point L foot to side with arms in 5th overhead playing both (1), L, roll (2, 3); Close foot in front, both on castanets (1), pause (2, 3); head is to the front as you point the foot to the side.

7. VUELTA DE PECHO (turn leading with the chest)

To Start
Arms: 5th position overhead.
Feet: 5th position, R foot front.
Castanets: both, L,   roll;   both, pause, pause;
               1,   2,   3;   1,   2,   3;

The Step
With a side bend in the body, head lifted, place R foot across L, drop arms outward to either side of body (rounded), turn revolving the body with the arms in that position and straightening up in 5th bringing arms up the front to 5th.

Performed 4 times with low arms, then twice to L (once with low arms and once with right arm in front and left arm starting in 5th lowering across body on turn and finishing with both arms opening out and up to 5th). Repeat to R twice (once with low arms and once with right arm starting in 5th, lowering across body on turn and with both opening out and finishing in 5th).

The Detail
Dropping chest sideways, place R foot across L, arms go to sides of body after the dig, castanets: both, (1),
Turn to L rolling body and straightening it, while both arms raise up front to 5th, play L, roll; (2, 3);
In 5th with foot and arms overhead play both, (1), pause (2, 3);

Repeat to left, repeat to right, repeat to left.

One turn to left, as before starting front foot, one turn starting back foot. Alternative arms: leave L arm up, take R arm down (3rd) bring R foot over to turn to L, on turn bring arm down to join R in front, take both outwards and up to 5th. Repeat both turns to R starting with L. Alternating arms.

8. VUELTA QUEBRADA ('broken' turn; bending at the waist)

To Start

Arms: 5th overhead.

Feet: 5th with R foot front.

Castanets:	both,	L,	roll;	both,	L,	roll;	both,	L,	roll;	both,	pause 2 beats;
(waltz)	1,	2,	3;	1,	2,	3;	1,	2,	3;	1,	2, 3;

The Step

Wait for 2 notes.

Step on R on place, low *rond de jambe* (*rodazán*) L across drop weight on L (front) foot, R at back on *cou-de-pied*. Step on R on place, *grand battement* L to side, place L behind turn under to L on a rise.

The Detail

Wait for 2 notes.

Arms 5th, step R in place, play both, (1),

Rodazán or circle the L foot across low and drop onto it, circling L arm outward castanet L, (2), and dropping onto it with L arm across front of body, R arm over head, playing roll; (3);

Step R (*coupé* under) taking L leg into *destaque* or kick to 2nd position on a rise, L arm up front to 5th overhead, play both, L, roll; (1, 2, 3);

Place L foot behind while arms circle outwards, and to side and slightly behind the back, playing both, (1),

Turn under to L, with body bending and straightening up to R bringing arms up front to 5th, playing L, roll; (2, 3);

Finish 5th facing front with L foot front arms 5th, play both, (1), pause (2, 3); Repeat to other side.

9. PIRUETA (Pirouette)

To Start

Arms: 4th position, R front.

Feet; 4th position, R front in lunge, weight on R.

Castanets:	L,	roll,	roll;	roll,	pause;
	1,	2,	3;	1,	2, 3;

The Step

Wait 2 notes.

Start lunge in 4th and turn to R, with arms starting 4th and opening to sides with L leg at back of knee, drop into 4th on a lunge, repeat side to side.
To reverse start in *plié* in 4th (Eloy Pericet, personal communication).

Note: the arms go 4th to 4th changing through low 6th while turning, and settle in 4th at the end.

The Detail
Wait for 2 notes.
With weight on R, front leg, *relevé* (rise) up on to R foot turning to R, with L foot at back of R knee, well turned out, playing L on the *relevé* (1), roll, roll; on the turn (2, 3);
Drop into 4th on a lunge with L leg in front and L arm forward, R at back, play roll, (1), pause for (2, 3);
Repeat 3 times forward to L, to R, to L.

Reverse the turns: travelling back with both legs bent in a *plié* to start:
Relevé onto L, lifting R foot across front of L knee and turning towards the R.
Finish by placing the foot down in 4th behind, both legs in *plié*. Timing is same as first four and it is repeated 3 more times alternating sides to R, L, R.

10. VUELTA TORDÍN O SALTO TORDO (jumped or 'hopped' turn)

To Start
Arms: 4th, R arm low across body in front, left across behind back.
Feet: 5th with R foot front.

Castanets:	both,	L,	roll;	both,	L,	roll;	both,	L,	roll;	both,	pause;
(waltz)	1,	2,	3;	1,	2,	3;	1,	2,	3;	1,	2, 3;

The Step
Wait for 2 notes.
Relevé in 5th, arms across body, jump turning and landing L front.

The Detail
Wait for 2 notes.
With R arm front, Left behind back, *relevé* in 5th playing both, L, roll; (1, 2, 3);
Demi-plié (half bend knees), arms remain same position, castanets both, L, roll; (1, 2, 3);
Jumped turn in air, changing arms across body playing both, L, roll; (1, 2, 3);
Straighten up knees, feet in 5th, castanets both (1), pause (2, 3);
Repeat three times alternate sides.

Note: *Tordin* is a type of bird. The jumped turn is descriptive of the way the bird hops. Several dictionaries were consulted and, other than the above, no word *tordin* or *tordo* could be found.

PRIMER CURSO: Grupo Primero

1. Abrir y cerrar

2. Tres cambiamentos bajos y tres altos

3. Golpe punta y talon, tres embotados step y vuelta fibraltada

4. Sease contra sease y vuelta de pecho

1. ABRIR Y CERRAR (open and close)
Music: Bolero Liso.

To Start
Wait for 3 notes (& 6 &).
Feet: 5th position, R foot front.
Arms: 5th position overhead, remaining there throughout the exercise.
Castanets: both, L, roll;

The Step
Échappé to 2nd position and jump into 5th, performed five times and knees straightened to end.

The Detail
Wait for 3 notes (& 6 &).
Jump high into the air landing feet apart at side, arms 5th play both, (1),
Jump high into the air landing feet in 5th, L front, arms 5th, L, roll, (2, 3);
Repeat closing alternate feet front 4 more times.
Straighten knees to end.

2. TRES CAMBIAMENTOS BAJOS Y TRES ALTOS (three changes and three split jumps in the air in 2nd position)
Music: Boleras de la Cachucha.

To Start
Wait for 3 notes (& 3; &).
Feet: 5th with R foot in front.
Arms: 5th overhead, remaining there throughout the exercise.
Castanets: both.

The Step
Three changes in 5th and three jumps with legs in 2nd *en l'air*.

3 changes (1, & 2), scissors (& 3);
                     scissors (& 1),
                     scissors (& 2),
3 changes (3; & 1), scissors (& 2),
                     scissors (& 3);
                     scissors (& 1),
3 changes (2, & 3);

Straighten up knees at end of exercise.
The Spanish Dance Society taped music requires that it ends on 3 changes and straighten knees.

The Detail
From 5th, with R front leap in air changing foot and land with L in front arms 5th, both (1),
Repeat landing with R in front, arms 5th, both on castanets, (&),

Repeat landing with L in front, arms 5th, both on castanets, (2),

From 5th leap in air extending legs to side, arms 5th (&),
Land with R foot in front (3); play both;
Repeat landing with L in front, play both (& 1),
Repeat landing with R in front, play both (& 2), straighten knees;
Jump in air on (&) to repeat from the changes.

Repeat the whole exercise etc. as required.

3. GOLPE PUNTA Y TALON, TRES EMBOTADOS, STEP Y VUELTA FIBRALTADA (stamp, toe
heel, dig front, three *retirés sautés*, step and *vuelta fibraltada*)
Embotada means blunt or dull. (French: Emboîté or dove-tailed)
Music: Malagueña *estribillo*.

To Start
Wait for chord.
Feet: 5th with R foot in front.
Arms: 5th overhead.
Castanets: both, L, roll; R L, roll, roll; R L, L, roll; both, L, roll; end on both (this one being the start of the next step if done continuously).

The Step
Stamp R foot 5th in front, dig L toe (turned in) and heel (turned out) at side,
Dig L in front, three skips back lifting L, R, L,
Jeté onto R, L in *attitude* in front (called 'step'). Face corner 1, head looks to corner 1.
Vuelta fibraltada to L.

The Detail
Stamp R foot front in 5th, taking L arm outward circle, play both, (1),
Turning leg in, dig L toe out at side, play L, (2),
Turned out dig heel at side, L arm is now down, play roll; (3); dig L toe front playing R L, (& 1),
3 skips back on L, R, L, taking arm to 5th play roll, roll, R L, (2, 3; & 1),
Jump onto R with L *attitude* front (face corner 1) leaning away from it, arms 5th play L, (2), look to corner 1, hold, roll (3);
Fibraltada jump turn to L, play both, L roll (1, 2, 3); both (1), hold or continue step, beginning left.

4. SEASE CONTRA SEASE Y VUELTA DE PECHO (*chassé* and a chest turn)
Sease comes from *se hace*, meaning to do or to make. The *contra* is to undo.
Music: La Maja y El Torero (16 bars of first part).

To Start
Feet: 5th position, R foot front.

Arms: 5th overhead,

Castanets:	L,	roll,	roll;	R L,	roll,	roll;	both,	L,	roll;	both,	pause.
	1,	2,	3;	& 1,	2,	3;	1,	2,	3;	1,	2,	3.

The Step

Wait for chord.

Preparatory small lift to *cou-de-pied* of R foot (&), *chassé* to R side with R, *coupé* L behind, place R foot in 5th behind, *chassé* to L to second, *coupé* R foot behind and step to side with L, chest turn to L. Repeat starting L.

Danced four times alternate sides to Spanish Dance Society tape.

The Detail

Starting with arms and feet in 5th, lift front (R) foot across the ankle, play R (&) making an outward circle with R arm, slide R foot to side, play L (1),

Bring L foot on *demi-pointe* behind, place R foot with small lift up and over L to 5th at back, R arm circles up front to 5th, play roll (2),

Close R foot behind play: roll; (3);

Repeat to L:

Again lift front (L) foot across the ankle, play R (&)

Making an outward circle with L arm, slide L foot to side, Play L, (1),

Bring R foot on *demi-pointe* behind, play roll, (2),

This time step to side with L (not behind as in the first one), arms 5th, play roll; (3); drop body forward and sideways and place R leg across L, open arms and place them low and rounded at sides of body, play both, (1), turn to L in a *vuelta de pecho* turn, L, (2), roll; (3);

End in 5th position of arms and feet, play both, (1), pause for 2 counts (2, 3).

Repeat to other side.

Note: when I was taught, I was told to make a distinction between the first *chassé* to R side with R, *coupé* L behind, place R foot in 5th behind, which is really a *coupé* changing the weight, while the second is *chassé* to L to second, *coupé* R foot behind and step to side with L, which is the start of the turn, although nowadays this interesting distinction is not carefully followed.

PRIMER CURSO: Grupo Segundo

1. Lisada por delante

2. Lisada por atras

3. Retortille dos pase de vasque y vuelta fibraltada

4. Escobilla hacia adelante tres destaques y vuelta quebrada

1. LISADA POR DELANTE (*glissade* in front)
Music: Bolero.

Note: some Spanish dance teachers say that *lisada* has nothing to do with the balletic *glissade* in French. I wish to note that in Italian *gl* is pronounced *lli*. In view of the influx of Italian dancers into the Spanish theatre in the eighteenth century, I cannot help wondering whether this is not the influence, excepting that the following two steps, although called *lisada* resemble a *glissade* in the first exercise and a *chassé* in the second.

To Start
As above wait for introduction before starting the step.
Feet: 5th, R foot front.
Arms: 5th overhead.
Castanets: L   Roll (& 1),   Both (2),   Both (3);
Timing: lift leg (&),   *chassé* (1),   *coupé* (2),   *assemblé* (3);

The Step
Chassé to second with R, *coupé* under with L, *assemblé* under with R,
Repeat the step alternately seven times and straighten knees to end.

The Detail
Slide R foot to 2nd position, R arm circles outward and down, L roll on castanet (& 1),
Place L foot behind with weight on it, keep arm down, swish R leg to side, play both, (2),
Assemblé feet together with R behind, arms go up front to 5th, playing both; (3);
Step goes from side to side starting each time with alternate feet.

2. LISADA POR ATRAS (DETRAS) (*glissade* at the back)
Music: Bolero.

Note: this is the step performed in Sevillanas Boleras, starting with 'stamp, stamp' or 'dig, stamp' or 'tip of toe, stamp'. This is the progression through which it evolved, having started with two flat stamps and performed today with the tip of the toe. All three are acceptable (Eloy Pericet, personal communication). In this exercise it is done from side to side; in the Sevillanas there is just a quarter turn (not a half turn to the partner's place) and then back to the starting point on the return (Eloy Pericet, personal communication).

To Start
Wait for 3-beat lead in to music's phrase.
Feet: 5th, L foot in front.
Arms: 5th overhead.
Castanets: both, (1), L, (2), roll, (3); both (&).

The Step
Wait for 3 notes.
Glissade with R to right, closing L in front, *jeté* (*pifla*) over onto R, L at back, arms circling outward and up to 5th. Repeat alternately. Close, and straighten legs.

The Detail

Stand still for 3 beats.

Step to side on R foot arms circling outward from 5th, play both, (1),

Close L front, arms down in front, play L, (2),

Jeté over on to R, swishing R and jumping arms 5th overhead with slight *épaulement*, play roll; (3); as you land; both (&) to start again. Looking over shoulder at sole of foot.

Repeat on L.

Note: the step goes from side to side with alternate feet, seven times to the Spanish Dance Society Tape. Usually it ends just closing the foot behind and straightening the knees (Eloy Pericet, personal communication).

3. RETORTILLE, DOS PASE DE VASQUE, Y VUELTA FIBRALTADA

Retortille means twisted and I take it that it refers to the *escobilla*: step to side, *chassé* across, with the body swinging over.

Music: La Macarena (the dance in which this step is performed).

To Start

Feet: 5th position R foot front.

Arms: 5th overhead.

Castanets:

A

Start L, roll on the preparation of *coupé* under and beat,

Then:

both,	L,	roll;	both,	L,	roll;	both,	L,	roll;	both,	L,	roll;
1,	2,	3;	4,	5,	6;	1,	2,	3;	4,	5,	6;

Two *pas de basque*; *vuelta fibraltada*;

B

R L,	roll,	roll;	R L,	roll,	roll;	R L,	L,	roll;
& 1,	2,	3;	& 4,	5,	6;	& 1	2,	3;

both,	start again: L,	roll etc.
4,	5,	6;

If put to music, the release of the foot for the *pas de basque* has to be timed for two beats of (5, 6); swishing it out to the side, arms 5th.

The Step

Starts on counts of (4, 5, 6); with no castanets, but could be (L, roll) if one wanted to play them. Eloy Pericet has the pianist play two chords, and starts on the second one before the music.

A

Coupé R under (4), pause (5),

Toe heel L at a diagonal, body slightly to corner 2 (& a),

and close R foot (6); behind with a stamp (like a *taconeo glissade*);

Step L to side (1), *chassé* across on R (2, 3), (the *escobilla*).

Repeat on L:
Coupé L under (4), pause (5),
Toe heel R at a diagonal, body slightly to corner 1 (& a),
Close L foot (6); behind with a stamp;

(The whole step is like a *taconeo glissade*.)

Step R to side (1), *chassé* across on L (2, 3); (the *escobilla*),
Coupé R under (4), pause (5, 6);

B
Two *pas de basque*: to L (1, 2, 3); to R (4, 5, 6);
A *vuelta fibraltada* turning to L (1, 2, 3);
Repeat step again starting A on (4, 5, & a 6);
After all repeats just hold for those three beats at end.

Greater Detail
A
The beaten step starting with R:
From 5th position of arms and feet,
Lift R foot behind and *coupé* it behind L, (play both) (4),
Release and lift L, (play L), (5),
Toe-heel beat with L, (& a) to direction of corner 2,
Close R behind (6); (play roll);

The Escobilla
Step to side on L, (play both), (1),
Step R across in small *rond de jambe* (*escobilla*) on the floor R arm in circle down (play L), (2),
Dropping across on R, (play roll); (3);

Repeat the beaten step, but with L:
Lift L behind, and *coupé* it behind R, (play both), (4),
Taking R arm up to 5th on (4),
Release and lift R, (play L), (5),
Toe-heel beat with R (& a) to direction of corner 1,
Close L 5th behind; (play roll); (6);

The Escobilla
Step to side on R (play both), (1),
Step L across with small *rond de jambe*, on floor play L, (2),
L arm opens out and down,
Dropping across on L (3); (play roll),
Coupé under with R, (play both), (4), with arm going to 5th.
Pause (5, 6); (L, roll); leg out on the way to *pas de basque*.

B

Note: arms from 5th make an outward circle with R on L *pas de basque*, with L on R *pas de basque.*

Pas de basque to L (1, 2, 3); (play R L), (& 1), roll (2), roll (3);

Pas de basque to R (1, 2, 3); (play R L), (& 1), roll (2), roll (3);

Vuelta fibraltada turning to L lifting L and changing feet in air. Arms remain in 5th, play R L, (& 1),

Turn to L, arms circle outward and up to 5th overhead, play L, roll; (2, 3);

Finish foot and arms 5th,

Take R foot back (4), (play both),

Play L, (5), roll; (& a 6); while starting the beaten step all over again.

Repeat the whole Step A and B to R starting on (4, 5, & a 6);

4. ESCOBILLA HACIA ADELANTE, TRES DESTAQUES Y VUELTA QUEBRADA (brushes forward to the front, three kicks and a turn under)

To Start

Music: La Maja y el Torero, the *jaleo* tempo.

It goes across the music 3 times with even timing for turn.

Feet: 5th position R foot front.

Arms: 5th overhead.

Castanets: both, L, roll.

The Step

Wait for two notes (6; &)

Step with R, *chassé* L across, *coupé* under with R into three *coupés* under and *grands battements* to 2nd, turn under with and to the L.

The Detail

Wait for two notes (6; &)

Step on the R, play (both), (1),

Chassé across with L, play (L, roll); (2, 3);

(R *cou-de-pied* at the back.)

Coupé under with R (both), (1), kicking L leg to side, play (L, roll); (2, 3); R arm circles down and up, leaning away from lifted leg (like an intake of breath).

Coupé under with L, (both), (1), kicking R leg to side, play (L, roll); (2, 3); dropping L arm in circle down and up, leaning away from lifted leg.

Coupé under with R; (both), (1), kicking L leg to side, play L, roll; (2, 3); dropping both arms in circle down, close L foot behind, play both, (1),

Vuelta quebrada turn to the L, circling both arms behind back and up front to 5th, play L, roll; (2, 3);

Repeat to other side.

PRIMER CURSO: Grupo tercero

1. Pifla y padebure (probably *pas de bourrée*)

2. Sobresu y bodorneo (probably from *soubresaut*. Bordoneo)

3. Vuelta de valse batararaña y vuelta con destaque (Possibly Matalaraña or 'killing of the spider', Angel Pericet Carmona said that there is no connection with this word, of killing a spider. (Eloy Pericet. Personal communication.)

4. Sisol dos jerezanas bajas y dos altas

1. PIFLA Y PADEBURE (*jeté* over and *pas de bourrée*)
As in Seguidillas Manchegas with a *sostenido* to start.
Music: Seguidillas Manchegas.

To Start
Arms: 5th overhead.
Feet: 5th, R foot front.
Head starts turned (looking) to R on the & beat.
As in *lisada por delante*, you look towards the sole of your raised foot.
Castanets: L roll; both both, L roll, L roll; both both.

The Step
Wait for chord in Spanish Dance Society music.
Introduction *sostenido*: dig R toe and stamp (& 6; L roll; & 1, both both),
Swish (2), *jeté* L leg over, (3),
Step R to side and *pas de bourrée* L behind, R side (4, 5, 6); close L front (1), Pause (2).

The Detail
Wait for chord.
Introduction: dig R toe in front (L roll); (& 6);
And lift (both)   (&) and stamp it, (both), (1), 1st time only, and does
not repeat when the step repeats:
Holding arms in 5th position, swish L leg, head changes to L, leg lifts, play (L roll),
                                                   (& 2),
Jeté over on L, (L roll);   (& 3); (arms remain 5th),
Step to side on R on toe, (both both),   (& 4),
Pas de bourrée to R: place L behind on pointe, (L roll), (& 5),
Step to side on R (L roll)   (& 6);
Close L in front (both both)   (& 1).

On the *pas de bourrée* the L arm circles outward and back up to 5th.

Repeat to other side starting with the R foot doing the swish, *jeté* over (L roll, L roll); (& 2, & 3);

2. SOBRESU Y BODORNEO (BORDONEO) (*glissade* and 'embroidery': turning toe in and out)
Music: Cachucha.

To Start
Feet: 5th R foot front.
Arms: 5th overhead.
Castanets: L, roll; R L, roll, roll; R L, roll, roll; R L, roll, roll; R L.

The Step
Wait for 4 chords.
Glissade to R, close L foot in 5th in front, step on R, lift L toe, turn it in bringing it over, lift the L heel bringing it forward turned out, repeat the in and out 3 times.

To end: step to side on R, *coupé* under with L, step forward on R and dig L foot behind.

The Detail
Wait for 4 chords.
Glissade over to right, ending L front, arms 5th (L, roll),
Stamp on R foot (*golpecito*) (R L),   (& 1),
L arm circles outward and down as you bring the toe of the L foot over, (heel remains on floor),
(roll),   (2),
Keep toe on floor and swivel heel forward, (roll);   (3);
Repeat stamp and the toe heel swivel (R L, roll, roll);   (1, 2, 3);
Repeat stamp and the toe heel swivel (R L, roll, r = oll);   (1, 2, 3);
Arm remains down in front on all three.
Step/stamp (*golpecito*) R behind close arm up to 5th (R L),
Repeat on L foot to L.

The Sequence
Long: one *glissade*, step, with 3 toe heels to R, stamp on R.
Long: one *glissade*, step, with 3 toe heels to L, stamp on L.
Short: one *glissade*, step, with 1 toe heel to R, stamp on R.
Short: one *glissade*, step, with 1 toe heel to L, stamp on L.
Long: one *glissade*, step, with 3 toe heels to R, stamp on R in 5th.

Note: may also be performed with a small *fibraltada* in regional dances instead of the *glissade*. The ending was choreographed for the Spanish Dance Society by Eloy Pericet.

3. VUELTA DE VALS, BATARARAÑA Y VUELTA CON DESTAQUE (waltzed turn, *glissade* to a point, and turn with *grand battement*).
Music: Maja y el Torero.

To Start
Feet: 5th, R foot front.
Arms: 5th.

Castanets:	L,	roll,	roll;	R L,	roll,	roll;	R L,	L,	roll;	both,	pause;
	1,	2,	3;	& 1,	2,	3;	& 1,	2,	3;	1,	2, 3;
	both,	L,	roll;	both,	pause,	pause;	both,	L,	roll;	both,	pause;

The Step
Wait for chord.
As described above.

The Detail
Wait for chord.
Vuelta de valse exercise to R playing first line of castanets;

Sostenido: Dig L toe front, stamp L, play both; both, (3; 1) arms 5th,

Glissade R, closing L front, R arm circles outward and down, play: L, roll; (2, 3); Point R to front corner 1, play both, (1), pause (2),
Close arm to 5th before lifting R leg to side (*grand battement*), play both; (3);
Bring leg in front and turn to L in *vuelta normal* using both arms as in exercise, outward and down in front and up front to 5th, play both, L, roll; both and hold. (1, 2, 3; 1, pause for 2 and 3);
Repeat to the left.
(Also performed without *sostenido*, counts changing accordingly.)

4. SISOL DOS JEREZANAS BAJAS Y DOS ALTAS (*sisol* has no known translation; Cyril W. Beaumont, in his *French-English Dictionary of Dance Terms*, thinks it is a corruption of *sissonne*; two *jerezanas*, 2 Low and 2 High)
Music: 2nd part of La Maja y el Torero.

To Start
Feet: 5th R front.
Arms: arms 5th overhead.

Castanets:	6;	& 1,	2,	3;	& 4,	5,	
1st Sisol	both,	L,		roll;	R L,	roll,	
(rep.) *Sisol* from*	roll;	R L,	L,	roll;*	R L,	roll,	
	roll;	R L,	L,	roll;	both,	L,	
	roll;	roll,	L,	roll;	roll,	pause,	
Jerezanas bajas:	both;	both,	L,	roll;	L,	roll,	
	both;	both,	L,	roll;	L,	roll,	
Jerezanas altas Choque;		both,	L,	roll;	L,	roll,	
Choque;		both,	L,	roll;	L,	roll,	pause;

REPEAT to return to front

Note 1: 6; 1, 2, 3, 4, 5, (start again with 6).
Bolero rhythms are usually counted, in 6 beats, crossing two bars of 3 beats.

Note 2: the movement of the arm is a very fluid circle and does not stop rigidly in 3rd. That is notated to show where the arm is at a given moment of the step.

The Step
Sisol
First line of castanets:
Step to 2nd with R (facing front) kicking L leg across body making half-turn to face back,
(1, 2, 3); (both, L, roll);   (arms 3rd, L arm across in front),
Step on L foot (4),   (arm to 5th),   (R L),
      (R arm starts circle out on next two steps)
Step behind with R, (5),   (roll),
to side with L,   (6);   (roll);
and point R to side, (1, 2, 3); (play first counts of second line of castanets: (R L, L, roll);
                (arms 3rd, R arm across in front);

Repeat with same foot facing the back and end facing front, but castanets play a different rhythm. (Begin with * second half of second line of castanets and play through count 4 of fourth line of castanets: (4, 5, 6; 1, 2, 3), (R L, roll, roll; R L, L, roll);

Hold foot pointed to side, Taking arm to 5th as before and play the underlined beats above: (4, 5, 6; 1, 2, 3, 4),   (both, L, roll; roll, L, roll, roll),

Dos Jerezanas Bajas

As noted above step on R,	(5), (pause),
Point L front, (arms 5th),	(6); (both),
Point L back, (arms to L hip),	(1), (both),
Low swish of L foot through forward,	(2), (L),
3 walks going to R round self: L, R, L:	(3; 4, 5), (roll, L, roll),

(arms open outward and up to 5th each time on the walks),	
Point R front (arms 5th),	(6); (both);
Point R back,	(1), (both),
Swish R foot through,	(2), (L),
3 walks finishing circle to face front:	R, L, R,
	(3; 4, 5), (roll, L, roll),

Repeat *jerezanas* but *altas*: with leg kicking back after the point in front, playing (*choque*), (5th), (both), (arm opening outward circle to 3rd as leg is up at back).

The Detail

Sisol

From 5th position of arms and feet:

With R step to 2nd facing front	(1), (both), (arms 5th),
Grand battement (kick) L leg across and to side making half turn to face back	
	(2, 3); (L, roll), (arm 3rd, L front),

(L arm circles up to 5th on step like a *pas de bourrée*):

Step (on place) on L,	(& 4), (R L),
Step behind on R,	(5), (roll),
Step to side L,	(6); (roll);

R arm then circles down to 3rd on the point to side:

Point R to side, (& 1, 2, 3); (R L, L, roll) (R arm is front, and then up on last two beats of hold – the L, roll).

(hold arms in 3rd with leg pointed to side).

(Thus the R arm has gone in an outward circle to hesitate in 3rd then returning up the front to 5th to start.)

Repeat this with R but starting to back and ending facing the front:

Step with R,	(4), (R L),
Grand battement (kick) L leg across making half turn to face front, arms 3rd as above,	
(5, 6); (roll, roll);	

(L arm circles up to 5th on step like a *pas de bourrée*): step (on place) on L,

	(& 1),	(R L),
Step behind on R,	(2),	(L),
Step to side L,	(3);	(roll),

R arm then circles down on the point to side:
Point R to side,   (4, 5, 6); (both, L, roll); (R arm is front, and then up on last two beats of hold – the L, roll)).
Thus the R arm has gone in an outward circle returning to 5th, (hold in 5th with leg pointed to side).

The Detail
Point (4), hold: 5, 6; 1; 2, 3; 4;   (both, L, roll; roll, L, roll; roll),
Count 5, is the first step of the *jerezana*

2 Jerezanas Bajas and 2 Jerezanas Altas
Jerezanas round self to L: castanet rhythm goes across two bars.

Step R,	(pause),	(5), arms 5th,
Point L front,	(both);	(6); arms going down front,
Point behind,	(both),	(1), arms down front to L hip,
Swish L through,	(L),	(2), (low, not high)

3 walks: arms go outward and up to 5th on all 3 walks:

	L (roll),	(3);
	R (L),	(4),
	L (roll),	(5),
Point R front,	(both);	(6); arms 5th,
Point R back,	(both),	(1), arms down front to R hip,
Swish R through,	(L),	(2),

3 walks: arms go slowly out and up to 5th, on all three walks:

	R (roll),	(3);
	L (L),	(4),
	R (roll),	(5),
Point L front,	(*choque*);	(6); arms 5th,
Kick L back,	(both),	(1), open L out,
Swish L through,	(L),	(2), arms 3rd going up, L front,
3 walks	L (roll),	(3); arm up to 5th on walks,
	R (L),	(4),
	L (roll),	(5),
Point R front,	(*choque*);	(6); arm 5th,
Kick R back,	(both),	(1), open R out,
swish R through,	(L),	(2), arms 3rd going up, R front,
3 walks	R (roll),	(3); arm up to 5th on walks,
	L (L),	(4),
	R (roll),	(5),
Point L foot;	(pause);	(6);

Repeat everything to the left.

At end: place foot in 5th in front to end on third walk: walk L, walk R, close L over in front.

SEGUNDO CURSO: Grupo Primero

1. Echape y tercera (French: *Echappé*)

2. Rodazánes en vuelta (French: *rond de jambe*)

3. Rodazán hacia adentro (dentro), rodazán hacia afuera (fuera), asamble y foete

4. Rodazán hacia dentro destaque y cuna

1. ECHAPE Y TERCERA (*échappé*, jump legs to 2nd and beat as you close)
Suggested music: if Bolero it is counted as below.
Cachucha:
e.g.   1,   2,   3;   pause 4
         5,   6;   1,   pause 2
         3;   4,   5,   pause 6;

To Start
Feet: 5th, R foot front.
Arms: 5th overhead throughout the exercise.
Castanets: both, L, roll.

The Step
As described above: six times and straighten knees to end.

The Detail
Jump into air   (&)
Landing feet apart in 2nd,   (both),   (1),
Jump up beating R foot front, (L),   (2),
Land in 5th with R foot behind (roll);   (3); pause (4).

Repeat with alternate feet beating front and closing behind.

2. RODAZÁNES EN VUELTA (*rond de jambe*s turning)
Suggested music: Bolero Liso, portion of the *copla*, stop and start again to other side.

To Start
Feet: 5th, R foot front.
Arms: 5th.
Castanets: both both, L roll, and do L rolls continuously after that.

The Step
Three *rodazán*es turning on self, facing front each time on 3rd one for each turn. This is done three times outward and *assemblé* the foot behind. Repeat turning to R doing inward *ronds de jambe* to R. Then repeat to the other side .

The Detail
Wait for counts of (4, & a 5).
Wait for first three beats.
Sostenido: dig step on R, (both both); (& 6);
Drop across with L (L) (&) arms into 3rd, R raised, L in front, step back on R foot (roll), (1), releasing L front in first *rodazán*.

Hopping on R turning to L do two more *rodazán*es with L in air (& 2), (& 3); end facing front,
Repeat with 3 more as above (& 4, & 5, & 6); ending front,

Repeat with 3 more as above (& 7, & 8, & 9), ending front,
Assemblé L leg behind (10), pause (11, 12),
Repeat without the *sostenido*:
Just step forward (like a *chassé*) on R (& 1), *rodazán* (9 counts) as above but turning inwards going to the R,
Assemblé in front on 10. Repeat to other side.

3. RODAZÁN HACIA ADENTRO (DENTRO), RODAZÁN HACIA AFUERA (FUERA), ASEMBLE Y FOETÉ (FOUETTÉ)

Step flat, *relevé rodazán* inwards with half turn, step flat, *relevé rodazán* outwards with half turn, *assemblé* R behind *entrechat trois*, *développé* L jumped, *assemblé* in front. (It is featured in the dance Zapateado de Maria Cristina's first step as described below, where it is often on a *relevé*).

Suggested music: Malagueña.

To Start
Feet: 5th, R foot front.
Arms: 5th.
Arms move from 3rd to 3rd.
Castanets: both, L, roll; both, L, roll; both, L, roll; both.

The Step
Wait for chord.
As above, step, *relevé rodazán* inwards with half turn to face back, step, *relevé rodazán* outwards with half turn to face front, *assemblé* R behind, *entrechat trois*, *développé* L on *sauté*, *assemblé* in front.

The Detail
Wait for a chord.
Step to R on R, extending L to side with half turn to face back (both), (1),
L arm has circled down to 3rd front,
Relevé and *rodazán* L inward (L, roll); (2, 3);
Take arm up to 5th.

Step on L *coupé* R to side half turn to face front, (both), (1),
R arm has circled out to 3rd front,
Relevé and *rodazán* R outward (L, roll); (2, 3);
Arm returns up front to 5th and remains there for:

Assemblé R behind (both),	(1),
Jump lifting L behind R (L),	(2),
Jump *développé* L in 2nd (roll),	(3);
Assemblé L foot in 5th, (both).	(1), pause for (2, 3).

Repeat with L to L.

4. RODAZÁN HACIA ADENTRO (DENTRO) DESTAQUE Y CUNA (round of the leg, kick and rock up on toes, not over on rolling ankles as in regional dances)
Suggested music: Malagueña *estribillo*.

To Start
Feet: 5th, R front.
Arms: 5th.
Castanets: both, L,   roll;   R L,   roll,   roll;   R L,   roll,   roll;   R L,   pause, pause.
         1,   2,   3;   & 1,   2,   3;   & 1,   2,   3;   & 1,   2,   3.

The Step
Step on R, *rodazán* L to side, drop across on it and rock on feet side to side (as in Sailor's Hornpipe), look over L arm.

The Detail
Step on R on place (both),   (1), L arm circles down outward,
Rodazán L at side (L),   (2),
Drop L across close to R foot (roll);   (3);

Arms stay in this position for rocks, feet move turned out rocking side to side where toes are in 5th.
Rock R under pushing over toes of L, (back foot) (R L),   (& 1),
Rock L over pushing over toes of R, (front foot) (roll),   (2),
Rock R under pushing over of L, (back foot) (roll);   (3);

Repeat stepping over on L. Change arms to 3rd with L up R in front, change head to look R over front arm.

Repeat to R but turning on self to R rocking 9 times and end on 10. Arm goes slowly up to 5th.
Repeat all starting with L.
Close 5th to end.

SEGUNDO CURSO: Grupo Segundo

1. Hecho y deshecho

2. Lazos dos bodorneos (bordoneos) y dos cambiamentos bajos

3. Tres pas de vasque echape y dos step (French: *pas de Basque* and *echappé*).

4. Cuatro balones dos pase de vasque y vuelta fibraltada (four *ballonnés*, two *pas de basque* and a jumped turn)

1. HECHO Y DESHECHO (to make and to unmake)
Suggested music: Bolero Liso.

To Start
Feet: 5th, R front.
Arms: 5th.
Castanets: both, L roll, L roll and continue with L roll, to end.

The Step
Wait for (& , 6 &).
Danced 6 times as follows:
From 5th jump into 2nd beating R front (both), (1), (can be without a beat 1st time), jump close beating R front and landing in 5th, R behind (L roll), (& 2),
jump open beating R front and landing in 2nd, (L roll), (& 3);

This can also be started with a plain *échappé* to second (Eloy Pericet, personal communication). This is how it is performed in Spain, however it is confusing as after that all *échappés* are beaten.

The Detail
Start with plain *échappé* to 2nd, or a beaten one.
Think of it as 3 steps using the R foot to beat each time. Then start from second and repeat it all with the left beating:

1st sequence of three steps with R beating front:
Jump up beat R front, landing in 2nd,
Jump up from 2nd beat R front, close R 5th behind,
Jump up beat R in front, land out in 2nd.

2nd sequence of three steps with L beating front:
Jump up beat L front, landing in 2nd,
Jump up from 2nd beat L front, close L 5th behind,
Jump up beat L front, land out in 2nd.

(End with beat R front, introducing that it now repeats with R):
Jump close beating R front, into 5th and close behind, pause.

Repeat alternately.

2. LAZOS DOS BODORNEOS (BORDONEOS) Y DOS CAMBIAMENTOS BAJOS ('Bows', two *bordoneos*, 'embroideries', and two low changes)
Suggested music: Polka.

To Start
Feet: 5th with L front.
Arms: 5th.

Music: If using the polka (music from *La Boda de Luis Alonso*) you play L roll, with pauses, throughout; the step remains the same (Eloy Pericet, personal communication). This can also be danced with only 3 quick *bodorneos* (*bordoneos*) and a pause. This brings it to start with the other foot, so it works alternately.

If using other music it is as follows:
Castanets:
Part 1: both, L,   roll; both, L,   roll; both, L   roll; both, pause, pause.
Part 2: both, L,   roll; R L,   roll,   roll; both, L,   roll; R L,   roll,   roll, etc.

Note: the foot is not lifted in the air.

The Step
Part 1
Wait for chord.
Arms go down in an outward circle.
Swivel (&) close 5th, (pause) (slow) both, (1), pause, L, roll, for (2, 3);
Swivel (&) close 5th, (pause) (slow) both, (1), pause, L, roll, for (2, 3);

Swivel (&) close 5th (quick) (both),   (1),
Swivel (&) close 5th (quick) (L),   (2),
Swivel (&) close 5th (quick) (roll);   (3);
Swivel (&) close 5th (quick) (both),   (1),
Pause for   (2, 3).

To repeat the exercise with alternate feet, pause after the 3rd quick one for that (1) beat as well as for (2, 3).

Repeat with arms going up to 5th, heels start swivelling out on (&);

Part 2
both, L roll;   R L,   roll, roll;
Turn foot in, out, jump close, *changement*, pause
Turn foot in, out, jump close, *changement*, pause
Turn foot in, out, jump close, *changement*, pause
Turn foot in, out, jump close, *changement*, pause

The Detail
Part 1
First swivel out of heels is silent then roll on each close in 5th:

Slow: swivel heels out (on *demi-pointes*)   (3);
Close down R foot front in 5th (1),   pause (2), both, L
Slow: swivel heels out, in 5th roll;   (3);
Close down L foot front in 5th (1),   pause (2) both, L
Slow: swivel heels out, in 5th roll;   (3);

Quick: swivel heels out close R front in 5th (both) (1),
Quick: swivel heels out close L front in 5th (L)   (2),
Quick: swivel heels out close R front in 5th (roll) (3);
Quick: swivel heels out close L front in 5th (both) (1),
Pause (2), pause (3);

The castanets will sound:
Slow: both (1),   L (2),   roll (3);   both (1),   L (2),   roll (3);
Quick: both (1),   L (2),   roll, (3); both (1),   pause (2, 3);

Repeat Part 1.

Part 2
              (1)   both (2) L roll (3); R L (1),   roll, roll (2, 3);
Swivel heels out, swivel toes out, jump foot 5th R front, *changement*, pause,
Swivel heels out, swivel toes out, jump foot 5th L front, *changement*, pause,
Swivel heels out, swivel toes out, jump foot 5th R front, *changement*, pause,
Swivel heels out, swivel toes out, jump foot 5th L front, *changement*, pause,

The Pericet step without music goes: R foot front: start L (back) foot – slow, slow, quick, quick quick, pause, repeat starting with R foot, repeat with L, repeat with R. The *bordoneo* step is danced four times after this sequence.

3. TRES PASE DE VASQUE ECHAPE Y DOS STEP (three *pas de basque*, *échappé* and two *jetés*)
Suggested music: Entrada section of La Maja y el Torero.

To Start
Feet: 5th, Right in front.
Arms: 5th.
Castanets: both,   L,   roll;
                L,   roll,   roll;

The Step
Wait for chord.
3 *pas de basque*, R, L, R
Échappé to 2nd, *jeté* R leg up, *jeté* onto R,
Échappé to 2nd, *jeté* L leg up, *jeté* onto L,
Échappé to 2nd, *jeté* R leg up, *jeté* onto R,
Échappé to 2nd, *jeté* L leg up, *jeté* onto L,
Ends with *échappé* to 2nd.
The *pas de basque* start from there with L on the repeat.

The Detail
Wait for chord.
Pas de basque to R (both, L, roll); (1, 2, 3); L arm circles outward and to 5th.
Repeat to L; R arm circles outward and to 5th.

Repeat to R; L arm circles outward and to 5th.

Échappé to 2nd (both), jump on L bringing R leg up (low *attitude* in front) (roll), *Jeté* on R bringing L leg up (roll); arms remain in 5th position throughout this part of the exercise.

Repeat lifting L then R, repeat lifting R then L, repeat lifting L then R.

End *échappé* in 2nd (both).

Repeat starting with L from second position, *relevé* on R lifting the L leg to the side, R arm circling down, to start the next sequence of *pas de basque*.

Note: when the *pas de basque* starts with the R leg, that is the leg that is lifted first on the *jetés*. When doing it starting L, then lift the L leg.

4. CUATRO BALONES DOS PASE DE VASQUE Y VUELTA FIBRALTADA (four *ballonnés*, two *pas de basque* and a jumped turn)

Suggested music: La Maja Jerezana.

To Start
Feet: 5th, R in front.
Arms: 5th.
Castanets:
On *ballonnés*: both, L, roll; both, L, roll; both, L, roll; both.
On *pas de basque* and jumped turn: L, roll, roll; R L, roll, roll; R L, roll, roll; R L

Direction: from corner 3 to corner 1 and then corner 1 to corner 2.

Note: the accent after the *ballonné* is in 5th, more a *chassé* than a balletic *ballonné* under the knee. It is exactly like the Cecchetti *ballonné*.

The Step
As described above.

The Detail
Step travels diagonally to corner 1.
Ballonné R, (both), (1), Right arm circles down outward,
Step on R, (L), (2), close L behind (roll); (3); arm completes circle up front to 5th.

Repeat the step with the same leg, but using L arm to circle outward and up.

Repeat the step with the same leg but using R arm again this time.

Repeat the step with the same leg but using L arm again this time,

Step on R to side (both), (1), and point L in front (pause). Arms 3rd, R up, L in front.

Pas de basque to L (L, roll, roll); (1, 2, 3);
Pas de basque to R (R L, roll, roll);

Vuelta fibraltada to L (R L, roll, roll);
Finish in 5th with L foot in front (R L), (& 1), pause 2, 3.

Repeat whole exercise starting with L travelling to corner 2.

SEGUNDO CURSO: Grupo Tercero

1. Asamble tres cuartas y cambiamento alto (French : *assemblé*)

2. Tamdecuip (Tam de cuip) (Probably French: *temps de cuisse*)

3. Tijera

4. Gorgollata (French: *gargouillade*)

1. ASAMBLE TRES CUARTAS Y CAMBIAMENTO ALTO (*assemblé*, three *entrechats quatre*, and a high scissor jump)
Suggested music: Bolero, complete *copla*. Step goes 5 times through the music and see special ending.

To Start
Feet: 5th with L in front.
Arms: 5th.
Castanets: both, L roll, L roll, L roll, both, pause.

The Step
Wait for (& 6, &) then as described above: *assemblé*, three *entrechats quatre*, and a high scissor jump.

The Detail
Arms in 5th. Wait for counts of (& 3, &).
R foot *assemblé* over (both) (1), R arm circles down,
Three *entrechats quatre* (beat R back front) (L roll, L roll; L roll) (& 2, & 3; & 1), arm remains in 3rd, R front,
Scissor jump in air changing feet. (both) (& 2), pause for (& 3);
Arms change on scissor jump: in one count R goes up front and L circles down, making 3rd with L down, R in front.

Repeats 4 more times on same foot.

Ending: Arms 5th.
R behind: *entrechat* (1), scissors (2), *entrechat trois* lifting R behind (3); circle R arm front, *coupé* R behind (&), *assemblé* L behind (4), arms to 5th.

Start again with R foot in front to repeat the whole exercise on the other side.

Note: This ending was specially choreographed for the Spanish Dance Society by Eloy Pericet.

2. TAMDECUIP (TAM DE CUIP ?) (possibly from the French *temps de cuisse*) *Temps* means time and *cuisse* means thigh. The French step is very different, a *sissonne* with the front foot lifted in flight, as it were.
Suggested music: Bolero Liso.

Feet: 5th, L in front.
Arms: 5th.
Arms open out and down on the first swish, and up to 5th on *jeté* (Eloy Pericet, 1965, personal communication).
Same arm as leg circles down on the *frappé* and up to 5th on the *jeté*, and lean away from working leg, turn head to side of working leg (Eloy Pericet, personal communication, 1997).
Castanets: both both, L roll, L roll, L roll, L roll.

The Step

Can be done with the *jeté* over as described below, or with *jeté* under travelling back.

Wait for first two notes then *sostenido* (dig L toe, step on it):

Frappé R leg and hop on L (supporting) leg,

Frappé R leg and *jeté* on to R.

The Detail

Wait for (& 6);

With *jeté* over:

Before the step do *sostenido*: tip L toe front, step (both both), (& 1),

Extend R leg to side and beat toes on the floor (*frappé* – to beat or knock) taking the foot across the calf at the back of supporting foot, (L) (&) R arm circles quickly down in 3rd,

Hop on L leg (roll), (2),

Repeat the *frappé* with the R (L) (&) to front of ankle

Jeté onto the R (roll); (3); R arm up front to 5th, releasing the L arm straight away for the next step.

Repeat this with the other foot, etc.

Assemble to end.

3. TIJERA (scissor)

Suggested music: Bolero Liso.

Note: when this step is used in regional dances the knees are turned in, here they are slightly turned out.

Feet: R foot pointed front, facing corner 2.

Arms: 3rd position with L arm raised over head and R across front, lean and turn top of body slightly (*cambré*) to R.

The arms change from 3rd to 3rd through 5th. The top arm opens out and down, the bottom arm goes up. '*Baja por fuera, sube por dentro*'. (Eloy Pericet, 1967, personal communication).

Castanets: L roll, L, roll on the *tijeras*, pause when pointing front and turn the top of the body slightly open over front leg (*cambré*).

In class Eloy Pericet performs this at half this speed with the following castanets: L, roll, L, roll, L, roll, L, roll, with a long pause after body twist.

Wait for beats of introduction (4; 5).

Jerezana R leg back, (L, roll); (6, 1);

Jump onto it to corner 1 with L in *jerezana*, (L, roll), (2, 3), changing arms to 3rd other side,

Point L to corner 1 (L, roll), (4; **5**),

Twist top of body to L (*cambré*) in that position (L, roll) (6; 1, 2, 3), Recover (4,5),

Step starts again on L:

Jerezana, L, roll (6, 1), *jerezana*, L; roll, (2; 3), point (L, roll) (4, 5); *cambré* (L, roll) (6, 1),

Step starts again *jerezana* (6; 1), *jerezana* (2, 3), point (4, 5), *cambré* (6; 1), Recover (2, 3, 4, 5),

Step starts again *jerezana* on (6, 1); as above etc.

Repeats alternately.

266 The Bolero School

The Detail
Wait for count of (4; 5),
Lift R foot sideways (knee turned out) (L, roll), (6, 1); arms 3rd, L arm up,
Jeté onto R with L leg kicking out and knee out (L, roll), (2, 3), change arms 3rd other side with R arm up,
Point L in front to corner to corner 1 (pause) (4; 5), arms remain in that 3rd position,
Cambré body by turning the top part over to L and away from the pointed L leg keeping R arm up and L across body (pause); (6, 1); hold and recover (2, 3, 4, 5),
Repeat with L at end of phrase (L, roll); (6); etc.

4. GORGOLLATA (*gargouillade*, in French, to gurgle; in the Russian school it is called *rond de jambe double*)
Suggested music: Bolero.

To Start
Feet: 4th position, R front.
Arms: 3rd, R in front.
Castanets: L, roll.
Eloy Pericet used Bolero rhythm for this in class.

The Step
Danced 8 times.
Rond de jambe (*rodazán*) outwards in the air with R foot, take R arm to 5th.
Leap into the air and do *rodazán* inwards with L foot close in front, circling L arm outwards and up, finish 3rd L front.
Repeat to left.
If doing a series, instead of closing, drop across on L using *épaulement* and *coupé* under with R to release L to start the repeat to L.

TERCER CURSO: Grupo Primero

1. Rodazán hacia adentro (dentro) destaque asamble y cuarta volada (French: *assemblé*)

2. Cuatro asambles con padebure y cuatro sostenidos en vuelta (French: *assemblé, pas de bourrée*)

3. Lisada con tercera por delante (Possibly from French: *glissade*)

4. Lisada con tercera por atras (Detras) (Possibly from French: *glissade*)

1. RODAZÁN HACIA ADENTRO (DENTRO) DESTAQUE ASAMBLE Y CUARTA VOLADA, (*rond de jambe*, *assemblé* and *entrechat cinque*)
Suggested music: Bolero. Wait for two beats of introduction.

To Start
Feet: 5th, R foot front.
Arms: 5th (but arm lowers down early on *sostenido*).

The Step
Sostenido with R (dig, stamp in front) to start dropping L arm,
Take L foot sideways from the back and *rodazán*, *relevé* (1),
Assemblé it in front (2), arm is still in position.
Leap into air and beat R foot front and end with it in *retiré* at back (3); look at back foot over shoulder.
Arm changes to R arm down on that last beaten jump.

The next *rodazán* starts from that lifted leg.

2. CUATRO ASAMBLES CON PADEBURE Y CUATRO SOSTENIDOS EN VUELTA,
(four *assemblés*, with *pas de bourrée* and four step-dig-steps, turning on self; it is really a *sissonne* to 2nd)
Suggested music: Introduction to El Vito.

To Start
Feet: 5th, R front.
Arms: 5th.
Castanets: both, both, L, roll, pause, pause, on 1st part
              R L, roll roll, on *sostenidos*.

The Step
Travels to side:

Bars:	3;	1,	&	2,	&	3;	
Bolero	6;	1,	2,	3;	4,	5,	
Castanets:		both;	both,	L,	roll,	–,	–,
	both;	both,	L,	roll,	–,	–,	
	both;	both,	L,	roll,	–,	–,	
	both;	both,	L,	roll,	–,	–,	
	both,	*choque*,	both.				

On the first jump, the arm drops to 3rd in front and remains for all four *assemblé*- step combinations:

Assemblé L over (6; 1), (both; both),
Jeté (*sissonne*) onto R, L in second *en l'air* arms in 3rd (2, 3), (L, roll),
Step on toe L behind (4), (L), step on toe R to side (5), (roll),
Repeating twice more and:
Assemblé in front, arms fifth. (6; 1), (both; both),

Sostenidos:
Castanets: R L, roll, roll, R L, roll, roll, R L, roll, roll, R L.

In circle around self:
Sostenido: pause while lifting L leg, (L), (–) (2),
Dig (3), (*choque*), step with L, (– , both), (4, 5), then:
Three times the entire *sostenido* step:

Step on R turning across self, to L, with R shoulder leading and back to audience (6; 1), (R; L),
Dig, step (2, 3); (roll, roll);

Step on R turning across self, to L, with R shoulder leading and back to audience (4, 5), (R, L),
Dig, step   (6; 1), (roll; roll),

Step on R turning across self, to L, with R shoulder leading and back to audience (6; 1), (R; L),
Dig, step, (2, 3); (roll, roll);

Close 5th behind. (6; 1), (R; L).

Repeat to L.

3. LISADA CON TERCERA POR DELANTE (*glissade* with beaten *jeté*)
Suggested music: Bolero.

To Start
Feet: 5th.
Arms: 5th.
Castanets: both both, L, roll, both both

The Step
Exactly as for *lisada por delante*, but beaten.
Chasse, coupé assemblé with a beat from side to side with alternate feet.

4. LISADA CON TERCERA POR ATRAS (DETRAS) (*chassé, coupé*, beaten *assemblé*)
Suggested music: Bolero.

To Start
Feet: 5th.
Arms: 5th.
Castanets: L, roll, both.

Exactly as for *lisada por atras*, but beaten.

The Step
Glissade with R to R (L, roll),

Jeté over on R with a beat of L leg in front and lift it at the back (both),
Arms open outward and up to 5th, look towards back foot, slight tilt of the body over the lifted leg.

TERCER CURSO: Grupo Segundo

1. Asamble y batuda (French: *assemblé*)

2. Espacada punta y talon

3. Balone y piroueta (French: *ballonné*)

4. Espacada doble y toldin

1. ASAMBLE Y BATUDA (*assemblé* and beat)
Suggested music: Bolero. The step goes across the music. A 2/4 time is really more suitable.

Bar:	&	1	&	2	&	3;
Bolero:	6;	1	2	3	4	5

To Start
Feet: 5th R foot front.
Arms: 5th.
Castanets: both, L, roll, pause.
Body leans away from the lifted leg and remains there for the whole sequence.

The Step
It is repeated with the same leg all the time.
Lean away from direction of travel.

With L *assemblé* over,	(6; 1), (– both), arms come down,
Jump in air and beat L behind	(2), (L),
Ending L leg in air in 2nd	(3), (roll)

Repeat step starting by the *assemblé* in front from the lifted leg, counting (4, 5): (6; 1):
Repeat   (2, 3):– (4, 5): –
Repeat *assemblé* R over (6; 1): and hold.

Repeat to the L with R foot doing *assemblé*.

2. ESPACADA PUNTA Y TALON ('Russian dance step' done by men)
Suggested music: Malagueña, *copla*, slowly.

To Start
Feet: 5th.
Exercise is performed with the same leg each time. Repeat on other leg.
Arms: 5th
One arm used in inward circle from low 1st out and up to 5th for each 3 steps, then down front inward for *plié* repeat.

Use the same arm as the supporting (R) leg, therefore the R arm is used if L leg is doing the toe, heel, at side.

Counts:	1, & 2, 3;
Castanets:	both, L, roll, roll, roll; repeat
Step:	*Plié*, toe, heel; repeat
Arm:	both 1st, out, circles to 5th; repeat

Note: toe is pointed turned in at side, then heel is on dig in same place with leg stretched out to side, leg turned out.

The Step

Slight jump into a deep *plié* down (feet on *demi-pointe*), both arms coming down front, (both), (1),

Jump up on R foot, (&)

R arm circles out and up to 5th, L arm is down in front and remains there, while L continues to make inward circles each time L foot is at side – going up to 5th during last (2, 3); counts.

R does toe, heel at side, hopping each time.

R arm circles up slowly down (1), and up outward to 5th (2, 3); during these three counts.

Repeat twice more and *assemblé* in 5th to end for repeat to the other side using R leg and L arm.

At end: close other arm to 5th, feet 5th.

3. BALONE Y PIROUETA (*ballonné* and *pirouette*)

Suggested music: First part of La Maja y el Torero.

To Start

Arms: 5th.

Feet: 5th, R front.

Castanets: L roll, roll, roll; (& 1, 2, 3); (a ria, ria, ria); repeat.

Note: the *ballonné* is danced on the diagonal.

The Step

Ballonné with R, (L) (&), step onto R,   (roll), (1),

Coupé under with L,   (roll), (2),

Chassé R into 4th front,   (roll); (3);

(Top, L arm comes down behind, making 4th with R in front),

Double *pirouette en dedans* (inward) with L behind (a ria, ria,) (1, 2),

close foot in front, (ria); (3);

Can end in 4th front, arms 4th, same arm in front as leg.

Quickly put arms up to 5th to restart the exercise.

Can be done outward (*dehors*) lifting front leg across in front:

Lifting front (R) leg and turning to R and closing behind.

4. ESPACADA DOBLE Y TORDIN

Music: La Maja y el Torero.

To Start

Arms: 5th.

Feet: 5th.

Castanets: both, L, roll; both, L, roll; both, L, roll; both, pause, pause.

The Step

Grand plié down arms coming inward in front, hands pointing down, (1, 2, 3); (both, L, roll);

Jump up on heels in 2nd, arms up in wide 5th (the Spanish Dance Society 2nd), (1, 2, 3); (both, L, roll);

Plié down arms turn inward and down front, R ending front and L behind (4th), (1, 2, 3); (both, L, roll);

Jump in air and tour en l'air from there, arms across body not 5th, (1), (both),

pause for   (2, 3); (–, –);

TERCER CURSO: Grupo Tercero (Superior)

1. Tercera y cuarta volada

2. Rodazán hacia afuera (fuera) tercera y cuarta volada

3. Briseles sencillos

4. Briseles dobles

5. Briseles del susu (French: *sus-suos* or *suos-sus*. G.B.L. Wilson suggests two sources: *dessus-dessous* or over-under from the French, and 'su e giu' from the Italian.)

6. Cuarta Italiana

7. Quinta

This group is technically difficult.

1. TERCERA Y CUARTA VOLADA
In circular pattern
Music: The Cachucha of Boleras de la Cachucha.

To Start
Arms start in 5th, move to 1st front (arms down) and then in 5th in a continuous circle.
Feet: 5th.
Castanets: both, both, (for the *sostenido*) L roll, continuously.

The Step
Turning on self in circle to right.
Only at start: *sostenido* with R in front: dig R, stamp, (both both), (on lead in music),
Brisé with L beating front, body over L, (arms low in front) (L roll), pause,
Entrechat cinque beating L front and closing and lifting L at back, body to R looking over R shoulder, (arms up in 5th), (L roll), pause.

Repeat twice more,
Assemblé over to end arms 5th.

Repeat on other side starting with R but do not repeat the *sostenido* as at start.

2. RODAZÁN HACIA AFUERA (FUERA) TERCERA Y CUARTA
Suggested music: Cachucha
I think Bolero more suitable.

To Start
Arms: 5th, drop to 3rd, 5th on *assemblé*.
Feet: 5th.
Castanets: both both on starting sostenido with L then:
L roll on each movement after that.

The Step
Wait for two beats.
Sostenido to start: toe dig L, stamp in front, (both, both),
Jump high doing *rodazán* outward with R at side, drop R arm, (L roll),
Brisé beating R front and closing behind (L roll), arms remain 3rd,
L now front, *entrechat quatre*.
Arms go up to 5th. (L roll),

Repeat with alternate feet.
Straighten knees to end.

3. BRISELES SENCILLOS
Music: Cachucha.

To Start
Feet: 5th, L foot front.
Arms: 5th, but move from 3rd to 3rd.
Castanets: L roll continuously.

No *sostenido* to start.

The Step
The L leg will be beating front each time:
Lifting R leg in a *retiré* behind,
Coupé R at back, L arm circles out and down and remains down, (L roll),
Brisé, lifting L front corner, beat front, close behind, (L roll),
Jump changing feet out to side (*tijera*), L now front, (L roll),
Beat L behind and end with it in air in 2nd to corner, (L roll),
Arms change quickly to third with the other arm in 3rd, as the repeat with the other leg starts.

Coupé to start repeat on other side (as above but with L).
Change arms through 5th to 3rd.

End with *coupé assemblé*, arms 5th.

4. BRISELES DOBLES TERCERA POR DELANTE (*brisé volé* and beaten *assemblé*, beat landing with leg in 2nd and restart with a *coupé* from there)
Music: Cachucha.

To Start
Arms: start 5th, move from 3rd to 3rd.
Feet: 5th, R foot in front.
Castanets: L roll.

The Step
Eloy described it as *brisé al aire, brisé al suelo y batuda coupé.*

If you say; *al aire, al suelo, batuda, coupé*, it gives the rhythm.

Start with *retiré* of R leg to *coupé* behind L (L roll),
Brisé volé: lift L front beat changing to R in air in front to corner 2, L arm down, (L roll),
Beat taking R beat front close R behind, face front, arm still in 3rd, (L roll),
Beat L behind and end in air to 2nd facing front, arms 5th, (L roll),
Coupé and repeat.

5. BRISELES DEL SUSU (*sus-sous* or *sous-sus*, *brise volé*)
Changes from corner to corner: two in front to 1, and 2,
Remain facing corner two for 1st one at back: two at the back to 4 and 3.

To Start
Feet: 5th.
Arms: 5th.
Castanets: L roll.

The Step
With arms coming down and remaining down;
Body changes to lean over front leg:
Brisé volé lifting R in front beat, end with L to corner 1,
Brisé volé lifting L in front beat end with R to corner 2.

Then the arms go up to 5th:
Body does not change but remains upright and arched:
Swish the lifted leg back and then changing to face other corner for the second one at the back,
Brisé volé lifting R to the back beat ending L to corner 4,
Brisé volé lifting L to the back beat ending R to corner 3,

End closing leg at back, arms 5th.

6. CUARTA ITALIANA
Music: Cachucha.

To Start
Feet; 5th position, R foot in front.
Arms: 5th position.
Castanets: L roll, roll, roll.

The Step
Assemblé
Entrechat quatre landing beaten foot to 2nd,
Performed repeatedly with foot lifted from second for the *assemblé*, repeat.

The Detail
Assemblé L foot over, L arm comes down on the *assemblé*, (L roll),
Jump up high beating L foot, back, front in air, take arms up to 5th, (roll),
Land on both feet legs open to 2nd, keep arms 5th, (roll).

Assemblé R front from 2nd by lifting the leg from 2nd for the *assemblé*.

7. QUINTA (*entrechat six*)

The Step
Assemblé back leg to the front. Same arm as leg comes down so that arms are in third, and in that position do:
Entrechat six, beating legs back, front, back before landing.

It repeats on the same foot each time.

SALUDO

The woman stands on the left foot with her right foot on the toe behind, holding her skirt in the right hand, she steps to the side opening the skirt to the side, places the left foot behind and curtseys down, lowering her skirt.

The man stands with his feet together, he steps to the right, places his feet together again and places his right hand with fingers extended, across his chest on his heart and bows.

CLASSICAL SPANISH PAS DE BASQUES

Travelling forward taught in 4 counts:
Start with feet and arms in 5th position, L arm circles outwards:
Step R foot to side (not on pointe) (l),
Bring L foot into 1st, slight bend of knees to facilitate next movement (2),
Slide it through into 4th on *demi-pointe* (3),
Close R foot behind in 5th on *demi-pointe* (4).

Repeat to L, coming down from pointe as you step to left.

Travelling backward also in 4 movements:
Step to side with R
Bring foot to 1st,
Slide it back onto *demi-pointe* in 4th at behind,
Close 5th on *demi-pointe.*

The counts and arm as above.
These are all danced with a small pause after each movement from counts 1–4.

Now do the same but in 3 counts:

Travelling forward:
Step to side,
Swing leg through first to 4th on *demi-pointe*,
Close other leg up on *demi-pointe* in 5th.

Travelling backward is different:
Step up on *demi-pointe* at side with R, (1),
Drop across in front on L, with R leg lifted at the back behind the knee, (2),
Coupé under with R on toe at the back, (3).

Pas de basque in Sevillanas
On place: step to side, drop across and *coupé* under.
Travelling: step to side, bring leg through first to 5th, close in 5th.

Pas de basque in Olé de la Curra

Forwards:

As above but arms are:

On one *pas de basque* with R leg: take arms from 5th, down and up to 5th (1, 2, 3);

On next *pas de basque* with L leg, take arms from 5th down to Left side (1, 2, 3);

Keep repeating the same.

Backwards:

Use arm in circle: R arm when L foot steps back.

Step slightly to corner with L (1),

Close R in front (2),

Step in place behind with L (a *coupé*) (3);

Start again with R foot taking it to other back corner (3).

ESCUELA BOLERA EXERCISES AT THE BARRE

The arm is used across the body as it comes forward and up or out when it is raised from 1st. The exercises are performed with the arm in 5th overhead.

Exercises at the barre holding with one hand are: *pliés*; *grand pliés* in 4th and 5th; *petits battements* on the ground and in the air; *rodazánes* (*ronds de jambe*) on the ground and in the air; *rodazán* outwards in the air, extend it to the side, close behind; *rodazán* inwards – extend it high to the side close in front; *destaques* (*grands battements*) four to the front, four to the side, four to the back; forward and back bends.

Facing the barre holding on with both hands: *échappés* and then removing the hands and placing them in 5th for equilibrium on the repeats of the *échappés*.

Part III
The Codified Dances

The Dances

BOLERO CON SEGUIDILLAS
(In the style of the Goya era)

These following two dances are usually performed together, one leading into the other.

The Bolero
It is a couple dance. The dancers work in mirror image, i.e. using opposite feet. The steps of the woman are described here.

Dancers face each other to start. Arms up. It must be noted that the arms are used in wide open positions, because the custom of the day was dictated by the heavy epaulettes worn by the men. In general, regional dances use this open 'Y' position.

The Bolero rhythm goes across two bars of music, thus the dance starts on the count of (6).

Music: instrumental, *bandurrias* and guitars.

Introduction resembling the *estribillo* of Sevillanas:
Coupé the R foot behind, releasing L in front	(6); (L);
With small unfolding of leg:	
Step forward on L, across partner	(1), (roll),
R arm up L arm front	
Dig R behind	(2), (*choque*),
Step back on R	(3), (both),
Dig L in front	(4), (L),
on dig in front L arm sweeps across, R behind	
Small unfolding of L leg	(5), (roll),

Crossing the partner on L to a more open position:
Turn: arm remains in that position for the three turns:
Step on L	(6); (roll);
Turn bringing (back) R foot in and turn to L	(1), (roll),
Step on R releasing L	(2), (roll),
Repeat turn:	

Step on L	(3), (roll),
turn bringing (back) R foot in and turn to L	(4), (roll),
Step on R releasing L	(5), (roll),
Repeat turn:	
Point it in front	(6); (roll);
Step on L	(1), (both),
arms out in 1st	
Step back on R	(1), (roll), (2), (*choque*),
arms front	
Step on R releasing L to point in front	(3), (both),
Facing to partner arms 3rd, L up.	

Copla or verse (1). This step and the repeats travel side to side:

Pause for	(4, 5), (– , –),
Placing weight onto L	(6); (–),
Assemblé R over	(1), (both), [arms 3rd, L up,
Sissonne to L with R to side	(& 2), (L roll), [as above]
Coupé R under	(&) (both) R arm lifts up front,
Assemblé L behind	(3), (both), R arm to wide 2nd,
Échappé to second	(& 4), (both),
Close with beating L front	(&) (L)
Landing 5th with L behind	(5), (roll),

Repeat (2). Arms as above but with R arm up, L in front on change

Jump changing feet	(6); (both);
Sissone to L with R to side	(& 1), (L roll),
Coupé R under	(&) (both)
Assemblé L behind	(2), (both),
Échappé to second	(& 3), (both),
Close with beating L front	(&) (L)
Landing 5th with L behind	(4), (roll),

Repeat (3). Exactly as first time:

Jump changing feet	(5), (both),
Sissonne to L with R to side	(& 6); (L roll);
Coupé R under	(&) (both)
Assemblé L behind	(1), (both),
Échappé to second	(& 2), (both),
Close with beating L front	(&) (L roll),
Landing 5th with L behind	(3), (roll),

Repeat (4). Exactly as second repeat:

Assemblé R over	(4), (both),
Sissonne to L with R to side	(& 5), (L, roll),
Coupé R under	(6); (both);
Assemblé L behind	(1), (both),
Échappé to second	(& 2), (both),

Close with beating L front	(&) (L)
Landing 5th with L behind	(3), (roll),

Ending:

Entrechat	(& 4), (L roll),
Entrechat	(& 5), (L roll),
Vuelta fibraltada to R	(& 6); (L roll);
Feet 5th	(1), (both),

The Seguidillas

Arms: held in wide second position:
Castanets: L (1), roll (& 2), roll (& 3); R (&) continuously throughout.

Estribillo
Step 1: *jetés*
12 *jetés* forward

Step 2: *punta y talon*, using R:

Step on L	(1),	
Dig R toe-heel side	(2, 3);	R arm dips down to side
Dig R toe in front,	(1),	R arm returns out
3 skips back R, L, R,		(2, 3; 1), both arms out

Repeat *punta y talon* on L:

Dig L toe-heel side	(2, 3);	L arm dips down to side
Dig L toe in front,	(1),	L arm returns out
2 skips back L, R,	(2, 3);	both arms out

Slow *vuelta fibraltada*:
Jump up kicking L leg and changing in air in front on landing to (1, 2),
Place R across (3);
Turn to L (1, 2, 3);

Copla step 1. *Careos*, one to pass, one to face:
With L cross partner face to face:
Careo stepping side on L (1), L arm up, R sweeping down
Step R behind (2), Step on place L (3); R arm goes up

One *careo* with R turning to face partner
Careo stepping side on R (1),   L arm up., L sweeping down
Step L behind (2), Step on place R (3); L arm goes up

Two *pas de basque* turning across partner back to back:
Step on L (1), turn to R,   R sweeping down
Step R behind (2), Step on place L (3); R arm goes up

Step on R (1), turn to L,   L sweeping down
Step L behind (2), Step on place R (3); L arm goes up
swinging back to:

Repeat *careos* and *pas de basque* to return to own position:
With L cross partner face to face:
Careo stepping side on L (1), L arm up, R sweeping down
Step R behind (2), Step on place L (3); R arm goes up

One careo with R to face partner:
Careo stepping side on R (1),   L arm up., L sweeping down
Step L behind (2), Step on place R (3); L arm goes up

Two *pas de basque* turning across partner back to back:
Step on L (1), turn towards R,   R sweeping down
Step R behind (2), Step on place L (3); R arm goes up

Step on R (1), turn towards L,   L sweeping down
Step L behind (2), Step on place R (3); L arm goes up

Repeat *punta y talon* step facing front and travelling sideways across partner, use foot furthest away from partner:

Punta y talon step using R:
Step on L (1),
Dig R toe-heel side (2, 3);   R arm dips down to side
Dig R toe in front (1),   R arm returns out
Use skips like a *pas de bourrée* behind, side front to cross partner:
3 skips back R, L, R, (2, 3; 1),   both arms out

Repeat *punta y talon* on L:
Dig L toe-heel side (2, 3);   L arm dips down to side
Dig L toe in front, (1),   L arm returns out
Use skips like a *pas de bourrée* behind, side front to cross partner:
3 skips back L, R, L, (2, 3; 1),   both arms out

Repeat *punta y talon* on R:
Dig R toe-heel side   (2, 3);   R arm dips down to side
Dig R to in front   (1),   R arm returns out

On place facing front do:
3 skips back R, L, R,   (2, 3; 1), both arms out

Turns across partner and back:
Step on L   (1),

Place R across and turn	(2, 3);
Step on L	(1),
Place R across and turn	(2),
Step back on L	(3);

Reverse direction and feet:	
Step on R	(1),
Place L across and turn	(2, 3);
Step on R	(1),
Place L across and turn	(2, 3);

Ending, facing front:

Step back on R	(1),	(both),
Partner steps back on L		

Now slightly back to back facing the front:

Point L foot front, man R foot	(2),	(*choque*),
Raise arms to 3rd, outside arm up in 5th,	(3);	(both).
	Inside arm front.	

BOLERO DEL CANDIL

(Goya era)

A couple dance. The woman waits while the man starts the dance:

Man

Introduction:

3 walks forward R, L, R

Vuelta fibraltada to L (hitch-kick turn)

Vuelta fibraltada to R

Place R foot behind.

Copla:

Paso de bolero:

Step forward on R, dig L behind,

Step back on L, dig R front,

2 limps round to R

Repeat to the L

Chassé to R, *coupé* with L *assemblé* R behind

Chassé to L, *coupé* with R *assemblé* L behind

3 *destaques* closing behind each time: with R, L, R

Vuelta fibraltada to L

Vuelta fibraltada to R

The man waits.

Woman

Standing R foot 4th in front:

3 *glissades* towards the audience (facing sideways):

Closing R front, behind, front

2 *jetés* on R and then L

3 *lazos* R, L, R

3 *jetés* L, R, L

Chassé to R, *coupé* with L, *assemblé* R behind

Coupé L over extending R to side

Pas de bourrée over, extending L to side

Pas de bourrée over, extending R to side

Pas de bourrée over, extending L to side

Pas de bourrée over, extending R to side

Place R over and turn to L

Woman waits.

Man

One *entrechat*

One *tijera* (a leap into the air extending legs to side)

One *entrechat*

One *tijera*

Woman joins in: one *vuelta* to L

Together
1 *paso de bolero*
1 Sevillanas
1 *paso de bolero*
Crossing: one-and-a-half turns crossing partner and facing on other side
1 *paso de bolero*
1 Sevillanas
Crossing one-and-a-half turns crossing partner and facing on other side
2 *entrechats*
Vuelta fibraltada to end. Hold position.

SEGUIDILLAS DEL CANDIL
(Goya period)

Soft shoes, *zapatillas*, are worn.

Music: Allegretto.
Castanets: (RL, & 1), (roll, roll, 2, 3). Unless otherwise stated, this is the rhythm played continuously. (–) denotes silent castanets.
Arms: move in circles as in Sevillanas.
Feet: tend to be jumped into 4th position facing the partner, with same arm as leg in front.
Note: the small jumps into 4th, so typical of this dance have become vague placings of feet into 4th or simply stepping back and pointing foot in front. This change has come about between the early 1960s, when I first learned it and the end of the nineties! It would be a pity to lose this feature.

First *Copla*:
Introduction:
Girl on the man's right, facing audience with R foot pointed in front. Girl holds man's right hand with her left, holds skirt with R hand;
Man with R pointed in front; man holds her L hand with his R;

Wait for 4 chords (1, 2, 3, 4), and (5, 6);

Salida. 2 walks forward, R, L:
Girl: walk forward R, L (1, 2), place R across (3), and turn under the L arm to the left ending with L foot front (4): pause (5, 6); R arm goes up to 5th on the turn.

Man: walks R, L, R, (1, 2, 3), places L in 4th front (4), facing her, and raises his L arm to 5th as the girl turns L under his R arm. She also ends feet 4th facing her partner, L in front. Hold (5, 6);

This introduction can vary according to the situation, of how it joins up in a suite of dances. Dancers may already be in place facing each other, or may walk in from a further distance than centre stage.

Step 1
Castanets: RL (& 1), roll, roll (2, 3), but first time L, roll, roll.
Arms: move in circles as in Sevillanas, R arm circling down first:

The Step:
Sevillanas step with a *jeté*, 4 times:
Step forward on R foot (1), across partner,
Dig L behind (2), step back on L (3),
Dig R in front (4), *développé* (5), forward *jeté* on R (6); (kicking L up bent at the back, not turned out).
Repeat on L,
Repeat first three counts on R,

Ending:

Point R in front on a *fondu* on R	(4),	(RL)	Hold R arm in front,
Kick R back	(5),	(both),	R arm in front,
Place R across and turn to R (6);		(*choque*);	taking arm to 5th,
	(1),	(both),	drop L arm 3rd in front,

Hold: feet in 4th arms 3rd for flourish in the music (2, 3), (-, -),

End facing partner, L front in 4th position of feet, 3rd with arms.

Step 2
Coupé chassé step behind (with the first count on the *coupé* in this step), (1, 2, 3), from side to side, 3 times to R, L, R. It starts on the count of 4. The body towards the leg each time, thus from side to side:

The Step:
Coupé onto L on (4),
Chassé to R with small 1/4 turn to go downstage (5), step L (6);
Coupé R (1), with small 1/4 turn to L to go upstage, (2), step R, (3),
Coupé L (4),
Chassé to R with small 1/4 turn to go downstage, (5), Step L (6);
Small jump with R ft behind in 4th, with L front (1, 2, 3), (-, -, -);
(The man goes downstage, upstage, downstage).

Step 3
1 *careo* crossing, 1 ending back to partner on his place looking back at him over L shoulder. *2 pas de basque* (*careos*) on place (with foot at back) looking back at partner over shoulder each time:

The Step:

Careo crossing with L	(4, 5, 6);
Careo on R to look partner over L	(1, 2, 3),
2 *pas de basque* from side to side, L and R	(4, 5, 6; 1, 2, 3),

The *pas de basque* are done stepping across self and turning with back to partner, looking over the shoulder at each other.

Repeat as before to return to original position:

Careo crossing with L	(4, 5, 6);
Careo on R to look partner over L	(1, 2, 3),
But do only one *pas de basque* to the L	(4, 5, 6);

Ending as in Step 1*:

Point R in front on a *fondu* on L	(1), (RL),	hold R arm in front,
Kick R back	(2),	(both),
Place R across and turn to L	(3),	(*choque*), arm 5th,
Hold: feet 4th, arms 3rd	(4, 5, 6);	(both, -, -); drop L arm front,
Girl finishes facing front,		
Man finishes facing back.		

However, both then do the following step facing front.

Step 4

Ballonné step 4 times from side to side facing front:
Subtly changing feet, the man uses opposite foot to that of his partner:
Castanets: RL, roll, roll continuously across the music:

The Step:

Ballonné with L: across front, back arms 3rd	(1, 2),	(RL, roll),
Chassé L, step R behind, step side with L	(3, 4, 5),	(roll, RL, roll),
Repeat with R to R	(6; 1),	(roll; RL),
	(2, 3, 4),	(roll, roll, RL),
Repeat with L:	(5, 6);	(roll, roll);
	(1, 2, 3),	(RL, roll, roll),
Repeat with R:	(4, 5),	(RL, roll),
Chassé L, step R behind, step side with L	(6; 1, 2),	(roll; RL, roll),
point L	(3),	(roll),

Ending:

Saut de basque to L	(1, 2, 3),	(RL, L, roll),
Hold facing partner;	(4, 5, 6);	(both, – –);

End of that musical phrase and on new one:

Beginning:
Saut de basque to L, man to R this time (1, 2, 3), (both, L, roll),
Girl ends facing back, man ends facing front, Hold, (4, 5), (both, –),

Step 5

Digs and walks round self and then partner; *choque* castanets in 5th then keep arms in 3rd, L up R front:

The Step:

Dig R in (6); (*choque* 5th); dig out to partner	(1, 2),	(roll, roll), in 3rd,
Dig R in (3), (RL in 3rd), dig out to partner	(4, 5),	(roll, roll), in 3rd,

Dig R in (6); (RL in 3rd);
To R: 3 walks round self to R: on R, L, R, (1, 2, 3), (roll, roll, RL),
        R arm across, L behind,
Place L foot 4th with L side to partner (4, 5), (–, –),

Repeat on L:
Dig L in (6); (*choque* 5th); dig out to partner (1, 2), (roll, roll) in 3rd,
Dig L in (3), (RL and continue this Sevillanas rhythm)
3 walks crossing partner L, R, L (4, 5, 6); take L arm up front to 5th;
(Crossing with L shoulders, and towards L when in partner's place into...)

Step 6
Sevillanas chorus step, the step as in 1 on R.

The Step:
Sevillanas step with a *jeté*, 4 times:
Step forward on R foot (1), across partner,
Dig L behind (2), step back on L (3),
Dig R in front (4), *développé* (5), forward *jeté* on R, (6); (kicking L up at the back).
Repeat on L,
Repeat on R,
Repeat first three counts on L, (1, 2, 3),

Ending with a kick back as before but with L:
Point L in front on a *fondu* on R   (4), (RL), hold L arm in front, R arm 5th,
Kick L back   (5), (both), hold L arm in front, R arm 5th,
Place it across and turn to R.   (6); (*choque*); arms 5th,
End feet in 4th   (1, 2, 3), (both, –, –).
L front with arms 3rd L in front.

Step 7
Sostenidos, step, dig, dig and *pas de bourrée* in partner's place.
Arms: in 3rd, L front, R up in 5th and remain there for.
Castanets: continuous RL, roll, roll, except where indicated (–).

The Step:
Step across partner on L   (1), (RL),
Dig R behind   (2), (roll),
Dig R behind placing weight on it   (3), (roll),

Step again across on L   (4), (RL),
Dig R behind   (5), (roll),
Dig R behind, placing weight on it (6); (roll);

A small *pas de bourrée* on place L side, R behind, L forward;
                                 (1, 2, 3), (RL, roll, roll),
Change bringing R arm down front, L up back to 5th.
Get to other side of partner with R shoulders together).
Point R foot in front, ending R shoulders together,
                                 (4, 5, 6); (RL, –, –);
Repeat entire step to R, crossing to L shoulders together as at start.
Ends away from partner girl slightly upstage.

Step 8
Chassé back to back, boy in front facing front, girl at back facing back.
Castanets: RL, roll, roll.

The Step:

Chassé to L	(1), (RL),
Step on R behind	(2), (roll),
Step L side	(3), (roll),
Repeat to R	(4, 5, 6);
Repeat to L	(1, 2, 3),
Point R in front and hold	(4, 5, 6); (RL, –, –);

These are done looking over shoulder at partner arms 3rd,

Playing castanets as above:
9 walks round partner crossing him on audience side returning to own original place to face partner:
R, L, R, L, R, L; R, L, R, (1, 2, 3, 4, 5, 6; 1, 2, 3), (RL, roll, roll 3 times),

Facing partner L foot front in 4th	(4), (RL),
Pause	(5, 6); (–, –);

The man faces back and turns to face front on 1st beat of next step.

Step 9

Ballonnés, both facing front crossing each other, so that the man uses opposite foot to that of his partner, sequence danced only 3 times to L, R, L.
Repeat of step 4 of 1st *copla* but with a slight difference, this time 8 in stead of 5 counts.
Castanets as before across the music.

The Step:

Ballonné with L front	(1), back (2), hop with *développé* L out (3),
Chassé L to side	(4), step R across (5), step side with L (6);
Step R behind R	(1), step L in front (2),
Ballonné with R front	(3), back (4), hop with *développé* R out (5),
Chassé R to side	(6); step L across (1), step side with R (2),
Step L behind	(3), step R in front (4),

Repeat 1st part with L:

Ballonné with L front	(5), back (6); hop with *développé* L out (1),
Place left across and turn	(2, 3), finish 4th R front, (4),

Ending:

Click castanets at sides, arms in 6th position,	(5),
Choque front,	(6);
Click castanets at sides, arms in 6th position.	(1),
Hold	(2, 3),

Step 10

Rodazánes (as in Escuela Bolera exercise but starting stepping under).
Castanets: continuous RL, roll, roll.
The turns at the end are done with arms opening out from 3rd to 3rd.

The Step:

Step behind with L foot	(4), *rodazán* R front in air	(5, 6),
Step to R on R	(1), sweep L across and step on it	(2, 3);
Repeat to R	(4, 5, 6); (1, 2, 3),	
Repeat first three beats to L:	(4, 5, 6):	
Step behind with L foot (4), *rodazán* in air R		(5, 6),
Kneel down in front of partner by placing leg back, arms in 3rd, L in 5th, R in front		(1, 2, 3);
Straighten up and *destaque* (kick) R		(4, 5),
Place leg across (6); and turn to L		

Arms: circle front arm to 5th, L circles outward, down and up front to 5th, and change arms in front on the turn to R front (usual flamenco turn).

Repeat turn to L using same arm movement:

Step L	(1),	
Place leg across	(2), and turn to L	(3),
Hold	(4, 5, 6);	(–, –);

Step 11

4 passes (Sevillanas arms), back to back crossing in front of man.
Castanets: RL, roll, roll, as before.

The Step:

Step on L	(1),
Lift R across (knee bent)	(2),
Step across on R	(3),
3 walks turning on self at other side of partner	(4, 5, 6);
Repeat on R crossing to place,	
Repeat on L crossing to partners place, as above,	
Repeat on R crossing to place as far away from partner as steps allow,	

4 *emboîtés* forward 4 *deboîtés* back to place:

Degagé L foot to side	(&) close in front	(1),
Degagé R foot to side	(&) close in front	(2),
Degagé L foot to side	(&) close in front	(3),
Degagé R foot to side	(&) close in front	(4), hold (5, 6);

Arms go outward and up to 5th,

Degagé R foot to side (&) close in behind		(1),
Degagé L foot to side (&) close behind		(2),
Degagé R foot to side (&) step back		(3),
Point L foot in front back to audience		(4), hold (5, 6);

Arms go outward and down, R to 1st but low in front, L behind,

Step 12

Careos as in last step of 4th verse of Sevillanas, girl crosses behind man, but facing the audience, then across front etc.

Arms: circles, same arm down as leg in front as usual.

The Step:

On L crossing partner,	on R *careo* turning to face partner;
On L, crossing partner,	on R *careo* turning to face partner;
On L crossing partner,	on R *careo* turning to face partner;
On L, crossing partner,	on R *careo* turning to face partner;

End step back on R with L foot 4th front and hold,

Woman finishes facing audience,
Man finishes facing back,
Arms across body L across front, R behind and stay there for:
2 *chassé* turns with L crossing partner (1, 2, 3), (4, 5, 6);
Step back on L (1, 2, 3), place R front in 4th and hold (4, 5, 6); arms same,
2 *chassé* turns with R crossing partner (1, 2, 3), (4, 5, 6); arms across body,
Step back on R (1, 2, 3), place L front in 4th and hold (4, 5, 6); arms same.

Arms cirle outward and up:
Jeté forward on L, R foot kicks back slightly in the air (1), (both),
    (Click castanets arms to sides in low 6th),
Place R foot across L (2), raise arms to higher 6th at sides and (both),
Turn to L, taking both arms up in 5th, (3), (*choque*),
Finish facing front with L foot front, man behind (4), (both),
Hold L shoulder to partners L (5, 6); (–, –);
Arms: drop L to 3rd across front, R up.

BOLERO DE CASPE
(A Regional Dance from Aragon)

Notated for the Spanish Dance Society with additional information.

This is a very old, regal Jota in 3/4 time, from Caspe in the region of Zaragoza, counted in rhythmic cycles of six beats. This Bolero rhythm is typical of Jotas. It may be a court Jota from as early as the eleventh or twelfth century (Pedro Azorín Ibañez, personal communication), although this is disputed. The entrance steps in the introduction, dropping forward on the front foot, are bows and seem very ritualistic, in the way old historic dances had acknowledgement to the king in their first steps.

Time Signature: 3/4, counted in cycles of 6 beats as is usual in the Bolero.

The man wears a hat and cape and discards them before the dance begins. The woman wears black leather shoes, not the usual rope-soled *alpargatas*. The shoe has a black velvet bow on the top. The big mantilla shawl is pinned in the front and allowed to hang loose, or a small white fichu is worn around the neck. The bodice is made of black satin, the skirt of brocade and a small apron is worn (Pedro Azorín Ibañez, personal communication). The dance is written out for the Spanish Dance Society, to be performed as a solo. When performed as a duet, the partners face each other and dance as a mirror image, with opposite feet and moving downstage and upstage, not in opposite directions, except when going round each other.

Start corner 4, L foot pointed to wall 6. Women hold skirt out to sides.

Introduction: wait for (1, 2, 3, 4, 5, 6; 1, 2),

A
Travelling towards wall 6:

Drop forward on L	(3, 4), 2 walks back R, L	(5, 6; 1, 2),
3 walks forward R, L, R	(3, 4, 5, 6; 1, 2),	
Drop forward on L	(3, 4), 2 walks back R, L	(5, 6; 1, 2),

Travelling towards corner 1:

3 walks R, L, R	(3, 4, 5, 6; 1, 2),
Drop forward on L	(3, 4), 2 walks back to centre R, L (5, 6; 1, 2),
2 steps R, L, to corner 1	(3, 4, 5, 6);

B
Facing wall 5: Arms raised to 2nd (a V or U position):

Assemblé R to *écarté* line in 2nd	(1, 2), *développé* R to side (3),
Pas de bourrée under R	(4, 5, 6);
Hop on R, lifting L in *attitude devant*	(1, 2),
Jeté L, lifting R in *attitude devant*	(3, 4),
Temps de flèche (hitch kick) kicking L through with *développé* (5),	
Jeté L kicking R through	(6);
Repeat B facing the back	(1–6);

Repeat B facing the front   (1–6);
Step forward R (&), *assemblé* on to demi-pointe facing the front (4), pause (5, 6);

C
Travelling to corner 3:
Step L, together R, step L, *grand battement* R with small hop (1, 2, 3, 4),
Drop on R, lifting L in *attitude derrière* with a small hop (5, 6);
Coupé under L (1) lifting R in low *attitude devant* with a small hop (2),
Repeat C starting R to corner 4 (3, 4, 5, 6; 1, 2, 3, 4),
Repeat C starting L to corner 2 (5, 6; 1, 2, 3, 4, 5, 6);
Repeat C starting R to corner 1 (1, 2, 3, 4, 5, 6; 1, 2),
Repeat C starting L to wall 7 (3, 4, 5, 6; 1, 2, 3, 4),
Repeat C starting R to wall 5 without the last *coupé* (5, 6; 1, 2, 3, 4),
2 small steps R, L (5, 6).

First *Estribillo*. Travelling round to L:
Step R (1), small *développé devant* L (2),
Step L (3), small *développé devant* R (4), step R (5), step L (6);
Repeat *estribillo* 4 times starting R each time,
Step *assemblé* to face the front (1–3).
Pause (4–6);

D
Travelling forwards and backwards to wall 5 and 7:
The shoulder and arm dips down on the slide across looking over it to partner:
Walk L to wall 5 (1, 2), slide R across L (3, 4), ball change (& 5), *jeté* L (6);
Walk R to wall 7 (1, 2), slide L across R (3, 4), ball change (& 5), *jeté* R (6);
Walk L to wall 5 (1, 2), slide R across L (3, 4), ball change (& 5), *jeté* L (6);
Walk R to wall 7 (1, 2), slide L across R (3, 4), ball change (& 5), *jeté* R (6);
Walk L to wall 5 (1, 2), slide R across L (3, 4), ball change (& 5), *jeté* L (6);
Walk R to wall 7 (1, 2), slide L across R (3, 4), ball change (& 5), *jeté* R (6);
Walk L to wall 5 (1, 2), slide R across L (3, 4), ball change (& 5), *jeté* L (6);

Ending:
Hop on L raising R at side *en l'air* with knee turned in (1, 2),
Hop on L turning R out in *attitude devant* (3, 4),
Coupé onto R extending L to side (5), *coupé* onto L extending R to side (6);

Second *Estribillo*. Turning to L on self:
Hops on L placing R toe across L (1, 2), extend R out (3, 4), R toe across L (5),
extend R out (6);
Hops on L placing R toe across L (1, 2), extend R out (3, 4), R toe across L (5),
extend R out (6);
Hops on L placing R toe across L (1, 2),
Lift R *attitude devant* (3, 4),
Temps de flèche L out in front (5), *jeté* L (6);
Coupé R over extending L to side (1, 2), L toe across R (3, 4), extend L out (5),

L toe across R (6);
Step forward L, *assemblé* feet together (1, 2, 3, 4), pause (5, 6);

In partners the next three steps are danced so that the partners end back to back and then return to their places.

E (i)
Facing corner 2:

Assemblé R, hop on L *développé* R to side	(1, 2, 3),
Pas de bourrée under	(4, 5, 6);
Hop on R bringing L across R knee	(1, 2),
Jeté L bringing R across L knee	(3, 4),
Two quick *jetés devant* R, L	(5, 6);

E (ii)
Facing wall 6:

Jump on R extending L to side	(1, 2),
Relevé on R lifting L *attitude devant*	
Turning towards the back to finish facing wall 8	(3, 4),

Facing wall 6:

Dig L, R (& 5), jump on L extending R to side	(6);
Relevé on L lifting R *attitude devant*	(1, 2),
Jeté R, lifting L *attitude devant*	(3, 4),
2 *jetés devant* L, R	(5, 6);

Repeat E (ii) with jump *coupé* onto L, turning towards the back to finish facing wall 6 on *relevé*

Repeat E (ii) with jump *coupé* onto R, turning towards the back to finish facing wall 8 on *relevé* deleting the last 2 *jetés*.

Ending facing wall 5:
Step L (&), step R (5), step L (6);

Third *Estribillo*:
6 times round room to L, as for first *estribillo*, but down on 5 & 6:
Step R (1), *développé devant* L (2),
Step L (3), *développé devant* R (4), step R (5), step L (6),
On steps (counts 5 and (6) bend knees to dip down slightly.)

F (i)

Step R to R, kick L to corner 1 (1, 2, 3),	
Jota turn to L	(4, 5, 6);

F (ii)

Jeté on R lifting L in *attitude devant*	(1), step L over R (2),
Hop on L lifting R in *attitude derrière*	(3),
Pas de bourrée under with R	(4, 5, 6);

Repeat F (ii) starting L
Repeat F (ii) starting R
Repeat F (ii) starting L

G (i)
Facing corner 2, corner 1, corner 2, corner 1:
Step and hop R (1, 2), *développé* L to front on heel (3),
Step R (4), place L toe across cou de pied (5),
Jeté L, lifting R in *attitude devant*   (6);

G (ii)
3 step hops on R, L, R turning to L finishing facing corner 1,
Repeat G (i) and (ii) 3 more times starting L, R, L,
Repeat G (i) starting R into picados R, L, R, L, R, L, R, L, R, L, R, L,
Step R, *jeté* L lifting R in *attitude derrière*, arms 3rd, R arm up.

BOLERAS DE LA CACHUCHA

Escuela Bolera, Pericet version
Suggested choreographies that can be interspersed with the Cachucha sections codified under the title Cachucha.

Escuela Bolera (danced in ballet shoes, *zapatillas*).

The order of the Boleras de la Cachucha is, 'A':
Introduction, first Bolero, coda into first Cachucha, concluding Bolero.
Introduction, second Bolero, coda into second Cachucha, concluding Bolero
Introduction, third Bolero, the finale or *exaltación*.
The arms: castanet rhythms and arm positions can be found in the syllabus.

However, to avoid stopping and starting over again, as was the custom a century ago, the small Coda used to continue and is brought in after both the first Bolero sequences. The order of the Boleras de la Cachucha is thus a continuous flow, selection 'B':

Introduction,   Bolero 1, coda, Cachucha,
                   Bolero 2, coda, Cachucha,
                   Bolero 3, finale or *exaltación*.

This makes an excellent dance, otherwise it can becomes tedious.

The Bolero Sections:
The three Bolero sections are free, *libre*, choreographically, so there are endless possibilities. Usually set steps are taken from the syllabus and combined in sequences.

The Two Cachucha Sections:
However, the two Cachucha sections, or *jaleos* between the Boleros, never vary in choreography. Two out of the three existing *jaleos* are selected from the set sequences. As can be seen above, only two Cachuchas are needed out of the three that are recorded in this book. Any number of these may be included if the dance is lengthened. It would become cumbersome if this was done.

   However, if the dance is lengthened, as Puig gives the reason for dances being called Boleras in the plural, that it was danced by more than one couple, and one can envisage this treated almost as a ballet, with various couples taking turns to dance the sections and perhaps ending with a finale of all joining in. That would relieve the tedium of a longer dance.

The Llamada:
The two stamps at the start of each Bolero section on the count of (6; 1), used to be danced as two stamps, then changed to dig stamp, and then to a *sostenido*: tipping the toe in front and a soft stamp or step (Eloy Pericet, personal communication). It is therefore up to the individual dancer what they choose to do, but I notate the original: stamp stamp.

Before each Bolero verse if choosing version 'A' is a:

Salida de Bolero:
Entrance:

Start corner 4 with foot nearest to partner pointed in front, the man holding the woman's left hand up with his right hand. She holds her skirt out to the side with her right hand and he has the top of his left hand on his hip, fingers facing back. In Spanish dance the man is usually on the woman's L side.

Wait for 8 bars introduction or: 1, 2, 3, 4, 5, 6; 1, 2, 3, 4, 5, 6; 1, 2, 3, 4, 5, 6; 1, 2, 3, 4, 5, 6;

On the next two sets of six counts: walk on (1, 2), walk (3, 4), in a measured way and then slightly more urgently into a run to the centre (5, 6); (1, 2), to face each other, the man steps forward on his right foot, with the left bent in behind, while the woman steps forward on her left foot (3), and on (4, 5, 6); turns under the upheld arm, to the left, both step on R (1, 2), step back on L, (3, 4), and then R, (5, 6); and point L foot in front (1), arms down in front in 1st position. Three chords follow. Pause on the first two. On the last chord the R arm is raised up over head to 3rd position with the left in front over the front foot (1).

Introduction:
Usual for Bolero, the introduction of two sets of 6 counts;
– 2, 3, 4, 5, 6; bring top arm down the front and making half an inward circle,
1, 2, 3, 4, 5, 6; Raise both arms out to the sides and up to 5th.

Destaque (lift) L leg to side	(1, 2), closing behind (3, 4),	(-,-,-,-),	(R arm circles down outward),
Chassé R across	(5),	(-),	(R arm to 5th),
Jeté over on L leg	(6); (*choque*)		(with arms in 5th);
Step side on R leg	(1), (both),		(arms in 5th),
Point L across partner in front,	(2, 3), (L, roll);		(arms come down front),
Point L back	(4, 5), (L, roll),		(arms now low in 1st)

(*Note:* arms come out and up to 5th on the next *développé*),

Small *développé* with L, step forward on it,	(6; 1),	(L, roll),	(arms 5th),
Dig R behind	(2),	(*choque*)	(arms 5th),
Step back on R	(3),	(both),	(arms in 5th),
Pas de bourrée with L behind, R side, dig L front,	(& 4, 5, 6);	(L roll, roll,);	

(arms open out and down to 4th, L front, R behind),

Two limps round to L on L	(1, 2, 3, 4),	(Roll, L, roll, L,),	(arms 4th, L front),
Step L, facing partner again,	(5),	(roll),	
Small *développé* with R, step forward on R,	(6; 1),	(L; roll),	(arms open out and up to 5th),
Dig L foot behind, step back on L	(2, 3),	(*choque*, both),	(in 5th),
Pas de bourrée R behind, L side,	(4, 5),	(L, roll),	(L arm is opened outward)

The llamada into the bolero:

Dig R Front; step on R,	(6;1),	(both; both),	(arms in 3rd R up, L down in front);
			(Body over to L,)

Step now moves to R, on the bolero section:
On this *pas de bourrée* the partners face the audience: (arms in 3rd R up, L down in front).
Now facing the audience, the woman on the man's right. The dancers will cross each other, one

partner will have to use the opposite foot, arms in 3rd with the same arm down as the leading foot.

Lisada por delante:
Hop on R, *chassé coupé assemblé* L behind, (2, 3, 4, 5), (circle L arm down and up to 5th),
Hop on L, *chassé coupé assemblé* R behind (6; 1, 2, 3), (circle R arm down and up to 5th),

Tres cambiamentos:
Rise in air for (4),
3 changes in 5th, R behind, front behind, (5, 6; 1), (arms 5th).

Échappé y tercera:
Échappé to 2nd, (2, 3), jump beaten close R behind, (4, 5), (arms 5th),
Échappé to 2nd, (6; 1), jump beaten close L behind, (2, 3), (arms 5th).

Repeat to other side.

Lisada por delante:
Hop on R, *chassé coupé assemblé* L behind, (4, 5, 6; 1), (circle R arm down and up to 5th),
Hop on L, *chassé coupé assemblé* R behind (2, 3, 4, 5), (circle L arm down and up to 5th),
Hop on R, *chassé coupé assemblé* L behind, (6; 1, 2, 3), (circle R arm down and up to 5th,

Tres cambiamentos:
Rise in air for   (4),
3 changes in 5th, L behind, front, behind,   (5, 6; 1), (arms in 5th)

Échappé y tercera:
Échappé to 2nd, (2, 3), jump beaten close R behind, (4, 5), (arms 5th),
Échappé to 2nd, (6; 1), jump beaten close L behind, (2, 3), (arms 5th),

Lisada por delante:
Hop on R; *chassé coupé assemblé* L behind, (4, 5, 6; 1), (circle R arm down and up to 5th),

Coda:
On the music of the introduction to join up to the Cachucha section:
2 *glissades* to L on L,   (2, 3), (4, 5),

Sevillanas *estribillo* step:
Small *développé* with L; step on L,   (6; 1),
Dig R behind and step on it,   (2, 3),
Pas de bourrée L behind, R, side, dig L front,   (4, 5, 6);
Step on L, limp on R behind, step on L   (1, 2, 3), (arms 4th),
Step forward on R, to partner,   (4), (circle R inward),
Step forward on L, dig R behind.   (5, 6); (1), (circle L up),
L arm is overhead, R behind, the Valencian position.
Counts 2 & 3 are the lead in to the:

First Cachucha *Jaleo*
Here will come a chosen verse of the Cachucha, usually the *bodorneo* (*bordoneo*) one.

Second Bolero Verse
Both partners facing front:

Llamada:
Stamp; stamp, L foot in front (6; 1),

Batararaña (*matalaraña*)
Glissade, with R, point R in front (2 & 3),

Sevillanas estribillo step:
Small *développé* with, step on R,	(4, 5),
Dig L behind; and step on it,	(6; 1),
Rodazán R,	(2, 3),
Pas de bourrée R behind, side,	(4, 5),
Step on R, *assemblé* L in front,	(6; 1),
3 *entrechats*	(2, 3), (4, 5), (6; 1),

Lisada por delante:
Chassé coupé assemblé to L

Repeat from the *llamada* with R

End:
Chassé coupé assemblé to R to face partner again

Coda:
On the music of the introduction to join up to the Cachucha section:
2 *glissade*s to L on L,   (2, 3), (4, 5),

Sevillanas *estribillo* step:
Small *développé* with L; step on L,	(6; 1),
Dig R behind and step on it,	(2, 3),
Pas de bourrée L behind, side, dig L front,	(4, 5, 6);
Step on L, limp on R behind, step on L	(1), (2, 3), (arms 4th)
Step forward on R, to partner,	(4, 5), (circle R inward)
Step forward on L, dig R behind.	(6; 1), (circle L up)

The dancers are now in the Valencia position, L overhead, R behind.

Second Cachucha *Jaleo*
Here will come a chosen verse of the Cachucha. The most beautiful one is the third one notated under Cachucha, the *Balanceo* with continual step hops passing back to back.

Third Bolero Verse
Both partners facing front.

Pifla y pas de bourrée danced facing front crossing the partner, as in the last verse of Bolero Medio Paso, Pericet version:

Llamada:
Stamp; stamp, L foot in front (6; 1), (both, both),

Pifla y pas de bourrée:
Glissade, glissade with R,   (2, 3, 4, 5), (L, roll, L, roll), (R arm up)
Jeté R across, *chassé* L,   (6; 1),
    (R arm circles up to *choque* in 5th on *jeté*, both on the *chassé*)
Pas de bourrée: (& 2, & 3), (RL, RL,)
Stepping behind with R, L to side, step R turning over L,
        (both arms circle down and up)
L foot stretches out on   (4), (L),

Lisada por delante:
Chassé L, *coupé* R, *assemblé*   (5, 6; 1) (roll, both; both),
        (L arm circles down and to 5th)

On next set of *glissade*s drop the back arm and look at partner as before.
Repeat exactly crossing partner to L (man R),
End up in centre, the man behind his partner,
When they do step and dig leg in front it is bent in 4th in front, turned to look over L shoulder at partner, the man does the opposite,
The woman L leg in front, turned to look over L shoulder at partner,

She goes from side to side: arms are low around body in 4th:
One beat for each movement:

Step on L, (*choque*) dig R, (both), look over R shoulder, (R arm in front)
Step on R, (*choque*) dig L, (both), look over L shoulder, (L arm in front)
Step on L, (*choque*) dig R, (both), look over R shoulder, (R arm in front)
Step on R, (*choque*) dig L, (both), look over L shoulder, (L arm in front)
Step on L, (*choque*) dig R, (both), look over R shoulder, (R arm in front)
Step turn: woman to the R Man to L away from each other,

Final position:
Step towards each other crossing outside leg over as the step is taken (6);
Step towards each other stepping open, dig L behind (man), woman R (&)
Middle shoulder closest to partner forward, arm in front, other arm up (1).
Look across partner to front corner.

The man is static, arms in 5th, but does (*choque*, both) in 5th overhead leaning from side to side as she turns to look at him.

Other Choroegraphies of Bolero Sequences
These are a couple of variations sometimes seen and when looking at the counting they are less succssful in accenting the stamp: stamp, on (6; 1).

Both partners facing front:

Llamada:
Stamp; stamp, L foot in front   (6; 1), (both; both),

Batararaña (*matalaraña*):
Glissade to R, point R foot to corner   (2, & 3),

Sevillanas *estribillo* step:
Small *développé* with R; step on R,   (4, 5),
Dig L behind and step on it,   (6; 1),
Dig R in front, *développé* R,   (2, 3),
Pas de bourrée R behind, side L,   (4, 5),
Dig R;   (6);
Step on R in front, *rodazán* L,   (1, 2),
Step on L in front, *rodazán* R,   (3, 4),
Step on R in front, *rodazán* L,   (5, 6);
Vuelta normal:
Step to side on L and turn L,   (1, 2, 3),

Lisada por delante:
Hop on R, *chassé*, *coupé assemblé* L behind; (4, 5, 6; 1), (circle R arm down and up to 5th),
Repeat to other side.

Coda on the music of the introduction to join up to the Cachucha section:
2 *glissades* to L on L,   (2, 3), (4, 5),

Sevillanas *estribillo* step:
Small *développé* with L; step on L,   (6; 1),
Dig R behind and step on it,   (2, 3),
Pas de bourrée L behind, R side, dig L front, (4, 5, 6);
Step on L, limp on R behind, step on L (1), (2, 3), (arms 4th),
Step forward on R, to partner,   (4, 5), (circle R inward),
Step forward on L, dig R behind.   (6; 1), (circle L up)
Now standing in the Valencian position of arms.
A variation of this section is with *destaques* instead of *rodazánes*.

Another variation:

Llamada:
Stamp; stamp, L foot in front   (6; 1), (both; both),
Glissade to R, *jeté* on to R,   (2, 3), (4, 5),
Glassade to L, *jeté* on to L,   (6; 1), (2, 3),

Assemblé R over,	(4, 5),
3 *entrechats quatre*	(6; 1), (2, 3), (4, 5),
2 scissor jumps with legs to second	(6; 1), (2, 3),
Repeat starting stamps on	(4, 5), (arms 5th),
End with 3 scissor jumps	(4, 5), (6; 1), (2, 3), (arms 5th),
Hop on R, *chassée*, *coupé*, *assemblé*,	(4, 5, 6; 1), (arms 3rd to 5th),

Coda on the music of the introduction to join up to the Cachucha section:

2 *glissade*s to L on L,	(2, 3), (4, 5),

Sevillanas *estribillo* step:

Small *développé* with L; step on L,	(6; 1),
Dig R behind and step on it,	(2, 3),
P.d.bourrée L behind, side, dig L front,	(4, 5, 6);
Step on L, limp on R behind, step on L,	(1), (2, 3), (arms 4th),
Step forward on R, to partner,	(4, 5), (circle R inward),
Step forward on L, dig R behind.	(6; 1), (circle L up),

The dancers are now in the Valencian position, L overhead, R behind.

BOLERAS DE MEDIO PASO
Escuela Bolero, Pericet Version

An Escuela Bolera dance for a couple in 3/4 time. There are three so-called 'verses'. Each 'verse' includes an opening introduction, a Bolero and a central *jaleo*, ending on a closing Bolero. The same construction is found in the Boleras de la Cachucha, where the *jaleo* section is the Cachucha.

This dance will be counted in Bolero time across two bars, making 6 counts.

Entrance
Start corner 4 with foot nearest to partner pointed in front, the man holding the woman's left hand up with his right hand. She holds her skirt out to the side with her right hand and he has the top of his left hand on his hip, fingers facing back. In Spanish dance the man is usually on the woman's L side.

Wait for 8 bars introduction or: 1, 2, 3, 4, 5, 6; 1, 2, 3, 4, 5, 6; 1, 2, 3, 4, 5, 6; 1, 2, 3, 4, 5, 6;

On the next two sets of six counts: walk on (1, 2), walk (3, 4), in a measured way, and then slightly more urgently into a run to the centre (5, 6); (1, 2). To face each other, the man steps forward on his right foot, with the left bent in behind, while the woman steps forward on her left foot (3), and on (4, 5, 6); turns under the upheld arm, to the left, both step on R (1, 2), step back on L, (3, 4), and then R (5, 6); and point L foot in front (1), arms down in front in 1st position. Three chords follow. Pause on first two. On the last chord the R arm is raised up over head to 3rd position with the left in front over the front foot (1).

Introduction
Usual for Bolero, the introduction of two sets of 6 counts:

–, 2, 3, 4, 5, 6; bring top arm down the front and making half an inward circle,
1, 2, 3, 4, 5, 6; Raise both arms out to the sides and up to 5th.

Destaque (lift) L leg to side	(1, 2), closing behind (3, 4),	(-,-,-,-),	(R arm circles down outward),
Chassé R across	(5),	(-),	(R arm to 5th),
Jeté over on L leg	(6); (*choque*)		(with arms in 5th);
Step side on R leg	(1), (both),		(arms in 5th),
Point L across partner in front,	(2, 3), (L, roll);		(arms come down front),
Point L back	(4, 5), (L, roll),		(arms now low in 1st)
	(*Note*: arms come out and up to 5th on the next *développé*),		
Small *développé* with L, step forward on it,	(6; 1), (L, roll),		(arms 5th),
Dig R behind	(2), (*choque*)		(arms 5th),
Step back on R	(3), (both),		(arms in 5th),
Pas de bourrée with L behind, R side, dig L front,	(& 4, 5, 6); (L roll, roll,);		
	(arms open out and down to 4th, L front, R behind),		
Two limps round to L on L	(1, 2, 3, 4),(Roll, L, roll, L,),		(arms 4th, L front),
Step L, facing partner again,	(5), (roll),		

Small *développé* with R, step forward on R,   (6; 1),   (L; roll),   (arms open out and up
                                                                         to 5th),

Dig L foot behind, step back on L   (2, 3),   (*choque*, both),   (in 5th),

Pas de bourrée R behind, L side,   (4, 5),   (L, roll),   (L arm is opened outward)

The llamada into the bolero:

Dig R Front; step on R,   (6;1),   (both; both),   (arms in 3rd R up, L
                                                      down in front);
                                                      (Body over to L,)

Step now moves to R, on the bolero section:

Verse 1

Part 1. Opening Bolero section as noted at end of introduction:

Sostenido: lowering L arm in an outward circle (look back at it) until it goes up to 5th on the *jeté*),
Dig R front; step R, (arms still 5th) (6; 1), (choque; both),

(Next step is like a *coupé chassé, pas de bourrée* but steps across)
Step L across front, *chassé* R to R side, (2, 3), (L, roll),

Pas de bourrée under: L behind, R side, L front (& 4, & 5), (RL, roll),
    (This crosses the partner L shoulders passing),
Jeté battu, lifting R up (on the 5th count) and beating it in front,
(left beating underneath and ending up in attitude in front,) (6); (–);
On landing on R foot, L in *attitude* front, arms 5th), (1), (both),
(Now partners are with backs to each other and will turn to face each other on next step.)

(Arms: open outward and down on *glissades* and up to 5th on the *assemblés*).

Slight lift of L in front (2), (L),
Step on L turning to face partner (now on her place and she in his), (3), (roll),

Side to side: 3 *jetés*: use both arms circling out and up to 5th on *glissade jetés*. Look to direction
of *jeté*:

Glissade to R   (& 4, & 5), (RL, roll), (arms open out and down to 1st),
Jeté on to R   (6; 1), (–; both), (arms up front to 5th),
Glissade to L   (2, 3), (L, roll), (arms open out and down to 1st),
Jeté on to L   (4, 5), (–, both), (arms up front to 5th),
Glissade to R   (6; 1), (L; roll), (arms open out and down to 1st),
Jeté on to R   (2, 3), (–, both), (arms up front to 5th),

Temps levé chassé coupé assemblé to L, (L arm circles to down on *assemblé*), (4, 5, 6; 1), (arms
3rd), (L, roll, both; both),
(L arm circles down and up and R lowers on the *assemblé*),
On the repeat below play (L, roll, RL, roll),

Repeat it all to return to original place:
(The last *coupé assemblé* (6; 1), takes the place of the dig step at the start).

Step L across front, *chassé* R to R side   (2, 3), (L, roll),
   (Lowering arm look back at it)
Pas de bourrée under, L behind, R side, L front   (& 4, & 5), (RL, RL),
   (This crosses the partner L shoulders passing),
Jeté battu, lifting R up (on the 5th count) and beating it in front,
   (left beating underneath and ending up in *attitude* in front), (6); (–);
On landing on R foot, L in *attitude* front, arms 5th), (1), (both),
(Now partners are with backs to each other and will turn to face each other on next step.)

(Arms: open down outward on *glissades* and up to 5th on the *assemblés.*)

Slight lift of L in front (2), (L),
Step on L turning to face partner (partners now back in original places) (3), (roll),

Side to side: 3 *jetés*: use both arms opening out and up to 5th on *glissade jetés*:

Glissade to R	(& 4, & 5), (RL, roll),	(arms open out and down to 1st)
Jeté on to R	(6; 1), (–; both),	(arms up front to 5th)
Glissade to L	(2, 3), (L, roll),	(arms open out and down to 1st)
Jeté on to L	(4, 5), (–, both),	(arms up front to 5th)
Glissade to R	(6; 1), (L; roll),	(arms open out and down to 1st)
Jeté on to R	(2, 3), (–, both),	(arms up front to 5th)

Temps levé chassé coupé assemblé to L (L arm down on *assemblé*), (4, 5, 6; 1), (arms 3rd), (L, roll, both; both),
This time to end: (L, roll, *choque*, both), (arms 3rd, R up L down in front).

Part 2. *Tiempo de Jaleo*
3/4 *piu vivo.* This has three sections.
Lead in of two beats (2 &, 3 &); man travels upstage, woman downstage.

Step A:
Sostenidos to R travels away from partner downstage, R arm up:
Step to R on R, tip step L front, (arms in 3rd); (1, 2, 3);   (L, roll, roll);
Step to R on R, tip step L front, (arms in 3rd); (& 1, 2, 3);   (RL, roll, roll);

Small steps:

R to side, L behind, R to side, (L arm to 5th),	(& 1, 2, 3);	(RL, L, roll);
Assemblé the L in behind, (arm 5th)	(1),	(both);
Lift L leg to side on a hop	(2, 3);	(L, roll);
Place L across and *vuelta normal* to R,	(&1, 2, 3);	(RL, roll, roll);

(Arms down and up front to 5th),
(L arm swings down to 3rd on next step),
Step R to side, *chassé* L across sweeping body over (& 1, 2, 3); (R L, roll, roll);
Small *pas de bourrée* on place:
Step R to side, step L behind, step on R on place, (& 1, 2, 3); (R L, L, roll);
Point L front towards partner, turning body towards it, (1), (both),
Lift arm to 5th   (2, 3); (–, –);

Repeat it all to L, travelling upstage.

Step B:
From side to side, as in *lisada por delante* but *vuelta normal* and not *de pecho:*
Chassé to R, place L behind, step R to side, R arm in 3rd front, (1, 2, 3); (L, roll, roll);
Chassé to L, place R behind, step L to side, L arm in 3rd front, (& 1, 2, 3); (RL, roll, roll);
Place R across and *vuelta normal* to L, (& 1, 2, 3); (RL, L, roll),
Swish R out *assemblé* in 3rd front (arm 3rd R front), (1), (both),
Entrechat quatre, (arm still in 3rd), (2, & 3); (L, roll);

Step C:
1 *sostenido*, 1 *pas de basque.*
Arms: travelling round partner to R to their place, arms third, R up on *sostenido*, take L, lower arm up to 5th on *pas de basque* ready for the *vuelta normal* using both arms.
Crossing partner do:
Sostenido: step to side on R, tip step L in front, (& 1, 2, 3); (RL, roll, roll);
In partner's place, *pas de basque*:
Step on R, *balancé* dig L front, step R, (& 1, 2, 3); (RL, roll, roll);
Vuelta normal to L in partner's place, (1, 2, 3); (both, L, roll);
Hold, arms 5th, bring R foot from back (1, 2, 3); (both, – –);

Repeat B and C exactly, crossing back to original place, but ending both facing front, arms 3rd, with foot nearest partner (woman L, man R) pointed slightly towards one another, ready to cross over from side to side facing audience. The woman's steps are described, the man does the opposite.

Part 3. Closing Bolero of Verse 1
Both facing front:

Step D:

Pause for two beats in that position	(4, 5),	
Point, point L foot, in front	(6; 1),	(both; both),
Arms change from 3rd to 3rd:		
Bend L leg across	(2),	(L),
Chassé, coupé, assemblé crossing partner	(3, 4, 5),	(roll, both, both),
Bend R leg across	(6);	(L);
Chassé, coupé, assemblé crossing partner	(1, 2, 3),	(roll, both, both),
Jump up into	(4),	(–),
Take arms to 5th and hold them in 5th for:		
Three changes,	(5, 6; 1),	(both, both; both),
Jump up into	(2),	(–),
Echappé, beaten close,	(3, 4, 5),	(both, L, roll),
Jump up into	(6);	(–);
Echappé, beaten close,	(1, 2, 3)	(both, L, roll),

Repeat, arms as above, with 3 crossings ending on partner's place:

Bend L leg across,	(4),	(L),

Chassé, coupé, assemblé crossing partner (5, 6; 1), (roll, both; both),
Bend R leg across   (2),   (L),
Chassé, coupé, assemblé crossing partner (3, 4, 5), (roll, both, both),
Bend L leg across,   (6);   (L);
Chassé, coupé, assemblé crossing partner (1, 2, 3), (roll, both, both),
Jump up into   (4),   (–),
Three changes   (5, 6; 1), (both, both; both),
Jump up into   (2),   (–),
Echappé, beaten close,   (3, 4, 5), (both, L, roll),
Jump up into   (6);   (–);
Echappé, beaten close,   (1, 2, 3), (both, L, roll),

Ending:
Bend R leg across,   (4), (L),
Chassé, coupé, assemblé crossing   (5, 6; 1), (roll, *choque*; both),
Release L pointed in front, arms 3rd, leaning towards partner, now returned to starting position on R side of partner facing front.

Verse 2

Introduction repeated as at start.
On first section step on L to face partner and point R foot front, arms 3rd.
It ends as before:
Pas de bourrée with R behind, L side,   (4, 5), (L, roll),
(*Note*: this time on *pas de bourrée* outward.)

Part 1. Opening Bolero Section

Arms: remain in 3rd until *rodazán* when they go up to 5th, lower left until *vuelta fibraltada* and repeat all when step repeats.

Lift R leg to side in preparation,   (6); (–);
Assemblé R foot in front,   (1), (both),
Entrechat quatre: entrechat quatre: entrechat quatre   (2, 3,: 4, 5,: 6; 1), (L, roll,: L, roll,:
L; roll),
Crossing partner do:
Temps levé on L *chassé* R   (2, 3),   (L, roll),
Coupé L (&), *chassé* R,   (& 4 &), (RL, roll),
Coupé stepping on L, now with back to partner   (5),   (L),
But swivel to R doing a *rodazán* (*rond de jambe*), (6);   (–); (arms 5th)
Now facing partner.

Step forward in open line across partner on R, L in *attitude* at back (1), (both), (arms 3rd L front)
Hop (R), *chassé* (L) across,   (2, 3),   (L, roll),
Coupé R (&), *chassé* L, with L,   (& 4, & 5), (RL, roll),
Coupé R lift L in front   (6);   (–);
Ending *vuelta fibraltada* to L (1), (both), turning on (2, 3), (L, roll),
(arms 5th and opening as usual for a turn, then to 5th at end)
Lift L leg   (4),   (L),

Chassé L, *coupé, assemblé* L behind,   (5, 6; 1), (roll, *choque*; both),
(L circles out and down to 3rd on *chassé* and 5th on *assemblé*).

Repeat it all to get back to starting place.

Part 2. *Tiempo de Jaleo* Section
Lift R foot and *rodazán* to side (2, 3); arm to 5th.

Part A
Step as in *rodazán y pas de basque* exercise:
Castanets: (L, roll, roll; RL, roll, roll); 6 counts:
Step R to side, low *rodazán* across, drop onto it, (1, 2, 3); (L, roll, roll);
Arms: 3rd in L front,
R arm circles down front:
Step R *rodazán* L to 2nd (1, 2, 3); (RL, roll, roll); (arms end in front crossed in 1st). Keeping arms down and using body movement to follow:
Chassé L behind, *chassé* R behind (1, 2, 3); (RL, L, roll); using body each time as foot goes behind, both arms front, R starts to lift back into 3rd.

Step hop crossing partner (this pass also appears in the Cachucha verses in Boleras de la Cachucha):
Step on L (1, 2), back to partner, hop with R in front (3); (both, L, roll); (arms 3rd, R arm up, L in front in opposition);

Sostenido, pas de basque, now on partner's place:
Step on R facing partner, tip L front on 3/4 point, step;
                    (1, 2, 3); (RL, roll, roll); (L arm 3rd in front);
Pas de basque to R (1, 2, 3); (RL, roll, roll); (raise L to 5th);
Vuelta normal to L (1, 2, 3; 1), (RL, L, roll, both),

Repeat exactly to return to original position.

Part B
This crosses partner and both face front and is written for the woman (use upstage foot, woman L, the man uses opposite R foot).

Step:
Woman crosses in front of the man, arms 3rd, lifts to 5th for *vuelta*:

Developpé L leg (R arm up in 3rd)	(2, 3); (–, –);	(L arm 3rd front)
*Step L, bring R together behind,	(1, 2, 3);	(L, roll, roll);
Step L, *developpé* R (kick),	(1, 2, 3);	(RL, roll, roll);
Place R across into *vuelta normal*,	(1, 2, 3);	(RL, L, roll);

(Use both arms for turn, drop into 3rd for:

Step facing front using opposite feet*:

Woman steps L on place	(1),	(both),
Developpé R in front	(2, 3);	(L, roll); (3rd R front)

(Man steps R on place (1), *developpé* L)
Pas de bourrée: R, behind, L, side, R, front, (1, 2, 3); (RL, roll, roll); (3rd)
Coupé, rodazán R in air, (1, 2, 3); (RL, roll, roll); (3rd)
Step on R towards each other, *vuelta normal* (1, 2, 3; 1), (RL, L, roll; both),
                    (arm raises to 5th and use both arms for turn).
Developpé R leg (man L) (2, 3);   (L, roll);

Repeat everything starting at * (woman L leg, man R leg).

End:
Finish *vuelta* facing front with inside foot pointed towards partner, (1), leaning over the pointed foot arms 3rd on the last (1) (both) above.

PART 3. Closing Bolero
Punta y talon variation. The womans beats are described the man's will be the opposite.
Arms change from 3rd to 3rd, same arm as leg in front, on *chassés* move through 5th.

Wait for two beats:
Sostenido: tip L front, step on it,   (6; 1), (both; both), (arms 3rd, L front),
R heel toe, in front,   (2 &), step on L, on place, (3); (L, roll);
R toe heel, in front,   (4 &), step on L, on place, (5), (L, roll),
Repeat to other side with other leg and arm in 3rd front.

Note: On the section marked *, turn slightly away from partner and on repeat towards partner.
Arms move in circles as normally, same arm front as leg

This step also towards and away from partner:
Lift L leg across supporting leg   (6); (arms 3rd L front),
Chassé, coupé step, to L   (1, & 2), (roll, RL), (L arm circles up),
Chassé, coupé step, to R   (3; & 4), (roll; RL), (R arm circles),
Assemblé L in front   (5), (roll), (L arm to 3rd, L front)
Entrechat quatre   (6; 1), (L; roll), (L arm remains in 3rd)
Entrechat quatre,   (2, 3); (L, roll); (L arm remains in 3rd)

Crossing partner:
Temps levé chassé   (4, 5), (L, roll), (L arm remains in 3rd)
Coupé assemblé   (6; 1), (both; both), (L arm up to 5th)

Repeat on other side in entirety from *.
End on (6; 1), with (*choque*; both), and foot closest to partner pointed to them, arms in 3rd.

Verse 3

Introduction repeated as at start.
On first section step on L to face partner and point R foot front, arms 3rd.
It ends as before:

Pas de bourrée with R behind, L side, (4, & 5), (L, roll), (both arms held in 5th after Sevillanas step forward on R),

PART 1. Opening Bolero Section
Travel to L side.

Step A:
Batararaña, last section of the introduction:
Step travels to L:
Sostenido: dig R front, step on it, (6; 1), (both; both), (arms held 5th)

Bataranaña:

Glissade with L to a point with L,	(2, & 3), (L, roll), (arms down in front),
Developpé L leg,	(4), (L) (arms circle out and up),
Step forward on L,	(5), (roll), (arms continue to go up),
Dig R behind;	(6); (*choque*); (arms reach 5th),
Step back on R,	(1), (both), (arms 5th),
Dig L front,	(2), (L), (L arm starts to circle out)
Developpé L leg,	(3), (roll), – down and up

Pas de bourrée L behind, R to side, dig L front (4, 5, 6); (RL, roll, roll);
 – up in 5th on the dig),

Chassé-	(1), (roll),
Coupé-chassé, crossing partner, (L shoulder),	(2, 3), (L, roll), (arms circle open)

The dancers have now reached their partner's place, and on place do:

Beaten *jeté en tournant* lifting L behind,	(4, 5), (–, both),
Hop on R, step on L,	(6; 1), (L; roll),

(arms circle open)

Beaten *jeté en tournant* lifting L behind,	(2, 3), (–, both),

(arms circling outward and up to 5th),
In the partner's place and end facing partner:
Hop *chassé-coupé-assemblé* to L, feet ending in 4th position not 5th, (4, 5, 6; 1), (L, roll, both; both).
(circle L arm down in 3rd).

Repeat exactly as above to return to original place.
On last hop *chassé-coupé-assemblé* to L, feet ending in 4th position not 5th (4, 5, 6; 1),
(L, roll, *choque*, both).
Use L arm circling down and up on *chassé-coupé* and R down on the *assemblé* to L.

PART 2. *Tiempo de Jaleo* Section
Wait for one of first two beats. Lifting R arm to join L in 5th, *choque* on next beat.

A:
Start arms 5th.

Careo with R leg crossing partner,	(1, 2, 3); (L, roll, roll);
Careo on place, to face partner	(1, 2, 3); (L, roll, roll);

Walk R, L, R, towards partner and point L foot in front, L shoulders together
Bend forward on the walks and straighten up on the point on (1),
(& 1, & 2, & 3); (& 1), (RL, RL, RL); (RL),
On (1), arms 3rd, (2), hold (–),
Tip L toe in front (3); (–)
Turning towards partner and in a circle on self:-

Sostenidos, stepping in front on 1:
2 steps L front, R travelling round self, tip toe front, (1, 2, 3);   (L, roll, roll);
Step L front, R travelling round self, tip toe front, (1, 2, 3);   (RL, roll, roll);
Vuelta normal to L (1, 2, 3); (arms down and 5th), (pause 1, 2), (arms 5th) (RL, L, roll); (both, –).
Lift R leg across under knee (3);

B:
The step: *chassé y contra chassé.*
Castanets: (L, roll, roll), (RL, roll, roll).
Chassé to R side, step behind with L, step on R, (1, 2, 3); (R arm circles),
Chassé to L side, step behind with L, step on L, (1, 2, 3); (L arm circles).
Step on L *vuelta normal* to R (1, 2, 3); (RL, L, roll); (arms down and up to 5th,
End facing outward, back to back with partner. (1, 2, 3); (both, –, –); (arms 5th).

Repeat *chassé y contra chassé* exactly, end facing partner.

C:
Repeat *careos*:
To partner's position:
Start arms 5th.
Careo with R leg crossing partner;   (1, 2, 3); (L, roll, roll);
Careo on place, to face partner;   (1, 2, 3); (L, roll, roll);

Returning to own place:
Careo with R leg crossing partner;   (1, 2, 3); (L, roll, roll);
Careo on place, to face partner;   (1, 2, 3); (L, roll, roll);

To partner's position:
Careo with R leg crossing partner;   (1, 2, 3); (L, roll, roll);
Careo on place, to face partner;   (1, 2, 3); (L, roll, roll);

Ending:
Step across partner with L, the man in front, and step turn across partner with R, the man in front.
The woman does step turn to R.
Step out on outside feet, pointing foot to partner, outside arm lifted, inside in front in 3rd (both, L, roll; both, –, –);

Part 3

Closing Bolero
Similar to the step in the Boleras de la Cachucha, but dropping the arm away from the direction of travel.

The step starts going away from the partner, the back arm is down and looking at the partner, the other arm is overhead. The step crosses and crosses again, finishing in the centre with the man behind his partner, he stands on his R leg, L at back in a dig. The woman starts to the L with the R, the man uses the R.
The *glissades* are more like limps with the foot at the back on the toe.
If you go to the L, the L arm is at the side of the body and circling to 5th.

Two starting beats (L, roll) (arms 3rd), the verses end in that position and remain there for the start of each verse,

Arms: Leave the arm that is down for the first *glissades* and look back at partner
Castanets: both, both, L, roll, L, roll
　　choque, both, R, L, R, L,
　　L, roll, both, both

The Step:
One often used as third Bolero section in Boleras de la Cachucha,
Sostenido: dig L front, step on it,
Glissade, *glissade* with R, *jeté* R, across, *chassé*, *pas de bourrée* (behind side, front turning L over L),
Chassé L, *coupé* R, *assemblé*.
L arm down on the *chassé*, up to 5th on the *coupé*, R arm down on the *assemblé*.

The Detail:
Sostenido: dig L front, step on it	(6; 1), (both; both),
Glissade, *glissade* with R	(2, 3, 4, 5), (L, roll, L, roll), (R arm up)
Jeté R across; *chassé* L	(6; 1),
(R arm circles up to *choque* in 5th on *jeté*; both on the *chassé*)	
Pas de bourrée:	(& 2, & 3), (RL, RL),
Stepping behind with R, L to side, step R turning over L, (both arms circle down and up)	
L foot stretches out on	(4), (L),
Chassé L, *coupé* R, *assemblé*	(5, 6; 1), (roll, both; both),
(L arm circles down and to 5th)	

On next set of *glissades* drop the back arm and look at partner as before.
Repeat exactly crossing partner to L (man R),
End up in centre, the man behind his partner,
When they do step and dig leg in front it is bent in 4th in front, turned to look over L shoulder at partner, the man does the opposite,

She goes from side to side: arms are low around body in 4th, one beat for each movement:

Step on L, (*choque*) dig R, (both), look over R shoulder, (R arm in front)
Step on R, (*choque*) dig L, (both), look over L shoulder, (L arm in front)
Step on L, (*choque*) dig R, (both), look over R shoulder, (R arm in front)
Step on R, (*choque*) dig L, (both), look over L shoulder, (L arm in front)
Step on L, (*choque*) dig R, (both), look over R shoulder, (R arm in front)
Step turn woman to the R, man to L, away from each other,

The man is static, arms in 5th, but does (*choque*, both) in 5th overhead leaning from side to side as she turns to look at him.

Final position:
Step towards each other crossing outside leg over as the step is taken, (6);
Step towards each other stepping open, dig L behind (man), woman R (&)
Middle shoulder closest to partner forward arm in front, other arm up (1).
Look across partner to front corner.

CACHUCHA
Escuela Bolera, Pericet version

The *jaleos* from the Boleras de la Cachucha
Escuela Bolera (ballet shoes, *zapatillas*)

The order of the Boleras de la Cachucha is:
Introduction, Bolero 1, Cachucha 1,
Introduction, Bolero 2, Cachucha 2,
Introduction, Bolero 3, finale or *exaltación*.

The three Bolero sections are free, *libre*, choreographically. However, the two Cachucha sections
or *jaleos* between them are usually always the same, therefore, only two are needed out of the
folowing three that exist.

Salida de Bolero

Introduction:
Usual for Bolero, the introduction of two sets of 6 counts;
– 2, 3, 4, 5, 6; bring top arm down the front and making half an inward circle, 1, 2, 3, 4, 5, 6;
Raise both arms out to the sides and up to 5th.

Destaque (lift) L leg to side	(1, 2), closing behind (3, 4),	(-,-,-,-),	(R arm circles down outward),
Chassé R across	(5),	(-),	(R arm to 5th),
Jeté over on L leg	(6); (*choque*)		(with arms in 5th);
Step side on R leg	(1), (both),		(arms in 5th),
Point L across partner in front,	(2, 3), (L, roll);		(arms come down front),
Point L back	(4, 5), (L, roll),		(arms now low in 1st)

(*Note*: arms come out and up to 5th on the next *développé*),

Small *développé* with L, step forward on it,	(6; 1),	(L, roll),	(arms 5th),
Dig R behind	(2), (*choque*)		(arms 5th),
Step back on R	(3), (both),		(arms in 5th),

Pas de bourrée with L behind, R side, dig L front, (& 4, 5, 6); (L roll, roll,);
(arms open out and down to 4th, L front, R behind),

Two limps round to L on L	(1, 2, 3, 4),(Roll, L, roll, L,),		(arms 4th, L front),
Step L, facing partner again,	(5),	(roll),	
Small *développé* with R, step forward on R,	(6; 1),	(L; roll),	(arms open out and up to 5th),
Dig L foot behind, step back on L	(2, 3),	(*choque*, both),	(in 5th),
Pas de bourrée R behind, L side,	(4, 5),	(L, roll),	(L arm is opened outward)

The llamada into the bolero:

Dig R Front; step on R,	(6;1),	(both; both),	(arms in 3rd R up, L down in front); (Body over to L,)

Step now moves to R, on the chosen bolero section, then the Cahucha introduction:

Three Jaleos from the Boleras de la Cachucha

Cachucha *jaleos* only:
The 3 sections come alternately between the Bolero sections.
Castanets: after the introduction are the same rhythms on all three *jaleos* (see last page).

Introduction to each verse:

Two *glissade*s forward with the L foot,	(2 & 3), (4, 5),
Small *développé* with L,	(6);
Step forward on L, dig R behind,	(1, 2),
Step back on R,	(3),
To L, *pas de bourrée* under, L behind, R side, L across	(4 & 5),
Dig R behind,	(6);
Limp onto L, pause,	(1, 2),
Walk R,	(3, 4),
Walk L into *posición Cachucha*:	(5, 6);
Dig R at back, L arm up, R behind.	(1),
Look over L shoulder at partner in front of you	
Pause,	(2),

First Cachucha, the *bodorneo* (*bordoneo*) *jaleo*:

Step 1:
The Cachucha step, the same in each *jaleo*.
This goes from side to side while facing the partner.
Arms: work inward circles on all *balanceo* steps.
Castanets: as indicated:

Ist *pica atrás* (touch with R tip of toe.)	(6); (ria);
The step, moving towards L:	
Coupé under with R foot (R shoulder to partner)	(1), (R, L),
Point L in front of you (face wall 6),	(2), (L),
Step on L;	(3); (roll);
Brush R toe through,	(4), (L),
Step on R,	(5), (roll),
Dig L at back;	(6); (roll);

Repeat step to R:	
Coupé under with L foot (L shoulder to partner)	(1), (R, L),
Point R in front of you (face wall 8),	(2), (L),
Step on R,	(3); (roll);
Brush L toe through	(4), (L),
Step on L,	(5), (roll),
Dig R at back	(6); (roll);

Repeat step to L:	
Coupé under with R foot (R shoulder to partner)	(1), (RL),

Point L in front of you (face wall 6),	(2), (L),
Step on L,	(3); (roll);
Brush R toe through,	(4), (L),
Step on R,	(5), (roll),
Dig L at back,	(6); (roll);

Repeat step to R:

Coupé under with L foot (L shoulder to partner)	(1), (RL),
Point R in front of you (face wall 8),	(2), (L),
Step on R,	(3); (roll);
Brush L toe through,	(4), (L),
Step on L,	(5), (roll),
Dig R at back,	(6); (roll);

Step 2. *Bordoneo* step:
Triple *bordoneo*:
R arm up in 3rd, L front.

Step to R on R, toe L in, heel forward	(1, 2, 3); (RL, roll, roll);
Step to R on R, toe L in, heel forward	(4, 5, 6); (RL, roll, roll);
Step to R on R, toe L in, heel forward	(1, 2, 3); (RL, L, roll);
Coupé with R,	(4), (both),
Arms go up to 5th on each *coupé* and stay there for the next step,	
subresu = *saut de basque* to L,	(5, 6); (L, roll);

Triple *bordoneo*:
L arm up in 3rd, R front.

Step to L on L, toe L in, heel forward	(1, 2, 3); (RL, roll, roll);
Step to L on L, toe L in, heel forward	(4, 5, 6); (RL, roll, roll);
Step to L on L, toe L in, heel forward	(1, 2, 3); (RL, L, roll);
Coupé with L,	(4), (both), (5th),
subresu = *saut de basque* to R,	(5, 6); (L, roll); (5th),

Single *bordoneo*:
R up in 3rd, front.

Step to R on R, toe L in, heel forward	(1, 2, 3); (both, L, roll);
Coupé with R,	(4), (both), (5th)
subresu = *saut de basque* to L,	(5, 6); (L, roll); (5th);

Single *bordoneo*:
L arm up in 3rd, R front.

Step to L on L, toe R in, heel forward	(1, 2, 3); (both, L, roll);
Coupé with L,	(4), (both), (5th),
Subresu = *saut de basque* to R,	(5, 6); (L, roll); (5th)

Step 3. *Sostenido* and step hops:
Sostenidos passing:

Step on R, dig, step L,	(& 1, 2, 3); (RL, roll, roll);

Step on R, dig, step L,   (& 4, 5, 6); (RL, roll, roll);

Arms: work inward on all *balanceo* steps (step hops). The arm sweeps behind the back with the leg at start, then the other comes down the front in opposition to the raised leg in front.

Step hop turning on self:
Step on R, sweep L back, step on it   (& 1, 2, 3); (RL, L, roll);
Step on R, swish,   (4, 5), (both, L),
(with L leg front *attitude*, R arm front, turning on self)
Hop   (6); (roll);

Sostenidos turning on self:
Step on L, dig, step R,   (& 1, 2, 3); (RL, roll, roll);
Step on L, dig, step R,   (& 4, 5, 6); (RL, roll; roll);

Step hop turning on self:
Step on L, sweep R back, step on it,   (& 1, 2, 3); (RL, pause, L);
Step on L,   (4, 5), (roll, roll),
(with R front *attitude*, turning on self)
Hop   (6); (roll);

Sostenidos passing (2):
Step on R, dig, step L;   (1, 2, 3); (RL, roll, roll);
Step on R, dig, step L;   (4, 5, 6); (RL, roll, roll);

Desplante:
Stamp R,   (1), (RL),
Point L front,   (2), (pause),
Pause;   (3); (pause);
Pas de bourrée L to face front:
L behind,   (4), (L),
R on place, face audience   (5), (roll),
Lift R, up,   (6); (roll);
Point in front leg and hold position   (1, 2, 3); (roll, –, –);
Continue playing the castanets throughout the introduction with no pause in castanets after the dance section into the next introduction.

Introduction 2
As before: standing, just playing castanets.

Second Cachucha. *Sostenido Jaleo*

Step 1:
Cachucha step as before.

Step 2. *Sostenidos y rodazán*:

Triple *sostenido*:

Step to R on R, dig step L	(& 1, 2, 3); (RL, roll, roll);
Step to R on R, dig step L	(& 4, 5, 6); (RL, roll, roll);
Step to R on R, dig step L	(& 1, 2, 3); (RL, L, roll);
Coupé with R,	(4), (both),
Rodazán L to high second,	(5, 6); (L, roll);

Triple *sostenido*:

Step to L on L, dig step L	(& 1, 2, 3); (RL, roll, roll);
Step to L on L, dig step L	(& 1, 2, 3); (RL, roll, roll);
Step to L on L, dig step L	(& 1, 2, 3); (RL, L, roll);
Coupé with L,	(4), (both),
Rodazán R to high second	(5, 6); (L, roll);

Single *sostenido*:

Step R, *rodazán* L across on floor	(1, 2, 3); (both, L, roll);
Coupé with R,	(4), (both),
Rodazán L to high second,	(5, 6); (L, roll);

Single *sostenido*:

Step to L on R, dig step L,	(1, 2, 3); (both, L, roll);
Coupé with L,	(4), (both),
Rodazán R to high second,	(5, 6); (L, roll);

Step 3:
Step hops passing, with *sostenidos.*

Step hops:

Step on R, *chassé* L across	(& 1, 2, 3); (RL, roll, roll);
Step on R, *chassé* L behind	(& 1, 2, 3); (RL, roll, roll);
quick *chassé* back with R	(& a) (RL),
Step L, hop lift R, passing partner,	(1, 2, 3); (L, roll, both);

(The R arm comes down across the front on the last quick *chassé* and then sweeps up at the back on the step hop)

Sostenidos:

Step R, dig step L,	(& 1, 2, 3); (RL, roll, roll);
Step R, dig step L,	(& 4, 5, 6); (RL, roll, roll);
Step R, slide L behind	(& 1, 2, 3); (RL, L, roll);
Step R, swish hop passing the partner	(4, 5, 6); (both, L, roll);

Repeat *sostenidos*:

Step L, dig step R,	(& 1, 2, 3); (RL, roll, roll);
Step L, dig step R,	(4, 5, 6); (RL, roll, roll);
Step L, slide R behind	(1, 2, 3); (RL, L, roll);
Step L, hop passing the partner	(4, 5, 6); (both, L, roll);

Desplante:

Stamp L,	(1), (RL),
Point R	(2), (pause),
Pause for	(3); (pause);

Pas de bourrée:

Behind R	(4), (L),
Side L	(5), (roll),
step on R	(6); (roll);
point L	(1), (roll),
Pause,	(2, 3); (–, –); facing audience:

Continue playing the castanets through the introduction.

Introduction 3
As before, castanets only.

Third Cachucha. *Balanceo Jaleo*

Step 1:
Cachucha step as before.

Triple:
Crossing partner, facing each other:

Step on R, *chassé* L behind,	(RL, roll, roll);
Step on R, *chassé* L over,	(RL, roll, roll);
Step on R, *chassé* L behind,	(RL, L, roll);

Step hop crossing back to back:
Step on R leg, swish, hop with L in *attitude* in front, (both, L, roll);

Repeat triple:
Crossing partner, facing each other:

Step on L, *chassé* R behind,	(RL, roll, roll);
Step on L, *chassé* R over,	(RL, roll, roll);
Step on L, *chassé* R behind,	(RL, L, roll);

Repeat step hop crossing back to back:
Step on L leg step hop with R in *attitude* in front; (both, L, roll);

2 singles. Play both, L, roll four times:
Step on R, *chassé* L behind; step R, hop crossing;
Step on L, *chassé* R behind, step L, hop crossing.

Step 3:
Sostenidos turning on self:

Step R, dig step L;	(1, 2, 3); (RL, roll, roll);
Step R, dig step L;	(1, 2, 3); (RL, roll, roll);
Step R, slide L behind	(1, 2, 3); (RL, L, roll);

Step R, hop passing the partner	(1, 2, 3);	(both, L, roll);

Repeat *sostenidos* turning on self:

Step L, dig step R;	(1, 2, 3);	(RL, roll, roll);
Step L, dog step R;	(1, 2, 3);	(RL, roll, roll);
Step L, slide R behind,	(1, 2, 3);	(RL, L, roll);
Step L, hop passing the partner,	(1, 2, 3);	(both, L, roll);

Sostenidos turning on self:

Step R, dig step L,	(1, 2, 3);	(RL, roll, roll);
Step R, dog step L,	(1, 2, 3);	(RL, roll, roll);

Desplante step and castanets as before but this time:

Stamp R,	(1),	(RL),
Point L front,	(2),	(pause),
Hold;	(3);	(pause);

Pas de bourrée L to face front:

L behind	(1),	(L),
R on place	(2),	(roll),
step L	(3);	(roll);
Point in front leg	(1),	(to face audience), (roll).
Hold position.		

End

Cachucha Castanets

Part 1:

A. The first beat of count 6 is the tip of toe at back:

& 1,	2,	& 3;	4,	& 5,	& 6;
				Pause	Ria
Pi Ta	Ta	Ria	Ta	Ria	Ria
Pi Ta	Ta	Ria	Ta	Ria	Ria
Pi Ta	Ta	Ria	Ta	Ria	Ria
Pi Ta	Ta	Ria	Ta	Ria	Ria

Part 2:

Pi Ta	Ria	Ria	Pi Ta	Ria	Ria
Pi Ta	Ta	Ria	Pam	Ta	Ria
Pi Ta	Ria	Ria	Pi Ta	Ria	Ria
Pi Ta	Ta	Ria	Pam	Ta	Ria

Part 3:

1,	2,	3;									
Pam	Ta	Ria									
Pam	Ta	Ria									
	Pam	Ta	Ria								
	Pam	Ta	Ria								

& 1,	2,	3;	& 4,	& 5,	& 6;	& 1,	2,	3;	4,	5,	6;
Pi Ta	Ria	Ria	Pi Ta	Ria	Ria	Pi Ta	Ta	Ria	Pam	Ta	Ria
Pi Ta	Ria	Ria	Pi Ta	Ria	Ria	Pi Ta	Ta	Ria	Pam	Ta	Ria
Pi Ta	Ria	Ria	Pi Ta	Ria	Ria						

Start the *desplante* on this bar below   **Pi Ta pause** Ta   Ria   Ria
Ria

EL OLÉ DE LA CURRA
Escuela Bolera, Pericet Version

A solo Escuela Bolera dance for a woman in 3/8 time. Performed in ballet shoes *(zapatillas)*. In the original choreography, this dance had no introduction. However, many teachers choreograph one to get onto the stage elegantly, thus avoiding starting centre stage (personal communication, Eloy Pericet). The introduction here is from Eloy Pericet.

Start offstage corner 3 and wait for 4 bars, holding skirt out to sides in both hands for the entire introduction.

Introduction:
Four *pas de basque* forward,
Step R, *développé* L,
Place across and turn to R,
battement frappé R front back point, back front step on R,
battement frappé L front back point, back front step on L,
Point R in front:

Arms: are the usual classical arms, using arms in circular movements from 5th overhead; in third using the same arm down in front as the working foot. Turns taken using the arms from 5th outwards, down and up the front to 5th again.

Step 1. *Sostenidos*:

Dig R in front; and point to side	(3; 1),	(*choque*; both)	
Hold	(2),	(L),	(arms 3rd)
Dig R in front; and point to side	(3; 1),	(roll; roll)	
Hold	(2),	(L),	(arms 3rd)
Dig R in front	(3);	(roll);	
Pas de bourrée on pointe to R,	(1, 2, 3);	(continuous rolls)	(arm up front to 5th)
Step to side on R, L pointed to front	(1),	(roll),	
Hold	(2),	(not on repeat)	

Repeat to L, L arm coming to front in 3rd.

Step 2. *Rodazánes* to side:
Castanets: both L, roll (or L, roll, roll) 8 bars.

High *rodazán* R in air to 2nd	(2, 3; 1),	(L, roll; both),	(R arm down)
Close 5th behind	(2, 3; 1),	(L, roll; both),	(R to 5th)
High *rodazán* L in air to 2nd	(2, 3; 1),	(L, roll; both),	(L arm down)
Close 5th behind	(2, 3; 1),	(L, roll; both),	(L to 5th)

Step 3. *Destaque*:

Destaque with R front to corner 1,	(2, 3);	(L, roll);	(R arm down)
Step, place L behind in 5th	(1, 2, 3);	(both, L, roll);	(3rd)
Step on R	(1),	(both),	(R goes up)
Destaque L with L front to corner	(2, 3);	(L, roll);	(arms 5th)
Place L across and turn R,	(1, 2, 3);	(both, L, roll);	

(Circle both outward and up to 5th)
Finish 5th front,   (1),   (both),   (arms 5th)

Repeat steps 1, 2 and 3 to the other side.

Drop into Valencian arm position with L arm back R arm over head, standing on the L foot, R pointed to corner 1

Step 4:
Arms: circle inwards.
Castanets: L, roll, roll; L, roll, both, repeat.
This is very difficult to explain and count precisely, as the arms move across the music:

Arm starts to circle down   (2, 3);   (L, roll);
Point R dig in across instep   (1),   (roll),
Circle R arm down   (&)   (arm simultaneously out and up)

Step R, *escobilla* step L to corner 1,   (2, 3); (L, roll)
(Complete circle with L arm outward, up and down the same time that the L leg does the *escobilla* or *rond de jambe à terre* over, while the R goes up outward simultaneously.)

Point R 2nd to corner 1   (1),   (roll),
Arm in Valencian position

Repeat.

Step 5:
Castanets: the *choques* are played in front.
Fondu L, R, foot 4th behind, arms behind   (1), (both),
Pause   (2), (–),
Point R 4th corner 1   (3); (*choque*); as foot comes through to point
to corner 1 (1), (both), (arms 3rd R across in front, L up)
Pause with R toe remaining pointed front   (2, 3); (–, –);

Repeat:
Fondu, on L, R foot 4th behind,   (1), (both), (arms behind)
Pause   (2), (–),
Point R to corner 1 and   (3); (*choque*); (arms in front)
As foot comes through to point corner 1   (1), (both), (arms 3rd R across in front, R up)
Pause with R toe remaining pointed front   (2, 3); (–, –);

Step 6:
Holding skirt.
Petit battement R   (2, 3); to point in 2nd on (1),
Petit battement R   (2, 3); step on R to side on (1),
Petit battement L   (2, 3); to point in 2nd on (1),
Petit battement L   (2, 3); to point in 2nd on (1, 2),

Dig L front at instep,   (3); (*choque*);

Step 7:
3 *sostenidos* turning on self to L, facing outward (face outward, going L on L, arms 3rd, R up over head).

Step on L, step R, toe dig L	(1, 2, 3);	(both, L, roll);
Step on L, step R, toe dig L	(1, 2, 3);	(RL, roll, roll);
Step on L, and turn to L	(1, 2, 3);	(RL, roll, roll);
Hold	(1),	(RL),

Step 8:
Pas de basque travelling forward and backward:
Castanets:

Hold	(2, 3);	(L, roll);
Pas de basque to L:	(1, 2, 3);	(roll, L, roll);
To R:	(1, 2, 3);	(both, L, roll);
Repeat these two rhythms 3 times,		
Turn	(1, 2, 3);	(RL, L, roll); both.

Arms: both up to 5th on *pas de basque* to L (L, roll, roll); (body leans to L, look R, arms 5th) and then both arms down to L hip. on *pas de basque* to R, (L, roll, both);
    (body leans to R, look L)

Start L: six *pas de basque* travelling forward, arms as above:

Pas de basque to L	(1, 2, 3);	(roll, L, roll);
Pas de basque to R	(1, 2, 3);	(both, L, roll);
Pas de basque to L	(1, 2, 3);	(roll, L, roll);
Pas de basque to R	(1, 2, 3);	(both, L, roll);
Pas de basque to to L	(1, 2, 3);	(roll, L, roll);
Pas de basque to R	(1, 2, 3);	(both, L, roll);
Vuelta normal to the L,	(1, 2, 3);	(RL, L, roll);
(both arms, open out, down and up),		
Hold feet in 5th	(1),	(both),

Start L to L, circle R arm down and up:
Start to R, circle L arm down and up;
Six *pas de basque* travelling back.

Castanets: RL, roll, roll, 6 times,
    RL, L, roll; both; on turn.

Arms: circle one arm outward and up on each *pas de basque*, same arm in front as leg:

Pause	(2, 3);	(L, roll);
Pas de basque to L	(1, 2, 3);	(RL, roll, roll);
Pas de basque to R	(1, 2, 3);	(RL, roll, roll);
Pas de basque to L	(1, 2, 3);	(RL, roll, roll);
Pas de basque to R	(1, 2, 3);	(RL, roll roll);

Pas de basque to L	(1, 2, 3);	(RL, roll, roll);
Pas de basque to R	(1, 2, 3);	(RL, roll roll);
Vuelta normal to the L,	(1, 2, 3);	(RL, L, roll);
Hold 5th	(1),	(both),
Pause	(2, 3);	(–, –);

Repeat steps 5, 6, 7 and 8 to the other side.

Step 9:
(Use of skirt) travels to R side:

Step on R, point L in front, step L	(1, 2, 3);
Step on R, point L in front, step L	(1, 2, 3);
Step on R,	(1),
Point L,	(2),
Step on L,	(3);
Point R,	(1),
Step on R,	(2),
Point L.	(3);

Repeat 9 to L

Step on L, point R in front, step	(1, 2, 3);
Step on L, point R in front, step	(1, 2, 3);
Step on L,	(1),
Point R,	(2),
Step on R,	(3);
Point L,	(1),
Step on L,	(2),
Point R.	(3);

Entrada into 5 *jerezanas altas*. Arms low in 4th on this section, same arm as leg pointed:
Counted in cycles of 6:

Kick R back (*jerezana*),	(4, 5),

5 walks to corner 1 point R foot on the next phrase,

Wait for	(6; 1),
2 stamps with R foot	(2, 3),
Tijera (inverted *pas de chat* to a point):	
Lift leg, jump on R	(4, 5),
Point L, pause	(6; 1, 2);
2 stamps with L foot	(3, 4),
Change weight onto it	(5),

Step 10:
Round the room, 5 *jerezanas altas* and 1 *baja*.
Castanets: *choque* both, L roll, L, roll 5 times:

1st *jerezana* travelling upstage to L:
Point R, front;   (6); (*choque*);   (arms 5th)
                                (R arm circles out and down as leg is lifted)
Hop kicking R leg back in air (1), (both), (R arm opens out)
                                (looking over R shoulder)
Swish R leg through (low)   (2), (L), (arms 3rd, R front)
                                (Start going upstage turning to L)
3 walks: Walk R, step up behind with L, walk R, (3, 4, 5), (roll, L, roll),
                                (R arm circles up to 5th)
(Head changes to looking over L shoulder for next step)

2nd *jerezana* continuing upstage:
Point L in front   (6); (*choque*); (arms 5th)
                                (L arm circles out and down as leg is lifted)
Hop kick leg back in (1), (both), (L arm opens out)
                                (looking over L shoulder)
Swish L leg through (low)   (2), (L), (arms 3rd, L front)
                                (continue going upstage, looking over L shoulder)
                                (L arm circles up to 5th on:
3 walks: Walk L, step up behind with R, walk L, (3, 4, 5),
                                (roll, L, roll),
                                (L arm circles up to 5th)
(Head changes to looking over R shoulder for next step.)

3rd *jerezana*:
Point R, front;   (6); (*choque*); (arms 5th)
                                (R arm circles out and down as leg is lifted)
Hop kicking R leg back in air (1), (both), (R arm opens out)
                                (Looking over R shoulder)
Swish R leg through (low)   (2), (L), (arms 3rd, R front)
                                (continue going upstage, looking over R shoulder)
                                (R arm circles up to 5th)
                                (roll, L, roll),
This time take the first walk to face the front:
3 walks: Walk R, step up behind with L, walk R, (3, 4, 5),
Head changes to looking over L shoulder for next step, but because the step is facing front, there
is less turn in the body.

4th *jerezana* facing front and coming forward:
Point R, front;   (6); (*choque*); (arms 5th)
                                (R arm circles out and down as leg is lifted)
Hop kicking R leg back in air (1), (both), (R arm opens out)
                                (looking over R shoulder)
Swish R leg through (low)   (2), (L), (arms 3rd, R front)
                                (start going upstage turning to L)
3 walks: Walk R, step up behind with L, walk R, (3, 4, 5), (roll, L, roll),
                                (R arm circles up to 5th)

(Head changes to looking over L shoulder for next step)

5th *jerezana* facing front and coming forward:
Point R, front;   (6); (*choque*);   (arms 5th)
                                                (R arm circles out and down as leg is lifted)
Hop kicking R leg back in air (1), (both) (R arm opens out)
                                                (looking over R shoulder)
Swish R leg through (low) (2), (L), (arms 3rd, R front)
                                                (continue coming forward, looking over R shoulder)
                                                (R arm circles up to 5th)
                                                (roll, L, roll),
3 walks: Walk R, step up behind with L, walk R, (3, 4, 5),
                                                (Head changes to looking over L shoulder for next step),

Jerezana baja: point L in front, point back stepping on it (6; 1), (*choque*; both),
Turn *vuelta normal* placing R foot over, (2, 3, 4), (L, roll, both),

Repeat steps with skirt and *jerezanas* to other (L) side.

Step 11:
Coda, to corner 1 starting arms in 5th.
Arms: circle on each *rodazán*, using same arm as working leg, second one remains in 3rd on step up and stays to accompany the next *rodazán* on the other side. This is repeated three times with third one having extra 'both' on castanets for accent.

To corner 1 on R:

Hop on L *rodazán* R in air in front,	(5, 6;)	(L, roll);
Step R,	(1),	(roll),
Destaque L front,	(2, 3),	(L, roll),
(circle L arm to 3rd in front and hold it there)		
Step on L, dig R behind	(4, 5),	(roll, both),
Hold in 5th on pointe	(6);	(–);
Bourrées back on pointe,	(1, 2, 3, 4),	(roll, roll, roll, roll),

Repeat with L to corner 2:
Repeat castanet sequence.

Hop on R *rodazán* L in air in front,	(5, 6);	(L, roll);
Step L,	(1),	(roll),
Destaque R front,	(2, 3),	(L, roll),
Step on R, dig L behind	(4, 5),	(roll, both),
Hold in 5th on pointe	(6);	(–);
Bourrées back on pointe,	(1, 2, 3, 4),	(roll, roll, roll, roll),

Repeat on L to corner 1 with different castanet sequence:

Hop on L *rodazán* R in air in front, step R,	(L, roll, roll)
Destaque L front, step on L,	(L, roll, roll)

Dig R behind, hold,   (both, both)
Bourrées back on pointe,   (roll, roll, roll, roll)

Step 12:
Rodazán L to 2nd   (5, 6);   (L, roll); (arm 3rd)
Close behind   (1),   (both),
Rodazán R to 2nd,   (2, 3),   (L, roll),
Close behind   (4),   (both),
Destaque L to 2nd   (5, 6);   (L, roll,);
Place across and turn to R   (1),   (both),
   (a *vuelta normal* taking both arms down & up)
Lift R and and kneel on L   (4, 5, 6);   (L, roll, both);
                                                                       (both arms 1st in front)

Rotate body right round to L for 6 counts   (continuous rolls)
Rotate body right round to L for 6 counts   (continuous rolls)

Rise up arms and feet 5th   (1, 2),   (–, –), (arms 5th)
Vuelta con destaque using both arms down and up to 5th:
Swish L   (3);   (–);
Assemblé L behind   (1),   (both),
Destaque L to side   (2),   (L),
And place it across R, turn to R   (3; 1)   (roll; both),
Pause   (2),   (–),
Step to side on R, point L front   (3; 1),   (–; both),
   (arms 3rd, L, front, R, 5th)
Pause 2   (2),   (–),
Step to side on L, point R front   (3; 1),   (*choque*; both),

The End

Note on step 2: in Andalusia I have seen, and in my own dance that I learned from Elsa Brunelleschi in London, the *rodazánes* in step 2, danced as: point foot in front on the floor with the knee bent (1), lift it in the air and *rodazán* in front (2, 3), step on it, and repeat with the other foot.

   In Andalusia they step forward onto it and in my dance it is stepped back, and then the direction changes to travelling forward to the corner with the *rodazán* step together step and *grand battement*, which gives it a rather attractive change of direction when the dance suddenly moves forward again.

Pas de basque travelling back, described at end of syllabus as well:
The Pericet *pas de basque* back for Olé de la Curra are different to the ordinary ones:

Stretch the leg to back corner, (1),
Step on it,   (2),
Close the other leg to it in front, step (*coupé*ing over) step on place with other leg.
                                (3);

Some variations:

I have also seen the *pas de basque* forward performed exactly as described above, but done travelling backward. Also the *pas de basque* first travelling forward and then back, reversed and travelled backward first and then forward.

JALEO DE JEREZ
Escuela Bolera, Pericet version

A dance of the Escuela Bolera from the nineteenth century in 3/4 time, Allegretto, performed in ballet shoes (*zapatillas*). The timing is in cycles of six counts (across two bars). Start off-stage (wall 8),

Introduction
Wait for introduction, run on to centre stage.
Facing front: Step on L, point R to side in and take arms outward and up to 5th position overhead.

Part 1
Sostenidos sequence as in Olé de la Curra.

A
*Dig R foot in	(6); (*choque* in 5th);
Point to 2nd	(1), (both), (R arm coming down in front),
Pause	(2), (L),

A repeat:
Dig R foot in	(3), (roll),
Point to 2nd	(4), (roll), (R arm down in front),
Pause	(5), (L),
Dig R foot in	(6); (roll);

B
Small *bourrées* on half pointe sideways to 8 (1, 2, 3), (continuous rolls) (arms up front to 5th),
Step stand on R	(4, 5), (roll, both),

C
Lift L	(6); (–);
Point L to front	(1, 2), (both, both), (arms 3rd L in front*)
Pause	(3), (–),

D
Point L to side on the floor	(4, 5,), (both, both), (arms stay 3rd),
Lift L leg side	(6); (–); (arms to 5th),

E
Assemblé L in behind	(1), (both),
Destaque (*grand battement*)	(2), (L),
Place leg across front and turn to R	(3, 4, 5), (roll, roll, roll),

Repeat to L all from * L until and including 1C) to *, leaving out 1D) go straight into E2) turning to L this time playing:

E2

Lift L leg side	(3); (–); arms to 5th,
Assemblé R behind	(4), (both),
Destaque (kick)	(5), (L), (arms 5th),
Place leg across front and turn to R	(6); (roll);
Continue turning slowly	(1, 2, 3); (RL, roll, roll);

   (on turn, circle both arms out, down and back to 5th);

Part 2

Similar to the one in Olé de la Curra circling arms.

Point L to side	(4), (RL), (L arm up) pause (5),

Arms: circle one at a time inwards.

Castanets: both, both, L, roll both, pause, pause.

A

Travelling sideways:

Dig L across front	(6); (both); (circle L down),
Step L to side	(1), (both), (circle starts to go up with:)
Escobilla R across	(2), (L), (R arm circles outward and up and)
Step across on R	(3); (roll), (R down front, L goes up outward),
Point L to side	(4), (both), (L up, R down in front),
Pause	(5), (–),

B

Dig L across front,	(6); (both); (circle L down),
Step L to side,	(1), (both), (circle down & goes up with:)
Escobilla R across & step across on R	(2), (L), (R down, L goes up),
Step across on L	(3); (roll), (L down, R goes up),
Point R to side	(4), (both), (R up)
Pause	(5), (–),
Hold position	(6); (–);

Repeat 2A to R
Repeat 2A to R
Repeat 2A to R

Part 3
Kneels.

A

Kneel down onto R knee	(1), (both), (arms behind back in 7th),
Straighten up	(2, 3);
Pointing R to side	(4), (both), (arms in 5th),
Hold	(5),

B

Transfer weight onto R in 2nd (6);

Keep L 2nd and point it	(1), (both), (arms up to 3rd, L in front)
Hold	(2),
Swish	(3); *assemblé* L behind (4), (both),
Destaque leg to 2nd in air	(5, 6); (L), continuous rolls to end:
Place foot across	(1), (roll), (arms open outward and down),
Turn to R	(2, 3); (roll, roll); (arms end in 3rd, L front),

Part 4

Repeats 4 times starting R, then L, R, L,
Arms: 3rd with L in front.
Castanets:
both (1), left (2), roll (3); R, L (4), roll, (5), roll (6);
RL, (& 1), left (2), roll (3); L (4), roll, (5), roll (6);
On subsequent repeats both becomes R, L.
RL, (& 1), L (2), roll (3); RL (4), roll (5), roll (6);
RL, (& 1), L (2), roll (3); L (4), roll (5), roll (6);

On 4th repeat end: both	(5), (6);

Arms: 3rd front, same arm down as working leg:

Destaque L (back ft) to front	(1, 2, 3); (both, L, roll)
Pas de bourrée: L behind	(4), R on place (5, 6), L in front,
	(RL, roll, roll);
Step on place R,	(1), (RL), (arm goes up to 5th),
Rodazán L in air to 2nd	(2, 3); (L, roll); (arms 5th),

Vuelta normal:

Step to side on L	(4), (L), (arms circle out and down)
Place R foot across (L) and turn to L front.	(5, 6); (roll, roll); arms down and end to 3rd with R in

Repeat starting R
Repeat starting L
Repeat starting R – ending both instead of roll.

Part 5

It goes across the music with 4 *pas de basque*, the first set and only 3 forward and 2 back on repeat of the whole step:

The Step:
4 *pas de basque* forward, *ballonné* over,
3 *pas de basque* back, *assemblé* over.

The Detail:

A
4 jumped *pas de basque* forward on R, L, R, L:
Arms as usual, circles with one arm for *pas de basque.*
Castanets: both, L, roll; for each *pas de basque.*

A1
Pas de basque on R (1, 2, 3); (both, L, roll); R arm up, L circles,
Pas de basque on L (1, 2, 3); (both, L, roll); L arm up, R circles,
Pas de basque on R (1, 2, 3); (both, L, roll); R arm up, L circles,
Pas de basque on L (1, 2, 3); (both, L, roll); L arm up, R circles,
3rd beat leads into

B
One *ballonné* with R (1), (both), pause (2, 3); (–, –); R arm across L behind (in 4th),

C
3 *pas de basque* travelling back:
Jeté over with R (1), step back with L (2), step tog. R (3); (both, L, roll); arm remains in 4th,
Pas de basque with L, (both, L, roll); L arm 4th front,
Pas de basque with R, (both, L, roll); R arm 4th front,
Assemblé L over in front (both, L, roll); arms in 5th.

Repeat all staring L foot but only 3 *pas de basque*:

A
Pas de basque on L (1, 2, 3); (both, L, roll); L arm up, R circles,
Pas de basque on R (1, 2, 3); (both, L, roll); R arm up, L circles,
Pas de basque on L (1, 2, 3); (both, L, roll); L arm up, R circles,
3rd beat leads into

B
One *ballonné* with R (1), (both), pause (2, 3); (–, –); R arm across L behind (in 4th),

C
3 *pas de basque* travelling back:
Jeté over with R (1), step back with L (2), step tog. R (3);
    (both, L, roll); arm remains 4th,
Jeté over with L (1), step back with L (2), step tog. R (3);
    (both, L, roll); L arm 4th front,
Jeté over with R (1), step back with L (2), step tog. R (3);
                        (both, L, roll); R arm 4th front,
Assemblé R over in front (both, –, –); arms in 5th.

Part 6
Travelling to corner 2.
Arms: on *développé* quickly drop both down front and circle L to overhead and R behind (Valencian position):

The Step:

A
Step on R, *développé* (6); Valencian position, also held for B.

B
3 *sostenidos* at the back:
Step on L, dig R in and back (1, 2, 3); (both, L, roll;
Step on L, dig R in and back (1, 2, 3); (RL, roll, roll);
Step on L, dig R in and back (1, 2, 3); (RL, roll, roll);

C
Step to side on L   (1), (RL),
Escobilla R leg over on floor (2), (–), R arm swings across,
Step on it (R)   (3); (*choque*), arms 5th,
Step on L at back   (1) (both),
Escobilla R leg back (1) (L) R arm swings back and L down *coupé*-ing L to front (2) (L, roll)
Arms are now in 4th, L front,
Posé turn to L (1, 2), *coupé* with R (3); (RL, roll roll);
Posé turn to L (1, 2), *coupé* with R (3); (both L roll).

Repeat from A to R:

A
Step on L, *développé* (6); (–) Valencian position, also held for B.

B
3 *sostenidos* at the back:
Step on R, dig L in and back (1, 2, 3); (both, L, roll);
Step on R, dig L in and back (1, 2, 3); (RL, roll, roll);
Step on R, dig L in and back (1, 2, 3); (RL, roll, roll).

C
Step to side on R   (1), (RL),
Escobilla L leg over on floor   (2), (–), R arm swings across,
Step on it (the L)   (3); (*choque*); arms 5th,
Step on R at back   (1), (both),
Escobilla L leg back   (2), (L) R arm swings back and L down,
*Coupé*ing R to front   (3), (L, roll) arms are now in 4th, L front,
Posé turn to R   (1, 2), (RL, roll,
Coupé with L   (3); (roll);
Posé turn to R   (1, 2), *coupé* with L (3); (both L roll);
End facing corner 2.

Part 6 ending or coda for former step:
Quick step on R to release L foot (&) for:
Arms: both arms start down at sides on *destaques* and are raised slowly up to 5th for the turn:

Face and travel towards corner 2:
Step on L and *destaque* R; (1, 2, 3); (L, roll, both);
Step on R and *destaque* L; (1, 2, 3); (L, roll, both);
Step on L and *destaque* R; (1, 2, 3); (L, roll, both);

Vuelta normal to R (hold arms in 5th), (1, 2, 3); (L, roll, both);

Part 7
Sease y contra sease:

A
Choque castanets 5th overhead (&).
Chassé to R *coupé* L behind close R behind, (1, 2, 3); (both, L, roll); (R arm circles outward and to 5th);
Chassé to L *coupé* R behind step L to side, (1, 2, 3); (RL, L, roll); (L arm circles outward and up to 5th);
Place R across L and *vuelta* (*normal*) to L; (1, 2, 3); (both, L, roll); ending:

B
Standing on R with L in dig (1), (both), (arms end in 4th in 4th, L front, R behind);
Swivel onto L (2, 3); (L, roll); (arms remain 4th but change to R across front), Pointing R to corner 2 (1, 2, 3); (both, L, roll);

C
3 *sostenidos* in front travelling round to L stepping on R with back to audience:
Step on R (1), dig step L in front (2, 3); (castanets strike R onto L each movement on (2, 3) arms being held in 8th at side);
Step on R (1), dig step L in front (2, 3); (castanets strike R onto L each movement arms being held in 8th at side);
Step on R (1), dig step L in front (2, 3); (castanets strike R onto L each movement arms being held in 8th at side);

Step on R (1), (both), pause (2, 3); (L, roll);

Repeat the *seasé* section A to the L until the turn (for only two counts) then the points are quicker and start on 3rd count, thus:

A
Choque castanets 5th overhead (&),
Chassé to L *coupé* R behind close L behind, (1, 2, 3); (both L, roll); (R arm circles outward and to 5th);
Chassé to R *coupé* L behind step R to side, (1, 2, 3); (RL, L, roll); (L arm circles outward and up to 5th);
Place L across R and *vuelta* (*normal*) to R; (1, 2), (both, L,),

Ending turn with R foot pointed in front on count of (3); (roll);
Change weight by stepping on R with L in front on (1), (both),
        pause (2, 3); (–, –);

2 *sostenidos* in front:
Travelling round self to R with back to audience:

Step across on L (1), dig step R in front (2, 3); (castanets strike R onto L each movement on (2, 3); arms being held in 8th at side);

Step on L (1), dig step R in front (2, 3); (castanets strike R onto L each movement arms being held in 8th at side);

Part 8
Sostenidos at the back travelling round room to R.

The Step:
Step, dig, dig; step dig, dig; step dig, dig; step *développé*:
Arms: move in inward circles on each *développé* same arm up as leg stepped onto, the other arm behind (Valencian position):
Castanets: both, L, roll; RL, roll, roll; RL, roll, roll; RL, L, roll. Repeated for each set:

Towards corner 1:
A
Step across on L (1), (both), pause (arms come down to sides),
Développé R leg to corner 1 (2, 3); (–, –); R arm up, L behind.

To new melody, go round room:

B
Step on R (1), dig L toe behind, dig back and step on it (2, 3); (both, L, roll); (R arm remains up).

B
Step on R (& 1), dig L toe behind, dig back and step on it (2, 3); (RL, roll, roll); (R arm remains up).

B
Step on R (& 1), dig L toe behind, dig back and step on it (2, 3); (RL, roll, roll);.

A
But arms and castanets are different:
Step forward on R (& 1), (RL), (R arm comes down, L circles over to 5th on–):
Développé L leg to back (2, 3); (L, roll); (L arm up).

The repeat with L leg:

B
Step on L (& 1), dig R toe behind, dig back and step on it (2, 3); (both, L, roll);
(L arm remains up and R behind).

B
Step on L (1), dig R toe behind, dig back and step on it (2, 3); (RL, L, roll);
(L arm remains up and R behind).

B
Step on L (1), dig R toe behind, dig back and step on it (2, 3); (RL, L, roll);
(L arm remains up and R behind).

The repeat with R:

A
But arms and castanets are different:
Step forward on L (& 1), (RL), (L arm comes down, R circles over to 5th on–):
Développé R leg to wall 6 (2, 3); (L, roll); (L arm up).

B
Step on R (1), dig L toe behind, dig back and step on it (2, 3); (both, L, roll);
(R arm remains up).

B
Step on R (& 1), dig L toe behind, dig back and step on it (2, 3); (RL, roll, roll);
(R arm remains up).

B) Step on R (& 1), dig L toe behind, dig back and step on it (2, 3); (RL, roll, roll); (R arm remains
up).

The repeat with L leg:

A
Step forward on R (& 1), (RL), (R arm comes down, L circles over to 5th on–):
Développé L leg to corner 2 (2, 3); (L, roll); (L arm up).

B
Step on L (1), dig R toe behind, dig back and step on it (2, 3); (both, L, roll);
(L arm remains up and R behind).

B
Step on L (& 1), dig R toe behind, dig back and step on it (2, 3), (RL, L, roll),
(L arm remains up and R behind).

B
Step on L (& 1), dig R toe behind, dig back and step on it (2, 3), (RL, L, roll),
(L arm remains up and R behind).

Towards corner 1:

A
Step across on L (1), (both), pause (arms come down to sides).
Développé R leg to corner 1 (2, 3); (– –); R arm up, L behind.

Part 9

Face and travel towards corner 1:
Arms go up slowly in outward circle to 5th:

A

Step on R and *destaque* L;	(1, 2, 3);	(both, L, roll);
Step on L and *destaque* R;	(1, 2, 3);	(both, L, roll);
Step on R (1), dig L behind step	(2, 3);	(both, L, roll);

B

Step on R (1), (both), then with back to audience:
Swish (2), (–), *jeté* over with R (3); (*choque*); arms down in front).

C

Travelling around to R:
Chassé to R, *pas de bourrée* behind (1, 2, 3); (both, L) side, (roll); step over and turn (*vuelta normal*) to R with arms 5th, (& 1) (RL), (2, 3); (roll, roll); end facing corner 2.

Face and travel towards corner 2 repeat with R:

A

Step on R and *destaque* L; (1, 2, 3); (L, roll, both);
Step on L and *destaque* R; (1, 2, 3); (L, roll, both);
Step on R and *destaque* L; (1, 2, 3); (L, roll, both).

Repeat but with different castanets and ending:

B

Step on L, (1), (both),
Swish (2), (–), *jeté* over with R (3); (–); (back to audience).

C

2 walks round to L:
L (1, 2, 3); R (1, 2), (both & continuous rolls),
Développé L to front (3); (continuous rolls).

Part 10

Repeat Part 4 side to side on L; R; L; R.
Castanets:
On *destaque*: both L, roll; (afterwards on repeats RL, L, roll)
Pas de bourrée: RL, roll, roll;
Step *rodazán* to side: RL, L, roll;
Vuelta: L, roll, roll; but on last vuelta just (both).

Coda

A
Careo to R (1, 2, 3); (L, roll, roll); L arm circles down and up,
Step across with L to face back, (1), both arms low across to L (roll),
Dig R behind (2), (both), (arms remain across to side), (3); (–);
Vuelta normal (1, 2, 3); (rolls) (arms down),
Continue to swivel on pointe to face front (rolls) (arms go up to 5th).

Repeat A to L.
Do only a swivel turning to L to face front with L pointed in front.

Ending:
Assemblé L foot behind, (1), (both),
Destaque L leg to side on a jump, (2), (L),
Place it across the R (3); (roll); and turn to R, (1), (both),
(Ending R in front with leg stretched to a point, arms 3rd).
Pause (2), (–),
Step on R (3); (–); and point L in front (1), (arms 3rd) (both),
Pause (2), (–),
Step back (3); (*choque*); and point R in front (2), (both), arms 3rd: R in front, L up in 5th.

LA MACARENA

Escuela Bolera, Rafael Pericet version, as taught by Eloy Pericet in Sitges, Spain (Spanish Dance Society 25th Anniversary, August 1990).

An Escuela Bolera dance in 3/4 time performed in ballet shoes *zapatillas*. The first half of La Macarena is danced with a fan held in the right hand and a mantilla is worn. After the fan and mantilla are discarded, castanets are played in the second half.

Terminology: to distinguish between the two types of 'rounds of the leg', in the air or on the ground, *rodazán* is used for the leg in the air and the *rond de jambe* on the ground refers to the Spanish term for it; *escobilla* (brush): step to side and *rond de jambe* over on the floor.

Arms move in 3rd positions with same arm as working front leg and turns as usual with both arms from 5th, open out, down and return to 5th. Begin centre back, face corner 2, R pointed to corner 2.

Part 1

Introduction of eight bars:
Wait for four bars, run into centre, step back on L with R pointed in front and raise fan outward and up overhead, L hand on hip (L hand remains on hip for almost the entire first section, the fan (F) is held across body, except where stated to be up over the head, when it is circled outward to 5th, then it is brought down across the front (inward circle):

Step 1:
Danced wearing a mantilla and using a fan, no castanets.
Travelling to corner 1 starting R: *pas de basque* (fan goes outward and to 5th, down across body) and *sostenidos*:

A
Pas de basque R	(1, 2, 3), fan sweeps 5th
Pas de basque L	(4, 5, 6); fan front
Walk R, L, R, point L to corner 1	(1, 2, 3, 4),
Pause	(5),
Tip L in (6); point L to corner 2	(1, 2), fan across body
Tip L in (3), point L to corner	(4, 5), fan across body
Tip L in (6); step L and turn L	(1, 2, 3, 4, 5, 6); fan circles outward and up and returns to front.

Repeat A travelling to corner 2 starting L: fan across body on 1st *pas de basque*, out and to 5th on second:
Pas de basque L	(1, 2, 3),	fan front
Pas de basque R	(4, 5, 6);	fan sweeps 5th
Walk L, R, L, point R to corner 2	(1, 2, 3, 4),	fan down front
Pause	(5),	fan held front
Tip R in (6); point R to corner 1 (1), hold (2),		fan held front
Tip R in (3), point R to corner (4), hold (5),		fan held front

Tip R in (6); step R and turn R (1, 2, 3, 4),   fan circles up and returns to front.

Step 2:
From side to side:
Rodazán exercise to R and L then 2 step *rodazánes* turning:

A
Rodazán R to side   (5, 6);
Step R (1), *rond de jambe* L *à terre* across R (2),   fan up
Drop across on L   (3),
Coupé with R (4), *rodazán* L to side   (5, 6);
Step L (1), *rond de jambe* R *à terre* across L (2),   fan front
Drop across on R,   (3),
Coupé with L (4), *rodazán* R to side   (5, 6);

Turning on self:

B
Step R and turn R to face back   (1),   fan up
Rodazán L to side   (2, 3),
Step L and turn to face front   (4),   fan front
Rodazán R to side   (5, 6);   fan front

Repeat *rodazán* exercise to R to end the musical phrase:

A
Step R (1), *rond de jambe* L across R   (2),   fan up
Drop across on L   (3),
Coupé with R (4), *rodazán* L to side   (5, 6);

Repeat *rodazán* exercise to L and R then 2 step *rodazánes* turning:
Step L (1), *rond de jambe* R *en terre* across L (2),   fan front
Drop across on R   (3),
Coupé with L (4), *rodazán* R to side   (5, 6);   fan up
Step R (1), *rond de jambe* L *en terre* across R (2),   fan up
Step L   (3),
Coupé with R (4), *rodazán* L to side   (5, 6);

Turning on self, on first *rodazán* fan follows leg up on next facing back flick fan inward in 5th:
Step L and turn L to face back   (1),
Rodazán R to side   (2, 3),   fan up
Step R and turn to face front   (4),   fan front
Rodazán L to side   (5, 6);
Ending: step L (1), *rond de jambe* R across L   (2),   fan up
Drop across on R   (3),
Coupé with L   (4),

Step 3:
Travelling to corner 1:

A

Rodazán R to side	(5, 6);	fan up
Step R to corner 1 on *demi-pointe*	(1),	
Close L to R on *demi-pointe*	(2, 3),	fan down
Step on R to corner 1	(4),	
Développé L to front	(5, 6);	fan up
Cross L over R and turn *vuelta normal* to R	(1, 2, 3, 4, 5),	
arm with fan comes down on the turn.		

Travelling to corner 2 repeat as to corner 1, fan still in R hand, as leg goes up so does the fan:
Grand battement L (6); step L *demi-pointe* (1),
Close R to L *demi-pointe* (2, 3), step L (4), *développé* R to front (5, 6);
Cross R over L and turn to L (1, 2, 3, 4, 5, 6);

Step 4:
Close fan start R and travel towards corner 1 doing *sostenidos*.
Hold L arm in front, beat fan with R hand onto forearm (pause on the step and, beat, beat on the dig, step):

A

Step R *demi-pointe*, tip L in behind R, step L	(1, 2, 3),
Step R *demi-pointe*, tip L in behind R, step L	(4, 5, 6);
Step R *demi-pointe*, tip L in behind R, step L	(1, 2, 3),

Open fan, travel to wall 8 with *escobillas*; on the first *rond de jambe* the fan circles down to the front and moves out and up to 5th on the second one for the *piqué* (*posé*) turns:

B

Step R, *rond de jambe* L across R, step L	(4, 5, 6);
Step R, *rond de jambe* L behind R, step L	(1, 2, 3),
Piqué (*posé*) turn to R on R	(4, 5, 6);
Piqué turn to R on R	(1, 2, 3),
Close R 5th front	(4, 5, 6);

Close fan, repeat A to corner 2 on L:

Step L *demi-pointe*, tip R in behind L, step R	(1, 2, 3),
Step L *demi-pointe*, tip R in behind L, step R	(4, 5, 6);
Step L *demi-pointe*, tip R in behind L, step R	(1, 2, 3).

Repeat B to L on L:
Open fan, travelling to wall 6 on L:

Step L, *rond de jambe* R across L, step R	(4, 5, 6);
Step L, *rond de jambe* R behind L, step R	(1, 2, 3),

Piqué turn to L on L	(4, 5, 6);
Piqué turn to L on L	(1, 2, 3),
Close L 5th front	(4, 5, 6);

Step 5:.
The next sections are danced with the fan closed and held in front.

Vuelta normal to R closing fan	(1, 2, 3),
Step R (4), *grand battement* L to corner 1	(5, 6);
Step L back	(1),
Step R in place	(2),
Rond de jambe L across R and step L	(3),
Coupé R (4), *rodazán* L to side	(5, 6);

Repeat to L on L:

Vuelta normal to L	(1, 2, 3),
Step L (4), *grand battement* R to corner 2	(5, 6);
Step R back	(1),
Step L in place	(2),
Rond de jambe R across L and step R	(3),
Coupé L (4), *rodazán* R to side	(5, 6);

Step 6:
Open fan, *vuelta de valse*, one with the fan up, one with the fan down.

A

Vuelta de valse turning to face back to R on R	(1, 2, 3),
Vuelta de valse turning to face front to L on L	
keep fan down in front,	(4, 5, 6);
Step R and turn R	(1, 2, 3,)
End feet in 5th	(4, 5, 6);

Repeat to other side as above, keep fan in front until end:

Vuelta de valse turning to face back to L on L	(1, 2, 3),
Vuelta de valse turning to face front to R on R	(4, 5, 6);
Step L and turn L	(1, 2, 3),
Assemblé L behind	(4, 5),
Grand battement L to side	(6);
Cross L in front and turn to R	(1, 2, 3),
Point R front to 2	(4, 5),
Step on R	(6);
Point L to corner 1	(1, 2),
Step L	(3),
Point R to corner 1	(4),
Pause	(5, 6);
hold fan across body in front.	

Close fan, run to side put fan down and take off mantilla.

Part 2

With castanets.

Castanets:

both (6); both (1), L (2), roll (3), both (4), pause (5),

Arms: inward circle on each *escobilla* L then R alternating :

A

| Tip R toe in | (6); stamp R | (1), *rond de jambe* L *en terre* (2), |
| Step L | (3), step back on R (4), hold (5), (L arm over), |

| Tip L toe in | (6); stamp L | (1), *rond de jambe* R *en terre* (2), |
| Step R | (3), step back on L (4), hold (5), (R arm over), |

| Tip R toe in | (6); stamp R | (1), *rond de jambe* L *en terre* (2), |
| Step L | (3), step back on R (4), hold (5), (L arm over), |

Tip L toe in (6); stamp L (1, 2),
Step R over twisting to the R to face the back (3),

B

Panaderos

Castanets: L, roll, roll, R 5 times

L, roll, *choque*, both, L, roll, both.

Arm: Inward circles as usual.

The Step:

Has the same timing as the Panaderos in Peteneras.

Facing back, start Panaderos:

Step L side, to wall 8, facing back	(4), (both),
Lift R across L	(5, 6); (–, –),
Step across on R	(1), walk L, R, (2, 3), (L, roll, roll),
(The start of the Panaderos castanets)
L behind turning to face back	(4), (RL),

Facing back 2nd Panaderos:

Step side R	(5), lift (6); (roll, roll);
Step across on L (1), walk R, L,	(2, 3), (RL, roll, roll),
R behind turning to face back	(4), (RL),

Facing back 3rd Panaderos:

Step side L	(5), lift R across L (6); (roll, roll);
Step R across	(1), (RL),
Step L behind facing front	(2, 3), (roll, roll),
Step R side	(4), (RL),
Start to lift L across R	(5), (–),
Lift L in *attitude* front	(6); (*choque*);
Step L cross R and turn L	(1, 2, 3), (both, L, roll),
(*Vuelta normal* finishing L across front, R behind),
Hold	(4, 5), (both, –),

Repeat from 1. starting on L moving to L.

C

Arms: 5th, no castanets:
Destaque L to corner 2, step on it (1, 2, 3),
Destaque R to corner 2, step on it (4, 5).

D

As in the *retortille* exercise:

To L:

Toe heel with L, stamp *coupé* L behind	(& a 6);	(–);
Step L to side, *escobilla* R across	(1, 2, 3),	(both, L, roll),
Coupé L under	(4),	(both),
Pause	(5),	(L),
Toe heel with R, stamp *coupé* L behind	(& a 6);	(roll);
Step R to side, *escobilla* L across	(1, 2, 3),	(both, L, roll)
Coupé R under	(4, 5),	(both, L),
Lift L front	(6);	(roll);
Vuelta fibraltada to L,	(1, 2, 3),	(both, L, roll),
(using both arms down and up to 5th on turn as usual),		
Pause, arms and feet 5th	(4, 5, 6);	(both, –, –);

Repeat the whole step to R:

C

Arms: 5th, no castanets:

Destaque R to corner 2, step on it	(1, 2, 3),
Destaque L to corner 2, step on it	(4, 5),

D

As in the *retortille* exercise.
Arms: circle out from 3rd to 3rd, same arm down as leg in front, both arms for *vuelta fibraltada*.

To R:

Toe heel with R, stamp *coupé* L behind	(& a 6);	(–);
Step R to side, *escobilla* L across	(1, 2, 3),	(both, L, roll),
Coupé L under	(4),	(both),
Pause as L goes to side	(5, 6);	(L, roll);
Pas de basque to L	(1, 2, 3),	
Pas de basque to R	(4, 5, 6);	
Vuelta fibraltada to L	(1, 2, 3),	
Pause, arms and feet 5th	(4, 5, 6);	

E

Escobillas over and behind travelling to wall 6.
Castanets: continuous rolls.

Arms: L up, R moves across front as foot crosses over the front and then behind as foot goes behind.

Step L, *rond de jambe* R *à terre* front, step across R	(1, 2, 3),
Step L, *rond de jambe* R *à terre* back, step across R	(4, 5, 6);
Step L, *rond de jambe* R *à terre* front, step across R	(1, 2, 3),
Step L, *rond de jambe* R *à terre* back, step across R	(4, 5, 6);
Step L, *rond de jambe* R *à terre* front, step across R	(1, 2, 3),
Step, *rodazán* R *en l'air*	(4, 5, 6);
Step R and turn R	(1, 2, 3),
Step back on R hold	(4, 5, 6);

End L pointing to corner 2, pause pick up skirt

F

Sostenidos travelling to wall 8, no castanets.

Making circles with skirt (as in Olé de la Curra):

Step L, dig step R	(1, 2, 3),
Step L, dig step R	(4, 5, 6);
Step L, dig step R	(1, 2, 3),
Step L, dig step R	(4, 5, 6);
Step L, dig step R	(1, 2, 3),
Step L, dig step R	(4, 5, 6);
Walks to wall 5 L, R, L,	(1, 2, 3), circle skirt on each walk,
Point R to front, step point L pause	(4, 5, 6); lift arms up front to 5th.

G

Travelling backward to wall 7.

Pas de basque L	(1, 2, 3),	(both, L, roll),
Pas de basque R	(4, 5, 6);	(both, L, roll);
Pas de basque L	(1, 2, 3),	(both, L, roll),
Pas de basque R	(4, 5, 6);	(both, L, roll);
Pas de basque L	(1, 2, 3),	(both, L, roll),
Step L and turn L	(4, 5,),	(both, –),

End pointing R to corner 1, pick up skirt,

Repeat F and G starting step on R. This can be deleted to improve the length of the dance for theatricality.

G

Repeat of *retortille* exercise to L.

To L:

Toe heel with L, stamp *coupé* L behind	(& a 6);	(–);
Step L to side, *escobilla* R across	(1, 2, 3),	(both, L, roll),
Coupé L under	(4),	(both),
Pause	(5),	(L),
Toe heel with R, stamp *coupé* L behind	(& a 6);	(roll);
Step R to side, *escobilla* L across	(1, 2, 3),	(both, L, roll),

Coupé R under	(4, 5, 6);	(both, L, roll);
Pas de basque to R	(1, 2, 3),	(RL, roll, roll),
Pas de basque to L (2 beats of it)	(4, 5),	(RL, roll),
Coupé lift R in preparation	(6);	(*choque*);
Vuelta fibraltada to R	(1, 2, 3),	(both, L, roll),
Pause, arms and feet 5th	(4, 5),	(both, -),

To R:

Toe heel with R, stamp *coupé* L behind	(& a 6);	(-);
Step R to side, *escobilla* L across	(1, 2, 3),	(both, L, roll),
Coupé L under	(4),	(both),
Pause as L goes to side	(5, 6);	(L, roll);
Pas de basque to L	(1, 2, 3),	(RL, roll, roll),
Pas de basque to R (2 beats of it)	(4, 5),	(RL, roll),
Coupé (lift L in preparation)	(6);	(*choque*);
Vuelta fibraltada to L	(1, 2, 3),	(both, L, roll),
Pause, arms and feet 5th	(4, 5, 6);	(both, -, -);

H
Finale.

Step R and turn R	(1, 2, 3),	(L, roll, roll),
Step on R	(& 4),	(RL),
Grand battement L to corner 1	(5, 6);	(roll, roll);
Pas de basque forward on L	(1, 2, 3),	(RL, roll, roll),
Pas de basque back on R	(4, 5, 6);	(RL, roll, roll);
Step L and turn L	(1, 2, 3),	(L, roll, roll),
Step on L	(& 4),	(RL),
Grand battement R to corner 2	(5, 6);	(roll, roll);
Pas de basque forward on R	(1, 2, 3),	(RL, roll, roll),
Pas de basque back on L	(4, 5, 6);	(RL, roll, roll);

I

Step R and turn R	(1, 2, 3),	(both, L, roll),
Assemblé R behind	(4),	(both),
Grand battement R to side	(5),	(L),
Cross R in front and turn L	(6);	(roll);
Point L to corner 2	(1),	(both)
Step L and point R to corner 2	(2, 3),	(L, roll)
Step R, L, stand R	(4, 5, 6);	(both, L, *choque*);
L pointed in dig behind	(1),	(both),
Hold the position	(2, 3),	(—), arms 5th.

PANADEROS DE LA FLAMENCA
Escuela Bolera, Pericet version

An Escuela Bolera dance in 3/4 time for a couple.

Within the Escuela Bolera, the type of shoes worn are dictated by the costume. Ballet shoes, *zapatillas* are worn if dressed in a classical costume of the nineteenth century; if from an earlier period, the era of the artist Goya, the heeled shoes, *chapines*, are worn. A different type of theatrical costume also allows for heeled shoes (see photograph of Susana y José).

There are several versions of this dance. The folk version has many *sostenidos* (step, dig behind, step on it behind), in place of the balletic version's steps such as *posé* in *arabesque*. The woman uses a fan for the introduction and then attaches it to a hook on the side of the skirt for the section with castanets. The Panaderos passes are timed differently, with the step behind on the count of 1. Another version uses the fan in the introduction, but with the classical version of the steps. As is noted in the section on the dances, this introductory section is a later addition to the dance, according to Maestro José Otero.

Detail of the Panaderos step (as for the Sevillanas pass, but with arm leading the way up, as in the Valencian position):
Step behind (6), step to side (1), lift leg up across knee (2); 3 walks passing partner and turning on self to pass partner: (3, 4, 5,) and the 6th beat is always at the back (6)–.

Directions are given for the woman. On Panaderos passes the man goes the opposite direction doing the same step, back to back with his partner.

Castanets for Panaderos step:
This is played only at start of step:
(6); (1), (2, 3), (& 4), (5), (6);
choque; both, L, roll; RL, roll, roll,
Then continuously:
RL(& 1), L, roll; RL, roll, roll;

Start corner 3, with the man to the left of his partner.

Introductory Andante Section
Wait for four bars of introduction in corner 3.
Entrance: andante with no castanets.
Arms: low across the body.

Step 1. *Vuelta de valse* (stepped, not jumped):
On diagonal to centre:
On R foot and then L foot: two *pas de basque*, one travelling and one turning on self,
4 walks and point R foot in front on 5.

Step 2. Low *attitudes* at the back,
2 *posé arabesques* around to R, (if danced as a couple, round partner),

Vuelta normal to R. (1, 2),
Step back into 4th with R, releasing L front (3),

Repeat steps 1 and 2 on L to L.
Finish facing front but keep dancing:

Step 3. *Destaques*:
Stamp L (1), *destaque* R to side (2), close front (3),
Stamp L (4), *destaque* R to side (5), close behind (6);

Two turns to the L:
One *normal*, (1, 2, 3),
One turning with 3 walks round self, L, R, L, (4, 5, 6);

Step 4. *Sostenidos*:
4 *sostenidos*: step on R, dig step L behind, (1, 2, 3),
4 *sostenidos*: step on R, dig step L behind, (4, 5, 6);
4 *sostenidos*: step on R, dig step L behind, (1, 2, 3),
Step on R, dig step turn L, (4, 5, 6);

If dancing with a partner the man gives his hand to his partner, who takes it with her right hand and turns under it.

Repeat steps 3 and 4 on other side, start stamp R.
End L pointed front, the man holds his partner's L hand up to side with his R hand.

Introduction to the Panaderos Section

Step 5
Walks around room starting R foot.
Wait for chords and 1 bar of introduction, place weight on L and do 10 andante walks around the room. (Angel Pericet just walks freely, not counting the walks, moving them freely across and not timed to each beat of the music, personal communication.) One hand is held on the hip, the other relaxed down at the side.

Preparation:
Step on R, point L (to audience), arms 3rd R up,
Step on L, point R (to partner), arms 3rd L up,
Step turn R half way round to point R in 4th front into:

Step 6. First Set of 4 Panaderos
Four Panaderos steps (described above) starting stepping behind on R then stepping out on:
L, travelling downstage, step behind with L,
R, travelling upstage, step behind with R,
Repeat L,
Repeat R, crossing partner.

Part 1

Step 7.
4 *desplantes* changing places with partner in semi-circle.
Castanets: L, roll, pause, L, roll, roll;
Arms: down on stamp, 5th on point, coming down on *pas de bourrée*:
Stamp L, point R; *pas de bourrée* under with R (1, 2, 3; 4, 5, 6);
Stamp L, point R; *pas de bourrée* under with R (1, 2, 3; 4, 5, 6);
Stamp L, point R; *pas de bourrée* under with R (1, 2, 3; 4, 5, 6);
Stamp L, point R; *pas de bourrée* under with R (1, 2, 3; 4, 5, 6);
Step L, *rodazán* R to 2nd,   (1, 2, 3),
Vuelta normal to R,   (4, 5, 6);

Step 8. Second set of 2 Panaderos:

Repeat as above:
Only two, one on L, travelling downstage, one on R, travelling upstage.

Part 2

Step 9. 2 *Escobillas*:
Castanets: L, roll, RL, roll, roll, RL: continue: roll, roll, RL.

Travelling to L:
Step L, point R,
Step R, point L,
Step L, point R small lift step, *pas de bourrée* with L to R,

Repeat to the R.

Step L, *rodazán* R to second,
Vuelta normal to R.

Step 10. Third set of 4 Panaderos.
Starting L foot:
The first one travelling downstage,
The second travelling across to left (crossing to partner's place).
The third travelling upstage on L,
The fourth travelling downstage on R.

Part 3

Step 11. *Rodazánes* and turn playing Panaderos rhythm:
Step on L, *rodazán* R to 2nd,   (1, 2, 3), circle R arm down and up,
Step on R, *rodazán* L to 2nd,   (4, 5, 6); circle L arm down and up,
Step turn to L,   (1, 2, 3), using both arms down and up,
Step on R, *rodazán* L to 2nd,   (4, 5, 6); circle L arm down and up,

Step on L, *rodazán* R to 2nd,	(1, 2, 3), circle R down and up,
Step turn to R,	(4, 5, 6); using both arms down and up.

Step 12. *Desplante* (as above) with L twice:
The girl advancing and on 3rd the girl stands R foot pointed front and bends back, head turned to L, R arm raised in 5th, L behind in waist, and the boy has travelled back and on the 3rd steps onto R leaning forward over her, R arm up, L behind. 2 counts (see photograph of Susana and José.)

Return to centre with 3 steps, the 4th being the start of:
6
Step 13. Fourth Set of 4 Panaderos:
Travelling upstage, passing partner, downstage and then upstage on own place without crossing.

Repeat Part 3 set of 4 Panaderos done in a square.

Part 4

Step 14:
7 *posé arabesques* playing (both) on each beat (musically it works out to 8):

To the L, shoulder to shoulder with partner, do 7 steps in *arabesques* in a circle and return to place. R arm up, L behind.

Step 15:
2 *desplantes*:
(*Note*: the semi-colon of the steps corresponds to that of the timing.)

Stamp L, point R; *pas de bourrée* under with R	(1, 2, 3, 4, 5, 6);
Stamp L, point R; *pas de bourrée* under with R	(1, 2, 3, 4, 5, 6);
Run round partner to L for six counts,	(1, 2, 3, 4, 5, 6);
Vuelta normal to L for three counts.	(1, 2, 3),
Face front, girl steps back on R,	(4, 5, 6);
Points L foot (1, 2,), R arm up, L front, partner steps back on L, points R foot	
Starting left do 3 steps forward: L, R, L	(3, 4, 5), into:

Step 16. Fifth set of Panaderos:
Note: starting with *R* foot.
4 sets crossing front of stage (from wall to wall, 6 & 8).

Part 5

Step 17:
Facing back, *destaques* with turns playing (both, L, roll);

Step on R kick L, arms 3rd R arm up	(1, 2, 3),
Step on L kick R, arms 3rd L arm up then R to 5th for the turn	(4, 5, 6);
Place R across and turn	(1, 2, 3),
Step L across R and turn	(4, 5, 6);

Step 18:
Facing partner, *desplantes* R:
Stamp R, point L; *pas de bourrée* under with L (1, 2, 3; 4, 5, 6);
Stamp R, point L; *pas de bourrée* under with L (1, 2, 3; 4, 5, 6);

Repeat step 17, *destaques* and turns.

Repeat step 18, *desplantes* with R.

3 steps: L, R, L,

Step 19. Sixth set of Panaderos
2 Panaderos crossing partner; start on R foot.
Drop arms, R across front, L across back for:

Coda:
Both facing front:

Step 20:
Rodazán y pas de bourrée (each set 6 counts):
Castanets:

1, 2,	3,	4,	5,	6;
L, L,	roll,	L,	roll,	R,

Step on L, *rodazán* R to 2nd, *pas de bourrée* under with R,
Step on L, *rodazán* R to 2nd, *pas de bourrée* under with R,
Step on L, *rodazán* R to 2nd, *pas de bourrée* under with R,
Step on L, *rodazán* R to 2nd, *pas de bourrée* under with R.

Step 21. *Sostenidos*:
6 *coupés* on pointe (both) travelling back to corner 3, L arm up, R in front.
Castanets: L roll, the roll played as the leg extends in front.

On L, extending R (1), close in front (&),
On L, extending R (2), close in front (&),
On L, extending R (3), close in front (&),
On L, extending R (4), close in front (&),
On L, extending R (5), close in front (&),
On L, extending R (6); close in front (&);
The 7th:
On L, extending R (1), is preparation for

Step 22:
3 turns to R to centre.
End pose: stand on L with R arm in 5th, L down in front, point R behind.

PETENERAS BOLERAS ANDALUZAS
Escuela Bolera, Pericet version

An Escuela Bolera Andaluza dance in 3/8 time.

Women: heeled shoes are worn.
Men: boots are worn, or shoes covered by long spats.

Note: for easier writing and reading back, a *rodazán* on the floor will be called *escobilla*, as the Spaniards do and the step we know as *escobilla* from corner to corner is called a 'complete *escobilla*'.

None of the three introductions in this dance are danced. On the first one the dancers stand with no castanets playing. On all the others the dancers end in the first position they make at the start of this dance and the castanet rhythm continues straight from the last step of each verse, playing continuously.

Arms: move inward on all steps connected with Bulerias, otherwise, usually in outward circles. Valencian position has one arm up in 5th, one back.

The timing of the *jerezana* step is unique to this dance (personal communication, Eloy Pericet).

First Introduction
Start centre, left foot pointed in front or in 4th position, left arm on hip, right dropped loosely at the side.
Castanets: *choque* (3) both (1), at end of the phrase.
Arms: front in 1st on the *choque* and on the both, the left arm goes to 5th outward and up and the right is taken low to the side behind the body. Arms move in inward circles on this step.

Part 1
Sostenidos.

Step 1:

Stamp L on place	(1),	(both), L arm up
Stamp, stamp R at back	(2, 3);	(L, roll); L arm up
Stamp L on place	(1),	(both), change L arm comes down front
		R outward and up to 5th
Escobilla R over	(2), (L), stand on it (3); (roll); R arm up	
Step back on L	(1), (both), pause (2), (–), R arm up	
Stamp, stamp R in front	(3; 1), (both; both), R arm up	
Stamp, stamp L	(2, 3); (L, roll); R arm up	
Stamp R on place	(1), (both), change arms, R arm comes down	
Escobilla L over	(2), (L), stand on it (3); (roll);L arm up	
Step back on R	(1), (both), pause (2), (–), L arm up	
Stamp, stamp L in front	(3; 1), (both; both), L arm up	

Stamp, stamp R	(2, 3); (L, roll);	L arm up
Point L in front	(1), (both), on pause (2, 3); change arms (inward) circle, L arm	
		down front R out and up to 5th on (–)

Step 2:
Paso de fandango.

A

Step to side on L (1), (both), *escobilla* R over	(2, 3);	(L, roll);
Step to side on L (1), (both), pause	(2), (–), (3);	(both);
Step to side on R (1), (both), *escobilla* L over	(2, 3);	(L, roll);
Step to side on R (1), (both), pause	(2, 3);	(—);
L arm continues to 5th on counts	(2, 3).	

B
Arms 5th, lean over raised leg:

Step to side on L	(1), (both), R *attitude* front	(2, 3); (L, roll);
Step to side on R	(1), (both), L *attitude* front	(2, 3); (L, roll);
Step to side on L	(1), (both), R foot across turn	(2, 3); (L, roll);
Castanet	(1), (roll),	
Pause on toes in 5th	(2, 3); (–, –);	

Arms for step 2:
Arms move R inward on *escobilla* L goes up,
Arms move L inward on *escobilla* R goes up then down,
L continues out and up to 5th,
On R in *attitude* front, arms are in 5th and lean over the R leg,
On L in *attitude* front, remain 5th and lean over the L leg,
On turn arms open outward this time and up to 5th,
remain up on toes, arms in 5th, look to L.

Step 3:
R arm circles outward on *chassé pas de bourrée*:

Chassé R,	(1),	(L), R arm circles out to 5th
Pas de bourrée L behind, R to side,	(2, 3);	(roll, roll);
Fifth on point, L front	(1),	(RL), arms 5th
Hold	(2, 3);	(*choque*, –);

5 *sostenidos* travelling in circle to L; L arm circles outward,

Stamp R	(1), dig step with L	(2, 3); (both, L roll); then
Repeat 4 more times playing:		(RL, roll, roll);
		(RL, roll, roll);
		(RL, roll, roll);
		(RL, roll, roll);

End stamp R, L foot pointed to the front		
	(1),	(RL), pause (2, 3); (–, –);

Position of arms: end R arm across chest, quite high, elbow bent, L behind.

Desplante:

Stamp L foot,	(1) (silent),	point R front (2, 3); (L, roll);
		lower R arm front
		slightly L behind – 4th position
Stamp R foot,	(1) (silent),	point L front (2, 3); (L, roll);
		change to L arm front
		lowered slightly
		R slightly behind
Stamp L foot,	(1) (L),	both arms front
Stamp, stamp R,	(2, 3); (R, L);	moving out and up
point L front	(1), (both),	arms 5th
Pause for	(2, 3); (–, –);	

L arm circles outward and up to 5th on next *pas de bourrée* step:

On place: *pas de bourrée* under, L behind,	(1), (L),
(L arm circles out, down and up in 5th)	
R on place,	(2), (roll),
L front,	(3), (roll);

Coupé under with a stamp R, *destaque* R high to 2nd (1), (RL), arms 5th

Rodazán L high in second	(2, 3); (–, –); arms 5th
Step on L, turn to L	(1, 2, 3); (both, L, roll);
Hold 5th on pointe looking to L	(1), (both), arms 5th
Pause in that position	(2, 3); (–, –);

Repeat step 2B: start R, arms sweep in outward circle, same arm up as leg. both arms down and up on turn up on pointe, same arm circles out and down as leg lifted in front:

Step to side on R	(1), (both), L *attitude* front	(2, 3); (L, roll);
Step to side on L	(1), (both), R *attitude* front	(2, 3); (L, roll);
Step to side on R	(1), (both), L foot across turn	(2, 3); (L, roll);
Pause in 5th on point looking to corner 2		(1, 2, 3); (–, –, –,);

Repeat step 2B: start L, at end R across and quick turn:

Step to side on L	(1), (both), R *attitude* front	(2, 3); (L, roll);
Step to side on R	(1), (both), L *attitude* front	(2,) (L),
Step to side on L	(3); (roll);	
R foot across quick turn	(1), (both),	
and hold in 5th on pointe	(2), (–),	
Step back on R	(3); (*choque*);	
L on dig front	(1), (both),	
Pause	(2, 3); (–, –); L arm front look over it, R slightly behind, Valenciana position.	

Play castanets L, roll, roll, R immediately while waiting there during the introduction as described below.

Arms:

R arm circles outward and up on *chassé pas de bourrée*.

On *sostenidos* L arm opens outward.

On stamp L arm behind, R arm across body, shoulder height.

On *desplante*'s first stamp and point arms remain in position but are lowered to a normal 4th in front.

On second stamp R and point, arms change to L 4th in front.

Stamp L, stamp, stamp R: arms go out and up to 5th as you point,

On *pas de bourrée* L arm circles out and ends up only as leg out to side, up to 5th

both arms down and up on the turn, Look to corner 2 (L).

Same arm front as leg up on the step to side lift leg front *attitude* outward circles = L, R, then after the turn = R, L

Use both arms opening outward and down and into 5th on the turn. End with L arm up R behind and stay there for Introduction.

Second Introduction

As described above, standing on R foot with L foot in dig front.

Arms: L arm up, elbow dropped, looking over L shoulder, R at the back, called the Valenciana position.

Castanets: L, (1), roll (2), roll (3); R (&)

At end arms go to front to play: (3); (*choque*);

Arms L elbow up and look under arm, R arm behind, (1), (both).

(Valenciana position).

Part 2. Panaderos

Step 1:

With a complete *escobilla*:

Travelling to left corner 2,

One arm circle with R for whole step.

A

Travel to corner 2:

Step on L	(1),	(both),	R arm circles out and –
Swish point R in front	(2, 3);	(L, roll);	up to 5th for, 1, 2, 3;
Step on R	(1),	(both),	R arm circles out and –
Swish point L in front	(2, 3);	(L, roll);	up to 5th for, 1, 2, 3;
Step on L	(1),	(both),	arms 5th,
Dig R toe front	(2),	(*choque*),	arms 5th,
Step R side	(3);	(both);	arms 5th;

B

Complete *escobilla*: *pas de bourrée*:

Arm starts to come outward and continues into next step.

Step L behind (1), R on place (2), (L, roll),

Instead of completing the *pas de bourrée*,

Start the next step.

Arms: outward circles, one to each swish point step, first R then L and up in 5th on *choque*.

L arm comes down slowly on *pas de bourrée* and continues for next step point:

Repeat A to R:
Travel to corner 1:

Swish point L in front	(3; 1)	(L; roll), L arm continues circle out
Step on L	(2),	(both), and up to 5th for 1, 2, 3;
Swish point R in front	(3; 1),	(L; roll),
Step on R	(2),	(both),
Dig L toe front	(3);	(*choque*); arms 5th
Step on L	(1),	(both),
Step R behind	(2),	(L),
Step behind on L	(3);	(roll);

(*Note*: after first Panaderos continue playing the Sevillanas rhythm.)

C
3 Panaderos to R, L, R.

1st Panaderos to R:

Stamp the step to side on R	(1), (*choque*) arms front	
Lift L	(2), (silent);	
		slowly lift R arm
Hold	(3); (–);	slowly L back
Step on L in front	(1), (L),	
2 walks turning on self to R:		
walk on R,	(2), (roll), arms front	
walk on L	(3); (roll);	
Swing R to behind	(1); (R L),	

2nd Panaderos to L:
Panaderos arms on passes, using same arm up as leg stepped onto:

Stamp the step to side on L	(2), (roll), L arm up & behind
Lift R	(3), (roll); R arm
Step on R in front	(1), (RL),
2 walks turning on self to L:	
walk on L,	(2), (roll), arms front
walk on R	(3); (roll);
Swing L to behind	(1), (RL).

3rd Panaderos to R:

Stamp the step to side on R	(2), (roll), [R arm up &
Lift L	(3); (roll); [L arm]
Step on L in front	(1); (RL), [behind]
2 walks turning on self to R:	
walk on R,	(2), (roll), arms front
walk on L,	(3); (roll);

Ending facing the back with L arm up R across front:

R foot pointed in front	(1), (RL),
Pause	(2), (–),

Ending:
Changing L arm down front,

Stamp, stamp R	(3; 1), (both; both),
Escobilla L over digging it front	(2), (L),
Step back on L	(3); (roll);

Repeat 3 Panaderos to R, L, R, circling arms inwards as above:

First Panaderos to R:

Stamp the step to side on R	(1), (*choque*), arms front
Lift L	(2), (silent), R arm up
Hold	(3); (–);
Step on L in front	(1), (L),
2 walks turning on self to R:	
walk on R,	(2), (roll),
walk on L,	(3); (roll);
Swing R to behind	(1), (RL),

Second Panaderos to L:

Stamp the step to side on L	(2), (roll),
Lift R	(3); (roll);
Step on R in front	(1), (RL),
2 walks turning on self to L:	
walk on L,	(2), (roll),
walk on R,	(3); (roll);
Swing L to behind,	(1), (RL),

Third Panaderos to R:

Stamp the step to side on R	(2), (roll),
Lift L	(3), (roll);
Step on L in front	(1); (RL),
2 walks turning on self to R:	
walk on R,	(2), (roll),
walk on L,	(3); (roll);
ending facing the front with:	
R foot pointed in front	(1), (RL),
Valenciana position, R arm up L back,	
Pause	(2), (–),

Ending:

Stamp, stamp R	(3; 1), (both; both),
Escobilla drop on over on L	(2), (L),
Stamp R,	(3); (roll);
Stamp R *coupé* L front at same time	(1), (both),

This time end in Valencian position of arms: R arm up L behind, body slightly turned in opposition. Drop arm to across body in 4th as for other *desplantes* as you stamp:

Desplante:
Arms as before.

Stamp L foot,	(1), (silent), point R front (2, 3); (L, roll);	
Stamp R foot,	(1), (silent), point L front (2, 3); (L, roll);	
Stamp L foot,	(1), (L),	
Stamp, stamp R,	(2, 3); (R, L);	
Point L front	(1), (both),	
Pause for	(2, 3); (both, –);	both arms 5th
On place: *pas de bourrée* under, L behind, (1), (L),		L arm outward R on place, (2) (roll),
L front,	(3); (roll);	
Coupé under with a stamp R, *destaque* R high to 2nd		
	(1), (RL),	arms 5th
Rodazán L high in second	(2, 3); (—);	arms 5th
Step on L, turn to L	(1, 2, 3); (both, L, roll);	
Hold in 5th on point	(1), (both),	arms 5th
Pause looking to L	(2, 3); (–, –);	

Instead of Step 2B as in 1st Verse, end with *rodazánes* in front in the air:

D

Step on R,	(1),	(both),	arms 3rd
Rodazán L in air	(2, 3);	(L, roll);	
Step on L	(1),	(both),	arms 3rd
Rodazán R in air	(2, 3;)	(L, roll);	
Step to R, and turn	(1, 2, 3);	(both, L, roll); arms 5th	
Hold in 5th up on toes	(1, 2, 3);	(both), (–, –);	

Repeat D

Step on L,	(1),	(both),	arms 3rd
Rodazán R in air	(2, 3);	(L, roll);	
Step on R	(1),	(both),	arms 3rd
Rodazán L in air	(2, 3),	(L, roll);	
Step to L,	(1);	(both);	Lift L up
Place L over and quick turn	(2),	(–),	arms 5th
Step back on R	(3);	(*choque*);	
L on dig front	(1),	(both),	
Hold	(2, 3);	L arm front look over it, R slightly behind	

Arms: L arm up, elbow dropped, looking over L shoulder, R at the back, called 'Valenciana' position

Third Introduction

As before throughout the introduction play:
Castanets: L, (1), roll (& 2), roll (& 3); R (&)
At end arms go to front to play: (3); (*choque*);

This is typical of a Bolero dance, to stand still and rest on the introduction playing castanets.

Arms: L elbow up and look under arm, R arm behind, (1), (both). (Valencian position).

Part 3. *Jerezanas*

Step 1. *Escobilla*:
To get the steps into one line in order to see the pattern of the step the abbreviations are St. for stamp of foot, (He) for Heel, (B) for both on castanet, (Ro) for roll. The timing is very even while the castanets cross the music:

Arms: in inward circles, start L up.

Step 1, Survey:
Castanets: Bolero rhythm, It goes across two bars:

1	2	3	4	5	6
both,	L,	roll;	L,	roll,	both;

St. L (1) (both), He R (2)(L), toe R (3) (Ro); He R (4)(L); St., (5), St. L; (6);
St. R (1) (both), He L (2)(L), toe L (3) (Ro); He L (4)(L); St., St. R
Stamp L (1) (both), heel R (2)(L), toe R (3) (roll); heel R (4)(L); stamp, stamp L
Stamp R (1) (both), place foot across and turn to right (2, 3); (L, roll);
Step back on R (4), (both),
Hold (5, 6); (–, –);

Step 1 (detail):

Stamp L,	(1), (both),
Heel R,	(2), (L), foot turns in as foot comes through
Toe R,	(3); (roll); foot straightens to facing front
Heel R,	(4), (L),
Stamp L,	(5), (roll),
Stamp L;	(6); (both);
Stamp R,	(1), (both),
Heel L,	(2), (L), foot turns in as foot comes through
Toe L,	(3); (roll); foot straightens to facing front
Heel L,	(4), (L),
Stamp R,	(5), (roll),
Stamp R;	(6); (both);
Stamp L,	(1), (both),
Heel R,	(2), (L), foot turns in as foot comes through
Toe R,	(3); (roll); foot straightens to facing front
Heel, R,	(4), (L),

Stamp L,	(5), (roll),	
Stamp L,	(6); (both);	
Stamp R,	(1), (both),	
Place foot across turn to R	(2, 3); (L, roll), using both arms	
Step back on R	(4), (both),	
Drop L arm back into Valanciana position R arm up, L back		
Hold;	(5, 6); (both) Take L arm up front to 5th	

Step 2:
Step kick, step together with outward arm circles:

Step forward on L	(1), (both),	
Kick R	(2, 3); (L, roll);	R arm circles outward.
Step R, together L	(1, 2, 3); (R L, L, roll);	(arm continues to 5th).
Step R	(& 1), (RL),	L arm circles outward
Kick L	(2, 3); (L, roll);	L continues up to 5th
(On next *pas de bourrée* behind, arms reach 5th and remain there.)		
Step L	(1), (L),	continues to 5th
Step behind R	(2), (roll),	remains in 5th
Step L on place	(3); (*choque*);	up in 5th
(continue to Jerezana step)		

Step 3:
Jerezanas with Bolero rhythm:

Point R front	(1), (both),	R arm circles outwards
Kick R back	(2), (L),	
Swish R forward	(3); (roll);	
Step on R	(1), (L),	goes up to 5th on walks
Step on L	(2), (roll),	
Step on R	(3); (*choque*);	in 5th overhead

Jerezana:

Point L front	(1), (both),	L arm circles outwards
Kick L bent back	(2), (L),	
Swish L forward	(3); (roll);	
Point L in front	(1), (both),	L arm doesn't complete circle
Hold	(2, 3); (–,–);	but arm moves back into Valencian position.

(*Jerezanas* counts are contrary to the usual count of *jerezanas*. Eloy Pericet, personal communication).

Step forward on L	(1), (both),	R arm circles down
Kick R, front	(2, 3); (L, roll);	outwards
Step R, together L,	(1, 2, 3); (RL, L, roll);	
Step R,	(& 1), (R L),	L arm circles down
Kick L, front	(2, 3); (L, roll);	outwards

(On next *careo* behind, arms reach 5th and remain there.)

Step L	(1), (L),	continues to 5th
Step behind R	(2), (roll),	remains in 5th
Step L on place	(3); (*choque*);	up in 5th

(Continue to *jerezana* step)

Jerezana with Bolero rhythm:

Point R front	(1), (both),	R arm circles down outward
Kick R bent back	(2), (L),	
Swish R forward	(3); (roll);	
Step on R	(1), (L),	
Step on L	(2), (roll),	
Step on R	(3); (*choque*);	arms 5th

Jerezana:

Point L front	(1), (both),	L arm circles down outward
Kick L bent back	(2), (L),	
Swish L forward	(3); (roll);	
Point L in front	(1), (both), end Valencian position, R up and L at back	

Desplante:

Danced in double time, arms are in 4th down across the body.

Stamp L on place	(1), (L), point R front (2), (roll),	R arm
Stamp R on place	(& 3); (RL); point L front (1), (roll),	L arm
Stamp L on place	(& 2), (RL), point R front (3); (roll);	R arm
Stamp R	(1), (RL),	both arms down in front
Stamp, stamp L	(2, & 3); (L, RL);	arms open outward to 5th
Point R	(1), (both),	arms 5th
Hold	(2, 3);	
Four steps under: R, L, R, L,	(1, 2, 3; 1), (L, roll, roll; roll),	arms remain 5th,
Rodazán the leg in front in the air	(2), (–),	arms 5th,
Jump on R lifting L *attitude* at the back	(3; 1), (*choque*; both),	arms behind back,
Pause	(2),	
Step back on L, pointing R front	(3; 1), (*choque*; both),	
		L arm up R at back

Repeat step 2B starting R:

Step to side on R	(1) (both),	L *attitude* front	(2, 3); (L, roll);
Step to side on L	(1) (both),	R *attitude* front	(2, 3); (L, roll);
Step to side on R	(1) (both),	L foot across turn	(2, 3); (L, roll);
Hold in 5th	(1) (both),	pause	(2, 3); (—)

Repeat step 2B start L. At end R across and quick turn:

Step to side on L (1), (both),	R *attitude* front	(2, 3); (L, roll);
Step to side on R (1), (both),	L *attitude* front	(2,) (L),
Step to side on L		(3); (roll);

R foot across quick turn   (1), (both),
and hold in 5th on pointe   (2), (–),
Step back on R   (3); (*choque*);
L on dig front   (1), (both),
Pause facing front   (2, 3); (–, –); L arm up look under it this time
R slightly behind, in Valenciana position.

Note arms as at start of *copla*: L up, R at back, but this time look under, not over the arm as it is the end.

SEGUIDILLAS MANCHEGAS
Escuela Bolera, Pericet Version

An Escuela Bolera dance in 3/4 time, performed in ballet shoes, *zapatillas*.

This is the classical version of a regional dance from La Mancha. It is considered by some historians to be the origin of many Spanish dances. It started from a verse form which was later set to music and this was then danced to. The nature and rhythm of the verse gives it a specific shape.

The dancers make an entrance walking around each other (typical of Seguidillas as opposed to Boleros, where the dancer waits immobile between verses). The dance consists of three verses. Each long verse, or *copla*, consists of three short verses and choruses joined together as a unit. The sequence of each *copla* is: walk around partner, stand in 5th position (arms 5th); a chorus step turning the dancer around self; a *copla*, which is a short burst of dancing, followed by a pass where partners change places, an *estribillo* and *copla* in the new place, *pass* the partner again, *estribillo* and *copla* in the dancer's original place and a *bien parado* (well held) ending with dancers immobile with the one leg held in the air.

The Seguidillas was first mentioned by Mateo Aleman at the end of the sixteenth century in his novel *Vida y Hechos del Picaro Guzmán del Alfarache*. The word Manchegas is derived from 'La Mancha', which comes from the Arabic word Almansha, meaning the dry land or wilderness, in its widest sense, the bare plain between the mountains of Toledo, Cuenca and the Sierra Moreno. It is described by Cervantes in his novel *Don Quijote de la Mancha*, where mention is made of the Seguidillas (published in the second book, 1615).

One feature that is very typical of a Seguidillas which in some versions has got lost is the three walks passing the partner (also found in the first pass of the third verse of Sevillanas as originally danced). The *estribillo* has this step with three walks on place, turning the dancer around himself and each small *copla* ends with the dancers passing with three walks to each other's places. According to Angel Pericet Blanco, grandson of Angel Pericet Carmona, who wrote down his knowledge of the eighteenth-century classical Spanish dance style, the Seguidillas should have these walks. However, they are often supplanted by limps. According to Angel Pericet, limps were never a part of the dance, but more typical of a Fandango Verdiales (personal communication).

Note: the music is anacrusic. The end of one step in an *estribillo*, for example, may lead into the start of the step of the *copla*. Often the lift of a leg, before an *assemblé* for example, needs a count of its own. Thus in a step notated with two counts, one is needed to lift the leg. The accented beat shows where the step or point actually takes place.

First Verse
Arms: used in outward circles. When arms are in third (*cuarto* in the Spanish term) the same arm is in front as the working leg. On turns both arms are used in outward circles as in *vuelta normal.*
Castanets: Seguidillas rhythm throughout.

Bar:	1),	(& 2),	(& 3,)	(&
Rhythm:	1,	2, 3,	4, 5,	6;
Castanets:	both,	L, roll,	L, roll,	both;
Also:	L, roll,	roll,	R,	

This can be played throughout if it is easier than following the specific rhythms noted below.

Steps are counted in phrases of six in order to get the accented, repeated rhythm of the counts (6; 1).

Wait for introduction 5 bars music,
Walk on and round partner for 5 bars,

Introduction:
Start feet 5th, L foot front.
Wait for 1 bar of melody (1, 2, 3, 4, 5, –); or (1 & 2 & 3 –) taking arms to 5th. This is where, on all the other repeats, you pass your partner with 3 walks.

On start of melody play: both, L, roll, L, roll.

Castanets play *choque* on (5), (–); as R leg extends to side and the jump starts:

Estribillo:
Assemblé R leg in front	(1),	(both),	3rd R front,
Hop taking it to side	(2, 3),	(L, roll),	3rd R front,
(under with R, L):			
Stepping R behind and L on place	(4, 5),	(L, roll),	R up to 5th,
Tip R front, step R,	(6; 1),	(both; both),	both in 5th,
Place L across turning to L	(2, 3),	(–, both),	circle out,
Complete the turn stepping on R,	(4, 5);	(–, both),	end 5th.

Repeat on L up to the dig step:
Assemblé L leg in front	(6; 1),	(–; both), 3rd front,
Hop taking it to side	(2, 3),	(–, –), 3rd front,
Pas de bourrée under with L, R	(4, 5),	(L, roll), 3rd front,
Tip L across front	(6);	(both); 5th,

Step 1:
Malagueña step, 3 1/4 times.
Castanet rhythm throughout: both, L, roll, L, roll, both.

Step back on the L	(1), circle R arm to 3rd,	(both),
Dig R in front	(2, 3), arm stays 3rd,	(L, roll),
Développé slightly to 2nd	(4, 5),	(L, roll),
Close R leg behind	(6; 1), arm to 5th,	(both; both),
Jump changing the feet – R to front	(2, 3), arm stays 5th,	(L, roll),
Jump changing the feet – R to back	(4, 5), arm stays 5th,	(L, roll),
Lift R leg on	(6); circle L arm to 3rd,	(both);

Repeat stepping back on R (phrase of 6 counts).
Repeat stepping back on L (phrase of 6 counts).

Last time:

Step back on R,	(1), (both),	arm 3rd,
Dig L in front	(2, 3), (L, roll),	arm remains,
Développé L in front	(4, 5), (L, roll),	arm remains.

The Pass:
(Always pass L shoulder to partner.)
This one is different to the other passes because it is evenly timed:

Step L behind the R	(6; 1), (–; both), (starting crossing partner)
Step R side	(2, 3), (L, roll),
Tip L toe in front	(4, 5), (–, both),

3 steps to cross to partner's place:

Step L, R, L,	(6; 1), (2, 3), (4, 5), (–; both, L, roll, L, roll),

Estribillo:

Assemblé R leg in front	(6; 1),	(both; both),
Hop taking R to side	(2, 3),	(L, roll),
Pas de bourrée under with R, L	(4, 5),	(L, roll),
Tip R front, step R, cross L over	(6; 1),	(both; both),
Complete the turn stepping on L, R,	(2, 3, 4, 5),	(L, roll, L, roll),

Repeat on L up to the dig step:

Assemblé L leg in front	(6; 1),	(both; both),
Hop taking it to side	(2, 3),	(–, –),
Pas de bourrée under with L, R	(4, 5);	(L, roll),
Tip L front	(6);	(both),

Step 2:

A

Pifla y pas de buret (*jetés*) as the exercise :

Step across on L into 4th	(1), (both),	(arms 3rd),
Swish R	(2, 3), (–, –),	(keep L up),
Jeté on to R (open)	(4, 5), (L, roll),	(keep L up),

(L shoulder to partner) take R arm to 5th on,
Steps side L, behind with R, side with L (6; 1, 2, 3, 4, 5),   (both; both, L, roll, L, roll),

B

Repeat jumping onto L leg: arm R up L front:

This time close foot (R) in 5th front on	(6; 1), (both; both),
Swish L	(2, 3), (–, –),
Jeté on to L (open)	(4, 5), (L, roll),

(R shoulder to partner) Take R arm to 5th on

Steps side R, behind with L, side with R (6; 1, 2, 3, 4, 5), (both; both, L, roll, L, roll),

Repeat as for A above: jumping onto R leg but this time no tip of toe.

Close L foot in 5th front on	(6; 1),
Swish R	(2, 3),
Jeté on to R (open)	(4, 5),

(L shoulder to partner) Take R arm to 5th on:
Steps side L, behind with R, side with L (6; 1, 2, 3, 4, 5), (both; both, L roll, L, roll),

Repeat as for B with jumping onto L leg:

This time close R foot in 5th front on	(6; 1),
Swish L	(2, 3),
Jeté on to L (open)	(4, 5),

(R shoulder to partner)

Step side R,	(6; 1),

The Pass:

Dig L behind	(2),
Step with R,	(3, 4),
Tip L in front	(5, 6);

3 steps to cross to partner's place:
Step L, (1, 2), R, (3, 4), L, (5, 6);

Estribillo as before:

Assemblé R leg in front	(6; 1),
Hop taking R to side	(2, 3),
Pas de bourrée under with R, L	(4, 5),
Tip R front, step R turning to L	(6; 1),
Complete the turn stepping on L, R,	(2, 3, 4, 5),

Repeat on L (up to the dig step):

Assemblé L leg in front	(6; 1),
Hop taking it to side	(2, 3),
Pas de bourrée under with L, R	(4, 5),
Tip L front	(6);

Step 3:
Punta y talon. Play basic castanet rhythm throughout, same arm as leg circles down:

Step on L on place	(1),
*Dig toe turned in at side	(2, 3),
Dig heel R at side	(4, 5),
Dig R toe in front of instep	(6; 1),
3 skips back on R	(2, 3), L (4, 5), R (6; 1),

Arm circles up to 5th on skips, 3rd skip is start, of next repeat as foot is placed down.

Repeat starting R foot* (dig toe turned in etc.);

Repeat starting L foot from *.

Repeat starting R foot from *.

Ending:
Jeté on to R, arms 4th, R arm up, L front.

Second Verse

Introduction:
Free, as before, usually walking around partner, and then standing in 5th, arms up.

Estribillo:
As before starting with R.

Step 1:
Paraditas con punteado. Step or point on accented beats:
Note: this was taught to me with two points in front on (5), and (1), and later I was shown the step with three points in front on counts (3), (5), and (1). The latter is described but the former is more usual. L, rolls can be played with pause after first point: both, both, pause for (2, 3).

Tip L in front	(6);
(Drop R arm to front across body in third, L arm up),	
1st time step open on L into 4th to corner 2	(1),
Point R front across partner	(2, 3),
Tap R toe in front across partner	(4, 5)
Tap R toe in front across partner	(6; 1),
(Take arm up to 5th),	
Close R 5th behind,	(2, 3),
Close L 5th behind,	(4, 5),
(Drop L arm to front across body in third, L arm up)	

2nd time step open on R into 4th to corner 1	(6; 1),
Point L front across partner	(2, 3),
Point L front across partner	(4, 5),
Point L front across partner	(6; 1),
(Take arm up to 5th),	
Close L 5th behind,	(2, 3),
Close L 5th behind	(4, 5),
(Drop R arm to behind back across body, L arm up.)	

3rd time step open on L into 4th to corner 2	(6; 1),
Point R front across partner	(2, 3),
Point R front across partner	(4, 5),
Point R front across partner	(6; 1),
(Take arm up to 5th),	
Close R 5th behind,	(2, 3),

Close L 5th behind,	(4, 5),

(Drop L arm to behind back across body, R arm up)

4th time step open on R into 4th to corner 1	(6; 1),
Point L	(2, 3),
Point L front across partner	(4, 5),
Point toe again in front	(6; 1),

The Pass:

Dig *coupé* L behind,	(2),
Step with R, (3, 4),	
Tip L in front	(5, 6);
3 steps to cross to partner's place: step L,	(1, 2), R, (3, 4), L, (5, 6);

Estribillo: as before starting with R.

Step 2:

Campanela step over and back:

Tip L front	(6);
Step L in front on place	(1),
Développé R, L arm up in 3rd	(2, 3, 4),
Step over in 4th on R	(5, 6);
Step L on place	(1),
Développé R, R arm up in 3rd	(2, 3, 4),
Step back in 4th on R	(5, 6);
Step on L, change to L arm up in 3rd lean over R	(1),
Hold	(2, 3),
Batararaña: *glissade* to R	(4, 5),
Point R.	(6; 1),
Two steps back in 5ths, R, L,	(2, 3), (4, 5),

Repeat to R

Step R in front on place	(6; 1),
Développé L to side, R arm up in 3rd	(2, 3, 4),
Step over in 4th on R	(5, 6);
Step R on place	(1),
Développé L to side, L arm up in 3rd	(2, 3, 4),
Step back in 4th on R	(5, 6);
Step on L, change to L arm up in 3rd lean over R	(1),
Hold	(2, 3),
Batararaña: *glissades* to L	(4, 5,)
Point L	(6; 1),

The Pass:

Dig *coupé* L behind,	(2),
Step with R,	(3, 4),
Tip L in front	(5, 6);

3 steps to cross to partner's place:

| Step L, | (1, 2), R, (3, 4), L, (5, 6); |

Estribillo:
As before starting with the R.

Step 3:
Rodazán (turn).

Tip L front	(6);
Step L in front on place	(1),
Développé R to side, L arm up in 3rd	(2, 3),
Step over in 4th on R	(4, 5),
Step L on place	(6; 1),
Développé R, R arm up in 3rd	(2, 3),
Step back in 4th on R	(4, 5),

Step on L, L arm up	(6; 1),
Rodazán R in front inwards arm stays up	(2, 3),
Destaque R, place R across,	(4, 5),
Turn to L changing to R arm	(6; 1, 2, 3, 4),
Place L 4th behind, change	(5),

Repeat to R	
Step R in front on place	(6; 1),
Développé L to side, R arm up in 3rd	(2, 3),
Step over in 4th on R	(4, 5),

Step R on place	(6; 1),
Développé L to side, L arm up in 3rd	(2, 3),
Step back in 4th on L	(4, 5),
Step R on place	(6; 1),
Rodazán L in front inwards over	(2, 3),
L arm up in 3rd	
End in *destaque* and place L across,	(4, 5),
Turn to R changing to both arms 5th	(6; 1),
Pause hold position on toes in 5th	(2, 3);
Hold	(4, 5, 6);
Jeté on to R, L *attitude* in front	(1),
Hold for	(2, 3, 4, 5, 6);

Third verse

Introduction free, usually walking round partner as before. Wait in 5th as before, arms down and up as before, then:

There are five complete sets of the *estribillo* step and the sixth one crosses without a turn, L shoulder to partner.

Estribillo:
As before starting with R, this time just continue turning second one to complete it to L, this makes two complete sets.
Arms: as before (for detail of arms with the steps see the explanation at the beginning of the dance).

Step 1:
3rd one: repeat the *estribillo* step turning on self to R
4th one: repeat the *estribillo* step turning on self to L
5th one: repeat the *estribillo* step turning on self to R
6th one: repeat the *assemblé* in front L (1), hop (2, 3),
Pas de bourrée under R (&) L (4, 5), touch R front (6);
Pass 3 walks crossing partner to change places, L, R, L,

Estribillo:
As before starting with R but continuing as above round self.

Step 2:
One passing partner with L shoulder as above to original starting position,
One turning round self in original place,
One passing partner,
One turning round self in original place,
One passing partner.

Estribillo:
As above turning round self.
Dig L toe behind, instead of tip in front, to start the skips travelling backward:

Step 3:
Woman starts L, man starts R.
Slow circles with both arms playing L, roll continuously:
22 *retirés* travelling backwards. The first 9 continue backward away from partner, the next 13 travel back facing the audience.
Step forward R, L, R (L roll, L roll, L roll –)
Jeté on to it (both) and hold it.

SEVILLANAS BOLERAS
Escuela Bolera, Pericet version

An Escuela Bolera couple dance in 3/4 time. Ballet shoes, *zapatillas*, are worn.

Arms: used in circular movements.
Castanets: are as usual. L, roll, roll, R. It has become the custom to play L, roll on all the first *coplas* of all the three verses. However, it is very possible to play straight Sevillanas, though more difficult and thus not the custom. There are many versions.

First Verse
The entrance steps in the introduction are written as taught to me by Eloy Pericet. The more ballet-trained the dancer the higher the legs are raised, and the higher on demi-pointe the dancer rises. This can be seen performed in Carlos Saura's film *Sevillanas*. It is a version endorsed by Eloy Pericet. Care must be taken when watching the film. Confusion can arise because some parts are filmed reflected in a mirror and if copied, the incorrect leg could be used as a result.

Start:
Standing on the R foot with the L foot pointed across in front, across from a partner, arms in 3rd: L front, R raised in 5th.
Wait for 9 counts (1, 2, 3, 4, 5, 6; 1, 2, 3):

Estribillo:
Introduction:
Castanets: L,   roll,   *choque*;   both,   L,   roll,   RL,   roll,   roll,   RL,
              4,   5,   6;   1,   2,   3,   & 4,   5,   6;   & 1,
See note at end of 3rd verse about castanets on the pass.

Note: I have joined the last counts (6, & 1), on to the *estribillo*, as is the custom, but it is really no man's land as the (6); is the end of the *estribillo* and the (1), the beginning of the verse's phrase.

Step 1:
Destaque the L leg to L, raising L arm to 5th, step on it (& 4), (castanets play: L),
Chassé the R leg across circling the R arm down and up (5), (roll), (some people *choque* on the & and play both on 6);
Jeté the L leg across   (6); (*choque*);
Step back on R   (1), (both),
Dig L in front   (2), (L),
Développé L in front   (3), (roll),
Small *degagé* and close L behind in 5th   (4), (RL),
Small *degagé* and close R behind in 5th   (5), (roll),
End of *estribillo* and 1st step of *copla*:
Tip L toe in front (6); (roll); and step on it on place or stamp in front (1), (RL),
(This originally existed in the Boleros as 'stamp, stamp', then became 'dig, stamp' – a *sostenido* – and eventually tipping the toe and a soft stamp. All are acceptable. Eloy Pericet, personal communication).

First *copla* or verse:

Here castanets play L, roll.

Note: on the *glissade jetés*, do *not* cross to your partner's place, only to face them a quarter of the way to the side (Eloy Pericet, personal communication).

The stamp with L as shown above	(1),
Glissade to R crossing partner quarter way to R	(2, 3), (L, roll),
Swish R foot (4), (–), beaten *jeté* across onto it	(5), (both),
Glissade to L crossing partner to place to L	(6; 1), (L, roll),
Swish L foot (2) (–), beaten *jeté* across onto it	(3), (both),
Swish R (4), (–), *assemblé* R in front	(5), (both),
Entrechat quatre	(6; 1), (–; both),
Glissade to L crossing partner quarter way to L	(2, 3), (L, roll),
Swish L foot (4), (–), beaten *jeté* across onto it	(5), (both),
Glissade to R crossing partner to place to R	(6; 1), (L; roll),
Swish R foot (2), (–), beaten *jeté* across onto it	(3), (both),
Swish L (4), (–), *assemblé* L in front	(5), (both),

Pass:

Relevé on R lifting L *attitude* in front	(6); (*choque*);
Step forward L	(1), (both),
2 walks crossing to partners place	(2, 3), (L, roll),

Estribillo:

Castanets: continue as for normal one, L, roll, roll, R, etc.

Coupé under with R	(4),
Step forward on L	(5),
Dig behind	(6);
Step back on R	(1),
Dig L in front	(2),
Développé L front (small)	(3), and close
With small *degagés* close L behind	(4),
Close R behind	(5),

2nd *copla* or verse:

Crossing partner on left side to original place, arms used in outward circles.

Castanets: RL, roll on step hop.

Tip L toe in front and step on it on place in front (6; 1), (roll; RL),

Hop on L with R leg in low *attitude* behind L arm down behind, R in 5th (face partner on this)	
	(2), (L),
Step forward on R	(3), (roll),
Hop on R with L leg in low *attitude* behind R	(4), (L),
R arm down behind, turning on self to R to face partner, arms 5th,	
step forward on L	(5), (roll),
Hop with *destaque* of R leg to 2nd, arms 5th	(6); (*choque*);
Assemblé behind, arms in 5th	(1), (both),

Hop with high *destaque* of R leg to 2nd, arms 5th   (2), (L),
Place Leg across   (3), (roll),
Turn to L   (4, 5), (RL, roll),

Repeat crossing back to partner's place with a quick turn:

Tip L toe in front and step on it on place in front (6; 1), (roll; RL),
Hop on L with R leg in low *attitude* behind L arm down behind, R in 5th (face partner on this)
(2), (L),
Step forward on R   (3), (roll),
Hop on R with L leg in low *attitude* behind R   (4), (L),
R arm down behind, turning on self to R to face partner, arms 5th,
step forward on L   (5), (roll),
Hop with *destaque* of R leg to 2nd, arms 5th   (6); (*choque*);
Assemblé behind, arms in 5th   (1), (both),
Hop with high *destaque* of L leg to 2nd, arms 5th (2), (L),
Place leg across, quick turn to L   (2, 3), (roll),
Step back on L   (4), (RL),
Forward on R   (5), (roll),

Pass:
Relevé on R lifting L *attitude* in front   (6); (roll);
3 walks crossing to partner's place   (1, 2, 3), (RL, roll, roll),

Estribillo:
Castanets: as for normal one, L, roll, roll, R, etc.
Coupé under with R   (4),
Step forward on L   (5),
Dig R behind   (6);
Step back on R   (1),
Dig L in front   (2),
Développé L front (small)   (3),
With small *degagés* close L behind   (4),
    close R behind (5),
Rise   (6);

3rd *copla* or verse:
Arms move in circles and castanets play Sevillanas rhythm.
From side to side.
Castanets: usual Sevillanas rhythm:

Careo onto L foot   (1, 2, 3),
Careo onto R foot   (4, 5, 6);
Careo onto L foot crossing partner   (1, 2, 3),
Careo onto R foot turning to R on self to face partner   (4, 5, 6);

Repeat exactly to return to original place.

Careo onto L foot	(1, 2, 3),
Careo onto R foot	(4, 5, 6);
Careo onto L foot crossing partner	(1, 2, 3),
Careo onto R foot turning to R on self to face partner	(4, 5, 6);
Step turn to L,	(1, 2, 3), (RL, L, roll); releasing L foot to front and hold. (both).

SECOND VERSE
Ballet shoes are worn.
Arms: move in outward circles.
Castanets: are as usual. L, roll, roll, R. It has become the custom to play L, roll on all the first *coplas* of all the three verses.

Start:
Standing on the R foot with the L foot pointed across in front, across from a partner, arms in 3rd, L front, R raised in 5th.
Wait for 9 counts, (1, 2, 3, 4, 5, 6; 1, 2, 3):

Estribillo:
Introduction as before.

Castanets:	L,	roll,	*choque*;	both,	L,	roll,	RL,	roll,	roll,	RL,
	4,	5,	6;	1,	2,	3,	& 4,	5,	6;	& 1

Step 1:
Destaque the L leg to L, raising L arm to 5th, step on it (& 4), (castanets play: L),
Chassé the R leg across circling the R arm down and up (5), (roll),
(some people *choque* on the & and play both on 6)

Jeté the L leg across	(6); (*choque*);
Step back on R	(1), (both),
Dig in front	(2), (L),
Développé in front	(3), (roll),
Small *degagé* and close L behind in 5th	(4), (RL),
Small *degagé* and close R behind in 5th	(5), (roll),

1st *copla* or verse:
Castanets: L roll:

End of *estribillo* and 1st step of *copla*:

Tip L toe in front	(6); (roll);
And step on it on place or stamp in front	(1), (RL),

Castanets: L, roll, L, roll, *choque*, both, L, roll,
Arms: 3rd with R arm up and L in front until the third *destaque*, when it moves to 5th up the front:

Castanets: L, roll continuously:

Glissade forward with R, closing L behind	(2, 3), arms 3rd,

Glissade forward with R, closing L behind	(4, 5), arms 3rd,
Destaque R to side closing behind	(6; 1),
Destaque L to side closing behind	(2, 3),
Destaque R to side closing behind	(4, 5),
Entrechat quatre	(6); (1), arms 5th, (–); (both)
Glissade forward with L, closing R behind	(2, 3), arms 3rd,
Glissade forward with L, closing R behind	(4, 5), arms 5th,
Destaque L to side closing behind	(6; 1), arms 5th,
Destaque R to side closing behind	(2, 3), arms 5th,
Step L behind, step R forward to pass	(4, 5), arms 5th, (L, roll),

Pass:

Relevé on R lifting L *attitude* in front	(6); (*choque*);
3 walks crossing to partner's place (L, R, L)	(1, 2, 3), (both, L, roll),

Estribillo:
Castanets: as for normal one, L, roll, roll, R, etc.

Coupé under with R	(4),
Step forward on L	(5),
Dig R behind	(6);
Step back on R	(1),
Dig L in front	(2),
Développé L front (small)	(3),
With small *degagés* close L behind	(4),
Close R behind	(5),

2nd *copla* or verse:
Punta y talon.
Castanets: as for normal one, L, roll, roll, R etc.
Pause before the *vuelta fibraltada*, both, L, roll on the turn,

Tip L toe in front and step on it on place in front	(6; 1),
R tip of toe turned in, heel turned out at side	(2, 3),
Dig ball of R in front of instep	(4),
3 skips back with R, L; R,	(5, 6; 1),
L tip of toe turned in, heel turned out at side	(2, 3),
Dig ball of L in front of instep	(4),
3 skips back with L, R: L,	(5, 6; 1),
R tip of toe turned in, heel turned out at side	(2, 3),
Dig ball in front of instep	(4),
1 skip back with R,	(5),
Pause	(6); (–);
Lifting L higher do *vuelta fibraltada* turn to L	(1, 2, 3), (both, L, roll),

Pass:
As above, returning to original place at start of dance.

Estribillo:
As before.

3rd *copla*:
Arms: both arms circling down and up the front, doing *choque* up in 5th as leg lifts in front.
Castanets: (*choque*; both, L, roll, L, roll) throughout.

The Step:
4 passes as described above, alternating L, R, L, R.
Ending: step to R, tipping L front with knee bent with tip of toe, arms 3rd R up L front (*choque*).

Castanets on turn: (both, L, roll):
Step turn to L, finishing with L in front on pointe, arms 3rd with L down in front and R up over the head (both).

Third Verse
Castanets: as usual, L, roll, roll, R. It has become the custom to play L, roll on all the first *coplas* of all the three verses. However, it is very possible to play straight Sevillanas, though more difficult.

Start:
Standing on the R foot with the L foot pointed across in front, across from a partner, arms in 3rd, L front, R raised in 5th.
Wait for 9 counts, (1, 2, 3, 4, 5, 6; 1, 2, 3).

Estribillo
Introduction as before:

Castanets:	L,	roll,	*choque*,		both, L,	roll,	RL,	roll,	roll,	RL,
	4,	5,	6;	1,	2,	3,	& 4,	5,	6;	& 1,

Step 1:

Destaque the L leg to L, raising L arm to 5th, step on it (castanets play: L),	(& 4),
Chassé the R leg across circling the R arm down and up	(5), (roll),
(some people *choque* on the & and play both on 6)	
Jeté the L leg across	(6); (*choque*);
Step back on R	(1), (both),
Dig R in front	(2), (L),
Développé in front	(3), (roll),
Small *degagé* and close L behind in 5th	(4), (RL),
Small *degagé* and close R behind in 5th	(5), (roll).

The *glissade*s: these are not jumped as in ballet but more stepped.

1st *copla*:
End of *estribillo* and 1st step of copla:
Tip L toe in front (6); (roll); and step on it on place or stamp in front (1), (RL),

With R foot 2 *glissade*s forward, L foot coming over, crossing to L side of partner, L arm lowers
behind, R arm up:

Glissade	(2, 3), (L, roll),
Glissade	(4, 5), (L, roll),
Pifla y pas de buret: *jeté* across on R	(6); (*choque*);

(L arm up the front to (*choque*) in 5th, on the (6);)
Step *pas de bourrée* with L:

Step side with L,	(1), (both),
Step behind with R,	(2), (L),
Step L, place R across and turn to L,	(3), (roll),

Arms circling down and going up whilst completing the turn,

L foot lifts across on	(4), (L),

to prepare for:

*Chassé L to side	(5), (roll),
Coupé behind with R	(6); (both);
Assemblé behind	(1), (both),

Repeat 2 and 3 to L, leaving out *.
With L foot 2 *glissade*s forward, R foot coming over, crossing
to R side of partner, R arm lowers behind, L arm up:

Glissade	(2, 3), (L, roll),
Glissade	(4, 5), (L, roll),
Pifla y pas de buret: *jeté* across on L	(6); (*choque*);

(L arm up the front to (*choque*) in 5th, on the (6);)
Step *pas de bourrée* with R:

Step side with R,	(1), (both),
Step behind with L,	(2), (L),
Step R, place L across and turn to R,	(3), (roll),

Arms circling down and going up whilst completing the turn,

Pass:
As before:

Coupé L foot behind	(4), (RL), or (L),
Step R to side	(5), (roll), or (roll),
Lift L in front (can be on a rise)	(6); (roll); or (*choque*);
Step L across	(1), (RL), or (both),
2 walks R, L,	(2, 3), (roll, roll), or (L, roll),

Estribillo:
As before (4, 5, 6; 1, 2, 3, 4, 5):
Castanets: as for normal one, L, roll, roll, R, etc.

Coupé under with R	(4), (L),
Step forward on L	(5), (roll),
Dig behind	(6); (roll);
Step back on R	(& 1), (RL),
Dig L in front	(2), (roll),
Développé L front (small)	(3), (roll),

With small *degagés* close L behind   (4), close R behind (5), (roll, RL),

2nd *copla*:
Punta y talon turning slowly on self to L:
Tip L toe in front and step on it on place in front (6; 1),
Punta y talon in front with R   (2, 3), arms 3rd R arm down,
(Turning on self towards L) step on R on place   (4),
Punta y talon in front with L   (5, 6); L arm down,

Note: each *punta y talon* must be to partner, so you have to get right round on the step each time.

Pas de basque to L   (1, 2, 3),   R arm circles up to 5th,

Repeat on R turning slowly on self to R:
Step on R   (4),
Punta y talon in front with L   (5, 6);   arms 3rd L arm down,
Turning on self to L step on R on place   (1),
Punta y talon in front with R   (2, 3),   arms 3rd R arm down,
Pas de basque to R   (4, 5, 6);   L arm circles up to 5th,
Vuelta normal to the L   (1, 2, 3),

Pass:
As before.
Coupé L foot behind   (4), (RL), or (L),
Step R to side   (5), (roll), or (roll),
Lift L in front (can be on rise)   (6); (roll); or (*choque*);
Step L across   (1), (RL), or -(both),
2 walks R, L,   (2, 3), (roll, roll), or (L, roll),

Estribillo:
As before (4, 5, 6; 1, 2, 3, 4, 5), ending pause on (6).
Castanets: as for normal one, L, roll, roll, R, etc.

Coupé under with R   (4),
Step forward on L   (5),
Dig R behind   (6);
Step back on R   (1),
Dig L in front   (2),
Développé L front (small)   (3), and close
With small *degagés* close L behind   (4), close R behind (5),
Pause   (6);

3rd *copla*:
8 complete times starting with alternate legs, passing partner on L.
Arms: R arm circles down and up to 5th.
Échappé in second   (1),

Hop on L and *ballonné* bringing R behind	(2),
Hop on L and *ballonné* bringing R in front	(3),

Arms: L arm circles down and up to 5th.	
Échappé in second	(4),
Hop on R and *ballonné* bringing L behind	(5),
Hop on R and *ballonné* bringing L in front	(6);

Repeating this crossing the partner, turning on self when you get to the partner's place and recrossing to own place turning to face partner.

Step and *vuelta normal* to left, ending with L foot pointed to front across partner, R arm up, L 3rd front. Look at partner over L shoulder.

Note: on the passes the castanets can be played:

Coupé L foot behind	(4), (RL), or-(L),
Step R to side	(5), (roll), or-(roll),
Lift L in front (can be on rise)	(6); (roll); or-(*choque*);
Step L across	(1), (RL), or-(both),
2 walks R, L,	(2, 3), (roll, roll), or (L, roll).

SOLEARES DEL MAESTRO ARCAS

Escuela Bolera Andaluza, Pericet version

An Escuela Bolera Andaluza dance in 3/8 time.
This dance is performed in heeled shoes.

Start centre stage, standing on left foot right pointed in front both arms in 8th behind.

Introduction of eight bars:
No castanets.
(Suggesion: walk in for four bars, take up position with right foot on a dig in front and raise the left arm for the next four.)
As taught: stand centre with R ft on dig in front. On introduction raise left arm over head to 5th for 8 bars.

Step1:
Arms: R across body ending up in 5th (4, 5, 6).
Castanets: both (1), L (2), roll (3); RL (& 1); pause (2, 3); 4 times.
Stamp R (1), lift right leg, knee bent, across (2), place L across (3); step on R (1), pause (2), stamp L (3);
Arms: L arm circles downward, R remains at back;
Repeat step 1 on L,
Arms: Move R in inward circle, R at back;
Repeat step 1 on R,
Arms: Move L in inward circle, L at back.

Ending:
Stamp L (1), place R foot across and turn to L (2, 3); ends with L foot pointed in front.

Step 2:
Castanets: both, L, roll; 4 times (last one goes into first *sostenidos* of next step, which starts on last phrase of this sequence:
Step on L, kick R leg up in front (*caballo*) (1, 2, 3);
Arms: R arm circles down,
Pas de bourrée the R: behind with R, step on L, step on R; (1, 2, 3);
Arms: R arm ends up in 5th and stays up on the:
Step L (1), *rodazán* R leg to 2nd (2, 3);
Castanets: both, L, roll of last sequence on 1st *sostenidos*, then RL (& 1), L (2), roll; (3);three more times.

Step R (1), (*sostenidos*) toe tip L front step on L (2, 3);
Step R (1), (*sostenidos*) toe tip L front step on L (2, 3);
Step R (1), (*sostenidos*) toe tip L front step on L (2, 3);
Step R (1), (sostenidos) toe tip L front step on L (2, 3);
Step R (1), (sostenidos) toe tip L front step on L (2, 3);
Arms: change to 3rd with R arm up, L across body in front

Repeat step 2 starting step on R and doing only 4 *sostenidos*.
Arms: 3rd with L up R across body.

Ending:
Stamp L (1), extending R (2, 3); castanets: both.
Arms: remain in 3rd.

A
Arms: used in inward circles.
Circle L down to behind back on 3 beats (1, 2, 3); R up;
Circle R down to behind back on 3 beats (1, 2, 3);
Circle both up outwards and up to 5th (1, 2, 3);

Castanets: For beats travelling back:
Both (on first stamp only), L, roll; R L, roll, roll,

Step 3:
8 stamp toe heels travelling back alternate feet:

Stamp R (1),	toe heel L (2 &),	toe heel R (3 &);
Stamp L, (1),	toe heel R (2 &),	toe heel L (3 &);
Stamp R (1),	toe heel L (2 &),	toe heel R (3 &);
Stamp L, (1),	toe heel R (2 &),	toe heel L (3 &);
Stamp R (1),	toe heel L (2 &),	toe heel R (3 &);
Stamp L, (1),	toe heel R (2 &),	toe heel L (3 &);
Stamp R (1),	toe heel L (2 &),	toe heel R (3 &);
Stamp L, (1),	toe heel R (2 &),	toe heel L (3 &);

Step 4:
Arms: circle outward and then up front to return to 5th.
Castanets: both, (1), pause (2), both, both (& 3);
Beats 6 times:
Stamp R, lifting L across R knee (1, 2), stamp L, stamp R (& 3);
Stamp L, lifting R across L knee (1, 2), stamp R, stamp L (& 3);
Stamp R, lifting L across R knee (1, 2), stamp L, stamp R (& 3);
Stamp L, lifting R across L knee (1, 2), stamp R, stamp L (& 3);
Stamp R, lifting L across R knee (1, 2), stamp L, stamp R (& 3);
Stamp L, lifting R across L knee (1, 2), stamp R, stamp L (& 3);

Ending:
Step to R and turn (1, 2, 3; 1, 2, 3); .
Arms: open outwards on turn, ending both behind back.
Castanets: both, L roll both.

Repeat step 1 starting R; 4 times side to side, turn.
Repeat step 1 starting L; 4 times side to side, turn.

Ending:
Redoble.
Stamp R (1), toe heel L (2), heel stamp R (& 3); stamp L (1) shooting R foot to point in front, pause (2, 3);
Castanets: Both, L, roll; both, pause, pause;

Step 5:
Castanets: both (1, 2), both (3; 1), both (2, 3); both (1), L (2) roll (& 3); both (1), pause (2, 3);

Beats travelling back:
Stamp.R, L, R, L
Redoble with R (as above) shooting L to point front.
Arms go outwards and up to 5th.

Repeat starting L,
Redoble wth L.

Step 6:
Arms come down the front.
Repeat Step 3 A beats: stamp toe heels travelling back 7 times, with the same arms and castanets. On the last one do not point foot front but go directly into next step with the ending:

Ending:
Step on L (1), *développé* R (2, 3);
Castanets: both, L, roll.

Step 7:
Step together step *développé*:
Step R (1, 2,) step together L (3);
Step R (1), *développé* L (2, 3); (travelling round to L)
Repeat with L,
Repeat with R. Stop feet together, lift skirt.

Arms: move from third to third, with outward circles.

Floor pattern:
You do this step three times with alternate feet making an S-shape on the floor. Start travelling to L to wall 6, then curling to the back and towards wall 8, curling round travel now to the R and wall 6 complete the S ending centre.

Castanets: ending both.

Step 8:
Beats (holding skirt) round room to L, 14 times and turn.
Stamp R, heel, toe heel L, toe heel R (1, &, 2 &, 3 & etc.);

Ending:
Turn to R, (1, 2, 3);
Arms: open outwards and up to 5th and down in front.

Redoble:
As before:
Stamp R (1)
Toe heel *redoble* with L, stamp L (2, 3); shooting R front (1) pause (2, & 3);
Arms: circle outwards and up again to 5th.
Castanets: both, L, roll; both, on the *redoble*.

Step 9:
Repeats step 5 completely with the single stamps and *redoble* travelling back, and the repeat Step 3 of the toe heels going back seven and stamp *coupé* L (1).

Step 10:
Arms: move from 3rd to 3rd as in the *rodazán* exercise in Cuarto Año.
Castanets: both, L, roll.

Rodazán R leg to side (2, 3); *
Step on R (1), step across (2, 3); step *coupé* R (1),
Repeat to L starting with the *rodazán* A with L,
Repeat to R as above A and B.

Ending:
Step on L, step on R across L, turning to L (*choque*), remain on R (castanets: both).
Arms: both go down outwards.
End: arms 3rd, L arm up.

ZAPATEADO DE MARIA CRISTINA
Escuela Bolera, Pericet version

An Escuela Bolera dance in 3/4 time performed in ballet shoes, *zapatillas*.

Start in corner 3:
Wait with L foot pointed *croisé* (to corner 1) in front.
Arms: 5th, do *choque* in that position at start.

The counting is sometimes in sixes.

Moderate tempo

First Verse

Step 1a:
Arms: move in outward circles.
Wait for 8 bars and on last beat –
Castanets:
Start: *choque;* (6); both, (1), L (2), roll (3); 4 times;
Continues: L, (4), roll, (5), roll,(6); RL, (& 1), roll, (2), roll (3); 4 times.

Travelling in a semi-circle around to the right, finishing centre do:

Step onto L	(1), arms 3rd, R in front,
Destaque R (*grand battement* on a hop or *enveloppés*),	(2, 3);
Chassé R to 4th	(4)
Dig tap, L foot behind	(5),
Step on it on pointe in 5th	(6); R arm raised to 5th.

Repeat with R, L, R, L, R, L
Thus this step is danced 7 times. Transfer weight onto L and:

Ending:

A quick *vuelta normal* turn to R	(& 1, 2), (RL, L), arms open outward
Land on *plié* in 5th	(3); (roll); arms down in 1st
Relevé in 5th	(4), (both), arms up to 5th.
Hold	(5, 6); (—);

STEP 1b:
Rodazán hacia adentro, rodazán hacia afuera, asemblé y foueté.
Arms: move from third through 5th to 3rd and 5th on *assemblé entrechat trois*,
Castanets: both, L, roll.

Step to R on R inward *rodazán* with L with half-turn to face the back wall (1, 2, 3); (both, L, roll);
left arm 3rd front
This is done on a *relevé* on *demi-pointe*.

Step L releasing R, turning body to R to *rodazán* R outwards with R, half-turn to face front (4, 5, 6); (both, L, roll); right arm 3rd in front. This is done on a *relevé* on *demi-pointe*.

Arms: move from 3rd through 5th to 3rd on *assemblé*.

Assemblé R behind	(1), (both), arms 5th,
Entrechat trois lifting L behind	(2), (L), L arm front,
Développé L to 2nd on a hop	(3); (roll); L arm front
Assemblé in front	(4), (both), arms 5th,
Hold	(5), (–), arms 5th
Lift leg to side on small rise	(6); (–); arms 3rd; L arm up.

Lower R arm to side to start the circling it for the *pas de basque*:

Two *pas de basque* from side to side to L and R,	(1, 2, 3); (L, roll, roll);
	(& 4, 5, 6); (RL, roll, roll):
Vuelta fibraltada to the L	(& 1, 2, 3); (RL, L, roll); arms circle
Hold up in 5th	(4, 5, 6); (both, L, roll);

Castanets have played:
Pam, ta, ria; Pam, ta, ria; Pam, ta, ria; Pam, –, –;
Ta, ria, ria; Pi-ta, ria; ria; Pi-ta, ta, ria; Pam, ta, ria;

Repeat the whole step to the L.
Step to L on L inward *rodazán* with R with half-turn to face the back wall (1, 2, 3); right arm 3rd front.
This is done on a hop on *demi-pointe*. R arm 3rd front.

Step R *coupé*ing L, *rodazán* L outwards with L,
Half-turning under to L to face front (1, 2, 3);
Also on a *relevé*.

Arms: move from 3rd through 5th to 3rd on *assemblé*.

Assemblé L behind	(1), arms 5th,
Entrechat trois lifting R behind	(2), left arm front,
Développé R to 2nd on a hop	(3); left arm front
Assemblé in front	(4), arms 5th,
Hold	(5), arms 5th
Lift leg to side on small rise	(6); arms 3rd; L arm up.

Drop R to side to start the circle for the *pas de basque*:

Two *pas de basque* from side to side to L (RL, roll, RL); and R (L, roll, RL);	

Vuelta fibraltada to the L	(1, 2, 3); (RL, L, roll);

Castanets on the repeat have played:
On the *rodazánes* (note the difference):
Pam, ta, ria; Pam, ta, ria; Pam, ta, ria; Pam, ta, ria.

On the *pas de basque*:
Pi-ta, ria, pi-ta; Ta, ria pi-ta;

On the *vuelta fibraltada*:
Pi-ta, ta, ria; Ta, ria, pi; The last 'pi' is on the sweep back below.

Start of Panaderos:
described below
**Step R back sweeping it behind L (4), (L),
Step out on L (5), (roll), lift R leg (roll); (6);
Folowed by 3 steps, R, L, R; (1, 2, 3);

Step 2:
Panaderos.
Castanets: Continuous rolls, starting with the L.
Arms: usual, with same arm up as leg that you step out on. Making inward circles.

Panaderos step seven times round room to L:
Slide R back:

1st pass on L with back to audience:
**Step on R behind (4), back to audience, (L),
Castanets: into continuous rolls on passes,
Step on L (5), lift R across knee (6); 3 walks coming round to face the audience, round self to R, L, R; (1, 2, 3);

2nd pass: repeat with L behind, step on R going wall 6.
3rd pass: repeat with R travelling upstage (turning).
4th pass: repeat with L going across the back.
5th pass: repeat with R travelling downstage (turning).
6th pass: repeat with L going across front (back to audience.).
7th pass: repeat with R going across the front.

Ending:
Vuelta girada.
Lift L leg across body in *attitude*, arms 5th (6); (*choque*);
Step side on L, place R across turn to L, (1, 2, 3); (both, L, roll);

Ending:
Step to side L, (4, 5), (L, roll), (arms 5th),
Drop across on R, arms 3rd (6); (*choque*);

Change to faster *Tiempo de Jaleo*.

Step 3a:
Rodazán y pas de buret.

The Step:
Arms 3rd, L up, R front,
Arms remain thus for whole step until *vuelta fibraltada*:

Coupé L behind.	(1), (both),
Rodazán R leg to side on a hop,	(2, 3); (L, roll);
Pas de bourrée under (R, L, R) end R front	(4, 5, 6); (L, roll, roll);
Coupé L behind	(1), (roll),
Rodazán R leg side on a hop	(2, 3); (L, roll);
Pas de bourrée under (R, L, R) end R front on	(4, 5, 6); (L, roll, roll);
Coupé L under	(1), (both),
and two *ballonnés* with R to corner 1	(2, 3; 4, 5), (–, both; –, both),

(One *ballonné* is across front, one across back,), (arms 3rd).

Vuelta fibraltada to the right, usual arms for *vuelta*: 5th to 5th.
Castanets: on the *vuelta*: (6; 1, 2, 3; 4, 5), (-; both, L, roll; L, roll),

Ending as above but with L leg:

Drop across on L	(6); (*choque*);
Coupé R behind(both), L leg out to side	(1), (both),

Repeat step 3A to L.

Vuelta fibraltada to the right, usual arms for *vuelta*: 5th to 5th.
Castanets: on the *vuelta*: (6; 1, 2, 3; 4, 5), (–; both, L, roll; L, roll),
Tip: (Dig) R foot in front (6); (*choque*);

Step 3b:
Piqués.
Explanation: like long *glissade*s on *demi-pointe* first closing the foot front then back. The arm that is over the *degagé* foot opens from 5th down and remains in 3rd until tht change over to repeat on the other side when it goes up to 5th.

The Step:
Step R to side on *demi-pointe* (1), releasing L low L to side, repeat alternately front and behind:
Castanets: continuous rolls starting L, on the little digs.
Arms: 3rd R up L in front.

E
Step 7 times travelling to the R side across the room:

Dig L front, step R to side,	(6; 1),
Dig L back, step R to side,	(2, 3);
Dig L front, step R to side,	(4, 5),
Dig L back, step R to side,	(6; 1),
Dig L front, Step R to side,	(2, 3);
Dig L back, Step R to side,	(4, 5),

On 7th at back:

Step toe on L in front,   (6);
Step full on R foot on last one   (1), (both),
Punta y talon with L at side toe, heel,   (2, 3; 4, *5*), (– both; – both);
Point tip of L toe on floor, in to R instep, (6; 1), (–; both),
Destaque (*grand battement*) L,   (2, 3); (L, roll);
Pas de bourrée dig: (4, 5, 6); (L, roll, *choque*);
Step L behind, step on R, dig across with L.

Repeat starting step L, to side, (1), but ending on the second count of (5),
Hold   (6); (both); (arms 3rd, L up);
Punta y talon with R at side toe, heel,   (1, 2, 3; 4), (both, –, both; –),
Dig R across front   (5, 6); (both, –);

Vuelta fibraltada to the R, (both, L, roll; L, roll, both);
Swing R foot back (4), and step on L (5), into Panaderos as above.

Change of music and tempo:

Repeat Step 2: The repeat of the Panaderos section.
Castanets and arms as before.

Ending:
Panaderos section with *vuelta girada*:
Step on R, Lift L leg across body in *attitude*,   (6); (*choque*);
Step side on L, place R across turn to L,   (1, 2, 3); (both, L, roll);
Step L,   (4, 5), (L, roll),
Drop across R,   (6); (both); (arms 3rd L up);
Step on L with *coupé*   (1), (both).

Change of music and tempo: 2nd 'chorus'

Step 4a:
5 *rodazánes girando dos vueltas con derecho*
2 *vueltas fibraltadas* repeat with the other foot in the other direction:
Do: 5 *rodazánes* with R, turning twice to R, on place.

Arms: remain 3rd.
Castanets: 5 L rolls, one on each *rodazán*.

Ending:
Vuelta fibraltada to R,   (1, 2, 3; 4, 5, 6);
Castanets: (both, L, roll; roll, roll);

Vuelta fibraltada to R,   (1, 2, 3; 4, 5),
Castanets: (both, L, roll, roll, roll),
Chassé L across   (6); (*choque*);
Coupé under with R   (1), (both) to:

Repeat Step 4a, the *rodazánes* turning to L on R.

Ending in 5th on pointe	(6); (*choque*);
Dig L behind	(1), (both),

Step 4b on *demi-pointe*
Castanets: continuous rolls.
Step as before, but:
6 on R foot from *degagé* L stepping *front* only (not front back as before),
Arms: L arm circles inward across body for 6 counts.

Repeat on L foot, but turning on self until end of phrase.

Arms: L arm opens outwards and down from 5th, (1, 2, 3); then as the R arm comes down inward, dropping the elbow, the L simultaneously goes back to 5th retracing its circle but back and out and up to start an inward circle; for 6 counts; Turning on self to R, with the R arm staying down: the L completes the inward circle coming inward down the front with dropped elbow to join the R (1, 2, 3), and then both go up outwards to 5th for the next 3 counts.

Degagé L over to dig front on (6);

Repeat all to L but end on (5), and straight into:

Step 5a:
Coda.

Drop across on R,	(6);
Step on L *rodazán* R,	(1, 2, 3); (both, L, roll);
Pas de bourrée under with R,	(4, 5, 6); (both, L, roll);
Step on L *rodazán* R,	(1, 2, 3); (both, L, roll);
Vuelta normal to the R, up on pointe	(4, 5, 6); (both, L, roll);

Repeat 5A to dropping across on L.

Step 5b:
Arms: 5th, going down outward and up on *vuelta normal*.

Swish L out and *assemblé* L, behind in 4th,	(1, 2), (both, L),
Destaque L, to side	(3); (roll); (arms 5th),
Place L across and turn to R,	(4, 5, 6); arms down and up to 5th, (both, L, roll);

Repeat with R arms as above:

Swish R out and *assemblé* R, behind in 4th,	(1, 2),	(both, L),
Destaque R, to side	(3);	(roll);
Place R across and turn to L, arms down and up to 5th	(4, 5, 6);	(both, L, roll);

End position *croisé*:

Step forward on R to corner 2	(both),
L pointed behind	(castanets: *choque*, both).

The back exit from
the Pericet studio in
Seville.
Photo: Robert Harrold

Bibliography

ABC newspaper, music section, authors unknown, 13 November 1992.

Anderson, Ruth Matilde. "Costumes", The Hispanic Society of America, New York, 1957.

Barbieri, Francisco Asenjo. "Cancionero Musical", Madrid 1890.

Barbieri, Francisco Asenjo. Editor Emilio Casares Rodicio. *Documentos sobre musica española y epistolario*. Fundación Banco Exterior, Madrid 1988.

Beaumont, Cyril. *"Complete Book of Ballets"*, Putnam, London, 1949.

Beck, Hans. "Fra Livet og Dansen", H. Hirschprungs Forlag, Copenhagen 1944.

Blasis, Carlo. "The Code of Terpsichore. A Practical and Historical Treatise on the Ballet, Dancing and Pantomime." Translated R. Barton. James Bulcock, London 1828.

Blas Vega, José. "La Escuela Bolera", Historia de la Danza.

Blas Vega, José. "Temas Flamencos", Dante, Madrid 1973.

Authors relevant to this book mentioned in it: Serfín Ramirez "La Habana de otros tiempos", 1928; Vicente T. Mendoza, "La Cachucha", 1949; Serafín Ramirez, "La Habana de otros tiempos", 1928; "Colección de las Mejores coplas..." etc. of Don Preciso.

Blas Vega, José. "Los Cantantes de Sevilla". Editorio Cintero S.A., Madrid 1987.

Blas Vega, José. Rios Ruiz, Mañuel. "Diccionario Encyclopedico Illustrado del Flamenco", Editorial Cinterco, S.L. Madrid 1988

Bourio, Juan Maria, (*Colleccion de Juan Maria Byrio*), *Archivo de Baile Español*, Ayuntamiento de Madrid, Centro Cultural de la Villa, Madrid 1992.

Bonald, Caballero. "Andalusian Dances", Editorial Noguer, S.A. Barcelona 1959.

Bournonville, August. "Mit Theaterliv", C.A. Reissel Copenhagen, 1840.

Bournonville, August. "Raad og Leveregler" Fra en aeldre till en Yngre Vän, Knud Arne Jürgensen, Gyldendal, Denmark 1989.

Brunelleschi, Elsa. "Antonio and Spanish Dancing", Adam and Charles Black, London, 1958.

Cabo, Ana. "Centenario de Angel Pericet Giménez", from the magazine "Por La Danza" No. 36, April 1999, Asociación de Profesionales de la Danza en la Comunidad de Madrid, Consejeria de Educación y Cultura; y Ministerio de Educación y Cultura, Instituto Nacional de las Artes Escénicas y la Musica.

Capmany, Aurelio. *Un Siglo de Baile en Barcelona*. Ediciones Librería Milla, Barcelona, 1947.

Cairón, Antonio. "Compendio de las principales reglas del baile traducido del Francés por Antonio Cairón y aumentado de una explicación exacta y metodo de ejutar la mayor parte de los bailes conocidos en España, tanto antiguos como modernos, Imprenta Repullés, Madrid 1820.

Calderón, Serafín Estébanez. "Escenas Andaluzas", Madrid, 1847.

Canyamares, Ferran, i Josep Iglesias. "La Dansarina Roseta Mauri" (1850 - 1923), Ediciones Rosa de Reus, Reus 1971, Publicacion Num. 46, Volume I, and Publicacion Num. 47, Volume II. Biblioteca D'Autors Reucs I D'Obres D'Interes Local.

Chase, Gilbert. "The Music of Spain", W.W. Norton & Company, New York, 1941.

Christensen, Charlotte. "O! Pepita!", i Gulnares Hus, Copenhagen 1990.

Clarke, Mary and Vaughan, David. "The Encyclopedia of Dance and Ballet', Pitman Publishing Ltd., London 1977. ISBN 0 273 01088 3

Concorsi Gran Teatro del Liceo, "Gran Teatro del Liceu", L'Avenc S.A. Barcelona, 1990.

Crivillé i Bargalló, Josep. Historia de la musica española, no.7 El Folklore musical, Alianza Musica, Madrid 1983.

Davillier, Baron Charles. Doré, Gustave. *Viaje por España: Le Tour du Monde* 1862-1873, Ediciones Castilla, Madrid 1957.

Don Preciso (Juan Antonio de Iza Zamácola)."Collección de las Mejores Coplas de Seguidillas, Tiranas y Polos que se han compuesto Para Cantar a la Guitarra". Madrid 1802.

Durand-Viel, "La Sevillana, Datos Sobre el Folklore de la baja Andalucia". Biblioteca de Temas Sevillanos, Servicio de Publicaciones del Ayuntamiento de Sevilla. 1983.

Durbin, Paula. "Four Teachers of Spanish Dance: A Three Part Series. Part III, an Interview With Eloy Pericet." *Jaleo* magazine, January/February 1984.

Davillier, Baron Charles. Doré, Gustave. *Viaje por España: Le Tour du Monde* 1862-1873, Ediciones Castilla, Madrid 1957.

Encyclopaedia Britannica

Escribano, Antonio. *Y Madrid se Hizo Flamenco*. Avapies, Madrid 1990. ISBN 84-86280-43-5

Esquivel de Navarro, Ivan. *Discursos Sobre El Arte del Dançado*, Juan Gomez de Blas, Seville, 1642.

de Galmés, Antonio. "Bailes Populares Baleares".

Fernández de Rojas, Juan. (Pseudonym Francisco Augustín Florencio). *Crotologia o Ciencia de las Castañuelas*. Imprenta Real, Madrid 1792.

Gautier, Theophile. "Viaje por España". Taifa Literaria, Barcelona, 1985.

Gosalvez Lara, Carlos José. La Danza Cortesana En La Biblioteca Nacional. Imagen, S.A. Sebastián Gomez, 5. Madrid. ISBN 84-7483-467-8

Guest, Ivor. "Gautier on Dance", Dance Books, Cecil Court, London, 1986.

Guest, Ivor. "Gautier on Spanish Dancing", Dance Chronicle, 1987, Pages 1-104.

Hartley, Gasquoine. "Things Seen in Spain", Seeley, Service & Co. Ltd., London 1912.

Huertas, Eduardo. "Teatro Musical Español en El Madrid Illustrado" Editorial El Avapies, S.A., Mayor 1, 28013 Madrid 1989.

Inzenga, Jose. "Cantos Populares de España", Antonio Moreno, Madrid 1887.

Ivanova, Ana. "The Dancing Spaniards", John Baker (Publishers) Ltd,London 1970.

Jürgensen, Knud Arne. "The Bournonville Ballets" A photographic Record 1844-1933, Dance Books London 1987.

La Meri. "Spanish Dancing", Barnes and Company, New York 1948.

Llorens, Pilar. "Historia de la Danza en Cataluña", C.G. Creaciones Graficas, S.A. ISBN 84-85332-17-2

Minguet e Irol, Pablo. *Breve tratado de los pasos del danzar a la española*. Oficina del Autor, Madrid 1764.

Mariemma (Guillermina Martínez Cabrejas). "I. Mis caminos a través de la danza. II. Tratado de La Danza Española", Fundación Autor, Calle Bárbara de Braganza, 7, 28004, Madrid. ISBN: 84-8048-078-5

Marin, Rodriguez (editor). *Cervantes*. Espasa Calpe S.A. Madrid 1957.

Marti i Mora, Enric (and Maria Teresa Oller i Benloch). "Panorámica de la la musica y la Danza Tradicional Valenciana", Universidad Politécnica de Valencia, 1998.

Martínez de la Peña,Teresa. *Danzas Españolas*. Biennal de Arte Flamenco y Fundación Machado, Madrid 1988.

Matos, García. "Danzas Populares de España, Castilla La Nueva", Altamira Rotopresss S.A., Madrid 1957.

Matos, García. "Danzas Populares de España, Andalucia", Altamira Rotopress S.A., Madrid 1971.

Matteo. "Woods that Dance", Dance Perspectives 33, New York. Spring 1968.

Neiiendam, Robert. Lucile Grahn: "En Skaebne i Dansen". Copenhagen 1963.

Otero Aranda, José. "Tratados de Bailes", Seville 1912.

Overskau, Thomas. "Den Danske Skueplads". Thieles Bogtrykkerie, Copenhagen 1864.

Pérez, Mariano. "Diccionario de la Música y los Músicos", vols I, II and III. Ediciones Istmo, S.A. 2000. ISBN 84-7090-139-7 Obra completa.

Pericet, Angel. "En Defensa de la Escuela Bolera", "La Familia Pericet", Associación Cultural Por La Danza, Madrid 27-1-1998.

Preciso (Don), (Juan Antonio Iza Zamácola) *Colección de las mejores coplas de Seguidillas, Tiranas y Polos que se han compuesto para cantara la guitarra*. Fermin Villapando, Madrid 1805.

Puig Claramunt, Alfonso. *Ballet y Baile Español*. Montaner y Simon, S.A. Barcelona 1944.

Rice, Cyril. *Dancing in Spain*. British Continental Press, London 1931.

Rioja, Eusebio. "Julian Arcas o los Albores de la Guitarra Flamenca", Bienal de Arte Flamenco VI, El Toque, Ayuntamiento de Sevilla, Area de Cultura, Expo'92.

Rodrígues Calderón, Juan Jacinto. *La Bolerologia o Quadro de las Escuelas Bolero,*

Tales quales eran en 1794 y 1795 en La Corte de España. Zacarias Poulson, Philadelphia 1807.

Ruiz, E. M. and de Pazzio Picorales. *Carl Linneus and the Enlightened Science in Spain.* Communidad de Madrid, 1998. ISBN 84-930363-1-5

Sand, George (Baroness Aurore de Dudevant), Translated by Robert Graves. "Winter in Majorca, Cassell and Co. Ltd., London1956

Pericet Blanco, Angel. Article in "Por La Danza" magazine, 1998

Pohren, D.E. "The Art of Flamenco", The Society of Spanish Studies, Madrid 1962. ISBN 0-933334-38-9

Sackville-West, Vita. "Pepita", Hogarth Press, London 1937.

Seymour, Bruce. "Lola Montez, A Life", Yale University Press/New Haven and London, 1996.

Sor, Ferdinand. "Le Bolero" from the "Encyclopedie Pittoresque de la Musique", Paris 1835.

Suarez-Pájares, Javier. Carriera, Xoán M. Garafola, Lynn (editors). "The Origins of the Bolero School", Studies in Dance History, The Journal of the Society of Dance History Scholars, Vol. IV Number I Spring 1993.

Subirá, José. "Historia de la Música Teatral en España", Barcelona collección Labor, 1945

Udaeta, José de. "The Spanish Castanets", Ulrich Steiner Verlag, Overath bei Köln 1985. ISBN 84-7628-062-9

Udaeta, José de. "La Castañuela Española, Origen y Evolucion", Ediciones del Serbal, Barcelona 1989.

Wilson, G.B.L. "The Dictionary of Ballet", Adam & Charles Black, London 1974.

Authors from Encuentro Internacional: La Escuela Bolera, Ministerio de Cultura, Co-ordinator Roger Salas, Madrid November 1992.

Cañibano, Antonio Alvarez. La Compania de la Familia Lefebre en Sevilla.

Carrasco-Benítez, Marta, Las Academias de Baile en Sevilla, page 25.

del Val, Carme. Rosita Mauri, page 102.

Blas Vega, Jose. La Escuela Bolera y el Flamenco, page 79.

Oztet, Montse. Joan Magriña y la Escuela Bolera en el Gran Teatre Del Liceo page 109.

Hutchinson Guest, Ann. Notación de la Danza Española, page 109.

Guest, Ivor. La Escuela Bolera en Londres en el Siglo XlX page 139.

Suares Pájares, Javier. El Repertorio Bolero en la Primera Mitad del Siglo XlX, page 171 and El Bolero page 187.

Programa La Escuela Bolera y el Ballet Baile Nacional etc. page 263 onwards

Falkoff, Laura. An interview with Angel Pericet in an unnamed Argentinian newspaper.

Marti i Mora, Enric. Escuelas Boleras Valencianas Siglos XVII y XIX, Departamento de Cultura de lo Rat Penat.

Various programmes and printed matter from newspapers, magazines and manuscripts.

INDEX

All the places in the text where *Bolero* and *Escuela Bolera* are mentioned cannot be listed in this index, because the entire book deals with this subject. French terms for ballet steps are also to be found in the codified syllabus on pages 229-280.

Abanicos (fans), 146
Abanicos de Calaña, 34
Académie Royale de Musique, 127, 156
Acosta, Hazel, 62
Aficionado, 80, 214
Agatha, Saint (religious order), 63
Agostini, Alfio, 89
Agudo (Agudillo), 32
Aguilar, Rafael, 185, 196, 206, 207, 208
Aguinaldo, Didi, 185
Aida, xii
Aire, Al (*En l'air*), 93
Aire, a Mi, 205
Albaicín, 92,
Albaicín, El, 170, 171, 184, 203
Albal, 66
Albéniz, Isaac (1860-1909), 26, 175, 183, 184, 208, 209
Albéniz (Teatro), 198
Albert Hall, 187
Alberti, Rafael, 50
Alborada del Gracioso, 183, 186, 197, 208
Alcarez, Antonio, 176.
Aldeana, La, 155
Alegría Enhart Company, 167
Alegrías, xiii (sequence), 26, 58 , 111, 179, 199, 209
Alemán, Mateo (1547-1614?), 13
Alexander, Vicente, 50
Alexandria Opera House, 170
Alfonso the Wise of Castile (1253-1284): see Cantigas de Alfonso, 58, 134
Algamesi, 66
Alhambra Theatre, Leicester Square, 214
Alicante, 68
Allegro de Concierto, 204, 208
Almería, 88, 122
Almonte, 41
Alonso, Alicia (b. 1917), 186
Alonso, Antonio, 207
Alonso, Juanito, 134
Alonso, Maestro, 124, 134

Alosno (town in the province of Huelva), 20
Alpargatas, 69
Alvarez, Amparo (see La Campanera).
Alvarez Cañibano, Antonio, 122, 221
Alzira, 128
Amaya, Carmen, xiii, 65, 88, 192, 206
American Ballet Theatre, 184
Amor Brujo, El, 174, 195, 197, 207, 208
Amparo, Nila, xii
Anacrusic, 22
Andaluces delicias, 121
Andalusia(n), 32, 34, 40, 58, 65, 66, 89, 109, 98, 121, 122, 134, 136, 140, 142, 143, 145, 146, 151, 156, 171, 205
Andersen, Hans Christian, 101
Andersen, John, 104
Anderson, Ruth Matilde, 68
Andorra, 179
Andrés, Elvira, 205.
Angiolini, Fortunata, 212 (relation Gasparo Angiolini, Pr. Ballerina Vienna)
Anguito, Serrano (dramatist), 142
Anta, Font de, 167
Antar, 209
Antibolerologia, 111
Antilles, 99
Antología de la Zarzuela, 180, 190
Antón, Conchita, 193,
Antonia Mercé y Luque), see Argentina, La
Antonio (Ruiz Soler 1921-1996), 52, 53, 59, 88, 167, *173*, 174, 181, 186, 204, 205, 207, 208, 214
Arab-Andalusian, 64, 68, 82
Arabesque, 159
Aracena, Carmen, 193
Aragon, 67, 190
Aragonese *Jota*, 8, 67, 190
Aragon, Rocio, 128
Aranda, Count de, 48
Aranda, Luisa, 61, 186
Arbeau, Thoinot (Jehan Tabourot, Canon of Langres), 39

Arcas, Maestro Julián (1832-1878), guitarist, 58, 133, 134
Archduke Carlos of Austria, 222
Arco de Cuchilleros, El, 187
Argentina, Antonia Mercé y Luque, La (1896-1936), 55, *175*, 177, 181, 196, 205, 214
Argentina (country), 27, 34, 107, 166, 167, 168, 169, 170, 172, 182, 193, 199
Argentina, Imperio (company), 170
Argentinita, La, (Encarnación López Julvez, 1895-1945), 50, 59, *175*, 206, 214
Argia, xv
Argüelles, Arantxa, 168, 176
Arista, A.S. (music book Colección de Bailes Populares), 129
Asociación de Coros y Danzas de, 167, 174, 180, 182, 198
Asociación de Coros y Danzas Francisco de Goya, 131
Asociación de Profesionales de la Danza de la Comunidad de Madrid, 198
Asturia(s), 65, 208
Atabalillos, 51
Aubert, Daniel François (composer, 1782-1871), 61, 107
Audeoud, Susana (b. 1919, see Susana y José), 203, 204
Australia, 192, 203, 210
Austria(n), 55, 91, 156, 203, 156
Autos Sacramentales (auto: a judicial decree), 49
Ávila, 32
Ávila, Lola, 180
Ávila, Maria de (b.1920), 159, 160, 169, *176*, 177, 182, 186, 191, 193, 196 200, 205, 207
Azagra, J. Ruiz, 193
Azorín Ibañez, Pedro, 180, 186, 190, 196, 197, 209
Azucarillo, 150

Badillo, Antonio, 134
Baética, 121
Bailadora/o, (Bailaor/a), 112
Bailarin/a, 112
Baile, 112
Baile antiguo, xiii
Baile de la Rosca, 32
Baile del Picador, xii
Baile de Luis Alonso, El, 121, 128 (illustration), 200, 219; colour plate 38
Baile de Pollo, 32
Baile de Torrent, 66
Baile Inglés, 162
Bailes de la Pradera, 82
Bailes del Candil, xii, 32, 81, 147; colour plate, 6
Balanchine, George (1904-1983), 191
Balearic Isles (Baleares), 63, 69-73, 79, 86
Balets de Barcelona, 194
Ballerina, The, (film), 186
Ballet Antología de Zarzuela, 180
Ballet de Barcelona, 177
Ballet de Festivales, 200
Ballet de Madrid, 182, 186, 206
Ballet de Mariemma, 194
Ballet de Murcia, 184, 205
Ballet de Wallonie, 195
Ballet Español de Madrid, 182, 184, 191, 197
Ballet Español de Pilar López, 188
Ballet Folkloric de Esbart Dansaire de Rubí, Barcelona, 179
Ballet Folklórico Español, 180
Ballet Nacional de España, 61, 153, 157, 159, 160, 168, 169, 171, 176, 177. 180, 181, 183, 185, 186, 189, 193, 194, 196, 197, 200, 201, 204, 205-209
Ballet Nacional de España (Lírico) - classical company, 59, 157, 177, 183, 190, 191, 207, 208
Ballet Nacional Español, 177, 189, 192, 195, 207
Ballet Nacional Festivales de España, 190
Ballet of Bulgaria, 200
Ballets de Barcelona, 194
Ballet Sihouetas, 186
Ballets Russes de Monte Carlo, 184
Ballet Vasco, 195
Ballonnée, 7
Ball Pla, 156
Ball Rodó, 156

Balls de Dolçaina, 74
Bandera, José Maria, 209
Bandurria, 21, 22, 32, 34, 70
Bangkok, 210
Baras, Sara, 59
Baratillo, Fernandillo el del, 124
Barberillo de Lavapies, El, 205
Barbier de Seville, 211
Barbieri, Francisco Asenjo (1823-1894), 56
Barbieri, Margaret, 168
Barcelona, xv, 12, 56, 69, 77, 85, 88, 121, 122, 126, 127, 138, 155, 156, 171, 174, 176, 178, 179, 189, 196, 202, 203, 221
Barrera, Manuel, 122, 161
Barrera, Miguel, 122, 161
Barrez, M., 107
Barrios, altos and *bajos*, 143
Bas, Daniel, 201
Baselga, Ana, 180
Bashkar Indian Dance Company, 184
Basílico de Mazencio, 192
Basque, xvi, 8, 9, 49, 78, 89, 110
Basque *Gabota*, 9
Bata de cola, xiii, 126, 178
Batararaña (see also matalaraña), 7, 8, 9, 38, 39, 114
Batterie (beats of the legs), 49, 79, 211
Bautista, Antonio, 176
Bayadères, 146
BBC, 66, 170
Beaumont, Cyril (b.1891, ballet historian, bookseller), 92, 94, 95, 98
Becker, Mavis (Marina Lorca, b.1940), 136, 209
Beck, Hans (1861-1952), 96, 104, 107
Bedells, Phyllis, 187
Beecham, Sir Thomas (1879-1960), 53
Béjart, Maurice (b. 1927), 201
Belgian Congo, 142
Belgium, 173
Bella Española, La, 131
Bella, Maria la, 214
Belles Artes Theatre, Mexico, 170
Bellini, Vincenzo (1801-1835), 222
Benamor, 205
Benavente, Quiñones de (1866-1954, author), 13, 193
Benguerel, Xavier (b.1931, composer), 201
Beniowsky, 98
Benois, Alexandre (1870-1960, Russian artist, designer for Diaghilev), 59

Berber, 58
Berlin, 189, 203
Berlin Scala, 189
Bern, 203
Biennale, 197
Bien parado, 19, 30, 43, 80, 117, 132
Bilbao, Antonio, El de (Antonio Vidal, 19th to early 20th century), 175, 198, 199, 203, 205, 214
Bishop of Orihuela, 49, 68
Bizet, Georges (1838-1875, composer), 26, 61, 208
Blacher, Deanna, 209
Blanco, Amparo, 167, 170, 171, 172
Blasis, Carlo (1795-1878), 6, 9, 89, 93
Blas Vega, José (b. 1942, author and bibliophile), 34, 45, 48, 78, 88, 134, 140, 142, 144, 168, 175, 187, 188, 202
Blood Wedding (Bodas de Sangre), 180, 207
Boccherini, Luigi (1743-1805, composer), 207
Boda de Luis Alonso, La, 121, 190, 219; colour plate 38
Bodas de Sangre, 208
Boigne, Charles de, 92
Bolera, La, 45, 47, 109
Boleras Amanchegadas, 86
Boleras a Ocho, 85, 156
Boleras Acuchadas, 86
Boleras de Cádiz, Las, 100, 213
Boleras de la Cachucha, 6, 9, 19, 49, 50, 78, 79, 86, 93, 97, 102, 129, 130, 131, 132, 133, 145; notation, 301
Boleras de la Charandel, 86
Boleras de la Madrileña, 86
Boleras de la Marica, 86
Boleras de la Matraca, 86
Boleras del Chocolate, 86
Boleras del Escondite, 87
Boleras del Tripoli (Tripili?), 212
Boleras de Madrid, Las, 85
Boleras de Medio Paso, 50, 79, 102, 131, 133, 165, notation 308
Boleras Jaleadas, 9, 85, 86
Boleras Orgia, 87
Boleras Sereni, 87
Boleras Tinta, 87
Boleras, various named by Alfonso Puig, 70, 85
Boleres antigues, 70
Bolero, 12, 14, 18, 19, 27, 30, 34, 40, 43, 45-62, 66 (Valencian), 69, 77 on-

wards, 106, 71 (Mallorcan), 74, 79, 85 (various named by Alfonso Puig), 153, 156, 183 (Ravel), 186, 197, 200, 208, 212, 217; colour plate 29

Bolero, comments by Caballero Bonald, 86

Bolero, foreign composers, 61

Bolero Antiguo, 82

Bolero à Quatre, 101, 102, 103, 106

Bolero Cachucha, 213

Bolero Carlos III, 86, 133

Bolero, Chocolate, 86

Bolero con Adagio, 85

Bolero con Cachucha, 84, 189

Bolero con Seguidillas, notation 283

Bolero de Algodre, 45, 63; colour plate 12

Bolero de Caspe, 46, 63, notation 297

Bolero de Castellón, 66, 68 (Castellón de la Plana)

Bolero de Fray de Luis León, 85

Bolero de L'Alcudia de Carlet, 9, 45, 64, 66, 68, 69, 179, 180, 203; colour plates 1, 14, 15

Bolero de la Caleta, 85

Bolero de la Civila, 85

Bolero de la Fragua del Vulcano, 85

Bolero de la Paloma, 70

Bolero de la Pradera, 82

Bolero de la Solitario, 85

Bolero del Canallita, 85

Bolero del Candil, 81, 84, 86; notation, 288

Bolero del Capricho, 85

Bolero del Confitera, 85

Bolero del Currito, 85

Bolero de los Bandos, 85

Bolero de los Canarios del Café, 85

Bolero de los Confitera, 85

Bolero de los Fanfarrones, 85

Bolero del Soledad, 85

Bolero del Zorongo, 85

Bolero de Madrid, 85

Bolero de Medio Paso, 49, 79, 84, 133, 189

Bolero de Pot Pourri, 85

Bolero de Sant Pere, (Pere, the Catalonian for Pedro) 70

Bolero de Sequeros, 32

Bolero de Torrent, 66, 179

Bolero de Torrente, 66

Bolero de Tres, 82

Bolero de Valldemosa, Parado, 71

Bolero, El, 45, 47, 76 (ill.), 109

Bolero Extranjero, 85

Bolero, Gallegada y, 66

Bolero in Algeciras, 64

Bolero in Seville, 34

Bolero Jaleadas de Madrid, 85

Bolero Jarabe, 85

Bolero Jarabe Americano, 85.

Bolero, Le, 45

Bolero Liso, xii, 9, 65, 69, 84, 87, 129, 189

Bolero Mallorquin, 63, 84, 133

Bolero of Liberty, 86

Bolero Piache, 85

Bolero Pla, 65

Bolero Robao (*Robado*), 82, 84, 85, 86, 156

Boleros Robados y Liso, 86, 97, 133, 156

Bolero Seco, 85, 86

Bolero, Smuggler's, 85

Boleros Nuevos, 69,

Bolero Toni Moreno, 70

Bolero, Valencian, 65

Boliche, Antonio, 112

Bolshoi Theatre, 95

Bonald, Caballero, 32, 86

Bonnat, Joseph-Leontin (artist, 1833-1922), 155

Borchsenius, Valborg (1872-1949), 96

Bordoneo, 8, 49, 107

Boronat, Teresina, 127

Borrull, Trini, 136, *177*, 178, 178, 194

Bosch, Aurora, 180, 196

Botella, Luis, 84, 146

Botkine, Vassili, 97

Bourbon, 86, 217, 218, 222

Bourbon monarchs, 217, 218, 222

Bournonville, August (1805-1879), 3, 7, 31, 35, 81, 86, 89, 90, 91, 94, 96, 98, 100-108, 110, 137, 137, 145, 154, 157, 158, 168, 169, 203

Bournonville, Helena (wife of August), 105

Braceo, xiii

Brandes, Edvard (writer, 1847-1931), 106

Brazil, 199

Brenaa, Hans (b.1910), 104, 145

Brenes, Juanito, 140

Breytenbach, Enrique (artist), 15, 17, 36

Brisé volé, 9, 49

Britain, Great, 207, 210

Brudfaerden i Hardanger, 101

Brunelleschi, Elsa (1908-1989), 3, 122, 187

Buenos Aires, 53, 107, 122, 166-171, 175, 184, 186, 199

Buen Retiro Court Theatre and Palace, 217, 218

Bugle, 75

Bulerias, 25, 58, 140, 145, 208

Burgos (a *Seguidillas* from), 32

Cabales, Los, 189

Caballé, Montserrat (soprano, b. 1933), 203, 204

Caballito Jaleada, 99

Cabriole, 8

Cáceres (singer), 154

Cáchuas, 27

Cachucha, 6, 8, 52, 55, 79, 82, 89, 90, 91, 92, 93, 93, 95, 97, 98, 102, 107, 132, 145, 150, 151, 154, 156, 157, 159, 168, 170, 212, 213, 319

Cachucha, Boleras de la, see *Boleras de la Cachucha*, notation 301

Cachucha, Bolero con, 84, 189

Cachucha de Mi Madre, La, 97, (see p. 96, same steps as in the Bournonville *Konservatoriet Cachucha*)

Cachucha, Double, 97, 98, 213

Cádiz, 12, 41, 42, 58, 77, 83, 88, 92, 111, 112, 114, 121, 136, 150, 180

Café Burrero, 134

Café Cantante (Cafes Cantantes), 87, 134, 165; colour plate (Zorn), 25

Café Concierto de Novedades, 88, 162

Café de Chinitas, 198

Café de Recreo, 88

Café El Teatro Suizo, 162

Café Silverio, 134

Cairón, Antonio, 30, 50, 81

Caja, 75

Calado, Alicia, 179

Calderón de la Barca, Pedro (1600-1681, the great dramatist and poet), 219

Caliphate of Córdoba, 151

Callipyge, Venus, 121

Calvo Sotelo, Joaquín, 193

Camacho, Pietro, 58

Cámara, Petra, 134, 153, 214; colour plate 36

Camargo, Marie (French ballet dancer, 1710-1770), 49

Camarón de la Isla, El, (cantaor b. 1950) 43

Cambré, 7, 80

Camino sin Retorno, 197

Campanela, 51

Campanera, La (19th century dancer, Amparo Alvarez), 12, 21, 49, 84, 87, 93, 122, 140, 146, 153, 161, 162

Campanero, El, 87

Campanillas, 16

Campo, Conchita del, 114

Camprubí, Juan (b. 1825), 126, 153, 156

Camprubí, Mariano (19th century *bolero*, partner of Serral), 11, 35, 53, 86, 89, 90, 91, 93, 101, 110, 126, 153, 156, 212; colour plate 23 and 26

Caña, 58

Canada, 171, 195, 199, 204

Cañada, Dámaso (composer), 81

Canario, 58, 111, 218

Canciones Españolas Antiguas, 40

Cándida, La, 134

Candil, 32, 80, 81

Cañete, José, 127

Cañibano, Antonio Alvarez (see Alvarez Cañibano), 122, 221

Canigó, 201

Cano Conquero, Consolación (Chelo), 15

Caños del Peral, Los (Theatre), 217

Cansino, Maestro, 164

Cante antiguo, xiii

Cante Jondo, Poema de, 53

Cantero, Carmen, 15

Cantigas de Alfonso el Sabio, Las, (Alfonso the Wise), 58, 134

Cap del Ball, *El*, colour plate 21

Cape Town, 209; illustrations: 60 and 62 *Bolero*, 133 *Boleras*, 136 *Olé*

Capitana, La (1913-1963; see Carmen Amaya), 88

Capmany, Aurelio (Catalan writer), 201

Capricho de Goya Nr 75, 203

Capricho Español, 195

Caracol, Manolo (1909-1973, Manuel Ortega Juárez, *cantaor*), 202

Caracoles, 50, 111, 131, 209

Caracoles, Los, 129

Caracolillo (Federico Casado Algrenti, b.1932), 191

Caragol, 69

Caraguells, 69

Carbonell, Arcadio, 192

Careo, 40

Careo del beso 39, 38 illustration

Caridad Theatre (Malaga), 217

Cariñosa, La, 185

Carlet, 66

Carlist War, First, 212

Carlos, Grand Archduke of Austria, 222

Carmen, 26, 186, 195, 203, 214

Carmen la Cigarrera, 135

Carmen on Ice, 199

Carnegie Hall, New York, 170, 199, 204

Carnestoltes, 201

Carpentier, Alejo, 99

Carpio, Adoració_, 209

Carpio, Roberto, 189

Carrasco Benítez, Marta, 87, 164, 165

Carrasco Salazar, Manuela (b. 1958), 43, 206

Carretilla (roll), 47, 54

Carthaginians, 68, 121

Casada Infiel, La, 208

Casa de Bernarda Alba, La, 185

Casa de España, 196

Casa de los Artistas, 163

Casas, Manuel, 153

Cascabeles, 16

Casetas, 40

Casonobas, 214,

Castanets, 47, 53, 54, 55, 60, 71

Castelau, Julia, 178

Castellana (in the *Alegrías*), xiii

Castellanas (*Seguidillas* in Castile), 32,

Castellana, La, 89

Castellón de la Plana, 68

Castellterçol, 179

Castile, 22, 32, 65, 66 (Castillians), 73

Castilla, 180, 209

Castilla de Sotarribas, 203

Castilla la Nueva (New Castile), 13, 14, 205

Castilla la Vieja (old Castile), 34, 205

Castilliana Bolero, 213

Castillo, Antonio (Cuquito de Barbate 1906-1976, singer), 176

Castizo, xi

Catalan/Catalonia, 65, 68, 73, 74, 89, 126, 127, 156, 180, 201, 204; colour plates 19 and 20;

Catalan-Valencian-Balearic-Romance, 68

Catalonian orchestra (cobla), 74, 154

Catholic Church, 49, 143

Cazuela, 79, 149, 150 illustration, 221

Cecchetti, Enrico, 3, 6, 7, 31, 80, 81, 110, 176

Celestina, La, 203

Celtic, 58

Centaura, La, 203

Centro Cultural, Barcelona, 171

Cerezo, Sebastián, 112

Cerrito, Fanny (1817-1909), 91, 98, 99, 100, 143, 144, 213

Cervantes Saavedra, Miguel de (1547-1616, author of Don Quijote), 13, 136

Chacón García, (Don) Antonio (1869-1929, *cantaor*), 187

Chacona, 14, 57, 151, 205, 209

Chambergas, 32

Chang, Lienz, 168

Chapines, 111, 129, 131, 134, 138, 142, 144

Charles II (Habsburg monarch, 1665-1700), 218, 222

Charles III, (Bourbon monarch, 1759-1788) 112, 222

Charrada(s) (Salamanca), 32, 190

Chase, Gilbert, 26, 61, 62

Chavalillos Sevillanos, Los, see Rosario and Antonio. 53, 88, *173*, 174, 214

Chile, 27, 34, 99, 169, 199

Chinchilla, Lázaro, 112

Chirimias (xeremies), 70

Chivo, El, 140

Chopin, Frédéric (1810-1849), 71, 73

Choreographers of Ravel's Bolero, 59

Christensen, Charlotte (Danish critic and writer), 100, 106, 144

Christmas Carol in Gerona, 56

Cid, Le (El), 68, 127

Cielo Protector, El, 197

Cigarrera, Carmen La (Associated with Olé Antiguo), 135

Cinta, La, 32

Circulo de Bellas Artes, 173, 200, 202

Ciro, Diez Handino, 181, 196, 197

Ciudad Real, 15, 17, 32, 34

Cizico, Eudoxio de (Eudoxus of Cyzicus), 121

Clarke, Mary (writer, critic, editor of The Dancing Times, London), 205

Classical composers (of *Seguidilla*), 26

Clave Flamenca, En, 180

Cobla, 75

Cohen, Ziva, 179; colour plate (*Mortitxol*), 3

Cojo, Enrique el (Enrique Jiménez Mendoza), 5

Cola, xiv (see also *bata de cola*)

Coliseo del Buen Retiro, 217, 218

Coliseo, Pepe el del, 140

Cologne, 203

Coloquio Internacional, "La Danza y Lo Sagrado" of UNESCO, 196

Compañas de Españolas de Ballet, 177

Compañía Andaluza de Danza, 187

Compañía de Antonio Márquez, 196

Compañía Folías, 191

Compañía Nacional de Teatro Clásico, 170

Compás(es), 10, 18, 19, 25, 26, 58, 134

Composers used by La Argentina, 175

Compte Arnau, El, 201

Concierto de Aranjuez, 188, 208

Concierto de Málaga, 209

Concierto para Clavinchenvallo, 200

Confidencen (Court Theatre at Ulriksdal Palace in Sweden), 217

Con Mi Soledad, 186, 209

Conmee, Ivy, 209

Conseille Internationale de la Danse, 188, 195

Conservatorio Dramático y Danza (Córdoba), 178

Conservatorium of Madrid, 167, 180, 190

Contemporary Ballet Theatre, 184

Contrabajo (three-stringed double bass), 75

Contretemps, 7

Copenhagen, 3, 35, 85, 90, 100-108, 137, 145, 157

Copla, 15, 16, 17, 19, 31, 32, 36, 37; referred to as verses: 39-43

Coral, Matilde, (Matilde Corrales Gonzalez, b. 1935), 6, 43, 126, 178

Coral, Pepa, 179

Coralli Peracini, Jean (1779-1854), 92

Córdoba (the city), 20, 58, 88, 122, 151, 203

Córdoba, Rafael de, 180

Cordobés, 40

Cornamusa, 70

Coronado, Jaime, 179; colour plate, 3

Coronas, Elvira, 153

Coronas, Maestro Carlos Perez Carillo, a Bailarín Bolero, 127, 153

Coros y Danzas, see Asociación de Coros y Danzas ...

Coros y Danzas de Madrid, 14, 142, 182; colour plate, 22

Corpus Christi, 14, 56

Corral (Corrales), 21, 151

Corral de la Cruz, 220

Corral de los Caños del Peral, 21, 77

Corral del Principe, Theatre, 21, 150, 220

Corral de Val Hubert and Olivera, 21

Corraleras, 21, 147, 153; de Sevilla, 212

Corraleros de Sevilla, 212

Cortés, Joaquín, 59, 96, 181, 207

Cosas de Payos, 187

Costumes of Murcia, The, 214

Coulon, Jean-François (ballet teacher 1764-1836), 8

Council of Castile, 221

Covent Garden, 21, 203, 212

Cristo Luz del Mundo, 192

Crivillé y Bargalló, Josep, 32

Crotalo, 53, 121; see also colour plate, 31

Cruz, Ramón de la (libettist of Zarzuelas, 1791-1794), 77, 219

Cruz (theatre in Madrid), 21, 217

Cruzados, 222

Cuadro, 50, 52

Cuadro Bolero, 52, 53, 88

Cuadro de Baile, 163

Cuadro Flamenco, 50, 52

Cuba, 45, 62, 99, 169, 180, 199

Cuban National Ballet, 186

Cubeles, Manuel, 74

Cuenca, 13, 32

Cuenca, La (Manuela García), 127, 134, 153, 156

Cuentos del Guadalquivir, 208, 183

Cuevas, Marquis de, 201

Cullberg Ballet, 177

Cultural del Ballet (Associación), 194

Cuna, 8

Curillo, 209

Curra, La, (associated with Olé de la Curra) 135

Currataco (showy, loud), 48

Cyprus, 210

Dama de Elche (Elx), 69

Dancing Master, The, 5

Dancing Times, 89, 205

Danish Ballet, Royal, 95

Dantes, Theo, 209

Danza Académica, 176

Danza, 112

Danza Castellana y Jota , 106

Danza de los Ojos Verdes, 185

Danza de Velatorio (Mourners' Dance, titled Mortitxol), 9-10, 66, 201; Doré (illustration), 4 and colour plate No.3)

Danza IX, 182, 185, 205, 209

Danza Española, 177

Danza Lorca, 62

Danza Prima (Asturias), 13

Danzas Cortesanas Francesas del Siglo XVII, 170

Danzas d'Artesa de Leida, 201

Danzas del Codice (Libro Vermell de Montserrat), 201

Danzas habladas, 217

Danzas Tortosinas, 74

Danza y lo sagrado, 196

Danza y Tronio, 169, 181, 182, 196, 207, 208

Davillier, Baron Jean-Charles, 9, 34, 43, 67, 84, 85, 136, 146, 162, 164

Dégagé, 7

Dégas, Hilaire-Germain Edgar (1834-1917), 156

Del Campo, Conchita, 114

Delibes, Léo (1836-1891), 61

Del Peral, Marqués, 77

Del Tres, 36

Del Medio, 36

Del U, 66

Del Uno, 36

Denmark, 3, 81, 168

Des Colores, 99

Deshayes, André Jean-Jacques (1777-1846), 98

Desplante, 66, 90, 140

Destaque, 7, 9

Destrucción de Sagunto, La, 190

Développé, 9

Devil on Two Sticks, The, 98

Devine, Henri, 156

Diable Boîteux, Le, 92, 94, 98, 150

Diablo Cojuelo, 200

Diálogo del Amargo, 184

Diaz, Rosita, 92

Diaz, Marcos, 134

Diaz de Quijano, Maximo, 198

Diccionario Enciclopedico Ilustrado del Flamenco, 174, 179, 188

Didelot, Charles-Louis (1767-1837), 49, 211

Diego, Emilio de (b.1942, guitarist/composer), 186, 207, 208

Diez Melodias Vascas, 208

Dimitri, 197

Diputación de Barcelona (Generalitat de Barcelona), 202

Directors of the Ballet Nacional de España, 190

Disfressades, 179

Ditlevsen, Grete, 103

Divínas de Pisa, Las, 185

Dolçaina, 74

Dolin, Anton (1904-1983), 59

Domingo, Adelita, 178

Domingo, Placido, 197

Dominique, Madame, 155

Doña Francisquita, 172, 180, 182, 190, 208

Don Giovanni, 183

Don Juan, 100, 180, 186, 207, 209

Don Preciso (Juan Antonio de Iza Zamácola o Ozerin), 18, 43, 112, 143

Don Quixote ved Camacho's Bryllup, 101

Doré, Gustave, 10, 49, 67, 87, 91, 117, 131, 138, 146, 162

Drottningholm (Theatre and Palace in Sweden), 217, 218

Duato, Nacho, 59

Dubinon, Manuela, 90, 93, 100, 126, 153, 212; colour plate 35

Duc d'Anjou, 218

Duchess d'Aulnoy, 218

Duende y Misterio del Flamenco, 173, 188, 189, 202

Duisberg, xii, 189

Dumas, Alexandre, 138

Dupont, Alexis, 100, 134, 149

Durand-Viel, Ana Maria, 37

Durban, 209

Durbin, Paula, 81, 179; colour plate 3

Durcal, Rocío, 190, 204

Double bass, 75

Duke of Parma, 86

Durán, Rosa (Rosita, b. 1922), 142, 206

Durón, Sebastian, 218

Duvernay, Pauline (1813-1894), 97, 98, 100

Echappé, 49

Echos d'Espagne, 61

Edinburgh, 20

Edo, Mariquita, 153

Egypt, 64

El Cap del Ball, 74; colour plate 21

"El Cojo" (Enrique Jiménez, 1912-85), 190, 202

Elias, Lourdes; 179; colour plates 3 and 20

Elizabeth II — See Queen Elizabeth II

El Jaleo, 184

El Punxonet, 74

Elssler, Fanny, 6, 55, 86, 91-98, 134, 137, 151, 154, 156, 212, 213; colour plate 27

Emboîture, 39

Embotadas, 39, 51

En Clave Flamenca, 180

Encuentro Escuela Bolera, (1992), 68, 158, 168, 171, 203,

England, 8, 192

Enric Majó company, 201

En L'Air, 93

Entrechat, 80, 86

Entrechat cinque, 9, 49

Entrechat six, 9

Entremeses, 151

Épaulement, 6

Esbart Dansaire de Rubí, Ballet Folkloric (Barcelona), xv, 9, 65, 66, 68, 69, 74, 179, 201, 203

Esbart Infantíl, 179

Esbart de San Cugat, 74

Esbart Santa Anna of Andorra, 179, 203

Esbart Verdaguer, 74, 179, 201

Escarramán, 14

Escobilla, xiii, 7

Escudero Award of Valladolid, Vicente, 173, 195

Escudero Uribe, Vicente (1885-1980), 175, 176, 205 (not the Escudero mentioned on p. 154 of 1838)

Escuela Bolera Andaluza 65, 111

Escuela Bolera (Classical school of Spanish dancing), 109, 129, 161, codified exercises of syllabus 225, codified dances 301-395

Escuela de Arte Dramático y Danza in Madrid, 195, 200

Escuela de Actividades Artisticas, Relatores, 199

Escuela de Coros y Danzas, 182

Esgarra (Engama), Rudolfo, 115

Esmeralda, Merche, 43, 180, 196, 197, 207

Espada, Jiminez de, 27

Espardenyes, 69

Espartero (a *Seguidillas*), 32

Esparza, Maria, 182

Espinosa, La Isabel, 134

Esplá y Triay, Oscar (1886-1976), 175

Espriu, Salvador, 201

Esquivel de Navarro, Ivan de, 5, 114, steps from 1642 noted: 114, 121

Estamos Solo, 197

Estampas del Siglo XIX, 200

Estampas Flamencas, 208

Estampío, El (Juan Sánchez Valencia y Rendón Ávila, 1879-1957), xii, 189, 202

Estébanez Calderón, Serafín (1799-1867), 78, 112, 122

Estrada, Padre Gregori, 201

Estrellas, 36

Estribillo, 16, 22, 30, 31, 32, 36, 37, 39, 40, 43, 69

Estudio de Danza Académica, 176

Eterna Castilla, 181

Eudoxio de Cizico (Eudoxus of Cyzicus, Greek navigator, Phrygia, 2nd century BC), 121

Extremadura, 205

Eyrol Minguet, Pablo, (see Minguet), 29

Fabianos, 155

Fabiani, Antonio, 156

Faíco, El (Francisco Mendoza Ríos, d. 1938), 65

Falla, Manuel de (1876-1846), 175, 198, 200, 208, 209

Falseta, xiii

Fan, 146

Fandango(s), 18, 27, 31, 34, 35, 58, 66, 71, 99, 106, 126, 144, 147, 156, 195, 208, 217; colour plate 9

Fandango Antiguo, 14, 82

Fandango de Hortunas, 11

Fandango de Soler, 209

Fandango del Candil, 14; costuming: colour plate 6

Fandangos de Huelva, 21, 31

Fandangos de Verdiales, 13, 30

Fantasía Galaica, 174, 186, 208

Far from Denmark, 35

Faraona, 206

Farnese, Isabel (Elizabeth), 5, 110, 218

Farinelli, 218

Farruca, 124, 159, 208

Farruca (Frasquillo famous for his), 199

Farruca Torero, 176

Farruco, El, (Antonio Montoya, 1936-1998), 178, 206

Farruquita, La, 206

Fenice, La (Theatre in Venice), 185

Ferdinand VI, 217, 218

Feria, 20, 40, 42; colour plate 30

Feria de Sevilla, La, 155; colour plate 30;

Fernández, Luisa, 88, 162

Fernández, Paco, 180, 181, 190
Festival de Mérida, 184
Festivales De España, Ballet Nacional de, 190
Feuillet, Raoul Auger (1675-1710), 54, 55
Fiestas de Madrid de la Pradera de San Isidro (Madrid's Patron Saint), 82
Fin de fiesta, 53
Fiorella, 107
Fiscorno (keyless cornet or bugle), 75
Fitzjames, Louise, 99, 100
Fitzjames, Nathalie, 100
Flamenco form, 22
Flaviol (flabiol), 75
Flindt, Flemming (b.1936), 106, 107, 203
Flor de Maravilla, La, 111, 155, 165
Florencio, Francisco Augustín (Juan Fernandez de Rojas), 53
Flores, Lola, xiii, 43, 204
Folía(s), 26, 111
Folie d'Espagne (pour une Dame), 54,
Folies d'Espagne Les, 211
Folklore Hidalguía (Casa de Castilla la Mancha), 182
Fondu, 114,
Font, Francisco, 90, 93, 126, 154, 212; colour plate 35
Font, Marta, 203
Fontalba Theatre, 173
Fonteyn, Dame Margot (Peggy Hookham, 1919-1991), 66, 97, 179, 201, 203
Foreigner from Santiago, 196
Fosas, Joan (b.1938), xv, 66, 68, 69, 74, *179*, 203; colour plate 1
France, 8, 89, 91, 127, 146, 156, 168, 181, 208, 218
Fracci, Carla (b.1936), 186
Francisco de Goya, Grupo, 131, 142, 182
Franco, General Francisco, 206
Frasquillo (Francisco León, 1898-1940), 124, 173, 187, 198, 199, 206
French, 49, 87, 122, 151, 200, 212, 214, 221
Fuensanta, Maria, 214
Fuentes, Luis, 180

Gabota, Basque, 9
Gades, Antonio (dancer, choreographer), 124, 135, 183, 184, 186, 189, 197, 200, 205, 206, 207, 208

Gadir, 121, 136
"Gaditano", 112
Gail, Wilhelm, 64
Gaita, 21
Galán, Carlos, 126
Galia, Adrián, 180
Galiano, Victor (maker of castanets), 56
Galician Gallegada, 66, 154
Gallardo, Maribel, 57, 168, *180*, 196, 207
Gallardo, Pepe, 153
Gallegada y Bolero, 66
Galmés, Antonio de, 69
Galop de Cortesia, 201
García Abril, Antón (Composer, b.1933), 183, 196, 207, 208
García Asensio, Enrique (conductor, b.1937), 169, 207
García Caffi, Juan José, 168
García, Felix, 152 (illustration)
García Lorca, Federico (1898-1936), 40, 50, 53, 142, 175, 206
García Matos, Manuel (1912-1974), 15, 16-21, 32, 34, 36, 77, 134
García, Manuela (La Cuenca), 127, 134, 153, 156
Gardner, Ava, 190
Garrotín, El, 65, 124
Gautier, Théophile (1811-1872), 90, 91, 94, 95, 98, 100, 124, 144, 149, 150, 153, 154, 156
Gavotte, Vestris (Gaetano Vestris, 1729-1808), 9, 10
"Generation of 1927", 50
George Washington University, 196
Germany, 87, 108, 127, 156, 189, 203, 204
Gide, Casimir, 92
Gilbert, Eliza — see Montez, Lola
Giménez, Jerónimo, 121, 219
Gipó, 73
Giselle, 98
Gitana, La, 95, 100; colour plate 28
Gitanas, 32, 92
Gitanes del Vallès, Les, 65, 201; colour plate 13 with Carmen Pous, Joan Fosas, Rosa Julià Fosas and Pedro Julià
Gitanilla, La, 183, 196, 208
Gitanilla, Madame, 209
Gitanillo de Triana, xiii
Gitanillos, xiii
Glasstone, Richard, 5, 9, 39, 142

Glinka, Mikhail Ivanovich, (1804-1857), 26
Glissade, 8, 114, 159
Godinov, Alexander, 176
Golfo de las Sirenas , El, 219
Golpe punta y talon, 7; notation, 240
Gómez, Aida (b.1967), 61, 168, *180*, 181, 205, 207
Gómez, José Carlos, 209
Gómez, Lupe, 171
Góngora, Manuel de, 142
González, Ana, 168, *181*, 207
Gonzáles Martinez, Francisca — see La Quica
Gordo Sobrino, Carmen, 15, 81, 86, 97, 122, 133, 135, *182*
Gorito, 153
Gosalvez Lara, Carlos José, 112
Gösta Berlings Saga, 98
Gounod, Charles-François (1818-1893), 155
Goya, Carola, 54, 55, 168, 199, 206
Goya y Lucientes, Francisco José de (1746-1828), 14, 32, 81, 82, 83, 86, 97
Goyescas, xii, 205
Gracia de Sevilla, La, 124
Gracia Theatre of Zaragoza, 217
Gráfico del Petenera, 142
Grahn, Lucile (1819-1907), 35, 91, 98, 100, 103, 104, 106, 134, 145, 157, 213   Graham, Martha, 184
Granada, 50, 58, 64, 88, 92, 97, 98, 127, 134, 147, 156, 197
Granadillo, 56
Granadína (Granaína), 126, 147, 154
Granados, Enrique (1894-1928), 175, 185, 205, 209
Grand battement, 80
Grande, Dolores, 153
Grands jetés, 159
Granero, José (choreographer), 59, 181, *182*, 190, 196, 197, 207, 208; colour plate 37
"Gran Pas", 89
Gran Teatro de Havana, 179
Gran Teatro del Liceo (Gran Teatre de Liceu), Barcelona, 127, 155, 156, 176 178, 179, 191, 194, 200, 201, 207, 222
Graves, Robert, 73
Great Exhibition (1851), 214
Greco II (Arroyo), José, 206

Greco, José (1964-2001), 59, 187, 189, 191, 201, 206
Greco, José Luis (composer), 183, 208
Greco (Arroyo), Lola (b.1964), *184*, 206, 207, 209
Greece, Greek, 53, 68, 69, 121, 210
Gregorian chant, 207
Grieg, Edvard (1843-1907), 175
Grisi, Carlotta (1819-1899), 100
Grote, Harriet, 96
Grupo de Danza de la Casa de Galicia (Buenos Aires), 170
Guadalajara, 32
Guadalquivir, 41
Guajiras, 26
Guajiras, Las, 124
Guaracha, 212
Gudenius, Carl, colour plate 3
Guerilla Band, 35
Guerrero, Manuel, 108, 138, 153
Guerrero, Maria, 214
Guerrero, Rafael, 143
Guest, Ivor, 96, 98, 100, 153, 154, 168, 211-214
Guillén, Gorge, 50
Guimard, Madeleine (1743-1816), 211
Guitar, 21, 32, 34, 36, 71
Guitarillo (also tipillo), 34
Guitarró, 70
Güito, El (Eduardo Serrano), 206
Gurgy, Burat de, 92
Guridi Badaola, Jesús (1886-1961), 207, 208
Gustav III of Sweden, King, 218
Gypsy(-ies), 8, 10, 25, 35, 45, 56, 58, 65, 68, 89, 95, 97, 98, 127, 141, 143, 187, 191
Guy-Stéphan, Marie (1818-1873), 100, 105, 134, 138, 139, 145, 213

Habanera, 61
Habsburg monarchs, 217, 222
Halffter, C. (composer), 208
Halffter, Ernesto (composer b.1905), 205, 207, 208, 209
Half-step Bolero (*Medio Paso*), 79
Hamburg, 203
Hamlet, 184
Hammond, Sandra Noll, 9
Harkness Ballet (company), 197, 203
Hartley, C. Gascuoine, 20, 112
Havana, 34, 99, 180
Haymarket, Theatre Royal, 21, 214
Hayworth, Rita, 164

Heller, Nancy, 179
Helsinki, 181, 197
Helsted, Edvard, 102
Hemiola, 25
Her Majesty's Theatre, 143
"Hermanas Pericet, Las", 161, 166
Hermosa o la Danzatrice Spagnola (*Cachucha*), 89
Hijo Pródigo, El, 192
Hileras, 42
Hilversum, 203
Hindberg, Linda, 105
His Majesty's Theatre, 98
Hispanic America, 34, 99
Hoecke, Mischa van (b.1945), 185
Holland, 195
Holm, Hanya (b.1898), 184
Holy Week (Semana Santa), 20, 40
Homage to La Argentina, 185, 196
Homenaje a Granados, 200
Hospital de la Santa Cruz (in Barcelona), 217
Huelva, 20, 42, 122
Huertas, Eduardo, 143
Hungary, 127, 156
Hurok, Sol, 195
Hutchinson Guest, Anne, 91, 168

Ibars, Leif, 204
Ibars, Maria, 204
Iberica: De lo arcaico a la actualidad, 196
Ibiza, 56, 196
Iberian, 68
Ida, xiii
Ihre, Marie-Louise, 43
Illustrated London Life, 96
Imperio, Pastora, 178, 206
India, Indian, 58, 146
Infante, xii
Institut del Teatro, Barcelona, (see also Theatre Institute), 201
Instituto de la Escuela de Folklore de Las Palmas, 178
Intermedio de Goya (Goyescas), 208, 209,
International Dance Alliance, New York, 188
International Festivals, 179
International Institute of Choreographic Arts, 188
Inzenga, José, 66
Iriarte, Tomás de, 13
Isabel Farnese, 5, 110

Isabel La Católica, Orden de, 173, 174, 175
Isabel II, Queen of Spain, 155
Iscar, 194
Israel, 204
Italian, 49, 77, 104, 212, 214, 217
Italy, 171, 210
Ivanova, Anna, 93, 112, 134, 220
Iza Zamácola, Juan Antonio de (Don Preciso), 112

Jabas Verdes, 34
Jácara, (see also *Xaquera*), 26, 53, 67, 151, 218
Jagoda, Flory, 142
Jaleada, 9
Jaleo, 9, 79, 121, 132, 145, 146, 150
Jaleo de Cádiz, 214
Jaleo de Jerez, 49, 87, 100, 102 (as Xeres), 106, 129, 131, 145, 146, 149 (illustration), 154, 155, 157, 335 (notation)
Jaleo, El, 184,
Jaleo Magazine, 81
James I of Aragon, 68
Japan, 193
Jarabe, 27, 99
Jensen, Inge, 105
Jensen, Richard, 103
Jerezana, 159
Jerez de la Frontera, 41, 42, 58, 111, 135, 145
Jeté, 31, 189
Jews, 140, 143
Jewish synagogue, 221
Jews, Sephardic, 142
Jijona, 67
Jiménez, Enrique — see "El Cojo"
Johannesburg, 209
Jondo, 25
José Antonio (J.A. Ruiz, b.1951), 59, 61, 168, 180, 181, 182, *185*-187, 191, 205, 206, 207, 208, 209
José Greco II, 206
Joseph, Saint, 56
Jota, xi, 9, 18, 27, 32, 47, 63, 66, 67, 89, 156
Jota Alcañiz, 176
Jota, Aragonesa, 61, 153
Jota de la Pradera, 14; colour plate 22
Jota Valenciana y Aragonesa, 66
Jotero, 47
Jowitt, Deborah, 53
Juanillo (innkeeper of Chiclana), 114

Juilliard School of Music and Drama, 179

Jurado, Rocío, xiii, 204

Jürgensen, Knud Arne, 35, 104, 106

Juvenal (Decimus Junius Juvenalis), 121

Karajan, Herbert von (conductor, b.1908), 195, 203

Kathak, 58

Keet, Marina, 62, 196, 209

Kennedy Center for the Performing Arts, John F., 179, 185, 195, 196

Kermesse i Brugge, 101

King Christian VIII of Denmark, 101

King John II, 151

King Ludwig (Louis) I of Bavaria — See Louis I of Bavaria

King of Naples and Sicily, 86

King's Theatre, 98, 211

Kirov, 170, 181, 186

Kloborg, Eva, 104, 107

Kniaseff, Boris, 202

Kragh-Jacobsen, Sven, 101, 107

Krøyer, P.S., 106

Kuursaal, 52, 88

Labanotation, 168

Laberinto, 181, 186, 207, 209

Ladino, 142

Lagerlöf, Selma (1858-1940), 98

Lago Lingustino, 41

Laguna, Ana, 177

Lalla Rookh, 99

Lander, Harald (1905-1971), xi, 59, 104, 158

La Quica (Francisca González Martínez, 1905-1967), 50, 124, 128, *187* (photo), 198, 199, 206

Las Hermanas de Sevilla, 101

Latido Flamenco, 187

Latin America, 22, 49, 195

Latorre, Javier, 59, 187

Latosti, 181

Lauchas, 27

Laud, 22

Lauesgaard, Elna, 103

Lavapies, 143, 172

Lavrovsky, 59

Lamyer, Francisco, 115

Lawyer of Farfulla, 26

Lazos, 7, 8, 80

Lefebre, 8 (Madame), 122

Legion of Honour, France, 173

Legrand, Lucien, 181

Lehman, Edvard, 35, 101, 102, 105

Lenguo, Paula, 153

León, 65

León, Francisco ("Frasquillo", 1898-1940) — See Frasquillo

León, Manuel, 153

León, Maria Mercedes Zúñiga, 12, 124, 128, 198, *199*

León, Mercedes — See Mercedes y Albano)

Lépic (artist), 155

Lérida, 203

Levy, Lorna, 133

Leyenda, 180, 183

Librán, Gloria, 174

Libre, 25

Libro Vermell de Montserrat, 179, 201

Liceístas, 222

Liceu (Liceo) — see Gran Teatro del Liceo, Barcelona

Liceu Filarmónico-Dramático, 222

Liceo de Montsio, 194, 222

Lifar, Serge (1905-1986), 59

Linares, Juanjo, 180, 190, 208, 209

Linnaeus, Carolus (Swedish: Carl von Linné, 1707-1778), 49

Lisbon, 212

Liso, 65

Llongueras, Carlos, 193

Llorens, Pilar (Pastora Martios), 127, 179, *187*

Loa, 53, 219

Lola de Valencia, 92

Lolita, La, 163

London, 168, 175, 203, 212-214

London Festival Ballet, 176

London Illustrated News, 213, 215

López, Encarnación López Julvez (La Argentinita, 1895-1945), 50, 59, 168, *175*

López, Pablo (pianist), 168

López, Pilar López Julvez (b.1912), xii, 24, 124, 167, 175, 181, 184, *188*, 190, 191, 197, 200, 206, 207, 208, 214

Lorca, Alberto (dancer and choreographer), xi, 58, 59, 61, 124, 180, 181, 182, 186, 188, *189*, 190, 197, 204, 206, 207, 208, 220

Lorca, Federico García, see García Lorca

Lorca, Marina, 136

Lorca, Nana (Djenana Modrego Vigaray, b.1937), 168, *190*, 191, 204, 205, 208 Loreto, Maleni, xiii

Lorquiana, 190, 191

Los Caños del Peral, 77

Louis I of Bavaria, 1786-1868, 100, 157

Louis XIV of France, 218

Lucena, 20

Lucena, Elvira, xi, 128, 169

Lucerne, 203

Luceros, 36

Lucía, Paco de, 207, 208

Luengo, Señor (Sandalia), 153, 212

Lund, José (composer), 127

Luisillo (Luis Pérez-Dávila, dancer and choreographer, b.1927), 59, 60, 180, 181, *191*-193, 197, 206, 207, 208

Luisillo y su Teatro de Danza Española, 192, 200

Lute, 21

Lyle, Bernie (Bernard), 209

Lyon, France (5th Biennale), 172

Macarena, La, 129, 143, 146; notation, 345

Macarrona, La, (Juana Vargas from Jerez de la Frontera, 1860-1947), xiii, 178

Machado, Manuel, 121

Madrid, xi, xii, 3, 14, 55, 63, 77, 82, 83, 88, 92, 97, 111, 121, 126-128, 131, 134, 145, 147, 149, 150, 153, 158, 162, 164, 166, 167, 168, 170, 173, 175, 182, 184, 186, 187, 189, 194, 196, 198, 199, 200, 202, 203, 210, 212, 214, 219

Madrilène, 61

Madrileños, 82

Madriles, Los, 143

Magic of Dance, The, 66, 97, 133, 170, 179, 201, 203

Magriña Sanroma, Juan (1903-1995), xi, 127, 167, 176, 178, 179, *193*, 194, 199, 200, 202

Mahar, 82

Maja, 14, 32, 48, 82, 83, 116, 144

Maja Jerezana, La, 131

Maja y el Torero, La, (also known as *La Malagueña y el Torero*) 90, 129, 131, 144, 145, 146, 154, 168, 169, 171, 175, 189

Majo, 14, 32, 48, 82, 83

Majó Company, Enric, 201

Majó, Nùria, 66, 69

Majos del Puerto, Los, 156

Makarova, Natalia (b.1940), 186

Málaga, 12, 20, 41, 77, 88, 122, 126, 134, 144

Málaga Escuela Superior de Arte Dramático y Danza, 171

Malagueña(s), xi, 31, 41, 126, 129, 131, 144, 145, 147, 189, 200

Malagueña y el Torero, La, 144, 146

Malena, La, (Magdalena Seda Loreto from Jerez de la Frontera, b.1870s) xiii

Maleras, Emma, 55, 58, 127, 203

Malgueñita, La, 214

Mallorca, 63, 70, 71, 72 and 74; illustrations, 73, 84, 86, 156

Malquerida, La, 193, 208

Mancha, La, 13, 66, 112

Manchegas, Las, 30

Manchegas Pias, 129

Mandolin, 36

Manet, Édouard (1832-1883), 53, 90, 92, 93, 155; colour plate 23

Manola, 48, 84; illustration, 143

Manola de la Favorite, La, 143,

Manola (Manolla), La, 143, 144; colour plate 34

Manolete, 180, 196

Manolo, 48, 84; illustration, 143

Mansha, Al, 13

Mantilla, 73, 143, 146

Manuel, Juan, 181

Map (distribution of *Seguidillas*), 17

Maria Estuardo, 183

Maria Luisa of Savoy, 218

Maria Magdalena, 180, 190, 196

Maria la Bella, 214

Maria Pia, 196

Maria Rosa, 180, 181, 186, 197, 204

Marianas, Las, 124

Marianna, 154

Mariemma, (Guillermina Martínez Cabrejas, b.1917), 59, 128, 169, 180, 181, 182, 184, 185, 190, *194*-196, 207, 208

Marina, 201

Marín, Manolo, 206, 208, 209

Marismas, las, 41

Marocco, 194

Márquez, Antonio, 184, *196*, 197, 207

Márquez, Mariana, 78

Marquis de Cuevas, 195

Marquis of Perales, 217

Marquis of Salamanca, 220

Marriage of Figaro, 186

Marti i Mora, Enric, 66, 67, 68

Martial (Marcus Valerius Martialis, Spanish-Roman poet AD c.39-103), 121

Martín, Maria, 196

Martinete, 173, 174, 209

Martínez, Juan, 194

Martinez, La, 164, 165

Martínez Ruiz, Enrique, 49

Martios, Pastora — See Llorens, Pilar

Masaniello (name used in England for Aubert's opera *La Muette de Portici*), 61

Mascaraque, Adela, 205, 209

Masón de la Fruta (Theatre in Toledo), 217

Masot, Mercedes, 166

Massenet, Jules-Émil Frédéric, (1842-1912), 175

Massine, Leonide de (1895-1979), 195

Matachin, 218

Mata, Juan, 168, *197*, 207

Matalaraña (see also *batararaña*), 9, 38, 39, 114

Matias, Don, 140

Matos, Manuel García — See García Matos

Matteo (Mateo Vittuci), 54, 56, 100, 149, 157, 168, 199, 206

Mauri, Pedro (1830-1906), 127, 156

Mauri, Rosita ("Roseta" in Catalan, 1849-1923), 127, 158, 153-156 (156 is Roger Salas's list of dances performed by Rosita such as: *La Feria de Sevilla, La Aldeana, La Rosa de la Macarena, La Flor de la Maravilla, La Tertulia, La Perla de Sevilla* and others), 158 (illustration)

Maxine Elliott Theatre, New York, 175

Maya, Mario, 207

Maywood, Augusta, 99

Mazilier, Joseph (1801-1868), 35

Medea 180, 182, 183, 186, 196, 197, 207, 208

Medino El Viejo (*cantaor*), 142

Mehul, Etiennes-Nicolas (1763-1817), 61

Melo, Salvador, 74

Mendoza, Vicente T., 99

Mengíbar, Milagros, 206

Menuetto, 218

Mérante, Louis (1828-1887), 155

Mercandotti, Maria, 8, 212

Mercé, Antonia (La Argentina), see Argentina, La

Mercedes y Albano (Mercedes León, 1923-2000, and Albano Zuñiga, b.1923), 19, 124, 128, 168, 187, 197, *198*, 206

Meri, La, 112

Mesonerilla, La, 26

Mexico (Mexican), 27, 34, 99, 191, 210

Mi Aire, A, 209

Michel, Jerane, 55

Migaja, 63

Millares, Francisco de, 194

Minguet, Pablo Eyrol, steps from 1764: 29

Ministry of Cultural Affairs, 196, 207

Minue Afandangado, 89

Minuet, 99

Miralles, Soledad, 142

Mirror scene, 105

Mi Vida, 175

Mojiganga, 219

Molina, Mercedes, 209

Molino, Amalia, 163

Molino y Mairena, 134

Monet, Enrique, 77

Montero, Dolores, 153, 156

Montes, Maria, 180

Montez, Lola (Eliza Gilbert, 1818-1861), 100, 153, 157, 213

Montiel, Sara, 190

Montilla, 20

Montsalvat, 188

Montsalvatge, Xavier (composer, b.1912), 207, 209

Montserrat Monastry, 179, 201

Moorish, 58, 69, 151, 221; see colour plate 31

Moorish heritage, 71

Moorish influence, 68

Moragas, Ricardo (1827-1899), 127, 153, 155

Morales, Eusebio, 116

Moreno, Antoñita, 204

Moreno Torroba, Federico (1891-1982), 193, 207, 209

Morente, Enrique (*cantaor*, b.1942), 187

Mori, Mlle, 212

Morocco, 194

Mortitxol, 9, 67; colour plate 3

Mother of the Marshes, 41

Museo del Prado, 83

Mourner's dance (*Danza del Velatorio*), 10, 48
Movimiento Perpetuo, 197
Muette de Portici, La, (see also *Masianello*), 154
Munich, 203
Murcia, 3, 32, 36, 65, 73, 80, 111, 190, (Ballet, 197), 205
Murcianas, 32
Murcianita, 36
Murillo, Bartolomé Esteban (1618-1682), 34

Naples, 211
Napoleon Bonaparte, 1769-1821, 111, 122
Napoleonic War, 212
Napoli, 104
Narros, Miguel, 170, 183, 186, 207
National Ballet of Spain, 168; See also *Ballet Nacional de España*
Navarrete y Ribera, 111
Navarro, Esquivel de, 5, 121
Navarro García, José Luis, 97
Negro, Rafael El (b.1932), 179
Neiiendam, Robert, 104
Nena, La, (Manuela Perea), 127, 136, 153, 213, 214, 215; colour plate 33
Nepompa, La, xiii
Neruda, Pablo, 50
Netherlands, The, 210
New York, 95, 196, 199, 203
New York City Ballet, 184
New Zealand, 192, 210
Nielsen, Augusta, 103
Nieto, José (composer), 186, 205, 207, 208, 209
Nijinska, Bronislava (1891-1972), 59
Noblet, Lise (1801-1852), 91, 100, 134, 149
Noblet sisters (Lise, Félicité and Mme Alexis Dupont), 106
Noche de San Juan de la Cruz, La, 185
Nogues, Maria Luisa, 194
Norma, 222
Norway, Norwegian, 35, 208
Nourrit, Alphonse, 92
Noverre, Jean Georges (1727-1810), 10, 211

Oboe, 75
Ocaña, Carmina, 180
Ocho Sevillanas Escogidas, 129
Off, August (artist), 155

Oleana, 157
Olé and *óle*, 135
Olé Andaluz, 131, 135
Olé Antiguo, 135
Olé Bujaque, El, 124
Olé de Cádiz, 155
Olé de la Curra, El, 49, 91, 96, 111, 121, 124, 129, 131, 131, 134, 135, 136, 137, 138, 171, 172, 175; notation 327
Olé, El, 137
Olé Gaditano, El, 111, 135, 138
Oliva, Pepita de — See Pepita de Oliva
Olivar, Antonio, 134
Oliver, Rita, 122
Ontin, Maestro, 180
O! Pepita — See Pepita de Oliva
Opera House in Alexandria, 170
Opéra, Paris, 9, 90, 154, 156, 212
Oración del Torero, La, 197, 205, 209
Orfeo Gitana, 203
Orihuela, Bishop of, 68
Oro, Pilar de, 180
Ortega, Rafael, 188
Ortega, Juan, 193
Ortega, Regla, 202
Österlind, Allan (1855-1938), 28, 41
Otero Aranda, José (1860-1934), xv, xvi, 29, 30, 65, 110, 121, 124 (social dances of the early 20th c.), 126, 134, 136, 138, 139, 140, 142, 153, 162, 164
Overskou, Thomas, 101

Padre Pitillo y Maria de los Reyes, 202
Pagán, Paquita, 204
Palacio de la Musica, 179
Palacio de UNESCO, 179
Palais Royale, 154
Palau de la Musica, 201
Palomino, Antonio (18th c.), 26
Palmas, 150
Palmeros, xiii
Pamies, Pauleta, 127, 176
Panaderos, 52, 81, 90, 121, 124, 142, 146
Panaderos de la Flamenca, 49, 66, 110, 129, 142, 147, 154, 165, 168, 172, 189; notation, 353
Panaderos de la Juerga, 131
Panaderos de la Tertulia, 129, 131, 135, 147, 155, 189, 204
Panaderos de la Vuelta de la Corrida, 131
Panaderos, Los, 124

Pandereta, 22
Pandorga, La, 34
Papal bull, 48
Paquita, 169
Parado, 71
Parado de Selva, 71
Parado de Valldemosa, 63, 70 (illustration showing the *rebozillo en amunt*), 71
Parejo, Carmen, 126
Paris, 85, 93, 96, 107, 126, 127, 143, 151, 153-156, 175, 194, 196, 206, 212
Paris Opera, 9, 90, 98, 107, 154, 156, 181
Parra, Nina, 181
Parramón, 56
Parrandas, Las, 36, 80
Pas de Basque, 39, 40, 159
Pas de bourrée, 6, 31, 39, 211
Pas de chat, 9, 159
Pas de Quatre, 102, 186
Pas de trois, 211
Paseo, 43
Pasión Gitana, 205
Paso de Cuatro (Sorazábal and Pittalugo), 200
Paso de Vasco (Pas de Basque), 7, 37, 39
Passacalle, 218
Passiegos, Los, 32
Pasqua, 201
Pas Venetien, 99
Patio Sevillano, El, 52
Patron Saint of Madrid, 82
Paulino, Don, 140
Paulli, Holger Simon (Danish composer), 35
Pavane, 203
Pavlova, Anna (1881-1931), 157, 175
Paya y Calé, 178
Pedralbes, Palacio de, 65
Pedrell, F., 143
Pemberton, Ralph, 17, 18, 19, 36, 37, 77, 93, 143
Peña, Paco, 207
Pepita de Oliva, (O! Pepita), 100, 106-108, 137, 138, 143, 157
Pepita Jiménez, 176, 186, 188
Perla del Guadalquivir, La, 129
Perla de Sevilla, 155
Perea, Manuela (see also Nena, La), 136, 152-154, 213, 214 (illustrations on ps. 213 and 214); colour plate 33

Perez, Carlos (Maestro Coronas), 127, 153

Perez, Manuel, 156

Peréz Padilla, Florencio (Rosario), 53, 167, 173, 174, 214

Pericet family, 11 (photograph), 97, 123, and chapter 8 from 161-172

Pericet Blanco siblings, 171 (photo)

Pericet Blanco, Angel ("El Jefe", b. Seville 1932), 97, 109, 140, 148 (photo), 159, 160 (photo), 161, 162, 166, 168 (photo), *169*, 171 (photo), 206, 209

Pericet Blanco, Carmelita, 97, 148 (photo), 161, 168, 169 (photo), *170*, 171 (photo), 206

Pericet Blanco, Eloy, xv, 9, 27, 28, 31, 38, 47, 97, 107, 111 (photo), 128 (photo), 131, 143, 145, 158, 161, 165, 166, 168, 169 (photo),170 (photo), *171* (photo), 206, 210

Pericet Blanco, Luisa, 161, 168 (photo), *170*, 206

Pericet Blanco, Maria del Amparo, 161, 168, 170 (photo), 171, *172*, 206

Pericet Carmona, Angel (Don Angel) (1877-1944), xi, 2 (photo), 3, 5, 11, 30, 84/85, 88, 123 (photo), 124, 128, 134, 153, 161, *162*, 163 (photo), 164, 166, 167, 168, 173, 198, 199

Pericet Carmona, José, 161, 164

Pericet Carmona, Rafael (1875-1956), 5, 88, 122, 123 (studio), 147, 158, 161, 162, *164* (photo), 165, 202, 204

Pericet Carmona, Salvador, 161, 164

Pericet Jiménez (1899-1973), Angel, 3, 110, 147, 157, 161, 162, 165-66 (photos), 167, 168, 202

Pericet Jiménez, Concepción (Concha, Conchita), xi, 161, 164, 166 (photo)

Pericet Jiménez, Luisa, xi, 123 photo, 161, 164, 165 (photo), *166*, 178, 189, 190, 202

Perla de Guadalquivir, La, 129

Perrot, Jules (1818-1892), 98, 99, 213

Peru, 27, 34, 45, 99

Peseta, La, 32

Peteneras, 6, 10, 19, 50, 65, 111, 129, 131, 139-142, 162, 184; notation, 358

Peteneras (Andalusian), 129, 136

Peteneras, (Flameco), 50, 65

Peteneras, (Valencian), 65

Petenera, La, 184

Peteneros, Los, 124

Petimetre, 48

Petipa, Marius (1818-1910), 7, 100, 157

Petipa-Ivanov, 100

Philippines, 192

Philip IV of Spain, 217, 218

Philip V of Spain, 6, 110, 217, 218, 222

Phoenicians, 121

Pia, Maria, 196

Piano accompaniment at saraos, 143

Piatoli, 154

Picasso, Pablo Ruiz y (1881-1973), 207

Picq, Charles Le, 211

Pifla, 6, 31

Palau de la Musica, 201

Palmas, xiii

Palmeros, xiii

Pilar Llorens — See Llorens

Pinto, Pepe, 178

Píteri, María, 134

Pito-Coloni, 115

Pitos, 36

Pla, 65

Plá, Mirta, 180

Playa de Windsor, En la, 162

Playeras, 32

Plaza de Toros, 34

Plaza Tirso de Molina no.20, 198, 199

Plié, 9

Plunkett, Adelina (1824-1910), 143; colour plate 34

Poema de Cante Jondo, 53

Poesio, Gianandrea, 89

Pohren, D.E., 52, 142

Polaca, La, 143

Polen, Danielle, 179

Polo, 18, 34, 61

Polonaise, 46

Pons, Aurora, 127, 129, 168, 180, 181, 191, 194, 196, 197, *200* (photo), 204, 205, 208

Pope Paul IV, 192

Pont de Diable El, 155

Por alto, 80

Portugal, 167, 194

Pradera, 82, 83

Prado, 14, 83

Prado, Enrique (guitarist of La Macarena), 146

Preciso, Don, (Iza Zamácola, Juan Antonio de), 112

Preobrajenska, Olga, 202

Price, Ellen, 101

Price, Juliette, 101

Price, Sophie, 101

Price, Valdemar, 101, 104

Prieto, Claudio, 209

Puelle gaditanae, 121, 136

Puerta del Sol, 143

Puerta de Tierra (Isaac Albéniz) 61, 171, 181, 190, 200, 208

Puig Aclaramunt, Alfonso, 84, 85, 88, 155, 178, 217

Puigserver, Fabià, 67, 201; colour plates 14 and 15

Punta y talon, 8, 49, 107

Punxonet El, 74

Quadrado, José, 73

Queen Elizabeth II, 65, 179

Queen of the Marshes, 41

Queen Regent, 212

Queen Sofia of Spain, 179

Queen of Spain, 126, 160, 212

Quica, La — see La Quica

Quijote, Don,13, 101, 169, 181, 192, 207, 208

Quijote's Vigil at Arms, Don, 26

Quintero, Juan, 208

Quiroja, 167

RAD — See Royal Academy of Dancing

Ralov, Kirsten (1922-1999), 96

Ramblas, Las(Barcelona), 222

Rameau, Pierre, 5, 6, 107

Ramerito (Antonio Ramires, 52

Ramirez, Serafín, 34

Ramos, Señoras, 212

Rango, 184, 185, 208

Ranz, Núria, 193

Raphael, 190

Rapsòdia per a piano i cobla, 201

Rat Penat, Lo, 67

Ravel, Joseph-Maurice (1875-1937), 59, 195, 207, 208

Real Academia de Nobles y Belles Artes de San Luis, 176

Real, Elvira, 167

Real Escuela Superior de Arte Dramático y Danza, 195

Real de San Vicente, El, 34

Real Montoya, Manuel (Realito, 1885-1969), 122, 124, studio 125, 153, 173, 174

Realito (see Real Montoya)

Rebozillo, ill. 70 illustration of *en amunt*, and description of *en amunt* and *en Volant*, 71

Recio, Antonio, 126

Recorder, 75
Redoble, 38
Reencuentros, 197
Reguero, Juan Manuel, 126
Renata Shotelius Ballet de Danz Moderna, 184
Renversée, 91
Requejo, 3, 5, 80, 81, 110, 131, 158
Retortillé, 159
Retrato de Mujer, 208
Reus, 127, 154, 155, 156
Rey, Blanca del, 206
Rey, Federico, 176
Ribera, Julián, 58
Rico, Paquita, 204
Rimsky-Korsakov,Nicolai Andreievitsch (1844-1908), 209
Rio, del, 199
Rioja, Eusebio, 133
Rios Ruiz, Manuel, 174
Ritmo y a Compás, Á, 209
Ritmos, 180, 181, 182, 190, 207, 208
Rivkind, Rhoda (Luisa Cortés), 209
Robbins, Jerome (b. 918), xii
Rocamor, Sabina, 179
Roche, Carmen, 177
Rocieras, 41
Rodazán(es), 5, 7, 9 *en vuelta*, 110, 135, 254 notation
Rodrigo, Joaquín (b. 1901), 207, 208
Rodríguez Calderón, Juan Jacinto, 111, 112, 114-119 steps and a class parodied as danced in 1794-95
Rodríguez de Hita, Antonio, (d. 1787), composer, 219
Rodríguez, Mercedes, 172
Rojas, Juan Fernández de, (pseudonym of an Augustinian monk: Francisco Augustín Florencio), 53
Rojo, José, 122
Roman, 53, 68, 121, 136
Romance, 208, 209
Romance de Luna, 186, 209
Romance Cordobés, 193
Romance del Carmen, 203
Romantic era, 35
Romeo and Juliet, 193
Romeras, 209
Romeria, 169
Romero, Paco, 196
Ronda, Lola de, 184
Ronda, 66
Rondeña, 127, 147

Rond de jambe, 5, 7, 49
Röök, Lars von, 76
Rosa del Azafran, La, 26
Rosa de la Macarena, La, 155
Rosa, Pedro de la, 29
Rosales, Antonio, 26
Rosario (Florencia Pérez Padilla), 53, 167, 173, *174*, 214
Rosati, Carolina, 99
Rosén, Maestro, 182
Rossi, Geltruda, 211
Rossini, Gioacchino Antonio, (1792-1868), 26, 146
Roy, Maestro, 12, 128
Royal Academy of Dance, Swedish, 173
Royal Academy of Dancing ("Royal Academy of Dance" since 2000), 6, 187, 209 Royal Ballet, 137
Royal Conservatory, Madrid, 204
Royal Danish Ballet, 35, 96, 101, 103, 104, 105, 203
Royal patronage, 77
Royal Proclamation, 48, 77
Royal Spanish Ballet, 214
Royal Theatre of Madrid, 77
Rubinstein, Ida (1885-1960), 59
Ruiz, Antonio, 153
Ruiz, Concepción, 154
Ruiz, (see José Antonio)
Ruiz, Martínez, 49
Ruiz, Paco, 196
Ruiz, Paulino, 139
Ruiz Soler, Antonio, see Antonio (1921-1996)
Rumores de la Caleta, 200
Russia, 8, 26, 87, 95, 127, 156, 168, 170, 181
Ryberg, Flemming (b.1940), 104, 105, 107, 145

Sackville-West, Vita (writer), 108, 143
Sacromonte, 97, 127
Sadler's Wells (Royal) Ballet, 168
Saeta, 25
Saint Joseph, 56
Saint-Léon, Arthur (1821-1870), 100, 138, 139, 143, 144, 213
Saint Teresa of Avila, 56
Saint Thérèse of Lisieux, 56
Sainete, 77, 219,
Sal de Andalucia, La, 131, 162
Salamanca, 32, 190
Salas, Antonio, 193
Salas, Roger, 127, 155, 158

Salazar, José, 193
Saldaña, Antonio, 179
Saldoni, Baltazar (1807-1889), 86
Salida, xiii, 22, 36, 37
Salinas, Pedro, 50
Salon, 82, 87, 88, 112, 115, 162
Salón del Recreo, Botillo's, 87
Salón Variedades, 88
Salón Concierto Filharmónico y Oriente, 162
Salud, Miguel, 127, 153
Salzburg Festival, 203
Sánchez, Felipe (b.1947), 128, 181, 185, 196, 207, 208
Sand, George (Amandine-Aurore-Lucile 'Lucie' Dudevant née Dupin, 1804-76), 71-74, 138 (her children Solange and Maurice), 71, 74 (illustration by Maurice)
San Francisco, 173
Sanlúcar de Barrameda, 193
Sanlúcar, Manolo (b.1943), 183, 186, 207, 208, 209
San Pedro de Ribas, 203
San Sebastian, 188
Sans i Aris, Albert, xvi, 67, 68, 74, 179, *201*
Santa Cruz de Mudela, 182
Santander, 195
Santelmo, Laura, 204
Santissima Virgen del Prado, La, 34
Santos, Carlos, 209
Sarabanda, 151
Sarao, 82, 143
Sarasate y Navasqués, Pablo Meltín Melitón (composer/violonist 1844-1908), 208
Sarau, el, 143, 201
Saura, Carlos, 21, 179,
Sauté, 159
Sayo, 73
Scala La, (Milan), 155, 173, 185, 186, 195
Scarf (Shawl) Dance, 34, 99; colour plate 16
Scarlatti, Domenico (1685-1757, lived in Madrid from 1729), 207
Schaufuss, Peter, 168
Schnell, Betty, 35
Scholl, Anna, 35
Scott, Captain, 98
Seanai, Yoko, 196
Sección Feminina del Movimiento Nacional de J.O.N.S., 20, 68, 70, 205

Seconde, á la, 7

Sedgwick, Nancy, 179; colour plate 1

Segovia, Enrique, 193, 209

Segovia, Rosita, 194

Seguidilla, 107

Seguidillas, xi, 8, 13-20, 22, 23, 25-36, 66, 68, 77, 107, 109, 132, 140, 142, 143, 147, 179, 218; colour plate 4

Seguidillas, 17 (map of distribution), 22 (music)

Seguidillas Antiguas, 82

Seguidillas Boleras, 45 and 47 (as Voleras), 83, 189; colour plates 10 and 11

Seguidillas Boleras y Jota, 34

Seguidillas de Andalucia, 100, 154

Seguidillas de Carlet, 64

Seguidillas d'Eco, 218

Seguidillas de la Pradera, 82

Seguidillas del Candil, 6, 14, 32, 81; colour plates 6 and 22

Seguidillas de Leciñena, 32, 45, 69

Seguidillas de Mondejar, 32

Seguidillas de Tarancon, 32

Seguidillas Jaleadas, 9

Seguidillas Manchegas, 13, 15, 16, 18, 26, 27, 28, 30, 31, 34, 35, 36, 77, 89, 94, 129, 131, 132, 171, 172, 204; colour plate 4; notation, p. 269

Seguidillas Meloneras, 32, 34

Seguidillas Mollares, 32, 146

Seguidillas Reliogosas, 33

Seguidillas Sevillanas, 20, 29, 36-43, 124, 129, 132, 142, 169-171; colour plates 7 and 9

Seguidillas Taleadas (corruption of *Jaleadas*), 89, 93

Seguidillas Voleras, 45, 46

Seguiriyas, 24, 25, 26, 32

Segura, Carmen Amanda, 155

Segura, Maestro Faustino, 12, 122, 134, 140, 161, 162, 164

Seis Sonatas para la Reina de España, 160, 207, 209

Seises, 48, 56

Semana Santa (Holy Week), 20, 40

Seneca, Lucius Annaeus, Spanish-Roman writer, c.4BC-65AD, 183

Serral, Dolores, 11, 35, 53, 88, 90, 91, 93, 101, 126, 137, 145, 153, 154, 212; colour plates 23 and 26

Setmana Santa, 201

Sevilla, Carmen, xi, 167

Sevilla, Jesús, 191

Sevillanas (film), 21, 43, 179

Sevillanas (see also references to specific *Sevillanas* and the *Seguidillas Sevillanas*), xi, 19, 21, 22, 23, 27, 32, 89, 139, 140

Sevillanas Boleras, 8, 21, 39, 40, 43, 50, 52, 132, 159, 168, 170, 171, 172; notation, 377

Sevillanas Corraleras, 21, 32, 147, 170

Sevillanas del Siglo XVIII, 40, 50, 169-172

Sevillanas, La Cava, 21

Sevillanas Rocieras, 41, 42

Sevillanas (*Seguidillas*), see *Seguidillas Sevillanas*

Sevillano, Trinidad, 176

Seville, 8, 11, 12, 15, 20, 42, 56, 58, 77, 87, 88, 92, 111, 112, 122, 124, 125, 126, 128, 134, 139, 146, 156, 162, 164-167, 169, 171, 172, 173, 178, 187, 196, 221

Seville Cathedral, 48, 56, 87, 153

Shawl dance, 34; colour plate 16

Shelton, Mary Ann, 179; colour plate 3

Shakespeare, William, 190

Shiraev, Alexandre, 100, 157

Sierra Morena, 13

Sinfonía Española, 184

Sinfonia Sevillana, 192

Sirilla, 34

Sisol, 7

Sisón, Manuel, 193

Sitges (Barcelona), 174, 199, 203, 204

Sittón, Nelson, 179; colour plate 3

Six Sonatas for the Queen of Spain, see *Seis Sonatas por la Reina de España*

Skorsiuk, Maria, 100, 157

Smith, Kaj, 104

Smithsonian Institution (Washington D.C.), 203

Smooth Bolero (*Bolero Liso*), 79, 129, 131, 133

Sociedad de Autores (SGAE), 167

Sol, Maria del, 190

Soleá, 181, 209

Soleá por Bulerias, 209

Soleares, 25, 56, 58, 111, 131

Soleares de Arcas, (*del Maestro Arcas*), 58, 111, 126, 129, 131, 133, 134, 169, 170; notation, 368

Soleares Granadinos, 129

Soler, Padre Antonio (1729-1757), 174, 184, 208

Solera y Duende, 169, 171, 172

Solo, 205, 209

Solo de Antonio, 197

Sombrero de Tres Picos (*Tricorne* or *The Three-Cornered Hat*), xiii, 27, 174, 180, 181, 186, 195, 197, 207, 209

Sonatas, 174, 181, 207, 208, 209

Sonatas de Padre Soler, 181, 204

Sor(s), Ferdinand, 4, 8, 45, 78, 79, 107, 111, 131

Sorazábal, Pablo (1897-1988), 62, 186, 190, 200

Soria, 155

Sorolla y Bastida, Juaquin (1863-1923), colour plate 7

Sostenidos, 8, 49, 132

Soto, Josefa, 145, 154

Soubresu, 7

South America, 206

South Africa, 192, 193, 209, 210

Soviet Union, 208

Spanish Dance Society, 6, 37, 54, 68, 179, 193, 198, 203, 204, 209, 210

Spanish Dance Theatre, Washington D.C., 68, 179, 196, 203, colour plates 1, 3, 20

Spanish Directorate-General of Theatre and Entertainment, 205

Spanish Galentries, 89

Spanish National Theatre Prize, 173

Spanish pas de deux, 89

Stockholm, 106

Stolen Bolero (Bolero Robado), 79, 82, 85

St. Petersburg, 95, 100, 143, 181, 194

Stuttgart, 203

Subirá, José, 33, 86

Sudra, 64

Suite Albéniz, 170, 171

Suite Española, 203

Sur, El, 184

Susana y José, (Susana Audeoud and José de Uadeta), 202, 203, 206

Swan Lake, 100, 157, 200

Sweden,(Swedish), 35, 98, 177, 204, 218

Switzerland, 127, 156

Sylphide, La, 35, 99, 101

Taberneras (Andalusian Seguidillas), 32

Tablao, xiii, 52, 178

Tabor, 21

Taft, Juana, 180, 180, 196

Taft, Karen, xii, 181, 186, 189, 190, 204

Taglioni, Filippo (1778-1871), 91, 95

Taglioni, Marie (1804-1884), 91, 95, 96, 99, 100, 126, 212, 213; colour plate 28

Taglioni, Paul, 35

Taleada (see *Jaleada*), 9

Tamayo, José, 190

Tango, El, 124

Tangos, 190, 209

Tapices de Goya, 200

Tarantos, Los, 180, 196, 207, 208

Tarara, 32

Tarragona, 65

Tarrida, Maestro, 127

Tati, La, (Francisca Sadornil Ruiz), 180, 206

Tavernes, 66

Teatro Albéniz, 198, 220

Teatro Avenida (Buenos Aires), 170, 171

Teatro Calderón, 196 (Valladolid), 220 (Madrid)

Teatro Casino (Buenos Aires), 167

Teatro Coliseo de Principe, 78, 219

Teatro Colón, 172, 184

Teatro Cómico, 122, 221

Teatro de la Comedia, 171

Teatro de la Cruz, 127, 212, 220

Teatro de la Zarzuela, 170, 190, 200, 205

Teatro del Circo (Madrid), 219, 220

Teatro del Maestranza, 197

Teatro del Principe, 127, 156, 212, 217

Teatro Español, 169, 188, 220

Teatro Esterpe in Reus, 156

Teatro Fontalba, 173

Teatro Monumental, 202

Teatro Nacional (Caracas), 163

Teatro Nacional Cervantes (Buenos Aires), 169

Teatro Palacio Edén, 162

Teatro Principal, 155, 217

Teatro Real de Madrid, 175, 220, 221

Teatro Romea, 58, 179

Teatro Santa Cruz, 222

Teatro Suizo, Gran Café El, 162

Tecnicas, pasos y aprendizase de la Escuela Bolera Andaluza, 167

Tejada, Carmen, 150

Telethusa, 121

Téllez, Marcos (sketches), 51, colour plates 10 and 11

Tena, Lucero, 206

Tenerife, 182

Tenora, 75

"*Tercetos*" 89

Teresa, Saint, 56

Teresa y Luisillo, 192

Teri, Robert, 179; colour plate 3

Terre à terre, 93

Tertulia, 147, 149, (*La*), 221

Théâtre Châtelet, 194

Théâtre de l'Académie Royale de Musique, 92

Théâtre des Variété, 90, 154

Théâtre du Palais-Royal, 90

Theatre Institute, Barcelona, (see also Instituto del Teatro) 200

Theatre Reform Council, 48

Theatre Royal, Haymarket, 21, 214

Theatres, 21, 217

Theresa of Lisieux, Saint, 56

Thiel-Cramér, Barbro, 106

Thorvaldsen, Bertel (scupltor), 101

Three-Cornered Hat— See *Sombrero de Tres Picos*

Tible, 75

Tientos, 171, 209

Tiersot, Julien, 61

Tijeras, 159, 265 (notation)

Timbala, 75

Tiplillo (*guitarillo*), 34

Times, The, 98, 212, 213, 214

Tirado, Angeles, 193

Tirana del Caramba, 143

Tirana del Contrabandista, 143

Tirana del Tripili, La, 169, 200

Tirana del Zarandillo ("Zarandillo" = energetic person), 14, 82, 143; colour plate 6

Tirananueva, 82

Tiranas, 18, 34

Tivoli (Theatre in Geltru, Catalonia), 156

Toledo, 34

Tomás Pacita, (Maria de la Paz Tomás Llory, b.1928), xi, 167, *202*

Tomlinson, Dudley, 133

Tonadilla, 151

Tonadillas Escenicas, 143, 151

Toreadoren, 101-108, 138, 145, 154, 168, 203

Torera, La, 155, 214

Tormo, Don José (Bishop of Orihuela), 68

Torneo, El, 66

Torras, 32

Torres, Paco, 196

Torres, Eduardo, 153

Tortosa, 74

Toscanini, Arturo (cellist/conductor, 1867-1957), 173

Totana, 36

Traje Corto, 134.

Tratado de Bailes, xv, xvi, 29 (other references under Otero)

Traviata, La, 200

Tres Danzas, 205

Triana, 97, 117, 170, 171

Triana, Antonio de (b.1909), 187

Triana, Gitanillo de ("diminutive flamenco 'bailaor'"), xiii

Triangle, 22, 75

Tricorne — See *Sombrero de Tres Picos*

Trieste, 197

Trio Pericet ("Las Hermanas Pericet"), 161, 166

Trombone, 75

Trumpet (trompeta), 75

Trythall, Richard (American composer in Rome), 62

Tuerto, Emilio el, 140

Tunis, 179

Turina, Joaquín (1882-1949), 175, 205, 208, 209

Turkey, 142

Tuteur Trompé, Le, 211

U (one), 66

Udaeta, José Luis de (b.1919), xi, 5, 54, 55, 56, 66, 97, 106, 108, 111, 112, 151, 158, 179, 189, 199, 201/*202*, 203, 204, 206

Uhlendorff, Gustav (Danish dancer), 103, 104

Ullate, Victor, 177, 196, 197

UNESCO, 188, 196

Union Musical Española, 40

United Kingdom, 210

United States of America, 45, 49, 151, 169, 171, 173, 182, 184, 191, 192, 195, 199, 200, 203, 206, 208

Urbeltz, Juan, xv, 10

Uruguay, 169, 199

USA — See United States of America

Ustinov, Peter, 186

Valencia(n), 5, 6, 10, 11, 20, 32, 45, 48, 63, 65, 66, 68, 69, 78, 80, 109, 128, 140, 141, 166; colour plates 17, 18 and 21

Valencia, Lola de, 93, 153, 154; colour plate 23

Valencianas, 66

Valladolid, 194, 195
Valle, Manuela (20th century dancer), 153
Valverde, Joaquín (1846-1910), 175
Vargas, Angelita, 206
Vargas, Antonio, 176
Vargas, Josefa, 153, 155
Vargas, Manolo (b. 1914), xii, 59, 124, 188, 189, 206
Vargas, Manuela, 184
Vargas, Martín, 209
Vargas, Mila de, 206, 209
Vargas, Orlando, 179; colour plate 3
Variaciones, 205
Variaciones Flamencas, 186
Variaciones Románticas, 197
Variétés, Théâtre des, 154
Vásquez, Maestro (b.1839), 126
Vaudeville theatre, 154
Vega Retana, Alejandro (1910-1980), xii, 176, 188
Vega, Antonio, 193
Vega, Mario de la, 190
Velada de San Juan, 162
Velásquez, Diego Rodríguez de Silva (1599-1660), 218
Venetien, Pas, 99
Ventana, La, 35, 101, 105, 107
Verdiales (see *Fandango de*), 28, 30
Vestris, Armand (son of Auguste, 1787-1825), 212
Vestris, Auguste (1716-1842), 211
Vestris, Gaetano (1729-1808), 10
Victoria, 174
Victoria Eugenia (Beti), 168, 180, 181, 186, 191, 196, *204*, 205, 208, 209
Vida Breve, La, 175, 195, 209
Viejo, Medino el, 142
Vienna, 95, 100, 197, 203
Viera Romero, Teresa, 192
Vihuela, 88
Villa, Joaquín (Joaquín Mediavilla, husband of Pacita Tomás), 167, 168, 202
Villafranca, dances from, 180
Villancico, 218
Villano, 111
Violin, 36, 71, 146
Virgen del Rocío, 41
Virgin of the Dew (tears), 41
Virgin of Magallón, 32
Visigoths, 68
Vito, El, 124, 129, 131, 132 (illustration), 165, 169; colour plate 32

Viva Navarra, 204
Vivancos, Gala, 188
Vives Roig, Amadeo (composer, 1871-1932), 208
Vivo, Maria, 193
Volero/Voleras, 45
Volière, La, 99
Volinine, Alexander (1882-1955), 202
Vuelta, 36, 167
Vuelta de valse, 7; notation, 234
Vuelta fibraltada, 7, 80, notation 234
Vuelta normal, 30; notation, 231
Vuelta de pecho, 116; notation, 235
Vueltas de la Corrida, 162

War of Spanish Succession, 218
Weber, Carl Maria von (1786-1826), 61
West Side Story, 184
Wexler, Sherrill, 210
Whitsun, 41
Wilson, G.B.L., 98
World Fair, New York, 173, 190, 199
World Fair, Thailand, 195

Xaquera Vella (Valencian for "Old Jácara"), 67
Xativa, 128
Ximénez, Roberto (b.1919), 59, 124, 167, 206
Ximénez/Vargas Ballet Español, 59, 184, 206
Xirimies (chirimias), 70

Yaravies, 27
Yerillo, 22, 32
Yerma, 185
Yoko Kumatsubara Ballet (Japan), 205
Yoscu, 197

Zafra, Roberto, 60, 193
Zagal, 26
Zamacola, see Don Preciso
Zambra, 142, 151
Zambra de Gitanos, 162
Zamora, 45, 63; colour plate 12
Zandt, Marguerite van, 106
Zapateado, xi, xiii, xiv, 34, 38, 85, 101, 134, 138, 139, 156, 157, 199, 208, 212
Zapateado de Cádiz, 213
Zapatedo de las Campanas, xii
Zapateado de Maria Cristina, 78, 131, 133, 138; notation, 390
Zapateado de Sarasate, 197

Zapatillas, 111, 129, 131, 132, 134, 142, 144
Zarabanda, 14, 29, 48, 112, 151, 181, 186, 209
Zaragoza, 168, 176, 193, 203, 207
Zarambeque, 29
Zaraspe, Héctor (teacher of ballet and folk dance, b.1931), 186, 191
Zarazas, Perete, 115
Zartmann, José, 169, 171, 172
Zarzuela(s), 85, 183, 190, 206, 218, 219
Zarzuela Antalogía Opera Company, 59, 190, 207
Zarzuela Theatre, 170, 190, 220
Zarzuelas, Fiestas de, 219
Zerezo, Conchita, 207
Zimmerl, Cristl, 91
Zombombos, 70
Zori "Muñeco" (Antonio Zori Ramírez), 193
Zorn, Anders (Swedish artist, 1860-1920): colour plate 25
Zorn, Friedrich Albert, 8, 91, 92, 96, 159, 168
Zorongo, 78, 192
Zuberoa, 10
Zúñiga, Albano de, (Mercedes y Albano), *198*
Zürich, 203

The dates for the Spanish dancers were taken from the "Diccionario Enciclopedio Illustrado del Flamenco" by José Blas Vega and Manuel Rios Ruiz, those for ballet dancers, musicians and artists from "A Dictionary of Ballet" by G.B.L. Wilson and the "Encyclopaedia Britannica" and "Diccionario de la Musica y los Musicos" (3 volumes) by Mariano Pérez. See bibliography for more information.